W9-CGN-612

THE
ULTIMATE
RESOURCE

THE ULTIMATE RESOURCE

BY JULIAN L. SIMON

PRINCETON UNIVERSITY PRESS

For our children
Rita's and mine
And yours

Acknowledgments

This book appears at the time and in the form that it does because of the professional and personal qualities of Sanford Thatcher, Assistant Director of Princeton University Press. Sandy suggested the present order of the topics, which I believe makes the book much better than it was before even if it asks more of the reader; he also advised wisely about where and how to cut a draft which was too long to be publishable or readable. He made sure that the book promptly got at least a fair shake in the process of editorial evaluation. And it was my faith in his word, based on the trust he built between us during the publication of my previous book, that gave me the heart to revise the long early draft even without any commitment from him, and while I had reason to doubt that anyone else would want to publish this controversial material.

The book has greatly benefited from, and I have delighted in, the help of two skilled copy editors. Richard Palmer policed the documentation and the syntax, and in the process improved the prose as much as I would let him; he also gave me the benefit of many amusing asides, some of which I appropriated. William Hively worked the book (and me) over sentence by sentence. He straightened, tightened, and sharpened the language, and detected troublesome errors in writing; he also contributed a good many helpful thoughts from his large stock of general knowledge. And with care and diligence he kept the book on track and away from dangerous derailings while in press. In a better job market for academics, these two talented men would be working on their own writings rather than my book; as the beneficiary, however, I can't help feeling grateful for this circumstance, and for the opportunity of getting to know them in the process.

Michael Aronson of Harvard University Press and Colin Day of Cambridge University Press helped me with their sound editorial judgments about the overall design of the book. Harold Barnett, Allen Chase, and Thomas Mayer generously read through most of the text and gave me copious, useful notes; where I did not take their advice, I hope they will forgive me. The anonymous referees also improved the revision. Stanley Trollip helped me choose the book's title. And James L. Smith read and made important corrections in the energy chapters. Alvin Weinberg also was kind enough to read several chapters and to comment upon them.

Douglas Love assisted in much of the data collection and computer work; he served intelligently and faithfully. James Bier created the excellent figures. And typists Phyllis Stout and Susan Walker contributed high skill and diligence to the making of the book.

The roots of this work go back to William Petty, Adam Smith, and Friedrich Engels; to Jules Verne and H. G. Wells; and to others who have, in their forecasts for the economy and society, given full weight to man's imagination and creative powers of solving the problems of people and resources. But it was in the more recent work of Simon Kuznets, Harold J. Barnett together with Chandler Morse, A. V. Chayanov, and Ester Boserup that I found this idea and was inspired by it.

My wife Rita strengthened me by agreeing with my point of view, just as my children David, Judith, and Daniel strengthened me by saying that my arguments about the topics of this book make sense, despite their not knowing the details of the arguments and in the face of having been told exactly the opposite by the newspapers and television.

Lastly, though I am not accustomed to dealing with organizations as if they have personalities or characters, I am happy to recognize that Princeton University Press has treated this book — and me — the way every author dreams of being treated but seldom is. The experience of having a book published usually feels to me like walking at snail's pace through a mine field; if I get through with the most vital organs, I can count on losing at least a few joints of major appendages, plus a big bunch of nerve endings, to what appear to be senseless, arbitrary blasts. Instead, during the publication of this book I have felt like a member of a partnership in which all partners work together enthusiastically toward a common goal; this has been a great joy, indeed.

I am grateful for all your help.

Urbana, Illinois
September 5, 1980

Contents

THE
ULTIMATE
RESOURCE

INTRODUCTION ───────────

What Are the *Real* Population and Resource Problems?

Is there a natural-resource problem now? Certainly there is — just as there has always been. The problem is that natural resources are scarce, in the sense that it costs us labor and capital to get them, though we would prefer to get them for free.

Are we now "entering an age of scarcity"? You can see anything you like in a crystal ball. But almost without exception, the best data — the long-run economic indicators — suggest precisely the opposite. The relevant measures of scarcity — the costs of natural resources in human labor, and their prices relative to wages and to other goods — all suggest that natural resources have been becoming *less* scarce over the long run, right up to the present.

How about pollution? Is this not a problem? Of course pollution is a problem — people have always had to dispose of their waste products so as to enjoy a pleasant and healthy living space. But on the average we now live in a less dirty and more healthy environment than in earlier centuries.

About population now: Is there a population "problem"? Again, of course there is a population problem, just as there has always been. When a couple is about to have a baby, they must prepare a place for the child to sleep safely. Then, after the birth of the child, the parents must feed, clothe, guard, and teach it. All of this requires effort and resources, and not from the parents alone. When a baby is born or a migrant arrives, a community must increase its municipal services — schooling, fire and police protection, and garbage collection. None of these are free.

Beyond any doubt, an additional child is a burden on people other than its parents — and in some ways even on them — for the first fifteen or twenty-five years of its life. Brothers and sisters must do with less of everything except companionship. Taxpayers must cough up additional funds for schooling and other public services. Neighbors have more noise. During these early years the child produces nothing, and the income of the family and the community is spread around more thinly than if the baby were not born. And when the child grows up and first goes to work, jobs are squeezed a bit, and the output and pay per working person go down. All this clearly is an economic loss for other people.

Almost equally beyond any doubt, however, an additional person is also a boon. The child or immigrant will pay taxes later on, contribute energy and resources to the community, produce goods and services for the consumption of others, and make efforts to beautify and purify the environment. Perhaps most significant of all for the more-developed countries is the contribution that the average person makes to increasing the efficiency of production through new ideas and improved methods.

The real population problem, then, is *not* that there are too many people or that too many babies are being born. It is that others must support each additional person before that person contributes in turn to the well-being of others.

Which is more weighty, the burden or the boon? That depends on the economic conditions, about which we shall speak at some length. But also, to a startling degree, the decision about whether the overall effect of a child or migrant is positive or negative depends on the values of whoever is making the judgment — your preference to spend a dollar now rather than to wait for a dollar-plus-something in twenty or thirty years, your preferences for having more or fewer wild animals alive as opposed to more or fewer human beings alive, and so on. Population growth is a problem, but not *just* a problem; it is a boon, but not just a boon. So your values are all-important in judging the net effect of population growth, and whether there is "overpopulation" or "underpopulation."

An additional child is, from the economic point of view, like a laying chicken, a cacao tree, a new factory, or a new house. A baby is a durable good in which someone must invest heavily long before the grown adult begins to provide returns on the investment. But whereas "Travel now, pay later" is inherently attractive because the pleasure is immediate and the piper will wait, "Pay now, benefit from the child later" is inherently problematic because the sacrifice comes first.

You might respond that additional children will *never* yield net benefits, because they will use up irreplaceable resources. Much of this book is devoted to showing that additional persons do, in fact, produce more than they consume, and that natural resources are not an exception. But let us agree that there is still a population problem, just as there is a problem with all good investments: Long before there are benefits, we must tie up capital that could otherwise be used for immediate consumption.

Please notice that I have restricted the discussion to the *economic* aspect of investing in children — that is, to a child's effect on the material standard of living. If we also consider the non-economic aspects of children — what they mean to parents and to others who enjoy a flourishing of humanity — then the case for adding children to our world becomes even stronger. And if we also keep in mind that most of the costs of children are borne by their parents rather than by the community, whereas the community gets the lion's share of the benefits later on, especially in developed countries, the essential differences between children and other investments tend to strengthen rather than weaken the case for having more children.

PREVIEW OF THE BOOK

Here are some of the topics covered in this book.

Food. Contrary to popular impression, the per capita food situation has been improving for the three decades since World War II, the only decades for which we have acceptable data. We also know that famine has progressively diminished for at least the past century. And there is strong reason to believe that human nutrition will continue to improve into the indefinite future, even with continued population growth.

Land. Agricultural land is not a fixed resource, as Malthus and many since Malthus have thought. Rather, the amount of agricultural land has been, and still is, increasing substantially, and it is likely to continue to increase where needed. Paradoxically, in the countries that are best supplied with food, such as the U.S., the quantity of land under cultivation has been decreasing because it is more economical to raise larger yields on less land than to increase the total amount of farmland. For this reason, among others, land for recreation and for wildlife has been increasing rapidly in the U.S. All this may be hard to believe, but solid data substantiate these statements beyond a doubt.

Natural resources. Hold your hat — our supplies of natural resources are not finite in any economic sense. Nor does past experience give reason to expect natural resources to become more scarce. Rather, if the past is any guide, natural resources will progressively become less scarce, and less costly, and will constitute a smaller proportion of our expenses in future years. And population growth is likely to have a long-run *beneficial* impact on the natural-resource situation.

Energy. Grab your hat again — the long-run future of our energy supply is at least as bright as that of other natural resources, though political maneuvering can temporarily boost prices from time to time. Finiteness is no problem here either. And the long-run impact of additional people is likely to speed the development of a cheap energy supply that is almost inexhaustible.

Pollution. This set of issues is as complicated as you wish to make it. But even many ecologists, as well as the bulk of economists, agree that population growth is not the villain in the creation and reduction of pollution. And the key trend is that life expectancy, which is the best overall index of the pollution level, has improved markedly as the world's population has grown.

Pathological effects of population density. This putative drawback of population growth is sheer myth. Its apparent source is faulty biological and psychological analogies with animal populations.

The standard of living. In the short run, additional children imply additional costs, though the costs to persons other than the children's parents are relatively small. In the longer run, however, per capita income is likely to be higher with a growing population than with a stationary one, both in more-developed and less-developed countries. Whether you wish to pay the present costs for the future benefits depends on how you weigh the future relative to the present; this is a value judgment.

Immigration. Immigration usually has a positive effect on most citizens. The few persons whom the immigrants might displace from their jobs may be hurt, of course, but many of them only temporarily. On balance, immigrants contribute more to the economy than they take, in the U.S. and most other places.

Human fertility. The contention that poor and uneducated people breed like animals is demonstrably wrong, even for the poorest and most "primitive" societies. Well-off people who believe that the poor do not weigh the consequences of having more children are simply arrogant or ignorant, or both.

Future population growth. Population forecasts are publicized with confidence and fanfare, but the record of even the official forecasts made by

U.S. government agencies and by the UN is little (if any) better than that of the most naive predictions. For example, experts in the 1930s foresaw the U.S. population as declining, perhaps to as little as 100 million people, long before the turn of the century. And official UN forecasts made in 1970 for the year 2000, a mere thirty years in advance, were five years later revised downward by almost 2 billion people, from 7.5 billion to 5.6 billion. Nor is the record better with more modern statistical methods. Perhaps most astonishing is a forecast made by the recent President's Commission on Population Growth and the American Future. In 1972 the commission published its prediction that "there will be no year in the next two decades in which the absolute number of births will be less than in 1970." But in the year *before* this prediction was made — 1971 — the number of births had *already* fallen lower than in 1970. The science of demographic forecasting clearly has not yet reached perfection.

World population policy. Tens of millions of U.S. taxpayers' money is being used to tell the governments and people of other countries that they ought to take strong measures to control their fertility. The head of the Population Branch of the U.S. State Department Agency for International Development (AID) — the single most important U.S. population official for many years — has publicly said that the U.S. should act to reduce fertility worldwide for its own economic self-interest. But no solid economic data or analyses underlie this assertion. Furthermore, might not such acts be an unwarranted interference in the internal affairs of other countries?

Domestic population activities. Other millions of U.S. taxpayers' funds go to private organizations making up the population lobby, whose directors believe that, for environmental and related reasons, fewer Americans should be born. These funds are used to propagandize the rest of us that we should believe — and act — in ways consistent with the views of such organizations as the Population Crisis Committee, the Population Reference Bureau, the Worldwatch Institute, the Environmental Fund, and the Association for Voluntary Sterilization.

Still more tens of millions of U.S. taxpayers' funds are being spent to reduce the fertility of the poor in the U.S. The explicit justification for this policy (given by the head of Planned Parenthood's Alan Guttmacher Institute) is that it will keep additional poor people off the welfare rolls. Even were this to be proven — and as far as I know it has not been proven — is this in the spirit or tradition of America? Furthermore, there is statistical proof that the public birth-control clinics, which were first opened in large numbers in the southern states, were positioned to reduce fertility among blacks.

Involuntary sterilization. Tax moneys are being used to involuntarily sterilize poor people (often black) without medical justification. As a result of the eugenics movement, which has been intertwined with the population-control movement for decades, there are now laws in thirty states providing for the involuntary sterilization of the mentally defective, and many thousands have been so sterilized. And these laws have led to perfectly normal women being sterilized, without their knowledge, after being told that their operations were other sorts of minor surgery.

In the chapters to come, you will find evidence documenting these statements and many others about resources, population, environment, and their interconnections. You will also find a foundation of economic theory that makes sense of the surprising facts. And you will find my offer to back with my own hard cash my forecasts about the things we can bet about — natural resources and energy. If you believe that scarcities are coming, you can take advantage of my offer and make some money at my expense.

ABOUT NUMBERS AND WRITERS

There are a good many numbers in the text, many of them in diagrams and tables; and an additional array of relevant data are in the Appendix. Numerical presentations are not popular. But without the numbers, the arguments in this book could not stand. If the conclusions reached here were not backed with hard data as proof, some would be instantly rejected because they violate common sense, and others would be rejected because they starkly contradict the main body of popular writings about population and resources.

You may look skeptically at some of the data I give — such as the statistics showing that world per capita food production and consumption are going up, even in poor countries, year by year. You may ask, "But what about the evidence that supports what everyone 'knows' — that the world is headed toward starvation and famine?" In this case, the simple fact is that there are no other data. The data presented here on food are UN and U.S. government data, the only data there are. If UN and U.S. officials often make statements inconsistent with these data, it is because

they have not looked at them, or because they are purposely disregarding
them. Some of the other data are more subject to argument. I have tried
to give you an honest shake on the data, but you will be the final judge
of that.

ABOUT THIS AUTHOR AND HIS VALUES

This book originated in my interest in the economics of population. In
order to show that population growth is not a straightforward evil, I had
to show that more people need not cause scarcities or environmental
decay in the long run. That's how this book came to be written.

Ironically, when I began to work on population studies, I assumed that
the accepted view was sound. I aimed to help the world contain its
"exploding" population, which I believed to be one of the two main
threats to mankind (war being the other). But my reading and research
led me into confusion. Though the standard economic theory of population (which has hardly changed since Malthus) asserts that a higher
population growth implies a lower standard of living, the available
empirical data do not support that theory. My technical book, which is
the predecessor of this volume, is an attempt to reconcile that contradiction. It leads to a theory that suggests population growth has positive
economic effects in the long run, though there are costs in the short run.

When I began my population studies, I was in the midst of a depression of unusual duration (whose origins had nothing to do with population growth or the world's predicament). As I studied the economics of
population and worked my way to the views I now hold—that population growth, along with the lengthening of human life, is a moral and
material triumph—my outlook for myself, for my family, and for the
future of humanity became increasingly more optimistic. Eventually I
was able to pull myself out of my depression. This is only part of the
story, but there is at least some connection between the two sets of mental events—my population studies and my increasing optimism.

One spring day about 1969 I visited the AID office in Washington to
discuss a project intended to lower fertility in less-developed countries.
I arrived early for my appointment, so I strolled outside in the warm
sunshine. Below the building's plaza I noticed a sign that said "Iwo Jima
Highway." I remembered reading about a eulogy delivered by a Jewish
chaplain over the dead on the battlefield at Iwo Jima, saying something
like, "How many who would have been a Mozart or a Michelangelo or
an Einstein have we buried here?" And then I thought, Have I gone
crazy? What business do I have trying to help arrange it that fewer

human beings will be born, each one of whom might be a Mozart or a Michelangelo or an Einstein — or simply a joy to his or her family and community, and a person who will enjoy life?

I still believe that helping people fulfill their desires for the number of children they want is a wonderful service. But to persuade them or coerce them to have fewer children than they would individually like to have — that is something entirely different.

The longer I read the literature about population, the more baffled and distressed I become that one idea is omitted: Enabling a potential human being to come into life and to enjoy life is a good thing, just as enabling a living person's life not to be ended is a good thing. Of course a death is not the same as an averted life, in part because others feel differently about the two. Yet I find no logic implicit in the thinking of those who are horrified at the starvation of a comparatively few people in a faraway country (and apparently more horrified than at the deaths by political murder in that same faraway country, or at the deaths by accidents in their own country) but who are positively gleeful with the thought that 1 million or 10 million times that many lives will never be lived that might be lived.

Economics alone cannot explain this attitude, for though the economic consequences of death differ from those of non-life, they are not so different as to explain this difference in attitude. So what is it? Why does Kingsley Davis (one of the world's great demographers) respond to the U.S. population growth during the 1960s with, "I have never been able to get anyone to tell me why we needed those 23 million"?[1] And Paul Ehrlich: "I can't think of any reason for having more than one hundred fifty million people [in the U.S.], and no one has ever raised one to me."[2]

I can suggest to Davis and Ehrlich more than one reason for having more children and taking in more immigrants. Least interesting is that the larger population will probably mean a higher standard of living for our grandchildren and great-grandchildren. (My technical book and a good many chapters in this book substantiate that assertion.) A more interesting reason is that we need another person for exactly the same reason we need Davis and Ehrlich. That is, just as the Davises and Ehrlichs of this world are of value to the rest of us, so will the average additional person be of value.

The most interesting reason for having additional people, however, is this: If the Davises and Ehrlichs say that their lives are of value to themselves, and if the rest of us honor that claim and say that our lives are of value to us, then in the same manner the lives of additional people are of value to those people themselves. Why should we not honor their claims, too?

If Davis or Ehrlich were to ask those 23 million additional Americans born between 1960 and 1970 whether it was a good thing that they were born, many of them would be able to think of a good reason or two. Some of them might also be so unkind as to add, "Yes, it's true that you gentlemen do not *personally* need any of us for your own welfare. But then, do you think that *we* have greater need of *you?"*

What is most astonishing is that these simple ideas, which would immediately spring to the minds of many who cannot read or write, have never even come into the heads of famous scientists such as Davis and Ehrlich — by their own admission.

The same absence of this basic respect for human life is at the bottom of Ehrlich's well-known restatement of Pascal's wager. "If I'm right, we will save the world [by curbing population growth]. If I'm wrong, people will still be better fed, better housed, and happier, thanks to our efforts. [He probably *is* wrong.] Will anything be lost if it turns out later that we can support a much larger population than seems possible today?"[3]

Please note how different is Pascal's wager: Live as if there is God, because even if there is no God you have lost nothing. Pascal's wager applies entirely to one person. No one else loses if he is wrong. But Ehrlich bets what he thinks will be the economic gains that we and our descendants might enjoy against the unborn's very lives. Would he make the same sort of wager if his own life rather than others' lives were the stake?

A last, very personal word: I may come through the print to you as feisty or even tough, and able to take care of myself in this argument. But I am not very feisty in person. I have been trying — mostly unsuccessfully — to get a hearing for these ideas since 1969, and though times have changed somewhat, the difficulties of espousing this unpopular point of view do get to me; until recently they were near the point of shutting me up and shutting me down. If there weren't a handful of editors like Sandy Thatcher of Princeton University Press, you wouldn't hear from me at all. Some others hold a point of view similar to mine. But there are far too few of us to provide mutual support and comfort. So this is a plea for love, printer's ink, and research grants for our side. All contributions gratefully accepted.

Now let's see if my facts and arguments persuade you of the claims I have made.

PART ONE

TOWARD OUR BEAUTIFUL
RESOURCE FUTURE

Necessity is the mother of invention.

RICHARD FRANCK, *Northern Memoirs*, 1694

1.

The Amazing Theory of
Raw-Material Scarcity

The Great Toy Shortage

Forget it, Virginia. Santa won't be leaving a "Star Wars" R2-D2
doll under the tree this year — just an I.O.U. promising you one
at some vague time between February and June. Don't count on
a Mego Micronaut kit for building your own robot either, or a
Milky the Marvelous Milking Cow, which drinks water when
its tail is pumped, moos plaintively and squirts a tiny pailful of
cloudy white "milk" from a detachable pink udder....

Not since the Grinch stole Christmas has there been such an
unseasonable shortage.

TIME, *December 19, 1977, p. 58*

The "Great Toy Shortage" clearly was a freak event. We don't worry
that there will be a long-run scarcity of Hula-Hoops, pencils, dental care,
radios, or new musical compositions. And we don't fear that a larger population will have an adverse effect upon the supply of these goods. Yet
people do worry about an impending scarcity of copper, iron, aluminum,
oil, food, and other natural resources. According to a typical Ehrlichian
pronouncement, "In the early 1970s, the leading edge of the age of scarcity arrived. With it came a clearer look at the future, revealing more of
the nature of the dark age to come."[1] That we are entering an age of
scarcity in which our finite natural resources are running out, that our
environment is becoming more polluted, and that population growth
threatens our civilization and our very lives — such are the propositions
continually repeated with little more evidence than that "everyone
knows" they are true.

The age-of-scarcity proposition has been used to justify almost any policy a writer has wished to put forth. For instance, in a *New York Times*

Magazine article about the U.S. political scene, the headline is "No Room in the Lifeboats," and the subheadline is "The Age of Scarcity and accompanying new 'lifeboat ethic' threatens some basic American beliefs...."[2] The author writes that "the cost of natural resources is going up.... Because of resource scarcity and the population explosion, the reserve army of the unemployable is becoming so vast [that it] begins to create social instability.... People without jobs, money or hope ... Draconian economics and brutal politics." And a leftist political economist, speaking of a "resurgence of racism," says, "It's no accident that it's coming at a time of economic scarcity."[3] In addition to these social catastrophes, a larger population is commonly thought to compound the threat of natural-resource exhaustion. As a spokeswoman for Zero Population Growth put it, "An exploding population with an increasing appetite is operating in a finite world with diminishing resources."[4]

What is the economic difference between extractive natural resources and Hula-Hoops or dental care? Is there really a difference? These are the questions that this chapter explores in a general theoretical way. The chapter draws examples from the metallic raw materials, which are relatively uncomplicated by government regulations or international cartels and which are neither "burned up" like oil nor grown anew like agricultural products. Energy, food, and land will be given special treatment in later chapters.

BETWEEN PIG COPPER AND DENTISTRY

The intuitive difference between how we get Hula-Hoops and copper is the notion that copper comes from a reservoir of natural copper in the earth, whereas a Hula-Hoop is not a "natural" resource. Each extraction of copper from the natural stockpile mines the most accessible lode as of that moment. Therefore mining operations successively work on less and less accessible lodes bearing successively lower grades of ore. If all else were equal, this trend would imply that the cost of mining copper must continually rise as less and less accessible lodes are mined. Hula-Hoops and dental care and radios *seem* different from copper because most of the cost of a radio, a Hula-Hoop, or dental care arises from human labor and skill, and only a small part arises from the raw material — the petroleum in the plastic hoop or the silver in the tooth filling. For good reason we do not worry that human labor and skill comes from progressively less accessible reservoirs.

But all this neat theorizing about increasing scarcity due to depleted lodes is refuted by a most peculiar fact: Over the course of history, up to this very moment, copper and other minerals have been getting less scarce rather than more scarce, as the depletion theory implies. In this respect copper follows the same historical trends as radios, undershirts, and other consumer goods (figures 1-1a and 1-1b). And it is this fact that forces us to go beyond our simple theory and to think more deeply about the matter.

At the end of this confrontation between theory and fact, we shall be compelled to reject the simple depletion theory. The revised theory will suggest that natural resources are not finite in any meaningful economic sense, mind-boggling though this assertion may be. That is, there is no solid reason to believe that there will ever be a greater scarcity of these extractive resources in the long-run future than there is now. Rather, we can confidently expect copper and other minerals to get progressively less scarce.

WHAT IS SCARCITY?

Here we must pause for an unexciting but crucial matter, the definition of "scarcity." Ask yourself: If copper—or oil or any other good—were much scarcer today than it actually is, what would be the evidence of this scarcity? That is, what are the signs—the criteria—of a raw material being in short supply?

Upon reflection perhaps you will agree that a complete absence of the material will *not* be a sign of scarcity. We will not reach up to the shelf and suddenly find that it is completely bare. It is obvious that the scarcity of any raw material would only gradually increase. Long before the shelf would be bare, individuals and firms, the latter operating purely out of the self-interested drive to make future profits, would be taking steps to hoard supplies for future resale so that the shelf would never be completely bare. Of course the price of the hoarded material would be high, but there still would be some quantities to be found at some price, just as there always has been some small amount of food for sale even in the midst of the very worst famines.

The preceding observation points to a key sign of what we generally mean by scarcity: a price that has persistently risen. More generally, cost and price—whatever we mean by "price," and shortly we shall see that that term is often subject to question—will be our basic measures of scarcity.

In some situations, though, prices can mislead us. The price of a scarce

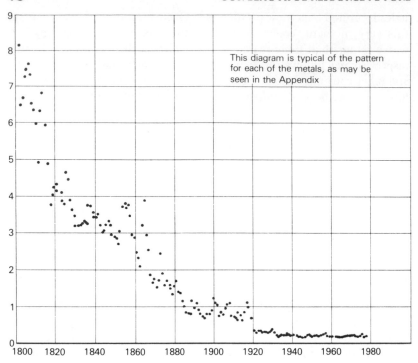

FIGURE 1-1a. The Scarcity of Copper as Measured by Its Price Relative to Wages

material may not rise high enough to "clear the market" — that is, to discourage enough buyers so that supply and demand come to be equal, as they ultimately will be in a free market (or even in a properly adjusted socialist system). If the price is deliberately held down, there may be waiting lines or rationing, and these may also be taken as signs of scarcity. But though lines and rationing may be efficient and fair ways of allocating scarce materials in the short run, in the longer run they are so wasteful that every sort of society tends to prevent them by letting the price rise enough to clear the market. Therefore we are not likely to see lines and rationing if there is a long-run (as contrasted to a temporary) scarcity of a raw material.

In general, then, if the scarcity of a raw material increases, its price will rise. But the converse need not be true; the price may rise even without a "true" increase in scarcity. For example, a strong cartel may

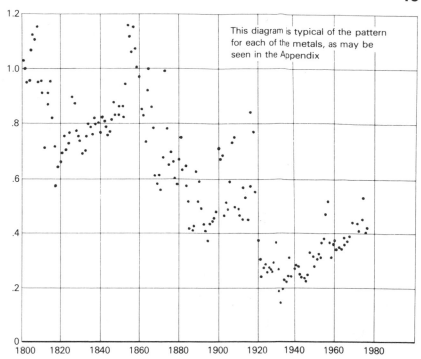

This diagram is typical of the pattern for each of the metals, as may be seen in the Appendix

FIGURE 1-1b. The Scarcity of Copper as Measured by Its Price Relative to the Consumer Price Index

successfully raise prices, as OPEC did in 1973 even though the cost of producing oil remained unchanged. This suggests that, in addition to the price in the market, we should consider production costs as an index of scarcity. But the measurement of production costs in money is not easy. Therefore we may turn to another measure of production costs and of scarcity, the amount of labor (and perhaps the amount of capital) needed to produce the material. Production costs measured in labor hours rather than in money may, however, be difficult to interpret because of wage changes. Hence, unless we have strong reason to believe that market prices do not reflect production costs, we should consider market prices as our primary measure of scarcity.

A more personal — but often relevant — test of scarcity is whether you and I (and other people) feel that we can afford to buy the material. That is, the relationship between price and income may matter. If the price of food remains constant but income falls sharply, then we feel that food is more scarce. By a similar test, if our wages rise while the price of oil remains constant, our fuller pockets lead us to feel that oil is getting less scarce.

A related test of scarcity is the importance of the material in your budget. You are not likely to say that salt has gotten appreciably more scarce even if its price doubles, because it accounts for an insignificant share of your expenditures.

So price, together with related measures such as cost and share of income, is the appropriate operational test of scarcity at any given moment. (We shall see later how this *economic* measure differs from a *technological* test of scarcity, which requires an estimate of how much material is available at a given moment.) What matters to us as consumers is how much we have to pay to obtain goods that give us particular services; from our standpoint, it couldn't matter less how much iron or oil there "really" is in the natural "stockpile." Therefore, to understand the economics of natural resources, it is crucial to understand that the most appropriate *economic* measure of scarcity is the price of a natural resource compared to some relevant benchmark.

Future scarcity is our interest. Our task, then, is to forecast future prices of raw materials.

WHAT IS THE BEST WAY TO FORECAST SCARCITY AND COSTS?

There are two quite different general methods for forecasting future costs of any kind: the economist's method and the engineer's method.[5] The engineering method is the one commonly used in discussions of raw materials; but I shall be arguing that the conclusions about costs reached with it are usually dead wrong because it is not the appropriate method.

With the engineering method, you forecast the status of a natural resource as follows: (1) estimate the presently known physical quantity of the resource on or in the earth; (2) extrapolate the future rate of use from the current use rate; and (3) subtract the successive estimates of use in (2) from the physical "inventory" in (1).

In contrast, the economist's approach extrapolates trends of past costs, if the trends can be reconciled with the theory (as they can be in the case of raw-material supply history). This is in sharp contrast to the technologist's physical analysis of the present state of affairs. Given this wide disparity between the two approaches, it behooves us to consider the conditions under which each is likely to be valid.

   The forecasting situation is analogous to that of a businessman who wishes to estimate costs of some piece of construction or production for the firm. Making sound estimates of costs and supplies is the businessman's bread and butter, the difference between solvency and bankruptcy. The extent to which a business uses one or the other method depends largely upon whether the organization itself has much or little experience with the type of project whose costs it wants to assess. Examples of jobs with which the organization already has a great deal of experience are a construction firm preparing a bid on a small parking lot or on an excavation of the sort that the firm has done many times before, and a chain franchising operation estimating the cost of adding another hamburger shop. In such cases the firm will, as a matter of course, estimate costs directly from its own records. In the case of the new hamburger shop, the estimate may simply be the average total cost of shops recently built, as already computed by the firm. In the case of the parking lot or excavation, the construction firm may be able to estimate with good accuracy the amounts required of the main components — labor and machine time — and their current prices.

   It is only when the firm does not have direct experience with the type of project being costed that it must and will make an *engineering* analysis of the project, together with estimates of the requirements for each element of the job. But the businessman, and the social analyst of natural resources too, should turn to engineering cost-estimates only in the unfortunate absence of reliable data from the past, because engineering estimates are much harder to make accurately, for a variety of reasons. An analogy may help. In forecasting the speed of a three-year-old race horse, would you rely more on a veterinary and anatomical inspection of the horse's bones and organs, or on the results of its past races?

   Considerable data showing trends in raw-material prices are available, as seen in the Appendix to this book. The overwhelming impression given by these figures is that costs for extractive materials have fallen over the course of recorded price history. The economist's first-approximation forecast is that these trends toward less scarcity should continue into the foreseeable future unless there is some reason to believe that conditions have changed, that is, unless there is something wrong with the data as a basis for extrapolation.

   In brief, the economist's and businessman's approach to price trends is to learn by experience — relevant experience. As P. T. Bauer put it, "Our predictions are firmly based on a study of the way these problems have been overcome in the past. And it is only the past that gives us any insight into the laws of motion of human society and hence enables us to predict the future."[6]

WILL THE FUTURE BREAK WITH THE PAST?

How should one judge whether a historical trend is a sound basis for a forecast? Specifically, how can we judge whether the data from the many decades in the past showing declines in raw-material costs are a good basis for prediction?

The question facing us is a problem in a scientific generalization. A good general principle is that you should generalize from your data if you can reasonably regard them as a fair sample of the universe about which you wish to generalize. It is prediction that concerns us, however, and prediction is not quite the same as generalization. Prediction is a special type of generalization, a generalization from past to future. Prediction is always a leap of faith; there is no scientific guarantee that the sun will come up tomorrow. It is purely your judgment and knowledge of your subject matter that supports your analysis, based on what happened in the past, that something similar will happen in the future.

A prediction based on past data can be sound if it is sensible to assume that the past and the future belong to the same statistical universe, that is, if you can expect conditions that held in the past to remain the same in the future.[7] Therefore, we must ask: Have conditions changed in very recent years in such a manner that the data generated over the many past decades are no longer relevant?

The most important elements in raw-material price trends have been (1) the rate of movement from richer to poorer ores and mining locations — that is, the phenomenon of "exhaustion"; and (2) the continued development of technology, which has more than made up for the exhaustion of the more accessible and richer lodes of ores.

We must also inquire: Is there reason to believe that the rate of development of such new technology is slowing up? The answer is to the contrary; the pace of development of new technology in general is increasing. Hence if the past differs from the present and future, our bias is likely to be in the direction of understating the rate at which technology will develop and therefore underestimating the rate at which costs will fall.

Besides extrapolating the overall trends of prices, the economist-businessman approach also extrapolates the trends of the most important elements in cost — extraction costs, rates of new discoveries in resources and methods, and the richness of the deposits available for exploitation. We know the direction of the trend of each of these elements, empirically as well as theoretically. But to my knowledge this research has yet to be done with sufficient precision so that we may then confidently combine the subtrends to produce a satisfying overall estimate.

Too often the response to the long trend of falling raw-material prices resembles this parody: We look at a tub of water and mark the water level. We assert that the quantity of water in the tub is "finite." Then we observe people taking water out of the tub and walking away. When we return, lo and behold the water level is higher (analogous to the price being lower) than before. We believe that no one has reason to put water into the tub (as almost no one will put oil into an oil well), so we figure that some peculiar accident has occurred, one that is not likely to be repeated. But each time we return, the water level in the tub is higher than before — and water is selling at an ever cheaper price. Yet we simply repeat over and over that the quantity of water *must* be finite and cannot continue to increase, and that's all there is to it.

Would not a prudent person, after a long train of rises in the water level, conclude that perhaps the process may continue — and that it therefore makes sense to seek reasonable explanations? Would not a sensible person check whether there are inlet pipes to the tub? Or whether someone has developed a process for producing water? Whether people are using less water than before? Whether people are restocking the tub with recycled water? Whatever the real explanation, it makes sense to look for the cause of this apparent miracle, rather than cling to a simple-minded fixed-resources theory and assert that it cannot continue.

The fall in the costs of natural resources decade after decade, and century after century, should shake us free from the idea that scarcity *must* increase *sometime*. Instead, it should point us toward trying to understand the way that technological changes are induced by the demand for the resources and for the services they provide, and the way that such changes reduced scarcity in the past.

Please notice that observing current prices does not mislead us about future scarcities. If there is reason to judge that the cost of obtaining a certain resource in the future will be much greater than it is now, speculators will hoard that material to obtain the higher future price, thereby raising the present price. So current price is our best measure of both current *and* future scarcity (more about this later).

Figure 1-1 and the Appendix to this book show the fundamental economic facts about natural resources: The costs and prices of most natural resources have been going down rather than up since at least 1800. However, cost and price can be slippery ideas and therefore require technical discussion in the Afternote to this chapter. Here I'll say but a few words on the matter.

The basic way to measure the cost of, say, copper, is with the ratios between the price of copper and the prices of other products. These ratios, as in figure 1-1, show us the terms of trade between copper and non-extractive products. One such measure is to examine the price of copper relative to wages, as shown in figure 1-1a. This price has declined very sharply (please notice the logarithmic scale in the figure). This means that an hour's work in the U.S. has bought increasingly more copper from 1800 to the present. The same trend has almost surely held throughout history, and similar trends are found for other raw materials, as seen in the Appendix. The decreasing price of copper relative to non-extractive products means that it now takes smaller quantities of haircuts or underwear to buy a ton of copper than it did a century ago.

The relative price between copper and other products is like a current-dollar price that has been adjusted for the cost of living. But we must remember that the other items in the cost-of-living index *also* have been produced progressively more cheaply over the years. Even if the price of copper had remained level relative to other items, our data would indicate that the scarcity of copper has diminished. But minerals have declined in price even faster than have the other products. That is, if all products were shown in diagrams like figure 1-1b, with their current prices adjusted for the cost of living, half the products would have to show a rising price. Therefore, the fact that the price of copper is seen to be declining relative to other goods is indeed a strong demonstration of its decreasing scarcity.

Another relevant concept of scarcity is the labor cost per unit of raw-material output. Labor cost, in constant dollars per unit of output of copper and other metals, has declined sharply although wages (labor costs per unit of labor) have risen markedly. If we calculate the outputs of copper and other metals per hour of labor input, we find a breathtaking decline in the cost of natural resources over the years.

(There are always some people who respond to such data by saying that the data do not reflect what happened last year or last week, and that the long-term trends no longer hold. There is no way of proving such statements wrong. But it is a safe guess from the history of such analyses that extrapolations from the recent past that run against previous long-term trends are more often wrong than are extrapolations of the long-term trends. More about this shortly, when I offer to back this judgment with hard cash.)

Another way to think about the cost of natural resources is to find the ratio of natural-resource costs to the total cost of all products. This measure also reveals a steady decline in cost. The absolute physical quantities of natural resources extracted have been rising, and the kinds of resources used have been increasing in number. But the expenditure on them has been falling as a proportion of total expenditures. "The gross value of extractive output [including agriculture, oil, and coal] relative to value of national product has declined substantially and steadily from 1870 to the present. In 1890, the extractive share was nearly 50 percent. By the turn of the century, it had fallen to 32 percent; and, by 1919, to 23 percent. In 1957, the figure was 13 percent and still trending downward",[8] a more recent figure is roughly 6 percent. And in 1972, minerals plus energy (but excluding food) accounted for only 3 percent of the U.S. GNP, and minerals (excluding energy sources) accounted for only about 1 percent of the GNP.[9] This trend makes it clear that the cost of minerals — even if it becomes considerably higher, which we have no reason to expect — is almost irrelevant to our standard of living; and hence a "scarcity" of minerals is not a real danger to our peacetime standard of living.

Of all the trends discussed so far, this last trend is the closest-to-home measure of changing raw-materials costs. Every trend leads us to the same conclusion, but these calculations of expenditures for raw materials as a proportion of total family budgets make the point most strongly: Raw materials have been getting increasingly available — less scarce — relative to the most important element of life, human work time. Taken together, the various data suggest the anti-intuitive conclusion that, even as we use coal and oil and iron and other natural resources, they are becoming less scarce. Yet this is indeed the appropriate economic way of viewing the situation. (If you want to explore further these measures of price and scarcity, see the Afternote to this chapter.)

A CHALLENGE TO THE DOOMSDAYERS TO PUT THEIR MONEY WHERE THEIR MOUTHS ARE

Talk is cheap, especially scare talk that gets newspaper attention and foundation grants. Where I come from, when we feel that someone is talking without having to take responsibility for the results, we say, "Put your money where your mouth is." I am prepared to back my judgment with my own cash. If I am wrong about the future of natural resources, you can make money at my expense.

If mineral resources such as copper will be more scarce in the future —

that is, if the real price will rise — you can make money by buying the minerals now and selling them later at the higher prices. This is exactly what is done by speculators who believe that the prices of commodities will rise (although for convenience' sake, they really buy contracts for the commodities, or "futures," rather than physical stocks, and let someone else handle the warehousing).

Please notice that you do not have to wait ten or twenty years to realize a profit, even if the expected changes in supply and demand will not occur for ten or twenty years. As soon as information about an impending scarcity becomes known and accepted, people begin buying the commodity, bidding up the present market price so that it reflects the future scarcity. Current market prices thus reflect the best guesses of professionals who spend their lives studying commodities and who stake their wealth and incomes on being right about the future.

An example of how expectations about future scarcity influence present prices was in a recent newspaper story about the large quantities of natural gas that Holland discovered in 1959 in Groningen Province. "The Dutch began signing contracts for their natural gas in the 1960s because they were fearful that nuclear power would make gas obsolete as a fuel source. Some of these export contracts won't run out until the end of the century."[10] Those who contracted for Holland's gas are (so far) the gainers, because they are now getting gas cheaper than the price that has ruled since the OPEC cartel sharply raised oil prices starting in 1973. And Holland is the loser — so far. But if the OPEC cartel breaks up and the price of oil comes down to anywhere near production cost, or if nuclear power does develop as the Dutch originally expected, Holland will profit from its long-term contracts and the buyers will be worse off.

The point is that both Holland and the long-run buyers backed their beliefs with their money. Will the doomsdayers who now say that minerals and other raw materials will get more scarce do the same?

A colleague of mine had the guts to do just that. He had been investigating long-run weather forecasting, and he forecast droughts for 1976 and 1977. He believed that harvests would fall and grain prices go up. Therefore he "sold short" in the grain market, which would have enabled him to profit if the price of grain rose. Unfortunately for him, but happily for consumers, the drought was neither grave nor universal. Furthermore, my friend did not allow for the capacities of farmers to make various adjustments to fight drought, such as digging new wells. The price of grain did not rise, but rather fell sharply as bountiful harvests came in. And my colleague therefore took a drubbing.

Another cautionary example is how Japan let itself be panicked by fears of future scarcities in the wake of the OPEC oil embargo and the resulting general price rise in 1973. Japan is now paying heavily for this blunder.

> The Japanese, and above all Japanese officialdom, were seized by hysteria in 1974 when raw materials shortages were cropping up everywhere. They bought and bought and bought [copper, iron ore, pulp, sulphur, and coking coal]. Now they are frantically trying to get out of commitments to take delivery, and have slashed raw materials imports nearly in half. Even so, industrial inventories are bulging with high-priced raw materials.[11]

You may say that I, too, should put my money where my mouth is. Fair enough. This is a public offer to stake $10,000, in separate transactions of $1,000 or $100 each, on my belief that mineral resources (or food or other commodities) will not rise in price. If you are prepared to pay me now the current market price for $1,000 or $100 worth of any mineral you name (or other raw material including grain and fossil fuels) that is not government controlled, I will agree to pay you the market price of the same amount of that raw material on any future date you now specify.[12]

Will the doomsdayers, who now say that minerals and other raw materials will get more scarce, also put their money where their mouths are? Paul Ehrlich, by contrast, has said, "If I were a gambler, I would take even money that England will not exist in the year 2000."[13] I imagine he would find a good many takers.

SUMMARY

The costs of raw materials have fallen sharply over the period of recorded history, no matter which reasonable measure of cost and price one chooses to use. This chapter has argued that these historical trends are the best basis for predicting the trends of future costs, too.

It is paradoxical that cost and scarcity decrease as more of the material is used. The following chapter discusses this paradox, and focuses on a couple of crucial theoretical matters that unravel the paradoxes: first, the definition of resources as the *services* they provide rather than as stocks of materials, and second, an analysis of the concept of *finiteness*.

ΛFT∈RNOT∈

The "True" Cost (Price) of Natural Resources

In this chapter we have seen why the cost (or the price) of a given resource falls or rises. But we have skimmed past the questions of the meaning of the price of a good and of which way is most appropriate to measure its cost.

We may measure the cost of a ton of copper by measuring the amount of workers' time necessary to produce it. But there are obvious difficulties with this approach. Capital equipment may be substituted for labor in order to economize on the use of workers' time; no allowance is made in this approach for the cost of the equipment. And some workers' time is more expensive than others'; an hour of a college-trained technician's time might be worth more in the market than that of a pick-and-shovel man.

A more sophisticated approach is to compare the market price of a ton of copper to the market price of some other good that seems to be unchanging — say, the price of grain. But the cost of producing grain (and most other things) has also been changing over the years owing to changes in seeds, fertilizers, technology, and so on. So if the cost of grain has been falling, then the cost of copper would be falling even if the relationship between the two prices — the terms of trade — has remained the same over the years.

A still more sophisticated approach would be to compare the price of copper to the price of a good that has changed little technologically for a long time — say, a haircut. But the wages of barbers have gone up, as can be seen from the fact that a barber in the U.S. now has a much higher standard of living than did a U.S. barber 100 years ago — because the wages of people in other occupations have risen owing to gains in technology and education. So this comparison, too, does not give us a "true" or "absolute" measure of changes in the price of copper.

Yet another approach is to examine the price trend of the source of the raw material — the price of farmland instead of the price of grain, for example, or the price of copper mines instead of the price of copper — relative to some other goods.[1] But the price of the source will rise if there is a technological improvement in production methods even if there is no change in the "scarcity" of the product; the price of good farmland in the U.S. rises when crop yields go up or when new machinery is introduced (though the price of poor farmland falls because it is no longer profitable to use such land at all).

And as yet we have said nothing about inflation. But the question of allowing for price changes in a commodity due to changes in the general price level raises a host of difficult questions.

What to do? We must accept the inevitable: There can be no "true" or "absolute" measure of cost or price. Rather, different measures of cost give different sorts of information, useful for different purposes. But this we can say with assurance: The average cost of all consumer goods taken together — an index of consumer prices — has fallen over the years in more-developed countries, measured in terms of what an unskilled worker can buy, as shown by the long-run increase in the standard of living. Therefore, if a raw material has remained at least level in price compared to the average of goods, its "real" cost has fallen. And in fact the price of mineral natural resources has declined even more sharply than has the average price of other commodities. Furthermore, all other measures of mineral costs have also declined over the long run. Hence we can be quite sure that the cost of mineral natural resources has declined substantially, by any reasonable test.

Do Technological Forecasts and Economic Forecasts Necessarily Contradict Each Other?

The most publicized technological forecasts of long-run natural-resource scarcity disagree with economic forecasts of the sort given in this book. But are these the best technological forecasts? And do economic and technological forecasts necessarily contradict each other? The answer is no to both questions. Some of the best-informed technological forecasters agree strongly with the optimistic economic extrapolations and disagree with the pessimistic technological forecasts. That is, the variation among technological forecasts is as great as the differences between technological and economic forecasts, though the pessimistic technological forecasts have gotten much more attention than the optimistic ones. This chapter delves into the bases of agreement and disagreement among technological and economic forecasts of raw-material availability, and the next chapter explains why the forces that produced the long-run decrease in scarcity are likely to continue indefinitely.

THE NATURE OF TECHNOLOGICAL FORECASTS: EXPLAINING THE PARADOX

The historical fact that natural-resource costs have fallen, as measured by all reasonable concepts of cost, flies directly in the face of the notion that diminishing returns must raise costs and increase scarcity. This paradox cries out for explanation. But the explanation is quite counter-intuitive. It contradicts "common sense" — at least until one has thought the matter through, after which this way of thinking constitutes obvious common sense.[1]

The approach of the technological writers is as follows: They estimate quantities and "qualities" of resources in the earth, assess the present methods of extraction, and predict what methods of extraction will be used in the future. With those estimates they then calculate the amounts of resources that will be available in future years, at various costs of extraction (in the better forecast) or just at the present cost (in the less-thoughtful forecast).

At the root of the technological view of natural resources is the assumption that a certain quantity of a given mineral "exists" in the earth, and that one can, at least in principle, answer the question: How much (say) copper is there? But the question of how much of a resource is "really" in the earth is like the question: Is there a sound in the forest when a tree falls but no one is nearby to hear it? The question as stated opens a Pandora's box of semantic confusion (as do many statements that contain the word "is").

Let us examine the matter. What do we mean by a "sound"? A physical disturbance? If so, we can put a sound meter in the forest. But what about a "resource"? We have no comparable instrument to measure the quantity of iron or oil in the earth. And even if we did, we probably would not be able to agree on just what ought to be measured—for example, on whether the copper salts dissolved in the sea should be included in the measurement of copper.

To sum up, this technological view of natural-resource measurement is hardly useful even in principle, let alone in operation. First, there is an almost insuperable difficulty in the definition of available "copper," "oil," and so on, because there are many different grades of each resource in places that vary in difficulty of extracting the resource and because the amounts at low concentrations (such as the quantities of metals on the sea bottom and in sea water) are extraordinarily large in contrast to the quantities we usually have in mind (the "proven reserves"). Second, we constantly create new supplies of resources, in the sense of discovering them where they were thought not to exist. (In the past, the U.S. Geological Survey and others thought that there was no oil in California or Texas.) Often, new supplies of a resource came from areas outside the accustomed boundaries of our system, as resources from other continents came to Europe in past centuries and as resources may in the future be brought from the sea or from other planets. New supplies also arise when a resource is created from other materials, just as grain is grown and nuclear fuel is "bred." (Here we must avoid getting hung up on the word "natural," as in "natural resources.")

Most people do not at first feel comfortable with this point of view. The philosophy of scientific definitions may help. Consider the definition of the potential supply of oil that is implicitly or explicitly used by many: the amount that would be recorded if someone conducted an exhaustive survey of all the earth's contents. This supply is apparently fixed. But such a definition is thoroughly non-operational, because such a survey is impossible even in principle. The operational supply is that which is known today, or that which we may forecast as being known in the future, or that which we estimate will be sought and found under varying conditions of demand. These latter two quantities are decidedly not fixed but rather are variable, and they are the ones relevant for policy decisions. (The next chapter will explore in greater depth this counter-intuitive idea.)

We must constantly struggle against the illusion that each time we take a pound of copper from the earth there is less left to be used in the future. Too often we view natural resources as we view the inventory in a paper-clips warehouse: Ship some of the paper clips, and fewer are left to ship. We must constantly remember that we create new paper clips and replenish the warehouse's inventory. The new clips may be somewhat different from the old clips in design or weight, but the new ones may be better rather than worse, so quality is not a necessary cause for concern. In exactly the same way, we create new supplies of copper and oil. That is, we expend time, capital, and raw materials to get them. Even more important, we find new ways to supply the services that an expensive product (or resource) renders, as we shall see shortly.

The commonly heard statement that the average American uses ninety times as much X as does the average Asian (where X is some natural resource) can now be seen as irrelevant. The average American also *creates* a great deal more of "natural" resource X than does the average Asian — on average, by the same proportion as the resource is used by Americans compared with Asians.

I realize that this approach probably still seems so anti–common sensical as to be impossible to believe; but please read on. Like many other important complex questions, this one can only be understood by coming to see the sense in what seems at first to be pure foolishness. Of course this requires a struggle, and a willingness to be open to radical rethinking of paradoxical propositions. Real understanding, however, often requires this price.

The Difficulties of Technological Forecasting

The most common technological forecasts simply divide the "known reserves" by the current rate of use and call the result "years of consumption left." This procedure is discussed more fully in the context of oil and energy (chapter 7), but a few words and data will be useful here.

The concept of known (or "proven") reserves is useful as a guide to the decisions a business firm must make about whether it is profitable

TABLE 2-1. Number of Years of Consumption Potential for Various Elements

	Known Reserves ÷ Annual Consumption	U.S. Geological Survey's Estimates of "Ultimate Recoverable Resources" (= 1% of Materials in Top Kilometer of Earth's Crust) ÷ Annual Consumption	Amount Estimated in Earth's Crust ÷ Annual Consumption
Copper	45	340	242,000,000
Iron	117	2,657	1,815,000,000
Phosphorus	481	1,601	870,000,000
Molybdenum	65	630	422,000,000
Lead	10	162	85,000,000
Zinc	21	618	409,000,000
Sulphur	30	6,897	na
Uranium	50	8,455	1,855,000,000
Aluminum	23	68,066	38,500,000,000
Gold	9	102	57,000,000

SOURCE: Nordhaus, 1974, p. 23.

to search for new deposits, just as a running inventory of a retail store tells the manager when to reorder. But known reserves are a thoroughly misleading guide to the resources that will be available in the future; see table 2-1, which compares known reserves with two other measurements of available resources. And in figure 2-1 we see how the known reserves of various raw materials almost all *increased* over the twenty-year period 1950–70 as demand for them increased — just the way a store inventory often increases because the store's sales volume increases. This should be strong proof, even for the doubting reader, that technological forecasts using the known-reserve concept — which includes most forecasts, especially the doomsday variety — are misleading to the point of being worse than useless.

To understand the concept of known reserves we must inquire into other concepts of physical reserves, including total crustal abundance and ultimate recoverable reserves, all expressed in terms of years of consumption remaining at the current consumption rate. Proven reserves are a ridiculously pessimistic floor for forecasting. At the other end — a ridiculously optimistic ceiling — is the total amount of a material in the earth's crust. The most economically relevant measure is that of "ultimate recoverable resources," which the U.S. Geological Survey presently assumes is one hundreth of one percent (.0001) of the amount in the top kilometer of the earth's surface; these are the figures given in the middle column of table 2-1, to be compared with proven reserves and total

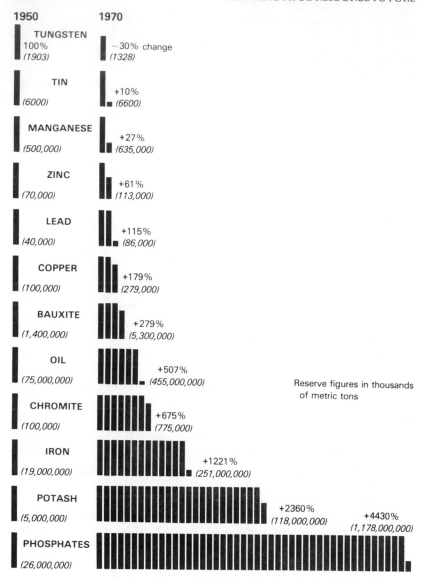

FIGURE 2-1. Known World Reserves of Selected Natural Resources, 1950 and 1970

annual abundance in the other columns. Even this "ultimately recoverable" estimate will surely be enlarged in the future when there are improvements in mining techniques or if prices rise.[2]

We must beware of confusing abundance in the earth with economic availability. Platinum, gold, and silver are far and away the least abundant minerals. But though they are used in industry, as well as for decoration and as stores of value, few people worry about a "shortage" of these materials, despite the fact that it has been progressively harder to find them.

A second difficulty with technological forecasts stems from an important property of natural resource extraction: A small change in the price of a mineral generally makes a very big difference in the potential supplies that are economically available — that is, profitable to extract. In technical economic terms, "Mineral supply . . . tends to be highly elastic in terms of prices. . . . The addition of currently paramarginal and submarginal resources would increase the 'reserve' category, not by modest amounts, but by multiples of itself."[3] Yet many technological forecasts are limited to supplies of the resource available at current prices with current technology. Given that the most promising lodes will always be mined first, this approach almost inevitably shows a rapid exhaustion of "reserves" even though this does not portend increasing scarcity.

A third difficulty with technological forecasts: The approaches that go beyond the "known reserves" concept necessarily depend upon more speculative assumptions than does the economic approach. They must make very specific assumptions about discoveries of unknown lodes and about technologies that have yet to be developed. In contrast, the economic approach makes only one assumption; to wit, the long-run cost trend will continue.

Fourth, the technological inventory of the earth's "contents" is at present quite incomplete, for the very good reason that it has never been worthwhile to go to the trouble of making detailed surveys. Why should you count the stones in Montana when you have enough to serve as paperweights right in your own back yard? This point was made sharply by the World Bank's *Report on the Limits to Growth:*

> We do not know the true extent of the resources that exist in, and can ultimately be recovered from, the earth. Nor will we know in the next two years or ten years. The reason why we do not know the absolute limits of the resources we have is simple and does not even require recourse to elaborate arguments about the wonders of technology. We do not know because no one has as yet found it necessary to know and therefore went about taking an accurate inventory.[4]

Last but certainly not least, technological forecasting depends heavily upon how well the forecaster can imagine the methods of extraction that

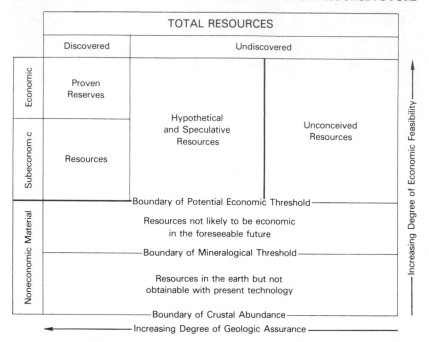

FIGURE 2-2. Concepts of Raw-Material Supplies — McKelvey's Box

will be developed in the future. Making the "conservative" (read "unimaginative") assumption that future technology will be the same as present technology would be like making a forecast of twentieth-century copper production on the basis of eighteenth-century pick-and-shovel technology.

All these difficulties in forecasting resource availability are well known to geologists, even though they are left out of popular discussions. To illustrate, figure 2-2 shows the place of known reserves in the overall scheme of total resources invented by Vincent McKelvey and adopted by the U.S. Geological Survey and the U.S. Bureau of Mines.

We must be wary of a tendency of experts in a given field to underestimate the scope of future technological changes and their impact on the economy. As Simon Kuznets says, "Experts are usually specialists skilled in, and hence bound to, traditional views; and they are, because of their knowledge of one field, likely to be cautious and unduly conservative."[5]

What would be the ideal technical forecast if it were possible to make it? All persons would agree, I believe, that what we want to know is how much of the raw material could and would be produced at each possible market price for each year in the future. The estimate for each future year, 19— or 20—, must depend on the amount of the resource used in years previous to 19— or 20—. Thus, if more was extracted in previous years, there will be less high-quality material left to extract, which tends to raise the price in 19— or 20—. But on the other hand, greater use in previous years leads to more exploration and more development of advanced technology, which in turn tends to lower the price. On balance, I'd guess that greater use in years prior to 19— or 20— means a lower rather than a higher price in 19— or 20—, respectively.

This idealized scheme paves the way to an answer for a most troublesome question: Among the wide range of technical forecasts and forecasters, which make the most sense? As we discuss this question, however, please remember my general advice on these matters: Prefer economic trend forecasts to any and all technological forecasts.

Among technological forecasters, the "best" are those who come closest to the ideal of making a price-dependent supply schedule that takes prior use into account and does so accurately. This immediately disqualifies most forecasters, because they do not make their predictions conditional on various prices. More specifically, this criterion knoccks out all forecasts based solely on the concept of known reserves. Among forecasts that do make the estimate conditional on price, you must judge a forecaster on how well he or she reasons about future technological developments with respect to resources in the land, ocean bottom, and sea. And this is a difficult judgment for any layman to make.

THE VAST DIFFERENCES AMONG TECHNOLOGICAL FORECASTS

Despite these reservations about technological forecasting, I shall briefly survey the results of some of the forecasters, mostly in their own words. My aim is to show that even with relatively "conservative" guesses about future extraction developments, many of the best-qualified forecasters report enormous resource availabilities — in contrast to the scare stories that dominate the daily newspapers. The central difficulty again is, Which expert will you choose to believe? If you wish, you can certainly find *someone* with all the proper academic qualifications who will try to give you as good a scare for your money as a horror movie. For example, the geologist Preston Cloud has written that "food and raw materials place ultimate limits on the size of populations . . . such limits will be reached within the next thirty to one hundred years";[6] and, of course, not too many years ago the best-selling book by Paul and William Paddock, *Famine—1975!*, told it all in the title. After this came similar forecasts from Paul Ehrlich and others, which we shall discuss later.

We begin with the assessment of the raw-materials situation by Herman Kahn and the Hudson Institute. Examing the evidence on the twelve principal metals that account for 99.9 percent of world and U.S. metal consumption, they classify them into only the two categories, "clearly inexhaustible" and "probably inexhaustible," finding *none* that are likely to be exhausted in any foreseeable future that is relevant to contemporary decisions. They conclude that "95 percent of the world demand is for five metals which are not considered exhaustible."[7]

An earlier forecast by one of America's greatest geologists, Kirtley Mather, was similar.

> Summing it all up, for nearly all of the important nonrenewable resources, the known or confidently expected world stores are thousands of times as great as the annual world consumption. For the few which like petroleum are available in relatively small quantities, substitutes are known or potential sources of alternative supply are at hand in quantities adequate to meet our current needs for many thousands of years. There is no prospect of the imminent exhaustion of any of the truly essential raw materials, as far as the world as a whole is concerned. Mother Earth's storehouse is far more richly stocked with goods than is ordinarily inferred.[8]

Mather deserves special attention because he is one of the few forecasters one might now quote who long ago established a successful forecasting record.

In a comprehensive survey of natural and technological resources for the next 100 years, Harrison Brown—a well-known geochemist who would not be described as a congenital optimist by anyone who knows Brown's work—nevertheless looks forward to a time when natural resources will become so plentiful that "mineral resources . . . will cease to play a main role in world economy and politics."[9]

And in an article sufficiently well regarded that it was the first article from the physical sciences ever republished in the *American Economic Review*, H. E. Goeller and A. M. Weinberg explored the implications of possible substitution in the use of raw materials that are essential to our civilization, with this result:

> We now state the principle of "infinite" substitutability: With three notable exceptions—phosphorus, a few trace elements for agriculture, and energy-producing fossil fuels (CH_2)—society can subsist on inex-

haustible or near-inexhaustible minerals with relatively little loss of living standard. Society would then be based largely on glass, plastic, wood, cement, iron, aluminum, and magnesium.[10]

As a result of that analysis of "infinite" substitutability, they arrive at an optimistic conclusion.

> Our technical message is clear: dwindling mineral resources in the aggregate, with the exception of reduced carbon and hydrogen, are per se unlikely to cause Malthusian catastrophe. But the exception is critically important; man must develop an alternative energy source. Moreover, the incentive to keep the cost of prime energy as low as possible is immense. In the Age of Substitutability energy is the ultimate raw material. The living standard will almost surely depend primarily on the cost of prime energy.[11]

Further, they accept that with some combination of breeder, fusion, solar, and geothermal power, it is possible to develop "satisfactory inexhaustible energy sources" at costs that will not disturb society.[12]

Am I quoting far-out types? Vincent McKelvey, until mid-1977 the director of the U.S. Geological Survey, said in an official *Summary of United States Mineral Resources:* "Personally, I am confident that for millenia to come we can continue to develop the mineral supplies needed to maintain a high level of living for those who now enjoy it and raise it for the impoverished people of our own country and the world."[13]

You may well be confused by the startling discrepancies between these assessments and those that you read in the daily newspapers. The best-known doomsday forecast of recent years is *The Limits to Growth,* and many newspaper stories have stemmed from that book. But the first and famous *Limits to Growth* book has been so thoroughly and universally criticized as neither valid nor scientific that it is not worthwhile to devote time or space to refuting its every detail. A few years ago the book was completely disavowed by its own sponsors, the Club of Rome. The sponsors now say that the conclusions of that first report are not correct and that they purposely misled the public in order to "awaken" public concern. (For details see Afternote to Chapter 20.)

With respect to minerals, Meadows (of *Limits to Growth*) predictably went wrong by using the known-reserves concept. For example, he estimated the world supply of aluminum to be exhausted in a maximum of 49 years. But aluminum is the most abundant metal in the earth's crust; Meadows counted only high-grade bauxite. Meadows estimated iron to run out in 154 years. But the U.S. Geological Survey says that, "because of the great amounts of identified iron-ore resources, no attempt is made to estimate quantities of hypothetical iron-ore resources beyond stating that they are enormous."[14]

SUMMARY

The potential reserves for all the important minerals are sufficient for many many lifetimes, on the basis of almost any assumption about whether resources are "really" finite or not. The point is brought out by this joke:

> A professor giving a lecture declares that the world will perish suddenly and certainly in seven billion years' time. One of the audience becomes very agitated, asks the professor to repeat what he said, and then, completely reassured, heaves a sign of relief: "Phew! I thought he said seven million years!"[15]

Technological forecasts of resource exhaustion are often unsound and misleading mainly for two reasons. (1) The physical quantity of a resource in the earth, no matter how closely defined, is not known at any time, because resources are only sought and found as they are needed; an example is the increase in the known supplies of such resources as copper, as shown in table 2-1 and figure 2-1. (2) More important, even if the physical quantities of particular closely defined natural resources were known, such measurements would not be economically meaningful, because we have the capacity to develop additional ways to meet our needs — for example, by using plastic instead of wood and metal, by developing new ways to exploit low grades of copper ore previously thought not usable, and by developing cheap atomic power to help produce copper. Thus the existing "inventory" of natural resources is *operationally* misleading; physical measurements do not define well what we will be able to use as future supplies. And hence the engineering method is not likely to produce sound forecasts.

> As a wise geologist puts it,

> Reserves are but a small part of the resources of any given commodity. Reserves and resources are part of a dynamic system and they cannot be inventoried like cans of tomatoes on a grocer's shelf. New scientific discoveries, new technology, and new commercial demands of restrictions are constantly affecting amounts of reserves and resources. Reserves and resources do not exist until commercial demand puts a value on a material in the market.[16]

To describe those who believe that the natural resources are available in practically limitless abundance, someone has coined the phrase "cornucopians," to contrast with "doomsdayers." But please notice: The school of thought that I represent here is not cornucopian. I do not believe that *nature* is limitlessly bountiful. I believe instead that the possibilities in the world are sufficiently great so that with the present state of knowledge, and with the additional knowledge that the human imagination and human enterprise will develop in the future, we and our descendants can manipulate the elements in such fashion that we can have all the mineral raw materials that we need and desire at prices ever smaller relative to other prices and to our total incomes. In short, our cornucopia is the human mind and heart, and not a Santa Claus natural environment. So has it been in the past, and therefore so is it likely to be in the future.

Can the Supply of Natural Resources Really Be Infinite? Yes!

Natural resources are not finite. Yes, you read correctly. This chapter shows that the supply of natural resources is not finite in any economic sense, which is why their cost can continue to fall in the future.

On the face of it, even to inquire whether natural resources are finite seems like nonsense. Everyone "knows" that resources are finite, from C. P. Snow to Isaac Asimov to as many other persons as you have time to read about in the newspaper. And this belief has led many persons to draw far-reaching conclusions about the future of our world economy and civilization. A prominent example is the *Limits to Growth* group, who open the preface to their 1974 book, a sequel to the *Limits*, as follows.

> Most people acknowledge that the earth is finite. . . . Policy makers generally assume that growth will provide them tomorrow with the resources required to deal with today's problems. . . . Recently, however, concern about the consequences of population growth, increased environmental pollution, and the depletion of fossil fuels has cast doubt upon the belief that continuous growth is either possible or a panacea.[1]

(Note the rhetorical device embedded in the term "acknowledge" in the first sentence of the quotation. That word suggests that the statement is a fact, and that anyone who does not "acknowledge" it is simply refusing to accept or admit it.)

The idea that resources are finite in supply is so pervasive and influential that the President's 1972 Commission on Population Growth and the American Future based its policy recommendations squarely upon this assumption. Right at the beginning of its report the commission asked, "What does this nation stand for and where is it going? At some point in the future, the finite earth will not satisfactorily accommodate more human beings — nor will the United States. . . . It is both proper and in our best interest to participate fully in the worldwide search for the good life, which must include the eventual stabilization of our numbers."[2]

The assumption of finiteness is responsible for misleading many scientific forecasters because their conclusions follow inexorably from that assumption. From the *Limits to Growth* team again, this time on food: "The world model is based on the fundamental assumption that there is an upper limit to the total amount of food that can be produced annually by the world's agricultural system."[3]

THE THEORY OF DECREASING NATURAL-RESOURCE SCARCITY

We shall begin with a far-out example to see what contrasting possibilities there are. (Such an analysis of far-out examples is a useful and favorite trick of economists and mathematicians.) If there is just one person, Alpha Crusoe, on an island, with a single copper mine on his island, it will be harder to get raw copper next year if Alpha makes a lot of copper pots and bronze tools this year. And if he continues to use his mine, his son Beta Crusoe will have a tougher time getting copper than did his daddy.

Recycling could change the outcome. If Alpha decides in the second year to make new tools to replace the old tools he made in the first year, it will be easier for him to get the necessary copper than it was the first year because he can reuse the copper from the old tools without much new mining. And if Alpha adds fewer new pots and tools from year to year, the proportion of copper that can come from recycling can rise year by year. This could mean a progressive decrease in the cost of obtaining copper with each successive year for this reason alone, even while the total amount of copper in pots and tools increases.

But let us be "conservative" for the moment and ignore the possibility of recycling. Another scenario: If there are two people on the island, Alpha Crusoe and Gamma Defoe, copper will be more scarce for each of them this year than if Alpha lived there alone, unless by cooperative efforts they can devise a more complex but more efficient mining operation—say, one man on the surface and one in the shaft. Or, if there are two fellows this year instead of one, and if copper is therefore harder to get and more scarce, both Alpha and Gamma may spend considerable time looking for new lodes of copper. And they are likely to be successful in their search. This discovery may lower the cost of copper to them somewhat, but on the average the cost will still be higher than if Alpha lived alone on the island.

Alpha and Gamma may follow still other courses of action. Perhaps they will invent better ways of obtaining copper from a given lode, say a better digging tool, or they may develop new materials to substitute for copper, perhaps iron.

The cause of these new discoveries, or the cause of applying ideas that were discovered earlier, is the "shortage" of copper — that is, the increased cost of getting copper. So a "shortage" of copper causes the creation of its own remedy. This has been the key process in the supply and use of natural resources throughout history.

Discovery of an improved mining method or of a substitute product differs, in a manner that affects future generations, from the discovery of a new lode. Even after the discovery of a new lode, on the average it will still be more costly to obtain copper, that is, more costly than if copper had never been used enough to lead to a "shortage." But discoveries of improved mining methods and of substitute products, caused by the shortage of copper, can lead to lower costs of the services people seek from copper. Let's see how.

The key point is that a discovery of a substitute process or product by Alpha or Gamma can benefit innumerable future generations. Alpha and Gamma cannot themselves extract nearly the full benefit from their discovery of iron. (You and I still benefit from the discoveries of the uses of iron and methods of processing it that our ancestors made thousands of years ago.) This benefit to later generations is an example of what economists call an "externality" due to Alpha and Gamma's activities, that is, a result of their discovery that does not affect them directly.

So, if the cost of copper to Alpha and Gamma does not increase, they may not be impelled to develop improved methods and substitutes. If the cost of getting copper does rise for them, however, they may then bestir themselves to make a new discovery. The discovery may not immediately lower the cost of copper dramatically, and Alpha and Gamma may still not be as well off as if the cost had never risen. But subsequent generations may be better off because their ancestors suffered from increasing cost and "scarcity."

This sequence of events explains how it can be that people have been using cooking pots for thousands of years, as well as using copper for many other purposes, and yet the cost of a pot today is vastly cheaper by any measure than it was 100 or 1,000 or 10,000 years ago.

It is all-important to recognize that discoveries of improved methods and of substitute products are not just luck. They happen in response to "scarcity" — an increase in cost. Even after a discovery is made, there is a good chance that it will not be put into operation until there is need for it due to rising cost. This point is important: Scarcity and technological advance are not two unrelated competitors in a race; rather, each influenes the other.

The last major U.S. governmental inquiry into raw materials was the 1952 President's Materials Policy Commission (Paley Commission), organized in response to fears of raw-material shortages during and just after World War II. The Paley Commission's report is distinguished by having some of the right logic, but exactly the wrong predictions, for its twenty-five-year forecast.

> There is no completely satisfactory way to measure the real costs of materials over the long sweep of our history. But clearly the man-hours required per unit of output declined heavily from 1900 to 1940, thanks especially to improvements in production technology and the heavier use of energy and capital equipment per worker. This long-term decline in real costs is reflected in the downward drift of prices of various groups of materials in relation to the general level of prices in the economy.
>
> [But since 1940 the trend has been] soaring demands, shrinking resources, the consequences pressure toward rising real costs, the risk of wartime shortages, the strong possibility of an arrest or decline in the standard of living we cherish and hope to share.[4]

For the quarter century for which the commission predicted, however, costs declined rather than rose.

The two reasons why the Paley Commission's cost predictions were topsy-turvy should help keep us from making the same mistakes. First, the commission reasoned from the notion of finiteness and from a static technological analysis.

> A hundred years ago resources seemed limitless and the struggle upward from meager conditions of life was the struggle to create the means and methods of getting these materials into use. In this struggle we have by now succeeded all too well. . . . The nature of the problem can perhaps be successfully over-simplified by saying that the consumption of almost all materials is expanding at compound rates and is thus pressing harder and harder against resources which whatever else they may be doing are not similarly expanding.[5]

The second reason the Paley Commission went wrong is that it looked at the wrong facts. Its report gave too much emphasis to the trends of costs over the short period from 1940 to 1950, which included World War II and therefore was almost inevitably a period of rising costs, instead of examining the longer period from 1900 to 1940, during which the commission knew that "the man-hours required per unit of output declined heavily."[6]

We must not repeat the same mistakes. We should look at cost trends for the longest possible period, rather than focus on a historical blip; the OPEC-led price rise in all resources after 1973 is for us as the temporary 1940–50 wartime reversal was for the Paley Commission. And the long-run trends make it very clear that the costs of materials, and their scarcity, continuously decline with the growth of income and technology.

RESOURCES AS SERVICES

As economists or as consumers, we are interested in the particular services that resources yield, not in the resources themselves. Examples of such services are an ability to conduct electricity, an ability to support weight, energy to fuel autos, energy to fuel electrical generators, and food calories.

The supply of a service will depend upon (a) which raw materials can supply that service with the present technology; (b) the availabilities of these materials at various qualities; (c) the costs of extracting and processing them; (d) the amounts needed at the present level of technology to supply the services that we want; (e) the extent to which the previously extracted materials can be recycled; (f) the cost of recycling; (g) the cost of transporting the raw materials and services; and (h) the social and institutional arrangements in force. What is relevant to us is not whether we can find any lead in existing lead mines but whether we can have the services of lead batteries at a reasonable price; it does not matter to us whether this is accomplished by recycling lead, by making batteries last forever, or by replacing lead batteries with another contraption. Similarly, we want intercontinental telephone and television communication, and, as long as we get it, we do not care whether this requires 100,000 tons of copper for cables or just a single quarter-ton communications satellite in space that uses no copper at all.[7]

Let us see how this concept of services is crucial to our understanding of natural resources and the economy. To return to Crusoe's cooking pot, we are interested in a utensil that we can put over the fire and cook with. After iron and aluminum were discovered, quite satisfactory cooking pots, perhaps even better than pots of copper, could be made of these materials. The cost that interests us is the cost of providing the cooking service rather than the cost of copper. If we suppose that copper is used only for pots and that iron is quite satisfactory for the same purpose, as long as we have cheap iron it does not matter if the cost of copper rises sky high. (But in fact that has not happened. As we have seen, the prices of the minerals themselves, as well as the prices of the services they perform, have fallen over the years.)

ARE NATURAL RESOURCES FINITE?

Incredible as it may seem at first, the term "finite" is not only inappropriate but is downright misleading when applied to natural resources, from both the practical and philosophical points of view. As with many of the important arguments in this world, the one about "finiteness" is "just semantic." Yet the semantics of resource scarcity muddle public discussion and bring about wrongheaded policy decisions.

The word "finite" originates in mathematics, in which context we all learn it as schoolchildren. But even in mathematics the word's meaning is far from unambiguous. It can have two principal meanings, sometimes with an apparent contradiction between them.[8] For example, the length of a one-inch line is finite in the sense that it is bounded at both ends. But the line within the endpoints contains an infinite number of points; these points cannot be counted, because they have no defined size. Therefore the number of points in that one-inch segment is not finite. Similarly, the quantity of copper that will ever be available to us is not finite, because there is no method (even in principle) of making an appropriate count of it, given the problem of the economic definition of "copper," the possibility of creating copper or its economic equivalent from other materials, and thus the lack of boundaries to the sources from which copper might be drawn.

Consider this quote about potential oil and gas from Sheldon Lambert, an energy forecaster. He begins, "It's like trying to guess the number of beans in a jar without knowing how big the jar is." So far so good. But then he adds, "God is the only one who knows — and even He may not be sure."[9] Of course Lambert is speaking lightly. But the notion that some mind might know the "actual" size of the jar is misleading, because it implies that there is a fixed quantity of standard-sized beans. The quantity of a natural resource that might be available to us — and even more important the quantity of the services that can eventually be rendered to us by that natural resource — can never be known even in principle, just as the number of points in a one-inch line can never be counted even in principle. Even if the "jar" were fixed in size, it might yield ever more "beans." Hence resources are not "finite" in any meaningful sense.

To restate: A satisfactory *operational* definition of the quantity of a natural resource, or of the services we now get from it, is the only sort of definition that is of any use in policy decisions. The definition must tell us about the quantities of a resource (or of a particular service) that we can expect to receive in any particular year to come, at each particular price, conditional on other events that we might reasonably expect to know (such as use of the resource in prior years). And there is no reason to believe that at any given moment in the future the available quantity of any natural resource or service at present prices will be much smaller than it is now, or non-existent. Only such one-of-a-kind resources as an Arthur Rubenstein concert or a Julius Erving basketball game, for which there are no close replacements, will disappear in the future and hence are finite in quantity.

Why do we become hypnotized by the word "finite"? That is an interesting question in psychology, education, and philosophy. A first likely reason is that the word "finite" seems to have a precise and unambiguous meaning in any context, even though it does not. Second, we learn the word in the context of mathematics, where all propositions are tautologous definitions and hence can be shown logically to be true or false (at least in principle). But scientific subjects are empirical rather than definitional, as twentieth-century philosophers have been at great pains to emphasize. Mathematics is not a science in the ordinary sense because it does not deal with facts other than the stuff of mathematics itself, and hence such terms as "finite" do not have the same meaning elsewhere that they do in mathematics.

Third, much of our daily life about which we need to make decisions is countable and finite — our weekly or monthly salaries, the number of gallons of gas in a full tank, the width of the backyard, the number of greeting cards you sent out last year, or those you will send out next year. Since these quantities are finite, why shouldn't the world's total possible salary in the future, or the gasoline in the possible tanks in the future, or the number of cards you ought to send out, also be finite? Though the analogy is appealing, it is not sound. And it is in making this incorrect analogy that we go astray in using the term "finite."

A fourth reason that the term "finite" is not meaningful is that we cannot say with any practical surety where the bounds of a relevant resource system lie, or even if there are any bounds. The bounds for the Crusoes are the shores of their island, and so it was for early man. But then the Crusoes found other islands. Mankind traveled farther and farther in search of resources — finally to the bounds of continents, and then to other continents. When America was opened up, the world, which for Europeans had been bounded by Europe and perhaps by Asia too, was suddenly expanded. Each epoch has seen a shift in the bounds of the relevant resource system. Each time, the old ideas about "limits," and the calculations of "finite resources" within those bounds, were thereby falsified. Now we have begun to explore the sea, which contains amounts of metallic and other resources that dwarf any deposits we know about on land. And we have begun to explore the moon. Why shouldn't the boundaries of the system from which we derive resources continue to expand in such directions, just as they have expanded in the past? This is one more reason not to regard resources as "finite" in principle.

You may wonder, however, whether "non-renewable" energy resources such as oil, coal, and natural gas differ from the recyclable minerals in such a fashion that the foregoing arguments do not apply. Energy is particularly important because it is the "master resource"; energy is the key constraint on the availability of all other resources. Even so, our energy supply is non-finite, and oil is an important example. (1) The oil potential of a particular well may be measured, and hence is limited (though it is interesting and relevant that as we develop new ways of extracting hard-to-get oil, the economic capacity of a well increases). But the number of wells that will eventually produce oil, and in what quantities, is not known or measurable at present and probably never will be, and hence is not meaningfully finite. (2) Even if we make the unrealistic assumption that the number of potential wells in the earth might be surveyed completely and that we could arrive at a reasonable estimate of the oil that might be obtained with present technology (or even with technology that will be developed in the next 100 years), we still would have to reckon the future possibilities of shale oil and tar sands — a difficult task. (3) But let us assume that we could reckon the oil potential of shale and tar sands. We would then have to reckon the conversion of coal to oil. That, too, might be done; yet we still could not consider the resulting quantity to be "finite" and "limited." (4) Then there is the oil that we might produce not from fossils but from new crops — palm oil, soybean oil, and so on. Clearly, there is no meaningful limit to this source except the sun's energy. The notion of finiteness does not make sense here, either. (5) If we allow for the substitution of nuclear and solar power for oil, since what we really want are the services of oil, not necessarily oil itself, the notion of a limit makes even less sense. (6) Of course the sun may eventually run down. But even if our sun were not as vast as it is, there may well be other suns elsewhere.

About energy from the sun: The assertion that our resources are ultimately finite seems most relevant to energy but yet is actually more misleading with respect to energy than with respect to other resources. When people say that mineral resources are "finite" they are invariably referring to the earth as a boundary, the "spaceship earth," to which we are apparently confined just as astronauts are confined to their spaceship. But the main source of our energy even now is the sun, no matter how you think of the matter. This goes far beyond the fact that the sun was the prior source of the energy locked into the oil and coal we use. The sun is also the source of the energy in the food we eat, and in the trees that we use for many purposes. In coming years, solar energy may be used to heat homes and water in many parts of the world. (Much of Israel's hot water has been heated by solar devices for years, even when the price of oil was much lower than it is now.) And if the prices of conventional energy supplies were to rise considerably higher than they now are, solar energy could be called on for much more of our needs, though this price rise seems unlikely given present technology. And even if the earth were sometime to run out of sources of energy for nuclear processes — a prospect so distant that it is a waste of time to talk about it — there are energy sources on other planets. Hence the notion that the supply of energy is finite because the earth's fossil fuels or even its nuclear fuels are limited is sheer nonsense.

Whether there is an "ultimate" end to all this — that is, whether the energy supply really is "finite" after the sun and all the other planets have been exhausted — is a question so hypothetical that it should be compared with other metaphysical entertainments such as calculating the number of angels that can dance on the head of a pin. As long as we continue to draw energy from the sun, any conclusion about whether energy is "ultimately finite" or not has no bearing upon present policy decisions. (For more discussion of finiteness in energy, see chapter 7.)

SUMMARY

A conceptual quantity is not finite or infinite in itself. Rather, it is finite or infinite if you make it so — by your own definitions. If you define the subject of discussion suitably, and sufficiently closely so that it can be counted, then it is finite — for example, the money in your wallet or the socks in your top drawer. But without sufficient definition the subject is not finite — for example, the thoughts in your head, the strength of your wish to go to Turkey, your dog's love for you, the number of points in a one-inch line. You can, of course, develop definitions that will make these quantities finite; but that makes it clear that the finiteness inheres in you and in your definitions rather than in the money, love, or one-inch line themselves. There is no necessity either in logic or in historical trends to suggest that the supply of any given resource is "finite."

AFTERNOTE 1._____

A Dialogue on "Finite"

The notion of non-finite natural resources is sufficiently important to this entire book, and sufficiently difficult to think through, that it is worth taking the time for an imaginary dialogue between Peers Strawman (PS) and Happy Writer (HW).

PS: Every natural resource is finite in quantity, and therefore any resource must get more scarce as we use more of it.

HW: What does "finite" mean?

PS: "Finite" means "limited."

HW: What is the limit for, say, copper?

PS: I don't know.

HW: Then how can you be sure it is limited in quantity?

PS: I know that at least it must be less than the total weight of the earth.

HW: If it were only slightly less than the total weight of the earth, or, say a hundredth of that total weight, would there be reason for us to be concerned?

PS: You're getting off the track. We're only discussing whether it is theoretically limited in quantity, not whether the limit is of practical importance.

HW: Okay. Would copper be limited in quantity if we could recycle it 100 percent?

PS: I see what you're saying: Even if it is limited in quantity, finiteness wouldn't matter to us if the material could be recycled 100 percent or close to it. That's true. But we're still talking about whether it is limited in quantity. Don't digress.

HW: Okay again. Would copper be limited in quantity if everything that copper does could be done by other materials that are available in limitless quantities?

PS: The quantity of copper wouldn't matter then. But you're digressing again.

HW: We're talking about scarcity for the future, aren't we? So what matters is not how much copper there is now (whatever the word "is" means) but the amounts in future years. Will you agree to that?

PS: That I'll buy.

HW: Then, is copper limited for the future if we can create copper from other materials or substitute other materials for copper?

PS: The size of the earth would still constitute a limit.

HW: How about if we can use energy from outside the earth — from the sun, say — to create additional copper the way we grow plants with solar energy?

PS: But is that realistic?

HW: Now it's you who are asking about realism. But as a matter of fact, yes, it is physically possible, and also likely to be feasible in the future. So will you now agree that at least *in principle* the quantities of copper are not limited even by the weight of the earth?

PS: Don't make me answer that. Instead, let's talk realism. Isn't it realistic to expect resources such as copper to get more scarce?

HW: Can we agree to define scarcity as the cost of getting copper?

[Here an extended dialogue works out the arguments about scarcity and price given in chapter 1. Finally PS says "okay" to defining scarcity as cost.]

HW: Future scarcity will depend, then, on the recycling rate, on the substitutes we develop, on the new methods we discover for extracting copper, and so on. In the past, copper became progressively *less* scarce, and there is no reason to expect that trend to change, no matter what you say about "finiteness" and "limits," as we just agreed. . . . But there is more. Do you really care about copper, or only about what copper does for you?

PS: Obviously what matters is what copper can do for us, not copper itself.

[Now you know why the name is Strawman].

HW: Good. Then can we agree that the outlook for the services that copper provides is even better than for copper itself?

PS: Sure, but *all* this *can't* be true. It's not natural. How can we use more of something and have it get less scarce?

HW: Well, this is one of those matters that defies common sense. That's because the common-sense view applies only when the resource *is* arbitrarily limited, for example, limited to the copper wire in your cellar. But that quantity is only fixed as long as you don't make another trip to the hardware store. Right?

PS: I may be Strawman but my patience is limited.

And so we close.

AFTERNOTE 2.

The "Law" of Diminishing Returns

"But the law of diminishing returns must come to bear *sometime*," people often say, meaning that eventually the cost of extracting mineral resources must rise, even if the cost will not rise in the near future.

Happily, there is no "law" that compels cost to rise eventually. The concept of diminishing returns applies to situations where one element is fixed in quantity — say, a given copper mine — and where the type of technology is also fixed. But neither of these factors apply to mineral extraction in the long run. New lodes are found, and new cost-cutting extraction technologies are developed. Therefore, whether the cost rises or falls in the long run depends on the extent to which advances in technology and new lode discoveries counteract the tendency toward increasing cost in the absence of the new developments. Historically, as we have seen, costs have consistently fallen rather than risen, and there is no empirical warrant for believing that this historical trend will reverse itself in the foreseeable future. Hence there is no "law" of diminishing returns appropriate here.

I hazard this generalization: In economic affairs, there are always diminishing returns in the small scale, but increasing returns in the large. For example, taking oil from one oil well will gradually increase the cost of successive barrels from that well. But taking oil from all the wells will eventually lead to lower costs for energy taken as a whole. This is partly because the oil is used in the growth of an economy that then has a greater capacity to develop cheaper energy sources and partly because people have an incentive to find new sources of energy (or whatever) when aggregate supplies are affected significantly. Eventually the new source turns out to be cheaper than the old one.

Famine 1985? Or 1995? Or 1975?

Food is the gut issue (pun intended) in any book on resources and population. It has been so at least since Malthus. Even if people do not worry about the effect of economic growth or population growth upon other resources, they may worry about food.

One after the other, official and unofficial forecasts about the future food supply are frightening. The UN Economic and Social Commission for Asia and the Pacific predicts "500 million starvation deaths in Asia between 1980 and 2025."[1] The head of the UN Food and Agriculture Organization (FAO) says that "the long-term trends in the food production of developing countries remain alarmingly inadequate."[2]

A book-length survey by the staff of the *New York Times* arrived at these purple-prose conclusions:

> From drought-besieged Africa to the jittery Chicago grain market, from worried Government offices in Washington to the partly-filled granaries of teeming India, the long-predicted world food crisis is beginning to take shape as one of the greatest peace-time problems the world has had to face in modern times.
>
> While there have always been famines and warnings of famine, food experts generally agree that the situation now is substantially different. The problem is becoming so acute that every nation, institution, and every human being will ultimately be affected.[3]

The Environmental Fund paid for a full-page advertisement in leading newspapers, signed by such dignitaries as author Isaac Asimov, Presidential adviser Zbigniew Brzezinski, author Malcolm Cowley, ecologist Paul Ehrlich, editor Clifton Fadiman, oilman J. Paul Getty, Time Inc. executive Henry Luce III, poet Archibald MacLeish, Nobel prize-winner Albert Szent-Györgyi, *Reader's Digest* founder DeWitt Wallace, U.A.W. President Leonard Woodcock, and many others, saying:

The world as we know it will likely be ruined before the year 2,000 and the reason for this will be its inhabitants' failure to comprehend two facts. These facts are:
1. World food production cannot keep pace with the galloping growth of population.
2. "Family planning" cannot and will not, in the foreseeable future, check this runaway growth.[4]

Novelist C. P. Snow dramatized the matter: "Perhaps in ten years, millions of people in the poor countries are going to starve to death before our very eyes.... We shall see them doing so upon our television sets...."[5] And the School of Public Affairs of Princeton is offering a course on "Problems of World Hunger" based on the premise that "Hunger ... has never been known on such a world-wide scale as today."[6]

Similar examples of widely publicized alarming forecasts could be multiplied by the dozens. This tiny sample, corroborated by your own memory of what you have read, should be plenty to establish that frightening food forecasts dominate the mass media. Perhaps the most influential was Paul Ehrlich's first lines in his best-selling book, *The Population Bomb:* "The battle to feed all of humanity is over. In the 1970's the world will undergo famines — hundreds of millions of people are going to starve to death."[7] Many writers believe the situation is so threatening that they call for strong measures to restrict population growth, "compulsion if voluntary methods fail," as Ehrlich puts it.[8]

Almost every schoolchild "knows" that the food situation has been worsening and that the world faces an impending crisis. If you doubt this, ask a few children of your acquaintance. A book for children puts it thus:

> When man first began to farm, there were fewer than 5 million people on earth, and it took more than a million years for the population to reach that figure. But populations increase geometrically — that is, they double (2, 4, 8, 16, 32, etc.). Food supplies, in contrast, increase only arithmetically, a much slower process (2, 4, 6, 8, 10, 12, etc.). . . .
>
> If the population continues to explode, many people will starve. About half of the world's population is underfed now, with many approaching starvation.[9]

Some influential people even see in these assertions the warrant for such policies as "triage — letting the least fit die in order to save the more robust victims of hunger."[10] It was the 1967 book by William and Paul Paddock *(Famine–1975!)* that applied this World-War-I medical concept to food aid, resulting in such Paddock judgments as:

Haiti	Can't-be-saved
Egypt	Can't-be-saved
The Gambia	Walking Wounded
Tunisia	Should Receive Food
Libya	Walking Wounded
India	Can't-be-saved
Pakistan	Should Receive Food[11]

Though some other matters discussed in this book, such as the supply of mineral resources, may not be as bad as commonly thought, the food situation really is bad and getting worse. Right?

Wrong. The record of food production absolutely contradicts these scary forecasts. The overall trend in recent decades has been an *increase* in food produced per person. This may be seen in table 4-1 and figure 4-1.

A few facts about the data in figure 4-1 should be kept in mind. First, these data are taken from recent U.S. Department of Agriculture (USDA) and UNFAO publications. The starting date of the series is the earliest given in those publications, chosen by them and not by me; this should reassure you that the starting date was not chosen arbitrarily so as to rig the results. (Such rigging is, however, not unknown in these discussions.) Second, though progress in food production has not been steady, there has been no year, or series of years, so bad as to support a conclusion of long-term retrogression. I emphasize this because I am now writing at a time when harvests have been particularly good, and some readers might wonder whether my assertions are overly influenced by recent events. In fact, the first draft of this material, for publication in my technical book,[12] was written in 1971 and 1972, when food production was having its worst time in recent decades. Third, some countries' experiences have been tragically different from the general trend, usually because of politics and war. More about these special cases later.

People to whom I show figure 4-1 sometimes ask, "Where are the other data?" When I ask, "Which other data?" the questioner usually replies, "The data the other guys quote to support their worried forecasts."

In simple fact there are no other data. The data shown in figure 4-1 were published by the USDA and the UN and were collected by the UN from the individual countries. Of course the data are far less reliable

TABLE 4-1. Index of World Food Production per Capita

Year	Excluding Mainland China (1952-56 = 100) UNFAO	Including Mainland China (1961-65 = 100) UNFAO	USDA	Combined Index (1948-52 = 100) UNFAO	USDA
1948–52	93			100	
1952	97			104	
1953	100			108	
1954	99			106	
1955	101			109	
1956	103			111	
1957	102			110	
1958	106			114	
1959	106			114	
1960	107			115	
1961	106			114	
1962	108			116	
1963	108			116	
1964	109	102		118	
1965	108	100		116	
1966	111	103		119	
1967	113	105		121	
1968		106		123	
1969		105		119	
1970		106		123	
1971		107		125	
1972		104		120	
1973		108		126	
1974		107	113	125	132
1975		108	113	126	132
1976		110	117	128	136
1977		110	118	128	137
1978			122		142
1979			118*		137

SOURCES: UN Food and Agriculture Organization, *Production Yearbook*, 1968, 1975, 1976, and *World Agricultural Situation*, January 1980.

NOTE: I am more inclined to believe the USDA figures for the years since 1974 because they are more recent and because the USDA has no institutional stake in showing a relatively poor world food situation, whereas the UNFAO does. The likeliest source of the difference is in population estimates rather than in aggregate food-production estimates.

*Preliminary estimate.

than one would like; economic data usually are. But these are the only official data, and no one quotes any other data. Standard data that would show a worsening trend in recent decades simply do not exist. If you

per capita food production (1948-52 = 100)

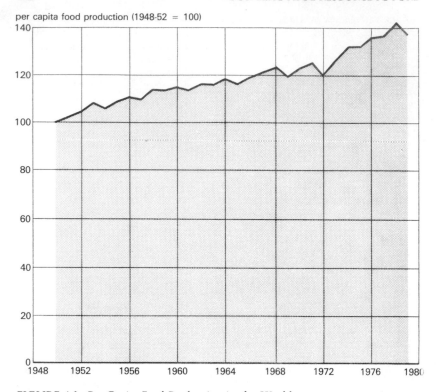

FIGURE 4-1. Per Capita Food Production in the World

doubt it, write to the authors of frightening forecasts, to the UN, or to the USDA.

Despite the mass-media consensus that we are heading toward agricultural crisis, the mainstream view among agricultural economists is quite the contrary, and has been so for years. Most agricultural economists agree that the trend has been toward improvement in the food supplies of almost every main segment of the world's population. For example, even before the recent years of bumper harvests, D. Gale Johnson said in an authoritative review (the President's Invited Lecture to the American Statistical Association):

> The available evidence indicates that the increase of the food supply has at least matched the growth of population in the developing countries, taken as a group, for the past four decades. This has been a period of very rapid population growth in the developing countries. . . . Thus

the recent achievement in expanding food supplies in the developing countries has been a significant one, food supply has at least kept up with population growth during a period of unparalleled increase in population. . . .

While there are undoubtedly exceptions, there is evidence that there has been a long term gradual improvement in per capita food consumption over the past two centuries.[13]

And in a "special compendium" entitled *Food: Politics, Economics, Nutrition, and Research*, published by the American Association for the Advancement of Science, the agricultural economists represented there speak nearly of a single voice: "The historical record lends support to the more optimistic view."[14]

Proof that the consensus of agricultural economists confutes the popular doomsday beliefs is found in the four major projections made at the height of the food worries, in the early 1970s, about the 1985 world food situation. As Johnson sums them up, "The four projections, singly or collectively, do not bear out the prophets of doom, gloom, and mass starvation."[15]

And since the calm assessments by the agricultural economists even in the face of the poor harvests of the early 1970s, conditions have improved spectacularly. Now the headlines say, "Corn, bean yields again set records";[16] "Wheat — there's too much despite drought, deluge";[17] and "World food supplies are just below record level."[18] Grain prices have fallen so sharply that U.S. farmers are complaining of disaster — from too much food.

It is a fact, then, that the world food supply has been improving. But it is also a fact that people resolutely try to ignore this silver lining and instead try harder to find the cloud. Consider, for example, this statement from a technical article: "During the last 25 years or so the average rate of increase of world food production has steadily deteriorated . . . it fell from 3.1 percent in the 1950's to 2.8 percent in the 1960's and 2.2 percent in the first half of the 1970's."[19] I shall leave aside the very large question of whether such apparent changes are statistically meaningful. What is interesting for now is the word "deterioration," which suggests that the world food situation is getting worse. But the data tell us only that the gain — the *improvement* — was greater in the 1950s than later.

Consider also figure 4-2, taken from *Business Week*. It seems at first glance to show population growing faster than food. That would mean a fall in food per capita, which would be a bad sign. But on close inspection we see that food per capita has increased, a good sign. It is ridiculous

The disproportions of people and food

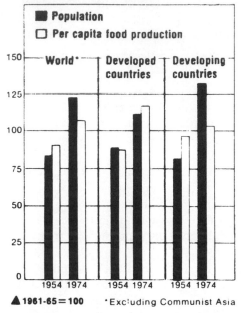

FIGURE 4-2. A Typical Misleading Diagram on Food Supply

and misleading to put a total figure (population) next to a per-capita figure (food per capita). Why is it done? People apparently want to believe
and to tell others that the world food situation is getting worse even
though it is really getting better.

FAMINES

Fear of famine is common. This is a typical statement: "Major famines
will occur in many of the developing countries of the world before their
population is brought under control. . . . When major famines develop,
their termination will become increasingly hopeless in the face of world
population increases."[20]

    The historical trend of famines is an important index of how well the
world's food supply has been doing. Famine is difficult to define and measure operationally, however, because when nutrition is poor many people die of diseases and not directly of starvation. Traditionally, historical
research on famine simply counts as a famine an event that people living

in a particular time referred to as a famine. There is no reason to believe that such accounts have been affected by a bias that would distort the long-term record. Therefore historians' studies of the occurrence of famines would seem to have considerable validity for our purposes.

Johnson, whose credentials to write about this difficult topic are at least as good as anyone else's, summarizes the incidence of famines as follows.

We might be inclined to deduce from the pictorial evidence of famine that we have seen recently on television, in newspapers, and in magazines that the world is more prone to famine now than it used to be. But the evidence is clearly to the contrary. Both the percentage of the world's population afflicted by famine in recent decades and the absolute numbers have been relatively small compared with those occurring in those earlier periods of history of which we have reasonably reliable estimates of famine deaths.

There has been a rather substantial reduction in the incidence of famine during the past century. During the last quarter of the nineteenth century perhaps 20 million to 25 million died from famine. If an adjustment for population increase is made, a comparable figure for the third quarter of this century would be at least 50 million and for the quarter century we are now entering at least 75 million. For the entire twentieth century to the present, there have been probably between 12 million and 15 million famine deaths, and many, if not the majority, were due to deliberate governmental policy, official mismanagement, or war and not to serious crop failure. . . .[21]

While there have been some deaths due to famine in the third quarter of the 20th century, it is highly unlikely that the famine-caused deaths equal a tenth of the period 75 years earlier.

There has not been a major famine, such as visited China and India in the past, during the past quarter century. There have been some near misses, such as in India in 1965–66, and the current sad situation in Africa should not be ignored because a relatively small population is involved. But the food supply has been far more secure for poor people during the past quarter century than at any other comparable period in the last two or three centuries. I should add that I do not attribute the diminished incidence of famine as much to improved food supplies as I do to improvements in communication and transportation, but whatever the reasons we have witnessed an improvement of great significance. . . .

The percentage of the world's population who find themselves subject to actual famine conditions is probably lower now than at any time in the past.[22]

Do you wonder how these optimistic trends can be reconciled with the pictures of starving children you have seen in national magazines, and with the FAO claim that "a lifetime of malnutrition and actual hunger is the lot of at least two-thirds of mankind"? (That claim has become the children's-book cliché that "about half of the world's population is underfed now, with many approaching starvation.")[23] This much-quoted FAO statement was made by the FAO director in 1950, within a year of the FAO's founding and in the aftermath of World War II, on the basis of no data at all. Later the UN did enough research to reduce its estimate of people in "actual hunger" to 10–15 percent of mankind. But even this estimate has been severely criticized by some experts as too high. Furthermore, the term "malnutrition" is sufficiently vague that it could include the diets of any of us.[24]

Casual as the original FAO conjecture was, a large amount of research about minimum or satisfactory dietary requirements, and the diets eaten in various countries, has been required to lay it to rest in a scientific cemetery. Yet the original statement comes back again and again in current discussion to "prove" that the food situation is bad and could not be getting better.

But—"The death of a single human being from starvation is an unspeakable human tragedy." That expression has been repeated often in the last few years. Logically it implies that even if the food supply is improving, it would be better to reduce the world's population so that *no* person would die from starvation. The value judgments that underlie this idea will be analyzed later. For now, let us note that if death from starvation is an "unspeakable human tragedy," then death from an auto accident or a fire would also seem to be the same sort of tragedy. But what are the implications for social action? The only way to avoid all such deaths is to have no people. Surely that cannot be intended. Hence this sort of phrase, dramatic and sincere though it may be, really is an emotional expression that tells us nothing about what should be done.

Paradoxically, a greater population density apparently leads to *less* chance of famine. The concentration of population causes better roads and transportation, and better transportation is the key factor in preventing starvation, as Johnson notes. The most recent illustration is the Sahel in West Africa.

"Sure, the food is pouring in," observed British Red Cross liaison officer George Bolton, "but how the hell are we going to get it to the people who need it? There isn't a tarred road within a thousand miles of Juba." Bolton wasn't exaggerating. While I was in Juba, I witnessed the arrival of 5,000 gallons of cooking oil, which had been diverted from the nearby state of Rwanda. Since the rickety old ferry was not strong enough to carry the oil shipment across the White Nile so it could be distributed to the needy in the interior, the oil was promptly unloaded on the riverbank and stored in Juba.

And this was not an isolated incident. I saw warehouses in Juba overflowing with millet, dried fish, cooking utensils, agricultural tools and medical supplies — all useless because nothing could be delivered to the people who needed it.[25]

The Sahel is a case study of food, population, and public relations. We read in *Newsweek*, September 19, 1977, that "more than 100,000 West Africans perished of hunger" in the Sahel between 1968 and 1973 due to drought. Upon inquiry, writer Peter Gwynne informed me that the estimate came from Kurt Waldheim's message to the UN Desertification Conference. I therefore wrote to Waldheim asking for the source of the estimate. A remarkable packet of three documents came back from the UN Public Inquiries Unit: (1) Waldheim's message, saying, "Who can forget the horror of millions of men, women and children starving, with more than 100,000 dying, because of an ecological calamity that turned grazing land and farms into bleak desert?" (2) A two-page excerpt from a memo by the UN Sahelian Office, dated November 8, 1974, saying, "It is not possible to calculate the present and future impact of this tragedy, on the populations. . . . Although precise figures are not available, indeed unobtainable . . . certainly there has been an extensive and tragic loss of life. . . ." (3) One page by Helen Ware, a respected Australian expert on African demography and a visiting fellow at the University of Ibadan in March 1975, when her memo was written specifically for the UN. Ware calculated the normal death rate for the area, together with "the highest death rate in any group of nomads" during the drought. Her figures made nonsense of the other two documents. She figured that "at an absolute, and most improbable, upper limit a hundred thousand people who would not otherwise have died, succumbed to the effects of famine. . . . Even as a maximum [this estimate] represents an unreal limit."

Ware's figures, which flatly give the lie to Waldheim's well-publicized assessment, were on page one of a document written for and sent out by the UN itself well before the UN Desertification Conference was held and Waldheim's message was publicized. Apparently, it was the only calculation the UN had. But it was ignored. More recently, UN press releases have retreated to the more modest, but still unprovable, assertion that "tens of thousands" died.[26] Ware's comment: "The problem with deaths in the Sahel is precisely that there was so little evidence of them — rather like the photograph of the dead cow which kept turning up in illustrations to every newspaper story."[27]

Now (July 10, 1980) the Associated Press credits the UN with asserting that a forthcoming "permanent food crisis . . . will be deeper than the 1972–74 drought, when 300,000 or more died in Ethiopia and the Sahel belt south of the Sahara."[28]

THE CASES OF SOME SPECIAL COUNTRIES

Sometimes a global picture obscures important parts of the world where the situation is quite different. Therefore, let's briefly consider a few countries of special interest.

India

Paul Ehrlich wrote in *The Population Bomb:* "I have yet to meet anyone familiar with the situation who thinks India will be self-sufficient in food by 1971, if ever." He went on to quote Louis H. Bean, who said, "My examination of the trend on India's grain production over the past eighteen years leads me to the conclusion that the present 1967–1968 production . . . is at a maximum level."[29] Yet, "net food grain availability" in kilograms per capita per year has been rising since at least 1950–51. And by September 1977 there was an "Indian grain reserve buildup of about 22 million tons, and U.S. grain exports to India . . . waned."[30] In 1977, India began to be faced with the problem of how to store the stocks "that overflowed warehouses and caused mounting storage costs" so that they would not be ruined by rain or eaten by predators.[31] (It is only fair to note, however, that many experts — ones that Ehrlich apparently had not met — have always said that India has a vast potential to increase food production.)

Why has India's food situation improved so dramatically recently? The cause seems straightforward. It is not an agronomic miracle but an expectable economic event: Price controls on food were lifted, and price supports were substituted for the controls. Indian farmers had a greater incentive to produce more, so they did. For example,

> Hari Mohan Bawa, a marginal farmer of this village 100 miles north of New Delhi, is richer by $300 this year.
> "I can marry off my daughter now," he said as he counted the

money paid by the Food Corporation of India, a government agency that bought all his rice crop. "Maybe I will pay off part of my debts, or I will buy a new pair of bullocks."

Beginning last year the Food Corporation offered a minimum support price that guaranteed profits. Banks and Government agencies came forward with loans to buy fertilizer and seeds. Mr. Bawa installed a tube-well that freed him of dependence on the monsoon rains.[32]

Is increased economic incentive to Indian farmers too simple an explanation? Simple, yes, but not *too* simple. Not simple enough for India's government to have removed price controls much earlier.

How did the Indian farmers increase production? Mostly by working longer hours — though they still work many fewer hours during the year than does the average American city worker or the Thai farmer — and also by planting more crops a year, on more land, and by improving the land they have.

You may wonder how Indian farmers, who are popularly thought to live in a country with an extraordinarily high population density, can find more land to cultivate. And this increase seems less surprising when one realizes that, contrary to popular belief, India (and Pakistan) are not densely populated compared with, say, Japan, Taiwan, and China. (Chapter 6 shows the data.) But India's rice yield per acre is low compared to those countries.

Bangladesh

When Bangladesh became independent after the devastating war in 1971, U.S. Secretary of State Henry Kissinger called it "an international basket case."[33] Since then the food supply has sometimes been so bad that some writers have advocated "letting Bangladesh go down the drain," whatever that means. Others organized emergency relief operations. A 1972 newspaper advertisement from the *New York Times* is shown in figure 4-3.

As of December 1976, however, there was optimism, largely because of an improved food supply from "two record annual harvests in a row. Storehouses are full, and food imports have been reduced."[34]

What about Bangladesh's future? "The land itself is a natural greenhouse; half of the cultivated 22 million acres is suitable for double cropping, and some could raise three crops a year."[35] But yields per acre are low. One reason is that "growing more than one crop required irrigation during the dry winter season, and only 1.2 million acres are irrigated."[36]

Why is so little land irrigated, and why are yields so low? According

FIGURE 4-3.
How Bangladesh's
Food Situation
Looked to Some
in 1972

"WHAT YOU DO IN THE NEXT ONE, TWO, OR THREE WEEKS IS IMPORTANT...

If help is delayed, it will have to be dropped on the graveyards of many, many Bengalis."

Dr. Abdur Rab Chaudhury, Coordinator External Assistance for Relief and Re-
habilitation, Office of the Prime Minister, Bangladesh.

Tons of food,
enough for several weeks,
lie in the harbors . . .

. . . but few bridges and trucks exist to carry it inland.

. . . 20 tons of food-grain
can be air-dropped
in 60 seconds. . . .
with YOUR HELP!

LEON HOWELL WRITING FROM BANGLADESH. . . .

"The elation that came with liberation and the joy in the near miraculous return of the revered Sheikh Mujibur Rahman has quickly given way to a grim wrestling with the nearly intractable problems of the world's newest—and eighth largest—nation.

The battle to sustain life with a disrupted transportation system is the most obvious problem confronting Bangladesh. . . .

GETTING FOOD GRAINS THROUGH THE SHAMBLES OF A TRANSPOR-
TATION SYSTEM TO PEOPLE WHO NEED FOOD IS THE PROBLEM. THE
PAKISTANI ARMY, AND THE SHORT WAR, DESTROYED MUCH RAIL-
WAY EQUIPMENT AND TRACK, ROAD AND RAILWAY BRIDGES,
FERRIES, TRUCKS AND BOATS."

By June the situation will be even worse. Once the monsoon rains begin to fall, almost half of Bangladesh will be under water. Roads will be impassable. There are only a few of the special rivercraft needed to travel the inland waterways.

THE ONLY WAY THROUGH IS UP! The organizers and operators of the food airlift to Biafra in 1969 formed the non-profit Foundation for Airborne Relief (FAR) to deal with just such emergencies as this. **THEY CAN AIR-DROP 20 TONS OF GRAIN IN 60 SECONDS.** They can get the food to the people to keep them alive . . . until transportation and employment are restored. But money is needed for the planes and crews . . . NOW!!!

The Bangladesh EMERGENCY RELIEF FUND, (ERF) a non-
profit organization directing funds to recognized relief agencies operating in Bangladesh, is joining hands with FAR and is seeking funds specifically for this urgently needed air-drop.

Thousands of Americans have been giving regularly to keep Bengalis alive until the monsoon harvest is completed. But now your contribution can help feed several hundred malnutritioned men, women and children by air-dropping food grains.

WITH YOUR HELP, FAR can start air-dropping huge loads of food to all parts of **BANGLADESH BY MAY 1.**

PLEASE SEND WHAT YOU CAN, AS QUICKLY AS YOU CAN!

Hon. Chester Bowles
Dr. Douglas Ensminger
Emergency Relief Fund
Campaign Co-chairmen

PLEASE COUNT ME IN TO GET THIS LIFE-
SAVING AIR-DROP OFF THE GROUND . . . NOW

Bangladesh
EMERGENCY RELIEF FUND
Box 1776
Washington, D.C. 20013
Enclosed is my tax-deductible contribution made out to the Emergency Relief Fund
☐ $1,000 Will sponsor delivery of one complete plane load.
☐ $500 ☐ $250 ☐ $100 ☐ $50 ☐ $25 ☐ ___

NAME ___

ADDRESS ___

CITY ___ STATE & ZIP ___

ATTENTION MR. LEONARD M. STUTTMAN, NATIONAL DIRECTOR

☐ I want to help. Please send me information on how I can organize my local community to support this effort.

☐ I have a better idea of how I can help. Please contact me.

☐ My organization is interested in a speaker on Bangladesh.

to a reporter, "Most farmers seem reluctant to grow much more rice than they themselves need. . . . They cite the high price of gasoline needed to run the [irrigating] pumps and the low price paid for their rice. The low price of rice is mostly due to the recent bumper harvests and the government's success in stopping massive smuggling of rice to India."[37] This analysis makes sense economically.

The U.S.S.R.

Because the U.S.S.R. bought a great deal of U.S. grain in 1972 and subsequent years, many people have concluded that its agriculture is in bad shape. In fact, as of 1975, "impressive gains have been recorded in the agricultural sector" of the U.S.S.R.[38] And the 1976 grain harvest set a record, even though the 1975 harvest was the smallest in ten years. The U.S.S.R. has been buying grain abroad mainly for cattle fodder in order to increase the quantity of meat in the Soviet diet.

ARE THERE ULTIMATE LIMITS TO FOOD PRODUCTION?

It is not necessary or useful to discuss whether there is an "ultimate" limit to the supply of any natural resource including food (as discussed in chapter 3.) We know for sure that the world can produce vastly more food than it now does, even (or especially) in such places as India and Bangladesh. If low-production countries were to produce even at the present level of agriculture in Japan and Taiwan, with present technology and without moving toward the much higher yields found under experimental conditions, world food production would increase dramatically and would more than feed any foreseeable population. Of course such an increase in output would impose costs in the short run, but it could reduce costs as well as improve the food supply in the long run.

In addition to the already proven methods of raising output, there are many promising scientific discoveries still being developed. These include such innovations as orbiting giant mirrors that would reflect sunlight onto the night side of the earth and thereby increase growing time, increase harvest time, and prevent crop freezes;[39] and meat substitutes made of soybeans that produce the nutrition and enjoyment of meat with much less resource input. Some of these ideas may seem like unrealistic science fiction to us. But we should remember that tractors and wheeled irrigation pipes, which are making enormous contributions today, seemed quite unrealistic a hundred or fifty years ago. Furthermore, nowadays we have the capacity to estimate the chances of successful new developments much more accurately than we did in the past. When scientists predict that a process will be commercially successful within a given number of years, the likelihood of it being so is rather good.

Radical food-raising methods are not just a desperate last resort. For example, General Mills recently reported that, after considerable research, it is setting up an indoor lettuce-raising factory because it is cheaper to raise lettuce indoors than by the standard method.

> General Mills Inc. plans to start a lettuce plant within the next year — that is, a factory for growing lettuce in.
> "We're going to have a commercial unit," E. Robert Kinney, chairman and chief executive officer, said in an interview. His statement was the first indication that General Mills will take its indoor lettuce growing venture, now in the fifth year of development, beyond the research phase and into the test market.
> In the factory, lettuce will be planted in a special medium in movable troughs. The troughs will move from light areas to dark areas to simulate day and night. The lettuce will be harvested and packaged for sale under the Kitchen Harvest brand. Lettuce produced that way in a small General Mills pilot facility is currently being sold in a few Minneapolis area supermarkets.[40]

Under which social and economic conditions will food supplies increase fastest? Little about this can be known for certain. But we can be quite sure that investment in research, especially research that shows how to adapt various combinations of seed, fertilizers, and cultivation patterns to particular conditions, has a big payoff. Additionally, almost all economists agree that a system of individual land-owning farmers operating in a free market, without price controls, leads to larger food production than does any other mode of organization (except the same system with price supports). And everyone with any knowledge agrees that good farm-to-market transportation, and political stability, are crucial in raising food production.

CONCLUSIONS

This chapter most certainly does not suggest that complacency about the food supply is in order, or that hunger is not a world problem. Some people are starving. And, although most people are not starving, they would still like to be able to purchase a more expensive diet than they now have (though for many of us a more expensive diet would be a less healthy one). But there is very strong reason to believe that the supplies of land and other natural resources do not now constrain the world's food supply, nor will they in the foreseeable future.

The main reason why more food has not been produced in the past is that there was insufficient demand for more food, either by subsistence-farming families or by the market. As demand increases, farmers work harder to produce crops and improve the land, and more research is done to increase productivity. This extra work and investment imposes costs for a while. But as we shall see in the next chapter, food has tended in the long run to become cheaper year after year, whether measured in terms of labor or relative prices. And production and consumption per capita have been rising. This is a solid basis for believing that these trends will continue.

But will a "population explosion" reverse these trends? On the contrary. Population growth increases food demand, which requires more labor and investment in the short run to meet the demand. (And there is always some lag before the supply responds to the additional demand, which may mean that some will suffer.) Yet there is little reason to believe that, in the foreseeable long run, additional people will make food more scarce and more expensive, even with increasing consumption per person. It may even be true that in the long run additional people actually *cause* food to be less scarce and less expensive, and cause consumption to increase. This theme will be developed in Part II.

Food in the 1970s: From Shortage-Crisis to Glut-Crisis

In chapter 4 we took the long view, decades and centuries. But what about recent food prices and the "food crisis"? Chapter 1 argued that price (and the cost of production, which is close to price over the long haul) is the most relevant index of scarcity for natural resources. The sharp rise in food prices in 1972–73 suggests an increasing food scarcity, by this test. Figure 5-1 shows how the situation looked then to Lester Brown. And that increase in price was indeed interpreted as a bad sign by a great many consumers, who saw it as a harbinger of a great crisis to come. For a better understanding, however, look at figure 5-2, which gives a longer historical perspective. The 1974 price jump is seen to be simply another fluctuation.

We must keep in mind, though, that price does not tell us the whole story about scarcity and social welfare. A product may be readily available, as measured by its price being low, and yet there may still be a social problem. For example, a daily ration of vitamin X may be very cheap, but if people are not getting enough of it there is a social problem. On the other hand, caviar may be particularly high priced and scarce this year, but few would consider that to be a social problem. Similarly, the price of food may be higher than in a previous year, but this may not indicate a social problem — if, for example, demand and price have risen because of an increase in income and a resulting increase in the amount of grain fed to animals to produce meat. So, though the price of food and the social welfare are often connected, they are not identical.

That understood, we are ready to analyze the causes and meaning of the sharp rise in food prices in the early 1970s. We begin, as in previous chapters, by examining the very long-run price trends. Figure 5-2 shows that the real price of wheat — the market price adjusted for inflation — has fallen over the long haul. And figure 5-3 shows details for corn and wheat over the past seven decades. This decline may come as a shock to you, especially when you consider the great increase in demand due both to world population increases and to world income increases. Yet the rise in food output was so great as to cause grain to become cheaper despite the large increases in demand from population and income. More shocking still, figure 5-4 shows how the price of wheat has fallen by another measure — relative to wages in the U.S.

(How and why did total output and productivity per worker and per acre increase so fast? Supply increased so fast because of agricultural knowledge gained from research and development *induced by* the increased demand, together with the increased ability of farmers to get their produce to market on improved transportation systems. These sentences are a lightning-fast summary of forces that take many books to document in satisfactory detail.)

The obvious implication of this historical trend toward cheaper food — a trend that probably extends back to the beginning of agriculture — is that real prices for food will continue to drop. Of course the interpretation of the data cannot be quite that simple; adjusted real prices are affected by monetary changes and by the method of price-level adjustment that is used. Yet the trend clearly has been toward cheaper grain; that is the all-important fact. It is also a fact that dismays American farmers and causes them to tractorcade to Washington.[1] And it is a fact that portends more drops in price and even less scarcity in the future, as discussed in chapter 4.

Despite the long-run trend, short-run fluctuations in food prices are inevitable. Though short-run prices carry little or no information about future long-run trends, we must nevertheless analyze the price rise in the early 1970s, at least briefly, because it made such an impression on so many people.

The sharp food-price rise in the early 1970s was caused by a chance combination of increased Russian grain purchases to feed livestock, U.S. policies to reduce "surpluses" and get the government out of agriculture, a couple of bad world harvests, and some big-business finagling in the U.S.

Though the high food prices of a few years ago were popularly viewed with alarm, it is to the credit of agricultural economists (with notable exceptions such as Lester Brown) that they did not view them that way, even in the midst of the "crisis." Even the UN World Food Conference in 1974, called to talk about the "crisis," produced rather unalarming forecasts. But there was no way to reduce public concern. When I passed on to my classes the prediction that these high prices would soon lead to increased supply, students asked, "How can you be sure?" And of course

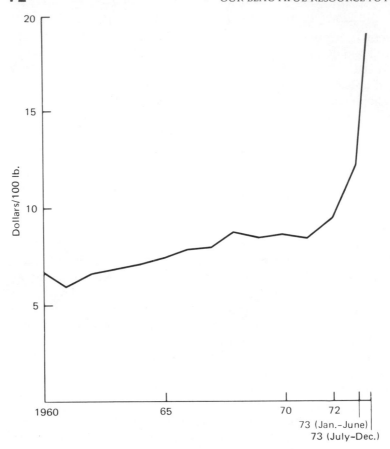

FIGURE 5-1a. How Short-Run Data Can Mislead: World Rice Prices, 1960–73

neither I nor anyone else could be sure. We could only rely on all of agricultural history and economic theory for our optimistic predictions.

History and economic theory turned out to be right, of course. And the consequences of the early 1970s increase in prices are far more important, and far better understood, than are the causes of the high prices: Farmers in the U.S. and elsewhere responded to the opportunity with record-breaking crops.

FOOD STOCKPILES

When in 1974 I showed people newspaper reports of a fall in grain prices—a clear indicator of increasing supplies—people said "Yes, but

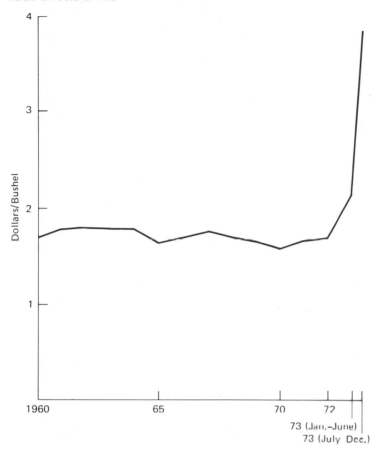

FIGURE 5-1b. How Short-Run Data Can Mislead: World Wheat Prices, 1960–73

what about stockpiles? Aren't they dangerously low?" Indeed, food stocks were then lower than they had been, but this does not necessarily mean that they were dangerously low. Rather, stocks — that is, U.S. and Canadian government-held stocks, which had originally been organized "as a means of holding unwanted surpluses off the market and thus sustaining farm prices"[2] — had come to be considered too high by the U.S. and Canadian administrations, and that is the main reason why stocks had come down.

Large grain stocks — "excess" in the eyes of farm policy-makers — had accumulated in the 1950s and early 1960s, and there was fierce price competition. Therefore, between 1957 and 1962, grain acreage in the U.S. and Canada was cut back sharply, and stocks fell as a result.[3] Then

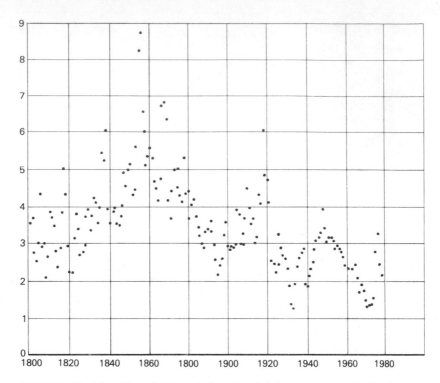

FIGURE 5-2. The Price of Wheat Relative to the Consumer Price Index

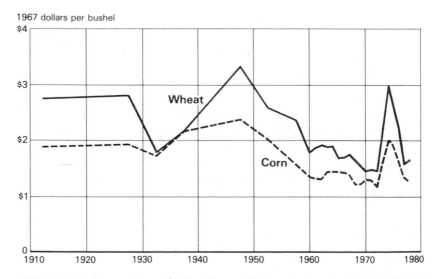

FIGURE 5-3. Export Prices of U.S. Wheat and Corn in Constant 1967 Dollars

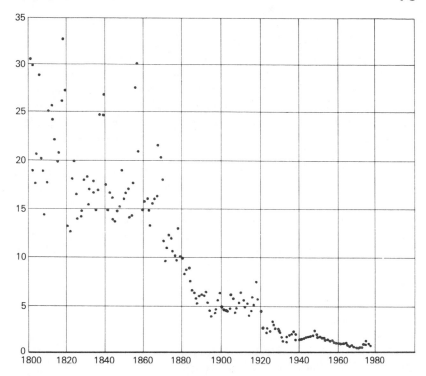

FIGURE 5-4. The Price of Wheat Relative to Wages in the U.S.

stocks inexorably began to rise again, after new free-market policies took effect in the U.S. and India. And now we are again at the point of glut. The free market has brought a bittersweet harvest for U.S. farmers, and the U.S. secretary of agriculture has been said to be "pessimistic" because of the record harvests and the "surplus" of wheat.[4] Prices are so low that farmers are reluctant to sell, and newspaper stories report that "huge grain crops trigger [a] need for bins as on-farm storage spreads in Midwest."[5] Manufacturers of storage bins "say sales are booming . . . [and] demand for metal bins is up 40% to 50%."[6]

Furthermore, the stocks of food that are necessary to supply a given margin of safety against famine become smaller as transportation improves. In the past, every isolated family and village had to maintain its own stock against a shortfall in the harvest. But now food can be moved quickly from areas of plenty to areas of shortfall. First the ship, then the train, and then the plane drastically reduced the total stocks that need be maintained.

AND NOW?

What will happen next? The most likely danger is not a "shortage" due to inability of farmers to produce. Rather, the likely danger is from reduced supply because of government-imposed incentives *not* to produce — such as subsidies for land kept out of production — and then price controls as production falls. These changes were clearly written in the Carter administration proposals to reduce planted acreage by 20 percent as of August 1977 (when the first draft of this chapter was written), and now similar suggestions are in the papers in 1980. Such a move to reduce production might well set the stage for another round of the sort of crisis that the world experienced in the early 1970s, because the U.S. exercises a crucial role in making up unexpected shortfalls in places where storage facilities are not available to carry over much food from one year to the next. The result might be a greater tragedy than last time, not because of physical limits to food production, but because of economic and political policies.

THE DROUGHT?

The drought of 1976–77 is an interesting case in modern food supply, the sort of episode that is likely to recur.

Curious it is that the huge recent crops, vast stockpiles, and falling prices documented earlier in this chapter have occurred in the face of widely publicized fears of drought. Throughout 1976 and 1977 there were news stories of droughts in various places and also worldwide. "Drought conditions similar to the one of 1977 faced Illinois farmers in 1956. Subsurface moisture was nil, wells were going dry, the weather forecast was gloomy" — in February 1977 just as in 1956.[7] Yet harvests were at or near record levels both in 1977 and in 1956. How can this be?

One reason that harvests were large despite the droughts is man's increased capacity to overcome adverse natural conditions. To illustrate, one of the most publicized droughts was in southern California.

> To thousands of Okies who fled the Midwestern dust bowl in the 1930s, California's San Joaquin Valley was the land of plenty. Aided by irrigation systems they laid down, the valley produced everything from grapes to almonds. But now the nation's most productive stretch of farmland lies parched by its second year of drought, and its farmers,

many of them dust-bowl immigrants or their children, are in danger of losing their land again.[8]

The southern California drought did not end. Yet by August the newspaper headlines said, "California Crop Yields Are Surprisingly Good Despite Long Drought." The explanation is, "California farmers, the nation's most productive, have been so successful at finding more water, and making wiser use of what they have, that California crop production is surprisingly strong despite the drought. Statewide cotton and grape crops are expected to set records, and many fruit, nut, and vegetable crops are up from last year. . . ."[9] The California farmers drilled new wells and substituted water-conserving sprinkler systems or trickle irrigation for flood irrigation.

Clearly it is not just luck that brought us safely past the 1976–77 drought, but rather our hard-won knowledge and skills, which are themselves products of natural crises and of population-induced demand.

Another reason why the droughts have had so little ill effect is that they simply have not been what they were cracked up to be. A drought in one country or state is dramatic and makes news; the ideal growing conditions in the next state or country seldom get reported. And "so huge is American farm geography [even more is this true of world farm geography] that it can absorb pockets of severe loss and still produce bountiful harvests."[10] Furthermore, people often assert that there is a drought when there has not *yet* been rain. This was the case in Illinois in 1977. But later, "Above average rainfall during August wiped out previous moisture deficits. . . . Despite a year-long drought followed by downpours that delayed harvest, Illinois farmers in 1977 grew a record 327 million bushels of soybeans and led the nation in production of both beans and corn."[11] And in California there was so much rain by the end of the "drought" year that "beleaguered state officials in Sacramento set up emergency relief — and quickly changed the name of the Drought Information Center to the Flood Control Center."[12]

At this writing, in August 1980, I am aware of this year's drought. Crops undoubtedly will be poorer than in 1979. But I'll bet that, though harvests will not set records, they also will not be as bad as the newspapers now say they will be, and that the year will be no disaster.

Modern technological capacities in league with modern transportation capacities, harnessed to farmers' ingenuity when offered a chance to make money, have vastly reduced the likelihood of a major disturbance in our food supplies. In the short run as in the long run, worldwide drought, like worldwide famine, is a receding rather than an approaching danger.

LUMBER

Lumber is an agricultural product. As such it fits more closely into this chapter than into a chapter about energy, even though it has been the main source of fuel in most places in the past.[13]

People have frequently worried about a wood shortage. In 1905 President Roosevelt said that "a timber famine is inevitable," a statement that culminated a national worry dating from as early as 1860. There was special concern over such woods as hickory. But despite the heavy use of wood since then, the picture is quite different now. A "glut of low grades of factory lumber exists . . . [and] a lack of market opportunities continues to set severe limitations on improvement of state and national forests. . . . [By 1951] hickory trees were taking over the eastern hardwood forest. . . . In spite of expanded uses of timber for pulp and paper, we are [in 1971] probably growing more cubic feet of wood annually than we were in 1910."[14]

That is, the amount of lumber that is being grown is now *higher* than in the past. Regarding more recent trends, the official Council on Environmental Quality tells us that "trends in net annual timber growth [total annual growth less mortality] show that the net annual growth of softwoods and hardwoods combined increased by 18 percent between 1952 and 1962 and another 14 percent between 1962 and 1970. This increase is a result of expanded programs in forest fire control, tree planting, and other forestry measures."[15] (See figure 5-5.)

The confounding of predictions, and the shift from an apparently impending "timber famine" to actual glut, was not fortuitous but rather occurred as a response to the perceived need. One response was that more timber was purposely planted. Even more important were conservation efforts due to higher prices, and research in wood and wood substitutes. We see the results in our homes: plastic bags substituted for paper bags; newsprint made thinner and yet stronger, as in airmail editions of overseas newspapers; and so on. Perhaps wood will not even be used for paper in the future, as recent news stories suggest:

KENAF PASSES TEST AS ALTERNATIVE NEWSPRINT FIBER

Peoria, Ill., September 12, 1977 — The first experimental press run using newly developed nonwood pulp newsprint has been made at the Peoria Journal Star.

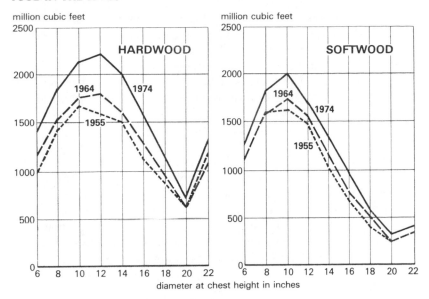

FIGURE 5-5. Timber Growth in North Carolina, a Representative State

The paper was made on a test basis from Kenaf, a fibrous plant related to cotton.[16]

KENAF MAY HOLD THE CURE FOR PAPER INDUSTRY WOES

Chicago, Ill., December 24, 1979 —

The American Newspaper Publishers Assn. has begun evaluating one-day tests conducted earlier this month by six newspapers that used the newsprint substitute, kenaf, a paper made from the pulp of a quick-growing relative of the hibiscus plant.

"There were no major problems in the test," said Erwin Jaffe, director of ANPA's Research Institute in Easton, Pa. But he emphasized that there are "still a tremendous number of things that need to be determined" before calling the test successful. . . .

The largest newspaper testing kenaf was the Miami Herald, which ran more than 3,000 copies of its Dec. 9 Sunday travel section from the slightly whiter paper.

"It passed the first test. It didn't tear apart," said Manny Gonzalez, the Herald's manager of engineering. "We got no complaints from readers and none from advertisers, that I know of. The average reader wouldn't know the difference between kenaf and newsprint. . . ."

(Industry sources told Advertising Age that kenaf production could become economical when the price of domestic newsprint hits about $400 a ton. The price currently is about $375.)[17]

We see, then, that fears in the past about running out of wood have been quite wrong. And there is no reason to believe that the trends of earlier decades are suddenly reversing their direction in this decade.

CONCLUSIONS

So — here we go again, it seems. There is a glut of food. Farmers — especially in the U.S. — are pushing for subsidies to reduce food production, and the U.S. government has already enacted such programs. Are we just at the top of another self-induced cycle, with a food crisis — real or imagined — at the bottom, just a few years away? If it happens, the main villain won't be population growth or income growth or physical limits, but rather the blundering of human institutions.

Are We Losing Ground?

Is the public being purposely misled about the trends in available land? Or are the scare reports just honest ignorance?

The title for this chapter comes from the 1976 book by Erik P. Eckholm, *Losing Ground.* That book is a product of the Worldwatch Institute. It was written "with the support and cooperation of the United Nations Environment Program," and contains a laudatory foreword by Maurice F. Strong, the executive director of the UN Environment Program. I draw attention to the auspices of Eckholm's book because we can consider it as representative of the "official" position of the interlinked world community of environmental and population organizations.

The thesis of Eckholm's book is that the world's land is deteriorating. In the language of Strong's foreword, "our delicately balanced food systems are being ecologically undermined . . . through deforestation, overgrazing, soil erosion and abandonment, desertification, the setting of irrigation systems . . . etc."[1] As a *New York Times* headline about the book put it, "Fertile Land Areas Dwindling in Poor Countries Despite Aid."[2] And, apparently associated with the appearance of Eckholm's book, the UN convened a conference on "desertification" in August-September 1977 in Nairobi. Front-page headlines in the *New York Times* reported "14 Million Acres a Year Vanishing as Deserts Spread Round Globe."[3] *Newsweek's* headline to a full-page story was "Lethal Spread of the Sands."[4] Children's books tell this story in simple terms: "Our Soil — Wasted and Lost."[5] The clear implication of these frightening statements is that the world's supply of arable land is decreasing.

It is not true. The world is not "losing ground" on a net basis, as this chapter shows. Of course arable land in some places is going out of cultivation because of erosion and other destructive forces. But, taken as a whole, the amount of arable land in the world is increasing year by year, in flat contradiction to the clear implications of the statements quoted above. How can this be?

Let us first step back and specify the questions that we should take up. As usual, it is not easy to formulate the right ones. We should first ask, What is the present trend in the supply of arable land? Next we ask, What is the effect of increasing affluence on the supply of agricultural land? And last, What is the effect of population growth upon the supply of agricultural land and recreational land? The first two questions are answered in this chapter; the last, in chapter 16.

THE TREND OF ARABLE LAND: LOSING GROUND?

Eckholm provides frightening ancedotes aplenty about how the world is "losing land" to deserts, dust, overgrazing, woodcutting, and salting due to irrigation — many of them taken from travelers' impressions and like evidence. But statistics he does not give. He says instead that "ideally, a book on the ecological undermining of food-production systems would include detailed national statistics. . . . Unfortunately, such comprehensive data are not available." In fact, comprehensive data *are* available. And when examined, these data contradict the picture suggested by the ancedotes.

Joginder Kumar has done an enormous amount of careful, headbreaking labor to collect and standardize the latest available data on land supply and use throughout the world. His finding: There was 9 percent more total arable land in 1960 than in 1950 in the eighty-seven countries for which he could find data; these countries account for 73 percent of the total land area for the world.[6] More details on this impressive gain of almost 1 percent per year may be found in table 6.1. Some of the places where the quantity of cultivated land is going up may surprise you — India, for example, where the amount of cultivated land rose from 1,261,000 to 1,379,190 square kilometers between 1951 and 1960.[7]

The trend that Kumar found from 1950 to 1960 still continues. The UNFAO now has collected data back to the 1960s showing that there was a rise in "arable and permanent cropland" from 1,403 to 1,507 million hectares in the world as a whole from 1961–65 to 1975, an increase of 7.4 percent for the roughly eleven-year period (table 6-2). Furthermore, the gain in the developing countries is particularly significant and heartening.

We begin, then, by taking notice of the fact that the amount of arable land in the world — and especially in the poor and hungry countries — is increasing, rather than decreasing as the popular press would have it. And this does not forebode diminishing returns in the long run due to successively poorer land being brought into use, because it is also a fact that average yields per acre are increasing.

TABLE 6-1. Changes in Land Use, 1950–60

	Arable Land as a Percentage of Total Area		Percentage of Arable Land That Is Cultivated		Cultivated Land as a Percentage of Total Land (1 × 3) and (2 × 4)		Agricultural Land (Arable and Pasture) as a Percentage of Total Area	
	(1) 1950	(2) 1960	(3) 1950	(4) 1960	1950	1960	1950	1960
Africa	14.27	15.30	36.21	42.72	5.2	6.5	46.50	49.02
Middle East	12.87	13.91	52.11	57.88	6.7	8.1	13.06	17.34
Asia	19.03	20.78	82.06	86.17	15.6	17.9	46.35	49.60
North and South America, U.S.S.R., Australia, New Zealand	6.88	7.75	82.75	82.96	5.7	6.4	34.27	38.59
Europe	30.79	30.98	89.02	90.06	27.4	27.9	45.63	46.10
All regions	10.73	11.73	82.74	83.99	8.9	9.9	37.35	41.07

SOURCE: Kumar, 1973, p. 107.

TABLE 6-2. Changes in Land Use, 1961–65 to 1975

	Arable Land as a Percentage of Total Area				Agricultural Land (Arable and Pasture) as a Percentage of Total Area			
	1961–65	1966	1970	1975	1961–65	1966	1970	1975
Africa	6.28	6.50	6.76	6.96	32.88	32.96	33.13	33.29
Middle East	6.25	6.38	6.54	6.79	21.91	22.12	22.32	22.62
Far East	28.87	29.37	29.88	30.73	33.08	33.62	33.80	34.56
North America	11.50	11.43	12.17	13.08	26.10	25.85	25.88	25.50
U.S.S.R.	10.24	10.24	10.39	10.37	26.83	27.34	27.09	26.97
Latin America	5.64	5.97	6.43	6.82	29.56	30.29	31.29	32.41
Western Europe	27.21	26.55	25.97	25.04	46.35	45.78	44.83	43.72
All regions	10.41	10.58	10.93	11.25	33.13	33.38	33.71	33.99

SOURCE: UN, Food and Agriculture Organization, 1976.

Where Is the Amount of Cultivated Land Declining?

The amount of cultivated land certainly *is* going down in some places — but where? In the U.S., that is where, as can be seen in figure 6-1. But this decline is by no means a bad sign. Both the total agricultural output and average yields per acre have been going up sharply in the U.S., to

millions of acres

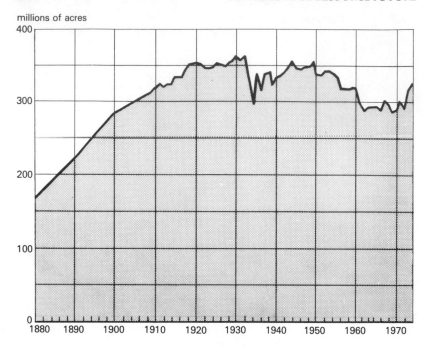

FIGURE 6-1. Cropland Harvested in the U.S. (48 states)

the extent that overproduction is a "problem." This high output is obtained in large part with huge farm machines that require flat land for efficiency. The combination of an increased productivity per acre of good land and the increased use of equipment adapted to flat land has made it unprofitable to farm some land that formerly was cultivated. For example, in New Hampshire between 1860 and 1950 the tillable area declined from 2,367,000 acres to 451,000 acres.[8]

There are, however, places where, for negative reasons — usually wars or fights about land tenure — good land that was formerly cultivated is no longer farmed. Mexico offers a typical recent example. Frustrated by the slow pace of agrarian reform, Mexican peasants began seizing land. The big estates then cut their investments in fear of more seizures. "The agrarian unrest has interrupted agricultural production and investment at a time of economic crisis. . . . Sonora's farmers, who grow more than half the country's wheat, complain that their 1977 production will be reduced as much as 15%, or 220,000 tons, because of the unrest."[9]

Even such persons who worry about the "loss" of land as Erik Eckholm acknowledge that it is in our own power to have more land if we will work for it: "Today the human species has the knowledge of past mistakes, and the analytical and technical skills, to halt destructive trends and to provide an adequate diet for all using lands well-suited for agriculture."[10]

Now we may proceed to our second question, leaving the last question, on the effects of population growth, for chapter 16.

Is Land Different from Other Resources?

Land, which many people consider to be a special kind of resource, is subject to the same processes of human creation as other natural resources, as discussed in chapters 1–3. Though the stock of usable land seems fixed at any moment, it is constantly being increased — at a rapid rate in many cases — by the clearing of new land or reclamation of wasteland. Land also is constantly being enhanced by increasing the number of crops grown per year on each unit of land and by increasing the yield per crop with better farming methods and with chemical fertilizer. Last but not least, land is created anew where there was no land. For example, much of Holland originally belonged more to the sea than to the land: "According to strict geographical determinism, one would expect to find there nothing but a fever-ridden delta and lagoons, the undisputed domain of sea fowl and migratory birds. Instead, we find a prosperous and densely-peopled country, with in fact the highest densities of population in Europe."[11] The new land was won by diking and draining: "This is essentially a triumph of human will; it is the imprint of civilization on the landscape."[12] A hundred years ago someone said of the Netherlands, "This is not soil: it is the flesh and blood and sweat of men."[13]

Holland was created by muscle power. But our potential for creating new land has increased as our knowledge and machinery and new power sources have developed. In the future, the potential for creating new and better land will be even greater. We will make mountains where there is now water, learn new techniques of changing the nature of soils, and learn how to develop and transport fresh water to arid regions.

The role of landbuilding in population history became clear to Malthus, who said of Germans in Roman times:

> ... when the return of famine severely admonished them of the insufficiency of their scanty resources, they accused the sterility of a country which refused to supply the multitude of its inhabitants; but instead of clearing their forests, draining their swamps, and rendering

their soil fit to support an extended population, they found it more congenial to their martial habits and impatient dispositions, to go in quest of "food, of plunder, or of glory," into other countries.[14]

The cooperative relationship between landbuilding, irrigation, population growth, and prosperity in prehistoric times is also well understood by historians of the ancient Middle East.

> In the great alluvial valleys of the Nile, the Tigris-Euphrates, and the Indus system collective effort had created artificial environments. . . . The organized exploitation of lands reclaimed from swamp and desert was yielding unprecedented supplies of corn, fish and other foodstuffs.[15]

But once built, land can be lost through neglect and depopulation, as happened in the same Tigris-Euphrates area. "Many of these districts have not been settled or cultivated in a thousand years or more, and have been deeply and cleanly scoured by wind erosion during that interval. . . ."[16]

Investment in land is as important in the modern world as it was in the ancient world. The key idea is that land is man-made, just like other inputs to farm production. "The productive capacity of a farm is the cumulative result of what has been done to the land in the past and is largely the result of investment. . . . The more progressive agriculture becomes, the smaller is its dependency on the natural endowments."[17]

Evidence that the amount of capital formation in subsistence agriculture can vary greatly, depending on people's motivations, is found in China. The amount of labor done by the average peasant rose 59 percent from 1950 to 1959 — from 119 days yearly to 189 days. Much of this labor went into improving the quality of the land and of the rural infrastructure (roads, waterworks, and utilities).[18] In fact, much agricultural investment has always come from the additional labor done by farmers during the off-season, when they are not engaged in crop work. For example, in agriculturally primitive Rapitok Parish in New Britain, "men of working age invest one-quarter of their manpower per year in the formation of new agricultural assets such as cocoa and coconut trees. This is a long-term agricultural investment."[19]

And in my hometown of Champaign-Urbana, Illinois, in the middle of some of the most valuable corn and soybean farmland in the world, people are surprised to learn that, before the pioneer farmers applied their labor and sweat (and lives) in developing this land, it was a malarial swamp. Though it was flat, it was also waterlogged, and therefore unproductive. "Until white settlers drained the prairie, Champaign County was very marshy.... Early settlers noted that the Indians built platforms high in the trees to escape the mosquitoes."[20] The schoolchild imagines a vast, untapped prairie frontier where the white man, if he was brave enough to stand up to the Indians, needed only to drop seeds in the earth to have a bountiful crop. This is simply a myth.

Nor is landbuilding a thing of the past, even in Illinois. In Champaign County, Harold Schlensker is a retired farmer whose farmholdings, which his sons work, were in 1977 worth more than a million dollars on paper. Much of the increase in the value of his land came from reclamation. "Pointing out the back window of his house, Schlensker indicated a drainage ditch that was one of his first improvements to try to upgrade a plot of land he characterized as 'just swampland.' He said, 'I put that ditch in and some tile, and brought it up to good productive land.'"[21]

In various parts of the U.S., cropland is being created at the rate of 1.25 (or another estimate, 1.7) million acres yearly by irrigation, swamp drainage, and other techniques. This is a much larger quantity of land than the amount that is converted to cities and highways each year, as we shall see in chapter 16. Compare this with the nightmarish *Limits to Growth* view that land is fixed in quantity and that agricultural land capacity is being "lost" to cities and highways.

The U.S. has been blessed with an endowment of land and water that has in the past made irrigation unprofitable. But now, with an increased demand for food and new technological advances, irrigation has become important in creating new land. California's San Joaquin Valley illustrates the miracle: "A century ago it was desert, but today a Rhode Island-size tract in California's arid San Joaquin Valley known as the Westlands Water District contains some of the richest farmland in the world—the product mainly of multi-billion-dollar Federal reclamation projects that irrigated the parched valley floor with water from government dams."[22]

Center-pivot irrigation is a landbuilding innovation so promising that it deserves special attention. Here is a dramatic account of the impact of center-pivot irrigation in the American West:

In its natural state, the land along the Columbia River in eastern Washington and Oregon is a forbidding expanse of shifting sand, sagebrush and Russian thistle, and only the hardiest of farmers or ranchers would try to wrest a living from it. The region is so desolate that the Navy uses some of the land as a bombing range. But for all this, the mid-Columbia region is one of the most thriving new agricultural areas in the world. Thanks to a remarkable new system of irrigation, the desert along the river is blooming. . . . With pivot irrigation, the water is pumped from the river to the center of a round field a half-mile in diameter. A giant arm of 6-inch pipe a quarter-of-a-mile long pivots around the center of the field like the hand of a clock, making one revolution every 12 hours. . . . Since much of the land is almost pure sand, it must be continuously fertilized, and here too the sprinkler system is used by feeding the appropriate nutrients into the water.[23]

We now see this process beginning to appear even in the most fertile spots in the U.S. By 1978 center-pivot irrigation had appeared in my home Champaign County, whose corn-and-soybean land is as rich as any in the world even without irrigation. In areas where water is scarce or saline, and where labor is scarce, the Blass system of drip irrigation (also called "trickle irrigation") may be utilized.[24]

But is there land capacity for still further expansion of agriculture? Yes, there is. UNFAO concluded that "there are 1,145 million hectares of [additional] land suitable for crops [excluding China], more than twice the 512 million hectares devoted to crops in 1962."[25]

What do "arable" and "suitable for crops" mean? Here again, economics cannot be separated from semantics. At one time most of Europe could not be planted, because the soils were "too heavy." When a plow was invented that could farm the heavy soil, most of Europe suddenly became "arable" in the eyes of the people who lived there. Most of Ireland and New England originally were too hilly and stony to be farmed, but with backbreaking toil the stones were removed and the land became "suitable for crops." In the twentieth century, bulldozers and dynamite have pulled out stumps that kept land from being cropped. And in the future, cheap water transportation and desalination will transform what are now deserts into "arable" lands. The definitions change as technology develops and the demand for land rises. Hence any calculation of "arable" land should be seen for what it is — a rough temporary calculation that may be useful for awhile but that has no permanent validity.

"You can even make agricultural land out of Mount Everest, but it would cost a fortune to do so," is a common reply to such optimism by those who worry that we are running out of land. But in many parts of the world new land can be bought and cleared right now for amounts that are considerably below the purchase price of already developed land in Illinois. Furthermore, the real cost of acquiring and clearing land nowadays is less than it was in the past, when tree cutting, stump pulling, and irrigation-ditch digging had to be done at great expense by hand or with the help of animals.

Then there is outer space and the planets. Buck Rogers stuff? Many respected scientists would disagree.

> Making plans so bold that they seem almost unbelievable, many of the nation's leading scientists are calling for immediate steps to begin colonizing space.
>
> Their goal is to make the vast reaches of space the natural habitat of man with Mother Earth remembered as the "old world. . . ."
>
> Peering into their crystal balls at the recent meeting of the American Association for the Advancement of Science, the scientists concluded that space colonization is inevitable — and sooner than we think.
>
> They reported:
>
> • The most important leap into space will begin in 1980, when the space shuttle takes its first payloads into Earth orbit. The shuttle is designed to make it easy for man to go into orbit and out again, almost like making transcontinental flights.
>
> • Mining the moon can begin in 1990. The material from 50 million tons of moon rocks can be used to make solar-power satellites that will provide all of the Earth's energy needs by 2000.
>
> • Space is an ideal location for many types of manufacturing, including the making of electronics equipment. Space manufacturing can begin in the 1980's becoming a multi-billion-dollar business in a few decades.[26]

CONCLUSION

My message is not one of complacency. I am not suggesting that we cease to care about our land, worldwide or regionally. Just as each homeowner must take care of his lawn lest it go to ruin, and just as every farmer must continually protect and renew his acreage, so must every country take care that its stock of good land is increased and improved.

What these land data do show is that there is no ground for the panic into which anecdotal accounts can throw us when they are not balanced by the larger picture of accurate figures. And there is no basis in these figures for opposition to continuing economic and population growth. (The *wisdom* of such growth with respect to land, as opposed to the feasibility, will be discussed in chapter 16.)

7.

When Will We Run Out of Energy? Never!

What will we do when the pumps run dry?
— Paul and Anne Ehrlich, *The End of Affluence*

Energy is an emotional topic now. In a recent Gallup poll of people who drive cars, 82 percent said that "the energy situation in the United States" is "very serious" or "fairly serious."[1] When asked their number one worry in September 1978, seven times as many people said "inflation" as "energy." By summer 1979, the numbers were roughly equal.[2] Energy is also a topic about which it is extraordinarily difficult to get any agreement among people on different sides of the controversy. But let us see how far we can get.

The main question before us is, What is the prospect for energy scarcity and prices? Here is the broad picture that this chapter draws. (This summary is at the beginning rather than at the end of the chapter to provide some guideposts for your exploration into the intellectual jungle of arguments about energy economics. You may wish to defer reading it until after the chapter, however.)

(1) Energy is the most important of natural resources because
    (a) the creation of other natural resources requires energy, and
    (b) with enough energy all other resources can be created.

(2) The most reliable method of forecasting the future cost and scarcity of energy is to extrapolate the historical trends of energy costs, for reasons given in chapter 1.

(3) The history of energy economics shows that, in spite of fears in each era of running out of whichever source of energy was important in that era, energy has grown progressively less scarce, as shown by long-run falling energy prices.

(4) The cause of the increasing plenty in the supply of energy has been the discovery of new sources and new types of energy, and the development of improved extraction processes.

(5) These new developments have not been fortuitous, but rather have been induced by increased demand caused in part by rising population.

(6) For the very long run, there is nothing meaningfully "finite" about our world that inevitably will cause energy to grow more scarce and costly. Theoretically, the cost of energy could go either up or down in the very long run. But the trends point to a lower cost.

(7) Forecasts based on technological analyses are less persuasive than historical extrapolations of cost trends. Furthermore, the technological forecasts of future energy supplies differ markedly among themselves.

(8) A sure way to err in forecasting future supplies is to look at currently known reserves of oil, coal, and other fossil fuels.

(9) An appropriate technological forecast would be based on engineering estimates of the amounts of additional energy that will be produced at various price levels, and on predictions of new discoveries and technical advances that will come about as a result of various energy prices.

(10) Some technologists believe that even very much higher prices will produce only small increases in our energy supply, and even those only slowly. Others believe that at only slightly higher prices vast additional supplies will be forthcoming, and very quickly.

(11) Causes of the disagreements among technological forecasters are differences in
> (a) scientific data cited,
> (b) assessments of political forces,
> (c) ideology,
> (d) belief or non-belief in "finiteness" as an element of the situation, and
> (e) vividness of scientific imagination.

(12) The disagreement among technological forecasters makes the economic extrapolation of decreasing historical costs even more compelling.

Now let's fill in this outline.

ENERGY, THE MASTER RESOURCE

Energy is the master resource because energy enables us to convert one material into another. As natural scientists continue to learn more about the transformation of materials from one form to another with the aid of energy, energy will be even more important. Therefore, if the cost of usable energy is low enough, all other important resources can be made plentiful, as H. E. Goeller and A. M. Weinberg showed.[3] For example, low energy costs would enable people to create enormous quantities of useful land. The cost of energy is the prime reason that water desalination is too expensive for general use; reduction in energy cost would make water desalination feasible, and irrigated farming would follow in many areas that are now deserts. And if energy were much cheaper, it would be feasible to transport sweet water from areas of surplus to arid areas far away. Another example: If energy costs were low enough, all kinds of raw materials could be mined from the sea.

On the other hand, if there were to be an absolute shortage of energy — that is, if there were no oil in the tanks, no natural gas in the pipelines, no coal to load onto the railroad cars — then our entire economy would come to a halt. Or if energy were available, but only at a very high price, we would produce much smaller amounts of most consumer goods and services.

Because energy plays so central a role, it is most important that we think clearly about the way energy is found and used. This is the common view:

> Money in the bank, oil in the ground.
> Easily spent, less easily found.
> The faster they're spent, the sooner they run out.
> And that's what the Energy Crisis is about.[4]

But this rhyme omits the key forces that completely alter the picture. We shall see that, with energy just as with other raw materials, a fuller analysis produces an entirely different outlook than does the simplistic Malthusian projection.

The analysis of the supply of mineral resources in chapters 1–3 identified four factors as being important: (1) the increasing cost of extraction as more of the resource is used, if all other conditions remain the same; (2) the tendency for engineers to develop improved methods of extracting the resource in response to the rising price of the resource; (3) the propensity for scientists and businessmen to discover substitutes for the resource — such as solar or nuclear power as substitutes for coal or oil — in response to increasing demand; (4) the increased use of recycled material.

The supply of energy is analogous to the supply of other "extracted" raw materials with the exception of the fourth factor above: Minerals such as iron and aluminum can be recycled, whereas coal and oil are "burned up." Of course this distinction is not perfectly clear-cut: Quarried marble is cut irreversibly and cannot be recycled by melting, as copper can; yet even cut marble can be used again and again, whereas energy sources cannot.

The practical implication of being "used up" as opposed to being recyclable is that an increased rate of energy use would make the price of energy sources rise sharply, whereas an increased use of iron would not affect iron prices so much because some of the additional iron could be drawn from such previously used stocks as dumps of old autos. All of this may seem to make our energy future look grim. But before we proceed to the analysis itself, it is instructive to see how energy "shortages" have frightened even the most intelligent of analysts for centuries.

The English Coal Scare

In 1865, W. Stanley Jevons, one of the last century's truly great social scientists, wrote a careful, comprehensive book predicting that England's industry would soon grind to a halt due to exhaustion of England's coal. "It will appear that there is no reasonable prospect of any relief from a future want of the main agent of industry," he wrote. "We cannot long continue our present rate of progress. The first check for our growing prosperity, however, must render our population excessive."[5] Figure 7-1 reproduces the frontispiece from Jevons's book, "shewing the impossibility of a long continuance of progress." And Jevons's investigation proved to him that there was no chance that oil would eventually solve England's problem.

What happened? Because of the perceived future need for coal and because of the potential profit in meeting that need, prospectors searched out new deposits of coal, inventors discovered better ways to get coal out of the earth, and transportation men developed cheaper ways to move the coal. Other countries did the same. At present, the proven U.S. reserves of coal are enough to supply a level of use far higher than the present level for many hundreds or thousands of years. And the use of coal must even be subsidized in some countries. Though the labor cost per unit of coal output has been falling,[6] the cost of other fuels has dropped even more. This suggests that *not enough* coal was mined in the past, rather than that the future was unfairly exploited in earlier years. As to Jevons's poor old England, this is its present energy situation: "Though Britain may reach energy self-sufficiency late this year or early next, with its huge reserves of North Sea oil and gas lasting well into the next century, the country is moving ahead with an ambitious program to develop its even more plentiful coal reserves."[7]

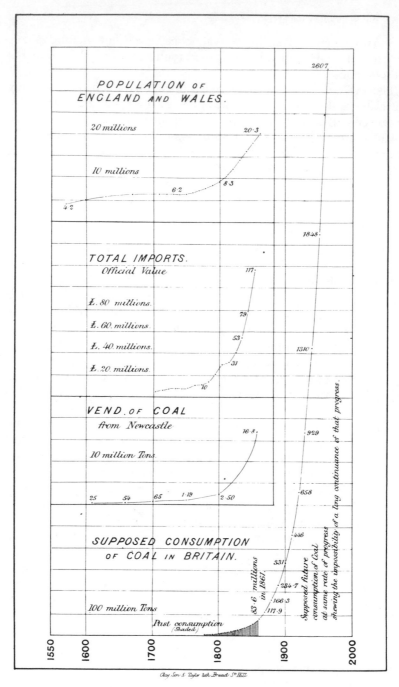

POPULATION OF
ENGLAND AND WALES.

20 millions

20·3

10 millions

6·2   8·3

4·2

TOTAL IMPORTS.
Official Value

117·

£. 80 millions.

79·

£. 60 millions.

53·

£. 40 millions.

·31

£. 20 millions.

·10

1848·

1310·

VEND. OF COAL
from Newcastle·

16·8·

10 million Tons.

·929

25   54   ·65   1·19   2·50

·858

SUPPOSED CONSUMPTION
OF COAL IN BRITAIN.

·446

331·

234·7

83·6 millions
in 1861.

166·3

100 million Tons

117·9

Past consumption
(Shaded)

2607·

Supposed future consumption of Coal at same rate of progress shewing the impossibility of a long continuance of that progress.

1550   1600   1700   1800   1900   2000

Clay Son S. Taylor lith Bread S°. Hill.

FIGURE 7-1. Jevons's View of Coal and of England's Future, as of 1865

The Long-Running Running Out of Oil Drama

Running out of oil has long been a nightmare. In 1885, the U.S. Geological Survey saw "little or no chance for oil in California," and in 1891 it prophesied the same for Kansas and Texas. In 1908, the Geological Survey estimated a maximum future supply of oil that has long since been exceeded. And since then, similar gloomy official prophesies by the Geological Survey, the Bureau of Mines, the Interior Department, and the State Department have regularly been made and subsequently proven false.[8] Of course this does not mean that every gloomy forecast about oil must be wrong. And forecasts can be overoptimistic, too. But it does show that expert forecasts often have been far too pessimistic. We therefore should not simply take them at face value.

THE LONG-RUN HISTORY OF ENERGY SUPPLIES

Enough anecdotes. Let's look at the statistical history of energy supplies to see that the trend has been toward plenty rather than toward scarcity. As was discussed at length in chapter 1, the relevant measures are the production costs of energy as measured in time and money, and the price to the consumer; and the relevant data are historical. Figures 7-2, 7-3, and 7-4 show these data for coal, oil, and electricity. Since chapter 1 discussed the relationship of such cost and price data to the concepts of scarcity and availability, that discussion need not be repeated here. Suffice it to say that the appropriate interpretation of these data is that they show an unambiguous trend toward less scarcity and a greater availability of energy.

The price history of electricity is particularly revealing because the price of electricity measures the price to the consumer, at home or at work. That is, the price of electricity is closer to the price of the service we get from energy than are the prices of coal and oil. And as discussed in chapter 3, the costs of the services we get interest us more than the costs of the raw materials themselves. The ratio of the price of electricity to the average wage in manufacturing (figure 7-4a) shows that the quantity of electricity bought with an hour's wages has steadily increased. Because each year an hour's work has bought more rather than less electricity, this measure suggests that energy has become ever less troublesome in the economy over the recorded period, no matter what the price of energy in current dollars. In short, the trends in energy costs and scarcity have been downward over the entire period for which we have data. And such trends are usually the most reliable bases for forecasts. From

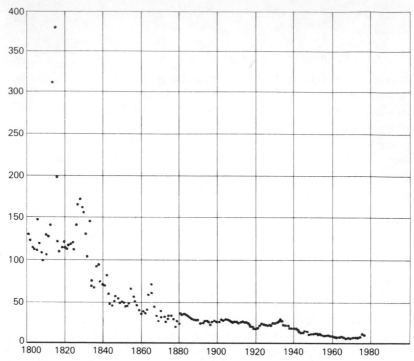

FIGURE 7-2a. The Price of Coal Relative to Wages

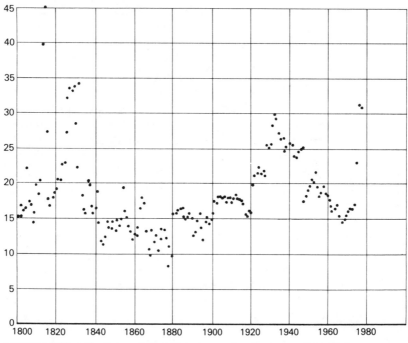

FIGURE 7-2b. The Price of Coal Relative to the Consumer Price Index

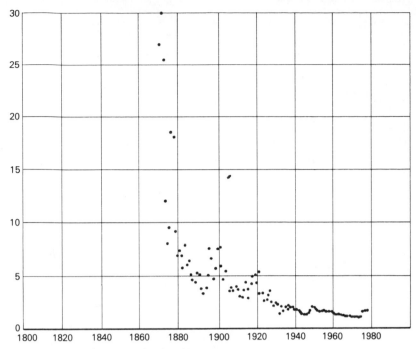

FIGURE 7-3a. The Price of Oil Relative to Wages

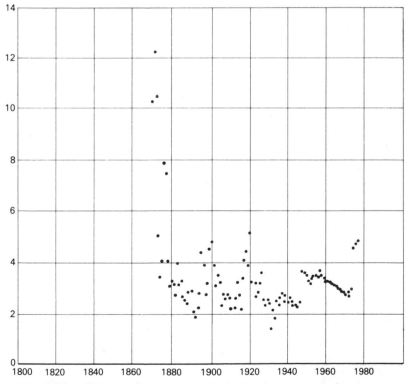

FIGURE 7-3b. The Price of Oil Relative to the Consumer Price Index

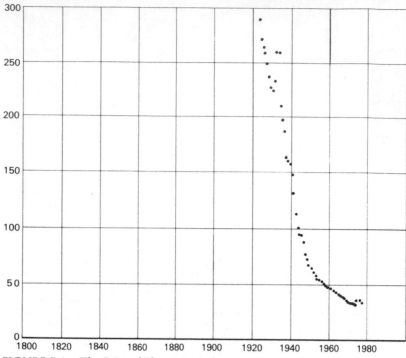

FIGURE 7-4a. The Price of Electricity Relative to Wages

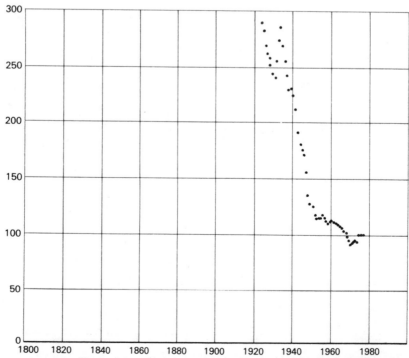

FIGURE 7-4b. The Price of Electricity Relative to the Consumer Price Index

these data we may conclude with considerable confidence that energy will be less costly and more available in the future than in the past.

Jumping Off the Eiffel Tower?

You may object that extrapolating a future from past trends of greater and greater abundance is like extrapolating, just before you hit the ground, that a jump from the top of the Eiffel Tower is an exhilarating experience. But for the tower jump we have outside knowledge that there is a sudden discontinuity when you reach the ground. In the case of energy and natural resources, there is no persuasive evidence for a negative discontinuity; rather, the evidence points toward positive discontinuities — nuclear fusion, solar energy, and so on. And historical evidence further teaches us that such worries about discontinuities have usually generated the very economic pressures that have opened new frontiers. Hence there is no solid reason to think that we are about to hit the ground after an energy jump from the Eiffel Tower. More likely, we are in a rocket on the ground that has only been warming up until now and will take off sometime soon.

THE THEORY OF FUTURE ENERGY SUPPLIES

Turning now from trends to theory, we shall consider our energy future in three theoretical contexts: (1) with income and population remaining much as they are now; (2) with different rates of income growth than now; and (3) with different rates of population growth than now. (The last of these will be discussed in chapter 15.) It would be neatest to separate the discussion of the U.S. from the world as a whole, but for convenience we shall go back and forth. (In general, the longer the time horizon of the discussion, the more the discussion refers to the world as a whole rather than just to the U.S. or the industrialized countries.)

The analysis of energy is quite similar to the analysis of natural resources and food, but energy has some special twists of its own that require separate discussion. With two exceptions, everything said earlier about natural resources applies to energy. (1) On the negative side, as noted above, energy cannot easily be recycled. (But energy can come much closer to being recycled than one ordinarily thinks. For example, because the fuel supply on warships is very limited, heat from the boilers is passed around water pipes to extract additional calories as it goes up the smokestack.) (2) On the positive side, our energy supplies clearly are not bounded by the earth. The sun has been the ultimate source of all our energy (other than nuclear). Therefore, though we cannot recycle

energy as we can minerals, our supply of energy is clearly not limited by
the earth's present contents, and hence it is not "finite" in any sense at
all — not even the non-operational sense discussed in chapter 3.

But let us turn back to earth, and to a horizon of time that is relevant
for social decisions — the next 5, 25, 100, perhaps 200 years. And let us
confine ourselves to the practical question of what is likely to happen to
the cost of energy relative to other goods, and in proportion to our total
output.

THE BOGYMAN OF DIMINISHING RETURNS AGAIN

First let us dispose of the "law of diminishing returns" with respect to
energy. Here is the way Barry Commoner uses this idea:

> . . . the law of diminishing returns [is] the major reason why the
> United States has turned to foreign sources for most of its oil. . . . Each
> barrel [of oil] drawn from the earth causes the next one to be more
> difficult to obtain. . . . The economic consequence is that it causes the
> cost to increase continuously.[9]

Another environmentalist explains her version of the "law of diminishing returns" with respect to oil:

> We must now extract our raw materials from ever more degraded and
> inaccessible deposits. This means that ever more of our society's pre-
> cious investment capital must be diverted to this process and less is
> available for consumption and real growth. Fifty years ago, getting oil
> required little more than sticking a pipe in the ground. Now we must
> invest several billion dollars to open up the Alaska oilfields to deliver
> the same product. *Economists, if they understood this process as well
> as physical scientists*, might call it the declining productivity of capital
> [law of diminishing returns].[10]

All that need be said here is that this is plain wrong; it costs less today
to get oil from the ground in prime sources than it cost fifty years ago to
get it from the ground in prime sources. (The Afternote to chapter 1
explains how there is no "law" of diminishing returns in general, and
hence why this line of thinking is fallacious.)

In brief, there is no compelling theoretical reason why we should eventually run out of energy, or even why energy should be more scarce and costly in the future than it is now.

THE BEST — AND WORST — WAYS TO FORECAST FUTURE ENERGY AVAILABILITY

The best way to forecast price trends is to study past price trends, if data are available and if there is no reason to believe that the future will be sharply different from the past. (The reasoning that supports this point of view is set forth at length in chapter 1 for natural resources in general.)

For energy there are plenty of past price data available, as we have seen in figures 7-2, 7-3, and 7-4. And there is no convincing reason to believe that the future will break completely from the past. Therefore, extrapolation of the trends in those figures is the most reasonable method of forecasting the future of energy supplies and costs, on the assumption that price has been close to cost in the past and will continue to be so in the future. This method of economic forecasting predicts progressively lower energy costs and scarcity.

Geologists and engineers, however, rely on technological rather than price-trend data in their forecasts of energy supplies. Because their forecasts have had so much influence, we must analyze their methods and meanings.

We must first dispose of the preposterous but commonly accepted notion that the energy situation can be forecast with the aid of presently known reserves. This notion is an example of the use of misleading numbers simply because they are the only numbers available. We briefly considered the uselessness of this concept of "reserves" in chapter 2 with respect to mineral resources. Now let us discuss it with respect to oil.

"Known reserves" are defined as the total amount of oil in areas that have been well prospected. Geologists are quite sure of their existence. Individuals, firms, and governments create known reserves by searching for promising drilling areas long in advance of the moment when wells might be drilled — far enough ahead to allow preparation time, but not so far ahead that the investment in prospecting costs will not obtain a satisfactory return. The key idea here is that it costs money to produce information about what are called "known reserves," and therefore people will create only as many known reserves as it is profitable to create at a given moment. The quantity of known reserves at any moment tells us more about the expected profitability of oil wells than it does about the amount of oil in the ground. And the higher the cost of exploration, the lower will be the known reserves that it pays to create.

"Known reserves" are much like the food we put into our cupboards at home. We stock enough groceries for a few weeks or days — not so much that we will be carrying a heavy unneeded inventory that bulges the cupboard and ties up an unnecessary amount of money in groceries, and not so little that we may run out if an unexpected event — a guest or a blizzard — should descend upon us. The amount of food in our cupboards tells little or nothing about the scarcity of food in our communities, because as a rule it does not reveal how much food is available in the retail stores. Similarly, the oil in the "cupboard" — the quantity of known reserves — tells us nothing about the quantities of oil that can be obtained in the long run at various extraction costs.

This explains why the quantity of known reserves, as if by a miracle of coincidence, stays just a step ahead of demand, as seen in figure 7-5. That's why Frank Notestein, the elder statesman of American demographers who is now well over seventy, remembers that, according to the news stories about known reserves, "We've been just about to run out of oil ever since I've been a boy." Yet most discussions of the oil and energy situation — among laymen and also among the most respected journalists — still focus on known reserves. Figure 7-5, taken from *Newsweek*, is typical. The graph apparently shows that the world's proven reserves have been declining, leading to the rhetorical threat above the picture: "End of the oil? . . . How much is left to find?"

Even more misleading is a graph of proven reserves in the U.S. alone, as in figure 7-6. As the U.S. turns to imports because they are cheaper than the home product, its proven reserves inevitably will fall. If one were to draw a graph of U.S. proven reserves of aluminum or gold, they also would appear frighteningly tiny. So what?

A more sophisticated — and even more misleading — approach is to project present growth in demand, assuming the price will remain constant, and then to compare that projection to known reserves, thereby indicating that demand will apparently outstrip supply very soon. This approach may be seen in figure 7-7. Even assuming that the growth in demand *at present prices* is reasonably estimated — and this would be difficult to do well — all that such a calculation would show is that price must rise in order to lower the demand and raise the supply until demand and supply meet. This basic economic way of looking at supply and demand is totally missing from the sort of diagram that is figure 7-7.

Equally misleading is the assumption underlying figure 7-7 that there will be no developments in oil production or in other energy sources that

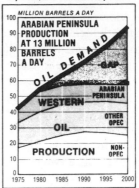

SOONER—OR LATER

If Arabian oil output is held at current levels, shortages could develop by 1981. Raising production limits would postpone the crunch. But even without any limits, one will eventually come.

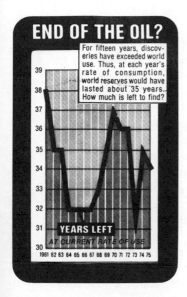

Above: FIGURE 7-5. The Confusion of the Proven-Reserves Concept
Right: FIGURE 7-7. Another Form of Hokum
Below: FIGURE 7-6. More Confusion

STILL IN THE GROUND

America's proven reserves of oil and gas are on the decline, but geologists estimate there may be a total of 1.6 trillion barrels of oil and potentially astronomical amounts of gas still to be found. The hitch: how much will it cost?

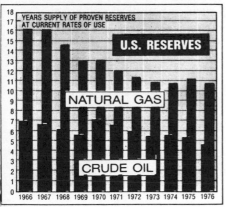

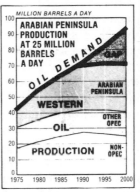

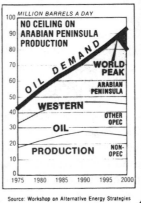

Source: Workshop on Alternative Energy Strategies

will make future energy costs lower than they would be with the present state of technological knowledge.

BETTER TECHNOLOGICAL FORECASTING METHODS

If one insists on making a technological forecast of the energy supply — even though such a forecast is likely to be inferior to extrapolations of past economic trends — how should it best be done? That is, how might one make a sound technological forecast for oil and energy in the near term — say over the next ten or twenty years?

During the next decade or two, increases in income and population in the U.S. and in the world may be assumed to be known, and therefore they can be taken into account as data rather than treated as imponderables. In addition, forecasts of the production of energy in the near-term future utilize two other kinds of information: (1) engineering estimates of the cost of extracting fuel with available technology from such currently unexploited sources as shale oil and windpower, based on calculations of the engineering inputs required for each type of energy source; and (2) economic estimates of how many conventional new wells and mines and reactors will be developed at various prices higher and lower than the present energy prices, based on past data about the extent to which firms in the oil, coal, and nuclear industries respond to changes in market prices.

Engineering calculations must play the dominant role in forecasts of the place of nuclear energy, shale oil, solar power, windpower, and other energy sources for which there are considerable uncertainties about technological processes and costs, due to a lack of experience with these sources. But where a source is currently being exploited sufficiently to produce a large body of data about the process of extraction and about producer behavior, as in the case of fossil fuels, empirical economic estimates of supply response to price changes should have the dominant role. The best overall energy forecast, therefore, would be a blend of both the economic and engineering approaches.

There is great variety, however, in the estimates of engineers and scientists about the costs of developing such energy sources as shale oil and nuclear power. Technologists also differ greatly in their guesses about the dangers to life from the various processes. And economists differ considerably in their estimates of the responsiveness of the energy industry to various price levels. For example, within three months three very different estimates of the amounts of natural gas likely to be produced at various prices were made by the U.S. Energy Research and Development Administration — the predecessor of the Department of Energy — on April 1, April 6, and June 3, 1977. The range was very great; at, say, a price of $1.75 per thousand cubic feet, the production estimates ranged from 260 to 775 trillion cubic feet![11] And such an enormous variation — one estimate being triple another — could (and probably did) arise simply as a result of political fiddling with the figures. With respect to still-undeveloped sources such as shale oil and artificial gas, the variation in estimates is much greater yet.

Why do estimates of supply response to price changes differ so widely? There are a host of reasons, including (a) vested interests — for example, the oil companies have a stake in keeping gas prices paid to gas suppliers low so that fewer gas wells will be drilled and more oil will be sold, and hence they want lower estimates of the responsiveness of natural gas supplies to changes in price; in contrast, gas companies have a stake in higher (unregulated) prices, and hence want higher estimates of gas supply responsiveness; (b) basic beliefs about the "finiteness" of potential supplies and about the likelihood of the human imagination to respond to needs with new developments; (c) differences in the scientific imaginations of the engineers and geologists making the estimates; and (d) professional differences among engineers and among economists due to differences in technical approaches.

Let us briefly note which facts all experts agree on, which matters are in dispute, and how the energy situation is tangled with conflicting interests, politics, and ideology.

Agreed-upon facts about oil. (a) Enough oil to supply the world for several decades can be produced in the Middle East at $0.05 to $0.20 per barrel (1978 currency). (b) Transportation from the Middle East to the U.S. and elsewhere costs $0.50 to $1.50 per barrel.[12] (c) The 1980 world market price for oil is roughly $35.00 per barrel. (d) Apparently, few believe strongly that the price of oil will sharply and continually go up in the future. If anyone really did believe that, it would make sense to buy and stockpile oil for long-term appreciation, even with the cost of storage. But no one is (though South Africa is said to have a seven-year supply because of its political-military situation). (e) Much of the world has not been explored systematically for oil. This may be seen in the numbers of wells that had been drilled in various parts of the world up to 1975: U.S. — 2,425,095; U.S.S.R. — 530,000; Latin America — 100,000; Canada — 100,000; Australia and New Zealand — 2,500; Western

Europe — 25,000; Japan — 5,500; Africa and Madagascar — 15,000; South and South East Asia — 11,000; People's Republic of China — 9,000; and the Middle East — 10,000.[13] The reason why so much more exploration has been done in the U.S. than elsewhere, and why so many wells have been drilled in the U.S., is not that the U.S. has had so much greater potential for oil production but rather that it has had a high demand for oil, plenty of production know-how, trade protection against imported oil until recently, and political stability. (f) Estimates of crude-oil reserves are highly sensitive to the definition of crude oil. The U.S. Geological Survey uses a definition that includes only oil that will come to the surface at atmospheric pressure. If one also includes oil that can be forced to the surface under pressure, plus naturally non-liquid oil in shale and tar sands and other sources, the estimate would be considerably greater.[14]

Agreed-upon facts about coal. (a) There are known quantities of coal in the U.S. and elsewhere that are vast compared with the known quantities of oil. (b) Coal is expensive to transport. (c) In energy yield, coal is clearly cheaper than oil or gas: "For deliveries to utilities in November [1976], coal's price represented 87 cents per million BTU's compared to $2.04 for oil and $1.13 for gas."[15] (d) The use of coal creates pollution that can raise coal's total cost above that of oil.

Agreed-upon facts about oil substitutes. The market price of oil may affect the market price of other fuels. For example, as soon as OPEC increased the price of oil in 1973, the price of coal and uranium jumped, apparently because the owners of those commodities perceived the greater demand for them. On the other hand, investment in coal and nuclear power is made risky by the possibility that oil prices might fall due to a collapse of the OPEC cartel, which would make investment in coal and nuclear power a financial disaster.

Agreed-upon facts about nuclear power. (a) Electricity can be produced from uranium at perhaps half or two-thirds the current price of oil.[16] This calculation is heavily dependent on the choice of interest rate (more precisely, the cost of capital). (b) In purely physical terms, the supply of nuclear power on this earth alone is awesome and inexhaustible on any human scale. (c) Nuclear fission creates radioactive wastes that raise storage and disposal problems; nuclear fusion is relatively clean, but not yet controllable as an energy source.

The following matters are in dispute.

The future supply of oil. Some technologists tell us that at present prices and rates of consumption, production of oil will peak around the year 1990 and decline thereafter. Other technologists confidently predict that vast new sources of oil will be found as needed.

The official spokesmen of various organizations put forth a cacophony of different views.

> The Department of Energy says — Energy Secretary James R. Schlesinger testified so last week — that the nation is short 500,000 barrels a day, and creeping toward 800,000 barrels. The Congressional Research Service says the shortage is only 80,000 barrels a day. The big oil companies say that, worldwide, it's 2.5 million barrels a day and so they must parcel out deliveries to make sure everyone gets a fair share. The General Accounting Office, Congress' investigative arm, finds that puzzling. It says that the companies are cutting the United States back 10 to 15 percent while at the worst the loss of Iranian oil puts it down only 4 percent.[17]

Also in dispute is the amount of oil and other fossil fuels that man can safely burn without creating excessive atmospheric levels of carbon dioxide.

The future supply of natural gas. The American Gas Association says that there is enough gas "to last between 1,000 and 2,500 years at current consumption. Experts in ERDA [Energy Research and Development Administration] have been trying to tell the White House [this] too."[18] According to these estimates, the price necessary to make these vast quantities profitable is $2.50 to $3.00 per thousand cubic feet, to be compared with the ceiling price of $1.75 proposed by President Carter in 1977. A 1977 price of $3.00 per thousand cubic feet is about equivalent to the present cost of an equal amount of heat from fuel oil, and less than a third the cost of the same amount of heat from electricity.

In stark contrast is the estimate quoted by President Carter in 1977. That estimate, made in 1974 by the U.S. Geological Survey, was "216 trillion cubic feet, 10 years supply . . . at 1974 technology and 1974 prices."[19] The difference boggles the mind: 10 years' supply versus a 1,000-2,500 years' supply!

A later official estimate, made in the midst of the congressional debate on energy in July 1977, by Dr. Vincent E. McKelvey, who was then director of the U.S. Geological Survey, was that "as much as . . . 3,000 to 4,000 times the amount of natural gas the United States will consume this year . . . may be sealed in the geo-pressured zones underlying the Gulf Coast region."[20] But this estimate ran contrary to what the Carter White House was saying, and within two months McKelvey was fired from his job as director — after six years as director and thirty-seven years at the Geological Survey, and after being nominated for the director's job by the National Academy of Sciences. As the *Wall Street Journal* put it, "Dr. McKelvey did not know enough to keep his mouth shut!"[21]

One gas issue that can hardly be in question is that U.S. gas-pricing policy has been ludicrous. At the same time that the controlled U.S. price was $1.45 per thousand cubic feet, and when President Carter later wanted to raise it to only $1.75, we agreed to buy Mexican gas at $2.60.[22] Then we haggled with Mexico that that was slightly too high, but at the same moment we agreed to buy Algerian and Indonesian gas at $3.42.[23] In the same newspapers[24] was the report of a congressional study that Devonian shale deposits in Appalachia could be brought to the market for $2.00 to $3.00 per thousand cubic feet — deposits that will not be developed if the U.S. ceiling is maintained at $1.45 or $1.75. And it is hardly likely that there is a sound political reason — or even an unsound political reason — behind this economic idiocy.

The controversy closed preposterously toward the end of 1978. The official views of the U.S. government had by then flip-flopped sufficiently so that Secretary of Energy Schlesinger announced at a press conference, "DOE is encouraging industries and utilities that now burn oil to switch, not to coal, but to gas."[25]

The potential effect of oil conservation measures. Some informed persons argue that it is possible to increase greatly the efficiency of oil use, that is, to waste less of it. Other informed persons are doubtful of any great benefits in this respect. Raising the price of gasoline to levels stratospherically high could affect consumption considerably, of course, but whether this makes economic sense is also in dispute, as chapter 10 discusses.

Whether the "alternative" energy sources are practical. Such possible sources as tidal power, ocean thermal power, geothermal power, windpower, fuel cells, conventional solar power, or geopressurized methane and alcohol might be able to compete with oil in the near or not-so-near future if the price of oil were to remain in the long run at the present level. On the other hand, they might not be important even if the price of energy were to double, triple, or quadruple.[26] Tidal power seems the best bet of the lot, especially in Great Britain, where a variety of devices that the sea compresses or bumps to convert its movements into electricity are well into the testing stages.[27] There is less dispute that shale oil, available in vast quantities in the U.S. and elsewhere, could be profitable at present energy prices; it was in use in Estonia long before the 1970s jump in world oil price and despite the lower price of oil within the Soviet bloc.[28] The most solid piece of recent research I could find concluded that, as of 1978, "Production of over 15 million barrels of shale oil per day [five-sixths of present U.S. oil consumption] is a profitable activity when the price of oil is only $18 per barrel (1975 dollars). . . . Even under quite conservative assumptions, production of two million barrels per day is economically feasible in the long run when the selling price of oil exceeds $12 per barrel."[29] Some others claim, however, that the cost would be much higher.

Also speculative are the possibilities of a variety of new and radical ways to harness solar power, some of which promise energy at remarkably low costs if they are developed. One such idea is a plan to launch huge orbiting satellites to convert solar rays into electrical energy, which would then be transmitted to earth by microwaves.[30] Another plan is to build mirrors in space that would turn night into day for agricultural areas and hence increase their food productivity, as well as increase the potential of solar-heating systems. A third scheme is the use of Ovshinsky's amorphous semiconductors as a spray-on liquid, or in other forms, to produce heat much more efficiently than conventional solar cells.[31] All three of these devices — and others, too — are backed by solid scientific evidence that they can work in principle, and by considerable engineering support that they might be practical in the foreseeable future.

The danger from nuclear energy. The mainline scientific position — expressed in the 1979 report of the National Academy of Sciences Committee on Nuclear and Alternative Energy Systems — concluded that "if one takes all health effects into account (including mining and transportation accidents and the estimated expectations from nuclear accidents), the health effects of coal production and use appear to be a good deal greater than those of the nuclear energy cycle." As to waste disposal, the "risks from the disposal of radioactive waste . . . are less than those of the other parts of the nuclear energy cycle . . . if appropriate action is taken to find suitable long-term disposal sites and methods."[32] An article in *Scientific American's* standard collection asserts that "the task of disposing of the radio-active wastes . . . is not nearly as difficult or as uncertain as many people seem to think it is."[33] And the geoscientist for the American Physical Society's study group on nuclear fuel cycles and waste management says much the same thing: "The problems, including hazards and waste disposal, about which much has been made, are not so serious as commonly pictured."[34] On the other hand, opponents of nuclear energy, such as those associated with the Sierra Club, assert that these assertions about waste-disposal risks are "not true," and are "myths."[35] This issue will be addressed briefly in the next chapter.

The most recent wide-ranging technological survey of long-run energy prospects is that of Herman Kahn and associates. After surveying the technological, environmental, and cost characteristics of all likely energy sources on the horizon, they concluded, "Energy costs as a whole are very likely to continue the historical downward trend indefinitely. . . ." The basic message is this: "Except for temporary fluctuations caused by bad luck or poor management, the world need not worry about energy shortages or costs in the future."[36]

CONCLUSIONS

Extrapolation of long-run cost trends seems to be the most reliable method for estimating future energy availability. Such extrapolation promises continually decreasing scarcity and cost, though this runs counter to popular opinion. At worst, the cost ceiling provided by nuclear power guarantees that the cost of electricity cannot rise far above present energy costs, political obstacles aside.

As to technological forecasts, the best we can do is examine the range of forecasts that are now available and try to learn from the history of such forecasts whether the higher or lower ones are more likely to be correct. In my judgment, Kahn and his associates do their homework best and are on firm technological ground when they say that energy costs are likely to decline indefinitely.

A fuller summary may be found at the beginning of this chapter, starting with the second paragraph.

Today's Energy Issues

Keynes's famous remark, "In the long run we're all dead," really was fatuous. Probably his love of a clever line overcame his good sense. Nevertheless, that remark captures our preoccupation with the present and immediate future. So let us now talk about current energy issues.

THE LATEST ENERGY CRISIS

The price data shown in figures 7-2, 7-3, and 7-4 cover a very long span of history, and they may mask major changes in the last few years. Therefore let us analyze the course of energy costs in the last few years, with special emphasis on the proximate cause of concern — oil.

The sharp rise of crude oil prices in the 1970s does not contradict our long-run conclusion that energy will become more available and less costly. The recent price rise is clearly due to the cartel agreements of the oil-producing countries' association, OPEC. It is the result of political power rather than of rising extraction costs. When reaching into the pocketbook, of course, the consumer in the U.S. and elsewhere is concerned only about the market price of oil, not the production costs. But if one is interested in whether there is, or will be, an *economic* shortage of oil, or if one wants to know about the world's capacity to produce oil, the appropriate indicator is the cost of production and transportation — and that cost is only a small fraction of the world market price.

During the years of the "energy crisis," the cost of oil production has not risen at all. It is far less than 1 percent of the selling price of crude — a cost of perhaps $0.05 to $0.15 per barrel, in comparison with a selling price of somewhere around $35.00 per barrel in 1980.[1] For perspective, we should remember that, not only have energy prices to the consumer been falling over the very long haul, but they have been falling over the recent past since World War II, as we saw in figures 7-2 to 7-4. Before the OPEC cartel got into action, oil prices had been declining relative to other commodities. The price of Iranian oil fell from $2.17 per barrel in

1947 to $1.79 in 1959,[2] and the price of oil at Rotterdam was at its lowest point in 1969; an inflation adjustment would show even more decline. The cost of electricity — and especially electricity for residential use — also had been falling rapidly in the decades prior to 1973. And the overall index of energy prices weighted by their values and deflated by the consumer price index fell steadily from 1950 to 1973, as follows: *1950*, 107.2; *1955*, 103.9; *1960*, 100.0; *1965*, 93.5; *1970*, 85.4; *June 1973*, 80.7.[3] The index was falling at an ever-increasing rate over this period.

A cartel such as OPEC, which has a variety of members with different interests, is subject to pressures that make it difficult to maintain whichever price maximizes profit for the cartel as a whole. There is a great temptation for individual countries to sell more than the quotas that have been given them. Furthermore, a sharp increase in price — as happened when OPEC raised prices in the early 1970s — reduces consumer demand. The result is an oversupply of oil and an underutilization of production facilities — a true "surplus" of oil rather than a scarcity — and this is exactly what has happened. Even as early as 1974 the press was reporting that,

> in the face of a world-wide oil surplus, Saudi Arabia and several other OPEC nations have cut their oil production by 10 percent this month in order to prop up oil prices. Industry sources attribute the decision to cut production to ARAMCO, owned jointly by Saudi Arabia, Exxon, Texaco, Mobil and Standard Oil of California. ARAMCO officials however, blamed "weather conditions" for the slash.[4]

By March 1975 the reports were, "Growing oil glut . . . sagging Western demand for oil has forced OPEC members to cut production sharply to maintain the current high price of crude.[5] By 1976, the price of fuel oil and gasoline had apparently fallen in real terms (adjusted for inflation).[6] And the OPEC members were fighting among themselves about whether to raise prices. At the beginning of 1978, OPEC decided not to raise prices at all, despite inflation, which meant a fall in the relative price of oil. Newspaper headlines again referred to an "oil glut."[7] The executive director of the International Energy Agency, though choosing not to speak of a glut, foresaw that OPEC and oil-producing countries "will face a slight overcapacity problem all the way into 1981–82 . . . [due to] inadequate demand for [OPEC's] oil for some years."[8] This sort of news has now become typical.

Even if the present price of oil should rise even higher, the costs of oil, and of energy in general, are not likely to be so high as to disrupt Western economies.[9] In the long run, however, it is reasonable to assume that economic forces will drag the market price of oil down closer to the cost of production, which implies a lower world-market oil price.

Some of the results of the 1970s "crisis" have been preposterous. A recent news story says that the Chicago gas utility, People's Gas, asked for a rate increase because people have been using *too little* gas; use of People's Gas dropped 7 percent during 1976 because of conservation.[10]

POLITICS AND THE CURRENT ENERGY "CRISIS"

About the "energy crisis" in the U.S. as of 1980: The facts and arguments about the energy situation are so tangled that it would take a whole book to even attempt a reasonable understanding of the situation. Vast areas of the subject must remain subject to dispute. The system of U.S. governmental regulation of energy is itself so complex that even a professional economist cannot understand it without a good deal of study.

In the oil market, for example, the price that oil producers are allowed to charge depends upon how long ago the well was drilled; this device is an attempt to keep "old" oil wells from getting a windfall gain from the rise in the world oil prices since 1973, but at the same time to provide an incentive to keep drilling new wells. Different amounts of taxes must be paid for "new" and "old" oil to equalize the market price. Then there are "entailments" that refiners get for purchasing old or new oil, allowing them to make other products of oil of different "ages"; these "entailments" can be bought and sold. This system is a patchwork quilt that hides the actual facts of oil supply from our view.

George Stigler once remarked that a business firm is a collection of devices to overcome obstacles to profit. For example, for *interstate* delivery the price of gas is controlled far below the price of oil for an equivalent amount of thermal energy. But in *intrastate* traffic gas prices are not controlled. The regulatory structure in which energy firms operate is a mine field of such obstacles to profit. Each obstacle, however, provides an opportunity to some firms just as it blocks others; it is an invitation to finagling. And sure enough, the finagling has not only begun, it has already been discovered.

July 14, 1978: Criminal charges against suspected oil-price chiselers may be coming. The Energy and Justice departments seek to bring criminal cases, not just civil suits, against companies that sold low-cost oil at illegally high rates. The first indictments may be brought by grand juries in Texas.[11]

July 21, 1978: Continental Oil Co. is under criminal investigation for alleged violations of federal oil-pricing rules.

According to government sources, Continental, the nation's ninth largest oil company, is the first major oil company to face possible criminal charges in a new crackdown by the Energy and Justice departments on improper oil-pricing practices during the years immediately following the 1973 Arab oil embargo. . . .

In separate cases, also in Texas, federal investigators are considering seeking indictments soon against several smaller companies that resell oil bought from major producers. The smaller concerns are suspected of participating in a criminal scheme to sell lower-priced "old" crude oil at the higher prices that apply to "new" oil.[12]

August 14, 1978: The Florida case involves a so-called "daisy chain" scheme during late 1973 and 1974. The government alleges that five oil companies sold fuel oil back and forth to raise their paper costs and, thus, the allowable price under federal regulations, before selling it to the buyer, Florida Power Corp.

And the government lawyers admit that "the oil pricing rules they are trying to apply may have been too confusing and vague."[13]

Some other headlines or news stories:

September 22, 1978: "Energy Agency Alleges Oil-Price Manipulation by Middleman Firms."[14]

December 11, 1978: "Possible Misconduct within Energy Unit Is Charged in Study of Oil-Pricing Cases."

Washington — Energy Department officials failed to move swiftly against suspected massive oil-pricing frauds in recent years and thus may have been guilty of serious, even criminal misconduct, a congressional report charged.[15]

February 9, 1979: "Kerr-McGee to Settle U.S. Oil-Price Claims: Firms to Refund $46 Million in Alleged Overcharges from 1973 through 1978."[16]

July 28, 1979: "Natural Gas Company to Pay $1 Million Fine."

Washington — Tenneco Inc. pleaded guilty of concealing the transportation of natural gas from federal regulation officials.[17]

November 9, 1979: "U.S. Is Accusing Nine Major Oil Concerns of $1.1 Billion in Consumer Overcharges."[18]

February 15, 1980: "Mobil Oil Ordered to Pay $500,000 Fine on Criminal Charges Involving Gas Sales," and "Indiana Standard Settles Price Case for $100 Million."[19]

February 22, 1980: "President's Price Council Plans to Report 11 Oil Concerns Violated U.S. Guidelines."[20]

February 25, 1980: "The Price Is Wrong — By $716 Million."
In recent months, leading domestic oil refiners have agreed to pay a total of $1 billion to settle charges of overpricing brought by the Department of Energy. Last week, DOE announced the biggest single settlement yet: a $716 million package arranged with Standard Oil Co. of Indiana.[21]

August 13, 1980: The Energy Department "has filed some 200 actions accusing the 15 top oil companies of violations amounting to more than $10 billion since 1973, and seeking restitution. [This] 'is the only good publicity we've got' says an official of the Energy Department."[22]

Furthermore, the government's price-regulating system is said by many informed writers to have the effect of supporting the OPEC cartel's price-fixing power and subsidizing their operations, though some other informed critics disagree.

Who would benefit by changes in energy policies? In 1977, the White House said that the deregulation of gas would be a "$70 billion ripoff" for the American consumer. Others say the consumer would be better off in the long run with deregulation and that any windfall gains would be a fair return to those who had the vision and courage to invest in the energy industries. Still others point out that a large — how large is also in dispute — proportion of the gains made by energy firms under gas deregulation would return to ordinary citizens because much of the stock of these companies is held by pension funds.

Similarly, with respect to the 1978 regulated domestic oil market, deregulation is said by some (the White House, for example), to be simply a gain for the big oil companies; others (including the *Wall Street Journal* editorial writers) argue that the present oil policy is a subsidy for OPEC — a transfer of funds from U.S. consumers to Middle East princes — and that deregulation would greatly reduce that outflow of funds.[23]

Rather than continue to multiply the details of who is saying what, much of which will be out of date by the time this book gets into print, let us instead try to get a feeling for the principles that govern the energy market. Let us imagine how it would feel from the inside, in some of the many different and conflicting roles within that industry. Imagine yourself, for example, as a California oil-well owner who can produce oil at a cost of $10 per barrel by forcing water down your well under pressure. (Remember, the production costs to OPEC are only five to twenty cents per barrel.) The world price is now $35 per barrel, so you think you might sell your oil at a nice profit. But you cannot, because it is "old" oil, whose price is fixed far below the market price by the U.S. government. So you do not produce and sell very much oil, because you hope that "old" U.S. oil might soon be deregulated. But you are happy as a clam at high tide with the regulation of gas prices because, if the price of gas were decontrolled, gas that is now kept out of the market would be profitably produced and sold at prices below what you could get for your oil, for the same energy content. Deregulation of gas would mean that you could sell less oil. It would also threaten the stability of the OPEC cartel. In fact, the world-market price of oil might fall — to, say, only ten or twenty times the cost of production and transportation from the Middle East — leaving you in the lurch. And if the world price of oil falls much below the government-fixed price per barrel that you now get for your "old" oil, you might as well plug up your well and raise pumpkins. So you lobby for the decontrol of oil prices, and you argue that if the price is freed, plenty of domestic oil will be supplied. But you are quite happy that the price of interstate *gas* is controlled, because that will discourage gas production and lead to a gas "shortage," to more demand for oil, and thus to political pressure to decontrol domestic oil prices.

Now assume you are the head of an international oil company — say Exxon or Shell. You make money by "lifting" oil for Middle Eastern governments and then marketing it worldwide. You are happy that the price of "old" oil is controlled in the U.S. because that keeps down the competition — especially because U.S. oil is the less-desirable "heavy crude." So you have a stake in having people believe that allowing U.S. suppliers to sell at a higher price will *not* produce much additional U.S. oil; you prefer that Americans believe that the world and the U.S. are running out of oil. And so you lobby against that "greedy" California driller; you want U.S. oil prices regulated. (One of the many comic and ridiculous sidelights of oil politics is that the U.S. oil companies see OPEC as simply a new cartel replacing an old one — the former one being the oil companies themselves. This may be seen in the remark by the executive vice-president of Exxon that, "since OPEC now controls the oil spigots, the companies are no longer as free to reduce surpluses as they were when they controlled the fields."[24]

Next imagine that you are a firm, such as Westinghouse, that specializes in constructing nuclear electricity plants. You want (a) the price paid for domestic supplies of oil and gas to be kept low by regulation so that there will be "shortages" of oil and gas, (b) a high world-market oil price, and (c) a negative U.S. balance of payments resulting from the expenditures for Middle Eastern oil. Such a situation, together with a panic that we are "running out" of fossil fuels, will induce the government to spend goodly sums on nuclear-power research and development, which will help you produce and sell more efficient nuclear plants in the future.

Now imagine yourself in early 1977 the owner of an oil well in Texas that could profitably produce a good deal of gas at the price the market will bear, say, $1.60 per thousand cubic feet. But the early-1977 regulated interstate gas price is $1.45. (The price picture gets complicated here, because much of the cost of gas is transportation and distribution rather than just the amount paid to the gas-well owner.) You lobby for deregulation of gas prices, of course. And you try to sell your gas within Texas at the unregulated, intrastate prices. But you find that gas is a glut on the intrastate market because every other Texas producer has the same idea. As a reasonable person, you will keep your gas down in the well and wait until sometime in the future when the price of gas rises (though this has its risks, too). If another bad winter hits in the meantime, and heating oil runs short, that will be the fault of national stupidity and not of your cupidity, of course.

Now let us go even further afield and make you a merchant seaman — or better yet, an official of the Marine Engineers Beneficial Association. You want more work for American seamen. So your organization contributes $200,000 to Jimmy Carter's 1976 campaign (this is for real now, not hypothetical). And by August of 1977 the "cargo preference bill" passes the House Merchant Marine Committee.[25] This bill provided that a fixed and rising percentage of all the oil imported into the U.S. must be carried on U.S. ships, despite the fact that "it costs about 23 times as much to operate a U.S. flag tanker as a foreign flag tanker at present.[26] Most of the extra money would come out of government subsidies to U.S. shippers. But if the U.S. oil-well owners could sell their oil at a decontrolled, untaxed price instead of being forced to sell under the present system, there would be less of a market for imported oil and, thus, fewer seamen's jobs. Hence the seamen also have a stake in domestic regulation and high oil prices.[27]

In each of these economic-political roles you find yourself fabricating reasons why your type of energy should not have its price controlled while the others' prices should be controlled, and why the government should finance research on your type of energy. One excellent all-purpose reason that you find, of course, is that the "supplies" of the other sorts of energy will soon run out, which makes your sort of energy the best hope to support. And you tie your arguments to expected economic and population growth, which will make the other fuels run out faster and make the need for yours that much greater.

Is it any wonder, then, that the rhetoric about energy is as impassioned and hard to untangle as it is? And is it now clear why population growth is dragged into the discussion by all sides as posing an immediate threat to our supply of energy, and as being a reason for special treatment of each particular industry?

This situation breeds not only tortured arguments and frightening forecasts, but also scams on a vast scale. For a single example: Prior to 1973, Westinghouse contracted to sell large quantities of uranium to nuclear power plants, uranium that it planned to buy from the producers at market prices. When OPEC boosted the price of oil in 1973, the price of uranium began a jump from $8 to as much as $53 a ton within three years.[28] This meant that Westinghouse might take losses of perhaps $2 billion. Along the way, Gulf Oil (a producer of uranium) got together with the Canadian government and other producers of uranium to keep the price of uranium high — which in the U.S. is illegal price-fixing, of course — so that Gulf and the others would profit from the final purchases of all consumers of nuclear electricity, and, incidentally, from Westinghouse. Sweet. The matter will be in the courts for years.

TOWARD A SOUND U.S. ENERGY POLICY

What is the best U.S. policy with respect to energy? Before anything else, let us take up the question of national security, because the rest is easy in principle — and, for that matter, the national security problem is not very difficult either, in principle.

If the U.S. has a large enough stockpile of oil and gas — say, a year's worth — no foreign nation can have much leverage, or pose much of a threat to our military security, through an energy shut-off. And there is no reason why the U.S. should not create such a stockpile. Oil could be stockpiled from imports or from such domestic reserves as the federally owned Elk Hills oil. Gas shortage is even less of a problem.

So, why doesn't the U.S. create such a stockpile? The answer is a combination of inertia and oil politics. As of 1980, the stockpile is scandalously behind the Department of Energy's schedule. It has accumulated only 92 million barrels — the equivalent of two weeks' imports — toward the goal of 750 million to 1 billion barrels. But "opposition to U.S. stock-piling runs strong in Saudi Arabia and in other members of the Organization of Petroleum Exporting Countries. They regard stockpiling as an unnecessary addition to world demand and a hostile act against producing countries...." The Saudi Arabian oil boss, Sheik Ahmed Zaki Yamani, "didn't leave any doubt regarding Saudi opposition to additions to the U.S. oil·reserve. 'We don't like to see any building of that strategic stockpile,' he said. 'We don't think it is necessary.'"[29] The Arab states have threatened reprisals if the U.S. buys more oil for stockpiles, because that would reduce their leverage. But sooner or later the job will have to be done. So why not sooner?

With national security taken care of, importing oil and gas poses little more threat than importing television sets or tourist services. The balance of payments is a weak reed as an issue, as free-trade economists know; we should import whatever buyers feel they want, and can get cheapest abroad. This will in general maximize our economic welfare.

Now which sources of energy should the U.S. government promote? The appropriate reasoning was stated clearly by the Paley Commission a quarter century ago as "the least cost principle." "This Commission believes that national materials policy should be squarely founded on the principle of buying at the least cost possible for equivalent values ... we cannot afford to legislate against this principle for the benefit of particular producer groups at the expense of our consumers and foreign neighbors, and ultimately with prejudice to our own economic growth and security."[30]

The Paley Commission perfectly previewed the 1980s situation. The government energy "program" has — among other things — led the trucking industry to lobby for an increase in the allowable weight of interstate trucks in the interests of energy conservation. Shipowners got a subsidy for rebuilding their engines included in the maritime omnibus bill. By the same argument, Greyhound and Trailways induced the House-Senate conference on the windfall-profits tax to give the bus companies a $36 million subsidy for new buses, and the conference also included billion-dollar tax credits for developing hydropower and coke-gas equipment.[31]

Which of these mechanisms will follow the least-cost principle most closely? There is little doubt that none of them can match the mechanism of a free market. No government decision-maker can come close to the efficiency of millions of individual buyers and investors who go comparison shopping among gas, oil, coal, and so on.

How can the solution be so simple when an entire multi-billion-dollar Department of Energy has hundreds of experts working out other kinds of schemes? Answer that for yourself. But please keep in mind that a very large proportion of U.S. economists would be likely to offer free-market solutions to U.S. energy problems exactly as simple as the one outlined above.[32]

In addition to the indirect but large costs of misallocation due to government controls, there are the direct costs of the energy bureaucracy.

> The Department of Energy will have an annual budget of $10.6 billion and will employ 19,767 people. This represents:
> — $500,000 per employee of the department; [or]
> — $50 for each and every person in the country; [or]
> — $266.871 for each of the 39,763 wells drilled in 1976; [or]
> — $58.35 for each of the 181,855,700 feet drilled in 1976; [or]
> — $3.59 for each barrel of domestic crude oil and $1.67 for every barrel of petroleum products consumed in 1976; [or]
> — 10 cents for every gallon of gasoline consumed in 1976. . . .[33]

ABOUT THE COSTS OF NUCLEAR POWER

Nuclear power is of special interest here because it provides the long-run ceiling to energy costs. Therefore, we must discuss the height of that ceiling and the practicality of nuclear power — including its dangers.

By now there is sufficient experience with nuclear power plants operating over the past decade and more to prove that nuclear plants can generate electricity at costs that are of the same order as the present costs of using fossil fuels. When I say "of the same order," I mean that some calculations indicate that electricity from nuclear plants is considerably cheaper than electricity from oil-burning plants (even at the prices of $7 to $10 per barrel in 1974) or than electricity from coal-burning plants. Other calculations might use different estimates for the cost of plant construction, for interest rates (the cost of capital), for preventing air pollution due to burning coal, and so on; and they might show nuclear power at no advantage or even at some disadvantage compared with oil at current prices. But even people who are not at all in favor of nuclear power — for example, Paul Ehrlich — acknowledge that nuclear power is no more expensive than conventional power. "Contrary to a persistent misconception, nuclear power is not particularly cheap today. . . . The largest nuclear generating stations are, even with their considerably hidden subsidies, just competitive with or marginally superior to modern coal-field plants of comparable size [in areas where coal is not scarce].[34] This implies that where coal is scarce, nuclear-generated electricity is considerably cheaper than other kinds, though the Ehrlichs wish to leave a different impression. And implicit in their statement is the fact that nuclear power is cheaper than oil, though this also is not a point they seek to bring out.[35]

Such calculations are of paramount importance to an electrical utility company. But to the consumer they do not matter. What *does* matter is that the calculations do *not* matter. It does not matter to our standard of living in the long run whether electricity is, say, 20 percent more or less expensive than it is now. Of course, an electricity bill 20 percent higher than now would hurt. But it would not much affect our future lives. Nor would an electricity bill 20 percent lower make our future much richer. And the longer we look into the future, the smaller will be the percentage of our total budget devoted to electricity, as our total incomes grow.

We must also consider technological developments. Fission is the source used at present. But in the longer run, a much "cleaner" nuclear fusion may well be practicable, though physicists cannot yet predict when — or even, with certainty, whether — fusion will be available. The main barrier seems to be know-how. As of 1969, Hans Bethe saw it this way:

> Finally there is the possibility of generating power from fusion of heavy hydrogen rather than from fission. The nuclear physics of this is simple and well known. But it has so far proved impossible to contain deuterium long enough at high temperature to make power extraction possible. It will probably take a long time for this problem to be solved, meaning perhaps 20, perhaps 100 years. Ultimately I believe it will be solved, and we evidently are in no hurry to solve it because there is a great deal of uranium fuel available.[36]

Recently, prospects for controlled fusion seem to have improved, perhaps in part because of the urgency provided by the run-up in oil prices. By the end of 1977, *Newsweek* could report that practical fusion-power "is closer than ever before."[37] And Herman Kahn and his associates conclude that "the consensus among scientists today is that the commercial feasibility of one of the magnetic fusion systems . . . is likely to be established by the early 1990's."[38]

If fusion becomes practicable, the possibilities are immense: By Bethe's estimate, even if we assume energy consumption a hundred times greater than at present, "the heavy hydrogen supply of the world will be sufficient to give us power for one billion years," at a price perhaps equivalent to that at present for fission power.[39]

NUCLEAR POWER, DANGER, AND RISK AVERSION

About the dangers of nuclear power: Because we do not have experience with a great many nuclear mishaps the way an insurance company has experience with millions of life patterns, estimating the danger of one or another sort of nuclear mishap obviously must be a highly technical matter, and it must depend fundamentally upon scientific and engineering judgment. For that reason, laymen such as you and I can do no better than consult the experts. And there is considerable controversy among the experts. One starting point on which it is fair to insist: When evaluating the safety of nuclear power, it is crucial to keep in mind the risks to life and limb that arise in producing energy in other ways, such as drilling accidents at oil wells, and mine disasters and pulmonary diseases in coal mining.

The likelihood of long-run danger from radiation is a crucial factor in our assessment of the risk from nuclear power. And prenatal radiation is thought to be the most dangerous. Therefore, this astonished me when I first read it, and perhaps it will astonish you, too:

> The juvenile cancer experience of children exposed prenatally in 1945 [from] the atomic bombs in Hiroshima and Nagasaki has [been] studied. There was no significant excess of mortality from leukaemia or other cancers.

That is, the children of pregnant survivors of the atom-bomb explosions in Japan have suffered no more than all other Japanese from cancer. I don't use many exclamation points, but this fact deserves one in my book! And an associated study of children who were up to ten years old when irradiated at Hiroshima and Nagasaki showed no cancer death until 1958, certainly no sign of greater mortality from cancer than non-irradiated Japanese.[40]

(Of course an atomic bomb explosion has nothing in common with a nuclear plant accident except that both involve the release of radiation. And of course I am not suggesting that the atomic bomb is "not so bad after all." The reason why the study of the Japanese children was made — and the reason it is mentioned here — is that vastly more radiation was received by the pregnant mothers in Japan than would be received by people in a peacetime accident under almost any conceivable conditions, and yet there was no excess incidence of cancer in the children. Tragedies though Hiroshima and Nagasaki were, we ought not to close our eyes to this useful lesson that they can teach us.)

Though there is little controversy that nuclear power's past record has shown it to be relatively safe compared with the best alternatives, and that it also has relative economic advantages, there remains the controversial matter of evaluating the risk of nuclear disaster. The opposing conclusions of the recent authoritative report from the National Academy of Sciences, and of anti-nuclear critics, were cited in chapter 7. It is not possible to compare the validity of these views without entering into an extensive technical analysis. Nor am I myself sufficiently familiar with the physical-chemical-geological-engineering calculations involved to offer an expert judgement, even though I am personally persuaded that the mainline view rests on thoughtful, sober, and relatively disinterested study. A couple of points can safely be made, however. First, a nuclear plant simply cannot explode, any more than can a jar of pickles, as physicist Fred Hoyle (with Geoffrey Hoyle) put it. Second, the problem of safeguarding the processed waste from year to year is much less difficult than is safeguarding the national gold supply at Fort Knox, and much less risky than safeguarding against terrorist explosions of nuclear weapons. The Hoyles illustrate the waste-disposal problem from a personal point of view, and they are worth quoting at length.*

Suppose we are required individually to be responsible for the long-term storage of all the waste that we ourselves, our families and our forebears, have generated in an all-nuclear energy economy.

It will be useful to think of waste in terms of the categories of [the table below].

CATEGORIES OF NUCLEAR WASTE AND THEIR LIFETIMES

	Lifetime (years)
High-level	10
Medium-level	300
Low-level	100 000
Very low-level	10 million

High-level waste is carefully stored over its 10-year lifetime by the nuclear industry. This is done above-ground in sealed tanks. It is not proposed to bury nuclear waste underground until activity has fallen to the medium-level category. . . . Instead of underground burial, however, we now consider that medium-level waste is delivered for safe keeping to individual households.

*From *Commonsense in Nuclear Energy* by Fred Hoyle and Geoffrey Hoyle. W. H. Freeman and Company. Copyright © 1980.

We take the amount of the waste so delivered to be that which has been generated over the 70 years from 1990 to 2060. . . .

. . . Over this period a typical family of four would accumulate 4 $\times$ 70 = 280 person years of vitrified nuclear waste, which for an all-nuclear energy economy would weigh about 2 kilograms. Supplied inside a thick metal case, capable of withstanding a house fire or a flood, the waste would form an object of about the size of a small orange, which it could be made to resemble in colour and surface texture — this would ensure that any superficial damage to the object could easily be noticed and immediately rectified by the nuclear industry.

The radioactive materials inside the orange would be in no danger of getting smeared around the house, not like jam or honey. The radioactive materials would stay put inside the metal orange-skin. Indeed the orange would be safe to handle freely but for the γ-rays emerging from it all the time. The effect on a person of the γ-rays would be like the X-rays used by the medical profession. If one were to stand for a minute at a distance of about 5 yards from the newly-acquired orange, the radiation dose received would be comparable to a medical X-ray.

Unlike particles of matter, γ-rays do not stay around. Once emitted, γ-rays exist only for a fleeting moment, during which brief time they are absorbed and destroyed by the material through which they pass. Some readers will be familiar with the massive stone walls of old houses and barns in the north of England. If a γ-ray emitting orange were placed behind a well-made stone wall 2 feet thick, one could lounge in safety for days on the shielded side, and for a wall 3 feet thick one would be safe for a lifetime.

Our family of four would therefore build a small thick-walled cubicle inside the home to ensure safe storage of the family orange.

After several generations, the waste inside the orange would have declined to the low-level category . . ., when the orange could be taken out of its cubicle and safely admired for an hour or two as a family heirloom. . . .

Such individual tedium would of course be avoided if the waste were stored communally. For 100 000 families making up a town of 400 000 people there would be 100 000 eggs to store. Or since it would surely be inconvenient to maintain a watch on so many objects the town would have the eggs reprocessed into a few hundred larger objects of the size of pumpkins or vegetable marrows. The whole lot could be fitted into a garden-produce shed, except that instead of a wooden wall, the shed would need to have thick walls of stone or metal.

This then is the full extent of the nuclear-waste problem that our own generation is called on to face. If by the mid-21st century it has become clear that nuclear fission is the only effective long-term source of energy, society will then have to consider the problem of accumulating waste on a longer time-scale. For the town of 400 000 people, a shed of pumpkins would accumulate for each 70 years, until the oldest waste fell at last into the very low-level category . . ., when it could be discarded. After 7000 years, there would be a hundred sheds, which could be put together to make a moderate-sized warehouse. In 100 000 years there would be about 15 medium warehouses, which could be accumulated into two or three large warehouses. Thereafter, the problem would remain always the same, with the oldest waste falling into the very low-level category as fast as new waste was generated. Of course, the 'warehouses' would be deep underground . . . , and there would be no contact between them and the population of the town. . . .

. . . The risk that each of us would incur, even if called upon to store our own waste, would be insignificant compared with the risks we routinely incur in other aspects of our daily lives.[41]

Yet there still remains the issue of public aversion to risk. Let's put the matter from the layman's point of view: Perhaps nuclear energy really is cheap enough to be a viable alternative to fossil fuels in generating electricity. And maybe it seems to be relatively safe. But what about the chance of a big catastrophe? Would it not be prudent to stay away from nuclear power to avoid that risk?

This is a sensible question once we accept that what economists call "risk aversion" is reasonable and normal. Risk aversion is evidenced when a person prefers to keep a dollar in hand rather than bet a dollar double or nothing, or even when the chance of winning is greater than 50-50. That is, if one were not risk averse, one would accept all gambles when the "expected value" — the probability of winning multiplied by the payoff if you do win — is greater than the amount you must put up to make the gamble. But a risk-averse person would prefer, for example, a one-in-a-hundred chance of winning $10 to a one-in-a-million chance of winning $100,000, even though the expected value is the same.

In the case of human affairs and the risk of death, a risk-averse society might rationally prefer taking many one-in-a-hundred chances of 10 persons dying to taking a single one-in-a-million chance of 100,000 or even

10,000 people dying. That is, the risk of a lot of small likely tragedies might be more acceptable than the risk of a very infrequent and less probable large tragedy. If so, that society would eschew nuclear energy even if it were to present a very small chance of a major catastrophe. This seems to be the logic that has underlain much of the opposition to nuclear energy.

The fact of the matter, however, is that there is practically zero chance of a nuclear-plant catastrophe that would cost tens of thousands of lives. The very outside possibility envisioned by the official committees of experts is a catastrophe causing 5,000 deaths. While indeed tragic, that number of deaths is not of a different order from the numbers of deaths in dam breaks, and it is smaller than the number of coal miners that we know for sure will die early from black lung disease.

So even a preference for risk aversion does not make nuclear energy unattractive. The size of the worst possible catastrophe is of the same order as other social risks that are accepted routinely, and hence we can judge nuclear energy according to the "expected value" of the mortalities it may generate. And according to expected-value calculations, it is considerably safer than other energy alternatives.

9.

More Pollution? Or Less?

According to the press and much of the academic community, the U.S. and the world are becoming increasingly polluted. A university newspaper quotes a speaker: "Man has been working to control nature for too long. Our natural resources are running out and pollution is taking its toll upon the land."[1] The top-of-page headline of a story in the *Chicago Tribune* is, "The Pollution of Earth: 'I'm Scared,'" with the subheadline "Air, Sea and Land — All Being Strangled":

> "I'm scared," said Joseph Sauris, 16, a sophomore at Main East Township High School, Park Ridge. . . .
> "I don't like the idea of leaving a dead world to my children. That might sound like a cliché, but it may be the truth someday."[2]

And grammar school texts fill young minds with unsupported assertions that mankind is a destroyer rather than a creator of the environment. Here are some samples from *Earth and Ecology*, a Golden Book text for children.*

> Our Dirty Air — The sea of air in which we live — our sky — is no longer sparkling clean. Once the smoke from chimneys was whisked away by winds and soon became lost in a clear sky. Then we believed that the sky could hold all the wastes we could pour into it. By some sort of miracle, we thought, the sky kept itself clean.
> Now there are too many chimneys pouring smoke, ashes, and poisonous fumes into our sky. Where the land has been scoured of grass and forests and there are no crops planted to hold the soil, the slightest breeze whips up choking clouds of dust that spill the dirt into the air.

*Adapted from *Golden Stamp Book of Earth and Ecology* by George S. Fichter, © 1972 by Western Publishing Company, Inc. Used by permission of the publisher.

Hour after hour, fumes from millions of automobiles' exhausts are spewed into the air . . . .

In many large cities, there are no clear days at all now. Over portions of the earth, there is a haze, darkest where the population is greatest. Each year air pollution becomes worse as we dump greater loads into the sky.

Yet, this is the air we must breathe to live. You can survive for days or even weeks without food, but without air, you will die in only a few minutes. Right now you are probably breathing polluted air. It is air containing poisons. Some of these poisons are kinds that do not kill immediately. They take their toll over the years, and more and more people are becoming victims of respiratory ailments. . . .

No more Clean Waters — Once the United States was a land of pure, sparkling waters. . . . But in the few hundred years since America's discovery, its waters have been almost totally spoiled by pollution. The greatest damage has come in very recent years.

Still, the people in many cities must drink the water from these lakes and rivers. They make it drinkable by loading it with purifying chemicals. But the chemicals make the water taste bad. There is also a point at which the chemicals used to purify water become poisonous to people, too.

Streams in the United States have indeed become open sewers carrying away wastes from industries and dwellings. The wastes are really only moved downstream to the next town or city, where more wastes are added, until the once-pure stream becomes little more than a sluggish stench.

Now Lake Erie is dead — killed by pollution.

Lake Michigan may be the next of the Great Lakes to be killed by man. Even sooner, a much larger body of water appears to be doomed — the giant Gulf of Mexico![3]

This is mostly nonsense — but dangerous nonsense, as we shall see shortly, after a bit of theory. The plan for this chapter is (1) To clarify how economics views pollution — as a trade-off between cost and cleanliness. (2) To study the trends of pollution as income and population have increased in recent decades. The finding is that, according to the most important measures, pollution has decreased, on balance. (3) To consider which is the best overall measure of pollution. Life expectancy seems to be the best, and by that measure pollution is decreasing sharply. (4) To study in a bit of detail some of the pollutions that have most worried people in recent years, such as the purity of the Great Lakes and the disposal of trash. The outlook for both examples is clearly cheerful.

THE ECONOMIC THEORY OF POLLUTION

Natural resources and pollution are the opposite sides of the same coin. For example, sooty air is undesired pollution; it may also be thought of as the absence of a desired resource, pure air. The key difference between the concepts of a natural resource and of pollution is that the goods we call "natural resources" are largely produced by private firms, which have a strong self-interest — the profit motivation — for providing consumers with what they want. A deal is made through the market, and people tend to get what they are willing to pay for. In contrast, the good we call "absence of environmental pollution" is largely produced by public agencies, in which the political mechanism that adjusts supply and demand is far less automatic and, for better or for worse, seldom uses a pricing system that would arrive at the same result as would a free market.

Another difference between natural resources and pollution is that natural-resource transactions are mostly limited in impact to the buyer and the seller, whereas one person's pollution is "external" and may touch everybody else. This difference may be more apparent than real, however. One person's demand for natural resources affects the price that all pay, at least in the short run; and conversely, the price that one person must pay for a resource depends upon the demand of all others for the resource. Much the same would be true for pollution if there were a well-adjusted system by which people had to pay for the privilege of polluting. But such a price system for regulating pollution is not easy to achieve. And hence the situations of resources and pollution do differ in how "external" they are.

The technologist views all emissions of pollutants as bad, and speculates how to get rid of them. But the economist asks about the optimal level of pollution. How much cleanliness are we willing to pay for? At some point we prefer to spend money to buy more police service or more skiing rather than more environmental cleanliness. The problem of pollution for economists is like the problem of collecting a city's garbage: Do we want to pay for daily collection, or collection every other day, or just twice a week? With environmental pollution just as with garbage, a rational answer depends upon the cost of cleanup as well as our tastes for cleanliness. And as our society becomes richer, we can afford and are prepared to pay for more cleanliness — a trend that we shall see documented below.

TRENDS IN U.S. POLLUTION

Sound discussion of this topic requires that we think about the many forms of pollution rather than just about a single, general "pollution." And it is useful to classify pollution as (a) health related or (b) aesthetic. Largely because it is easier to talk objectively about the former than the latter, we shall concentrate on the health-related pollutions.

Life Expectancy and Pollution

The danger of an airplane falling on your house is infinitely greater now than it was a century ago. And the danger from artificial food additives is now many times greater than it was 1,000 years ago. You may or may not worry about such dangers as these, but an alarmist can *always* find some new man-made danger that is now increasing. We must, however, resist the tendency to conclude from such evidence that our world is more polluted now than it was before airplanes or food additives or whatever danger you please.

How may we reasonably assess the trend of health-related pollutions? It would seem reasonable to go directly to health itself to measure how we are doing. The simplest and most accurate measure of health is length of life, summed up as the average life expectancy. To buttress that general measure, which includes the effects of curative medicine as well as preventive (pollution-fighting) efforts, we may look at the trends in causes of death.

In the U.S. (and the Western world as a whole) there has been a long upward climb in life expectancy for many hundreds of years. This all-important fact may be seen in figure 9-1 for the twentieth century. And in the rest of the world life expectancy has been climbing steadily for decades. Surely this historical view gives no ground for alarm. Of course, history may change course tomorrow and we might be headed directly into a cataclysm. But there is no reason to believe this. And despite speculation to the contrary, life expectancy is still increasing in the U.S., and even faster than before, according to latest reports.[4]

Next let us turn to specific causes of death. In the past, most people in the U.S. died of environmental pollution — that is, of infectious diseases such as pneumonia, tuberculosis, or gastroenteritis. Nowadays, people die of the diseases of old age, which the environment does not force upon the individual — heart disease, cancer, and strokes (figure 9-2). And there

expectation of life in years

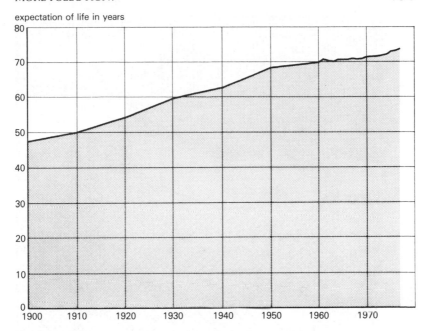

FIGURE 9-1.   Expectation of Life at Birth by Year of Birth in the U.S.

seems to be no evidence that the increase in cancer is due to environmental carcinogens; rather, it is an inevitable consequence of people living to older, more cancer-prone ages. The decline in accident deaths,
despite increased auto use, may also be seen as an improvement in the
health environment.

The worldwide picture begins to show the same characteristics. Small-
pox, for example, once was a common killer; now it has been wiped out.
And cholera, purely a pollution disease, is no longer an important factor
in the world.

In sum: Life expectancy is the best index of the state of health-related
pollution. And by this measure, pollution has been declining steadily
and sharply for decades. Hence it is reasonable to say that taken together
the health-affecting "pollutions" (using that term in its widest sense)
have been diminishing.

AIR AND WATER POLLUTION

Pollution of the air and water are, for most people, the major environmental problems. And the popular impression is that the situation is get-

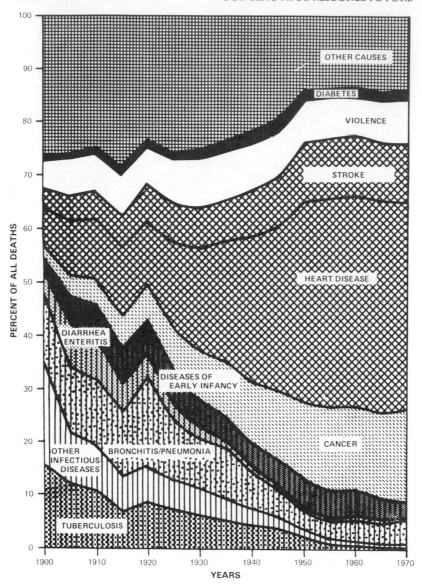

FIGURE 9-2. Trends in the Leading Causes of Death in the U.S. This figure clearly shows the diminution of the most important life-destroying pollutions in the twentieth century. The increase in the proportion of deaths from cancer is statistically inevitable simply because fewer people are dying at younger ages.

ting worse. One reason for this impression is the widely reported Environmental Quality Index of the National Wildlife Federation. The *New York Times* headline for the 1976 report was "Environmental Quality Held Down," and the story begins, "The nation's overall environmental well-being declined slightly in 1976. . . ."[5]

Despite the impressive name of the index, and its numerical nature, it is, according to the National Wildlife Federation, which prepares and disseminates it, "a subjective analysis [that] represent[s] [the] collective thinking of the editors of the National Wildlife Federation Staff." That is, the Environmental Quality Index represents casual observation and opinion rather than statistical facts. It includes such subjective judgments as that the trend of "living space" is "down . . . vast stretches of America are lost to development yearly." (Chapter 16 shows the facts on that particular non-pollution issue.)

If we look at objective facts instead of "subjective analysis," we see that the quality of the environment is improving rather than worsening. The governmental Council on Environmental Quality's data on major air pollutants show sharp improvements in the last decade. Whereas the Environmental Quality Index has the quality of air declining from 1970 to 1973, the data collected from 1970 to 1974 by the official Environmental Protection Agency show a steady decline in the most important air pollutants, "particulates" and sulfur dioxide, as can be seen in figure 9-3.

Whereas the Environmental Quality Index says that "in cities, air quality is improving, but in the country it's getting worse," data for 1968–70 (I couldn't find a later study) show improvements in air quality in all population-classified living areas (figure 9-4).

The Environmental Quality Index says "Water: Down," and their graph shows a steady deterioration from 1970 to 1977. It would be interesting to know how the National Wildlife Federation formed this impression — apparently in ignorance of the Council of Environmental Quality's 1975 report, which describes the situation as shown in figure 9-5, based on U.S. Geological Survey data. The proportion of water-quality observations that had "good" drinking water rose from just over 40 percent in 1961 to about 60 percent in 1974. And the 1976 report concluded that "progress has been made in controlling municipal and industrial point sources of pollution. Major improvements in the quality of polluted streams have been documented in the preceding pages and in CEQ's previous Annual Reports."[6]

Longer-run data are hard to come by. But most students of the subject

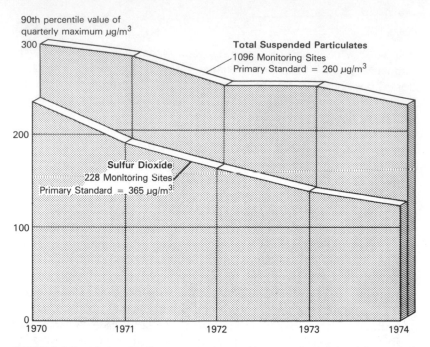

FIGURE 9-3a. National Pollution Trends in Sulfur Dioxide and Total Suspended Particulates

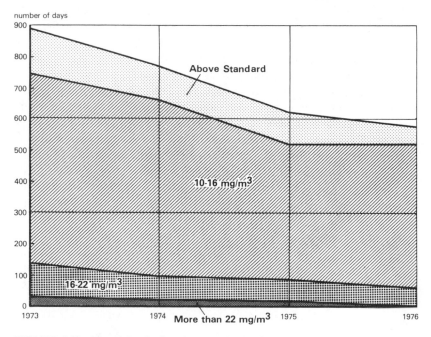

FIGURE 9-3b. Trends in Carbon Monoxide Levels in 13 Cities
Note: A darker shade represents a higher level of pollution.

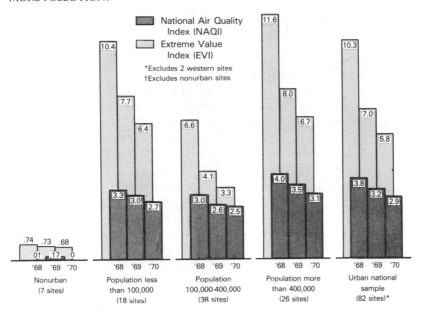

FIGURE 9-4. Trends in Air Pollution in the U.S.

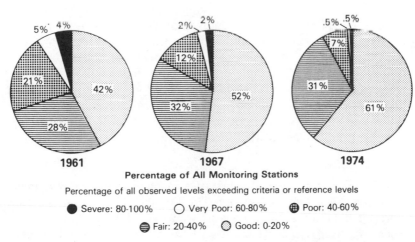

FIGURE 9-5. Trends in the Quality of Drinking Water in the U.S.

would probably agree with this assessment by Orris Herfindahl and Allen Kneese:

> Serious deterioration in some aspects of environmental quality did take place between, say, 1840 and 1940.
>
> By most measures the quality of air and water deteriorated, sometimes severely. Wild areas were brought under development, and their beauty frequently was impaired or destroyed. Game populations diminished rapidly, and in many cases ugly and congested cities were created.
>
> Since 1940, however, the quality of the environment has in some respects markedly improved. Rivers have been cleaned of their grossest floating materials; cities have substantially reduced the particulate matter in their atmosphere; some of the worse slums have been eliminated; public health, at least so far as infectious diseases are concerned, has been greatly improved; much land has been returned to a wild state, and many important varieties of wildlife have been encouraged to increase spectacularly.[7]

In brief: Air and water are getting purer. And the public is being taken to the cleaners by such environmental groups as the National Wildlife Federation, which tell people just the opposite of the facts.

WHERE AND WHEN WAS (IS) POLLUTION LESS?

If we know the circumstances under which there will be less pollution, we can either try to change the local conditions or we can move to where there is less pollution. For the U.S., two invidious comparisons are commonly made: to socialist countries and to the past. Let us see whether the grass is greener elsewhere. (These comments are not intended as a comparison of capitalism with socialism, or of the present with the distant past; I have found no environmental data for such comparisons, and anecdotes alone are not a sound basis for them. My aim is simply to show that if one lifts one's eyes from one's own yard to others', one may see that things are not necessarily better over there.)

Socialist Countries

The Eastern European socialist countries are no paragons of environmental virtue. "Blue Only a Memory: The Danube Is Filthy," says a *New York Times* headline. "A dozen years ago we could swim in the Danube. Today the river is so dangerous it is illegal to swim in it," said the head of the Czechoslovak Research and Development Center for Environmen tal Pollution Control. . . . Brastislava [the capital of Slovakia] has the most polluted atmosphere and the worst environment among . . . other European cities."[8]

The Soviet Union, too, is beset with environmental problems.

In Russia, a huge chemical plant was built right beside a beloved tourist attraction: Yasnaya Polanya, Leo Tolstoy's gracious country estate. Unmonitored fumes are poisoning Tolstoy's forests of oak and pine, and powerless conservationists can only wince. With equal indifference, the Soviet pulp and paper industry has settled on the shores of Lake Baikal. No matter how fully the effluents are treated, they still defile the world's purest waters.

The level of the Caspian Sea has dropped 8½ feet since 1929, mainly because dams and irrigation projects along the Volga and Ural rivers divert incoming water. As a result, Russia's caviar output has decreased; one-third of the sturgeons' spawning grounds are high and dry. Meanwhile, most municipalities lack adequate sewage treatment plants, carbon monoxide chokes the plateau towns of Armenia, and smog shrouds the metallurgical centers of Magnitogorsk, Alma-Ata and Chelyabinsk.[9]

Life expectancy is high and has been rising, in the socialist countries as in the U.S., of course. But perfect environmental purity has yet to be achieved there, just as in the West.

Pollution in the Past

There is a common tendency to compare the present to a hypothetical pristine past when lakes and streams were clean and when cities were free of the nuisances of modernity. But it wasn't so. Contrast a major Western metropolis today with London of 1890:

The Strand of those days . . . was the throbbing heart of the people's essential London . . . But the mud! [a euphemism] And the noise! And the smell! All these blemishes were [the] mark of [the] horse. . . .

The whole of London's crowded wheeled traffic — which in parts of the City was at times dense beyond movement — was dependent on the horse: lorry, wagon, bus, hansom and 'growler', and coaches and carriages and private vehicles of all kinds, were appendages to horses . . . the characteristic aroma — for the nose recognized London with gay excitement — was of stables, which were commonly of three of four storeys with inclined ways zigzagging up the faces of them; [their] middens kept the cast-iron filigree chandeliers that glorified the reception rooms of upper- and lower-middle-class homes throughout London encrusted with dead flies, and, in late summer, veiled with living clouds of them.

A more assertive mark of the horse was the mud that, despite the activities of a numberous corps of red-jacketed boys who dodged among wheels and hooves with pan and brush in service to iron bins at the pavement-edge, either flooded the streets with churnings of 'pea soup' that at times collected in pools over-brimming the kerbs, and at others covered the road-surface as with axle grease or bran-laden dust to the distraction of the wayfarer. In the first case, the swift-moving hansom or gig would fling sheets of such soup — where not intercepted by trousers or skirts — completely across the pavement, so that the frontages of the Strand throughout its length had an eighteen-inch plinth of mud-parge thus imposed upon it. The pea-soup condition was met by wheeled 'mud-carts' each attended by two ladlers clothed as for Icelandic seas in thigh boots, oilskins collared to the chin, and sou'westers sealing in the back of the neck. Splash Ho! The foot passenger now gets the mud in his eye! The axle-grease condition was met by horse-mechanized brushes and travellers in the small hours found fire-hoses washing away residues . . . .

And after the mud the noise, which, again endowed by the horse, surged like a mighty heart-beat . . . and the hammering of a multitude of iron-shod hairy heels . . . , the deafening, side-drum tatoo of tyred wheels jarring from the apex of one set to the next like sticks dragging along a fence; the creaking and groaning and chirping and rattling of vehicles, light and heavy, thus maltreated; the jangling of chain harness and the clanging or jingling of every other conceivable thing else, augmented by the shrieking and bellowings called for from those of God's creatures who desired to impart information or proffer a request vocally — raised a din that . . . is beyond conception. It was not any such paltry thing as noise. It was an immensity of sound. . . .[10]

There may not be overwhelming evidence for saying that in general the pollution situation has been getting better. There is (in my judgment) even less basis for saying that things have been getting worse. What is clear, however, is that there has been an increase in *concern* about pollution in the past decade. At the very same time that air and water pollution were decreasing, people were becoming progressively more worried about it, a trend that may be seen in these poll data:[11]

Q. Compared to other parts of the country, how serious, in your opinion, do you think the problem of air/water pollution is in this area — very serious, somewhat serious, or not very serious?

A. Very Serious or Somewhat Serious:

	Air	Water
1965	28%	35%
1966	48%	49%
1967	53%	52%
1968	55%	58%
1970	69%	74%

Herfindahl and Kneese wisely note that "the present concern with environmental quality may stem as much or more from increased demands [for a clean environment] as deterioration in supply."[12] But the cause of the concern is not fundamental to our theory; what does matter is the fact that people want a purer environment strongly enough to create it.

It is also clear that advanced economies have considerable power to purify their environments. And the key element in purification is well known. England's top anti-pollution bureaucrat, Lord Kennel, identified it precisely. "With rare and usually quickly solved exceptions, there is no contaminating factor in the environment, including noise, that defies a technical solution. All it takes is money."[13] In other words, purification requires the will to devote the necessary part of a nation's present output and energy to do the job. Many kinds of pollution have lessened in many places — for example, filth in the streets of the U.S., buffalo dung in the streams of the Midwest, organic impurities in our foods, soot in the air, and substances that killed fish in the rivers of England.

> British rivers . . . have been polluted for a century while in America they began to grow foul only a couple of decades ago. . . . The Thames has been without fish for a century. But by 1968 some 40 different varieties had come back to the river.[14]

> Now to be seen [in London] are birds and plants long unsighted here. . . . The appearance of long-absent birds is measured by one claim that 138 species are currently identified in London, compared with less than half that number 10 years ago. . . . Gone are the killer smogs. . . . Londoners . . . are breathing air cleaner than it has been for a century . . . effect of air pollution on bronchial patients is diminishing . . . visibility is better, too . . . on an average winter day . . . about 4 miles, compared with 1.4 miles in 1958.[15]

And here is a U.S. success story:

> Long used for recreational purposes, Lake Washington [an eighteen-mile-long body of fresh water bordered by Seattle on its western shore

and a number of smaller communities on its eastern shore] began to deteriorate badly soon after World War II when ten newly built waste-treatment plants began dumping some 20 million gallons of treated effluents into its water every day.

Algae thrived on the phosphorous and nitrogen in the sewage discharge, and each time more of the burgeoning aquatic plants died, so did a little bit of the lake — in the form of oxygen lost in decomposition. The lake became cloudy and malodorous, and the fish died along with the algae.

Alarmed, the state legislature in 1958 created a new authority — the Municipality of Metropolitan Seattle — and charged it with sewage disposal for the Seattle area. With the support of local residents, Metro, as the agency soon became known, built a $121 million integrated system that funnels all of the area's effluents far out into Puget Sound. In that way, the wastes are dissipated by tidal action.

Starting in 1963, the system was far enough along for the plants that had been dumping their nutritive wastes into the lake to begin, one by one, to divert their output into the new system and Puget Sound. The results were obvious in the clearer, cleaner water and the return of fish populations. "When the phosphorous levels fell off, so did the algae blooms," says one zoologist, "and so did the pollution." What Lake Washington demonstrates, of course, is that pollution is not irreversible — provided the citizenry is really determined to reclaim the environment, and willing to pay for past years of neglect.[16]

And, most astonishing of all, the Great Lakes are not dead — not even Lake Erie! Though the fish catch in Erie fell in the 1960s, it has recently increased, and in 1977 10 million pounds of fish were caught there. Ohio beaches on Lake Erie are reopening, and "trout and salmon have returned to the Detroit River, the Lake's biggest tributary."[17] For the Great Lakes as a whole, the catch was at its lowest in history in 1965 (56 million tons), but has since rebounded to 73 million tons in 1977, not far from the average since World War I. By 1977 Lake Michigan had become "an angler's paradise . . . the finest fresh-water fishery in the world," a $350-million-a-year sport fishing industry.[18]

What about all the other possible pollutants — PCB's, mercury, the environment warming, the environment cooling, and the rest? Because their number is as large as the environmentalist's imagination, it is not possible here or elsewhere to consider, one at a time, all the past, present, and future pollutions. The possibility of a dangerous or unaesthetic polluting effect may be raised against almost any substance we have ever produced or ever will produce. And if we act as if all *possible* dangers of a substance are also *likely* dangers, then we will become immobilized.

May I now introduce, as a surprise witness, Ralph Nader? His qualifications in the fight against pollution are almost beyond question. Here is his testimony about sodium azide, which is used in air bags for automobiles. (He is responding to a report publicized by Congressman Shuster that this chemical may cause mutations and cancer.)

> Sodium azide, if you smell the gas or taste it, is very, very unsafe. So is gasoline. So are the additives in gasoline. So are battery additives. So are tire wear and tire flakes that get into the air. So are hydrocarbons. So is the nitrogen oxide, and so is carbon monoxide.
>
> It strikes me as eroding the credibility of some of these opponents who suddenly become full of such concern for these toxic substances because it happens to be in accord with what certain special industrial interests want, and so unconcerned with the massively more pervasive, massively more poisonous array of chemical substances that we too charitably call pollution.
>
> I also spoke with Dr. Bruce Ames (chairman at the Genetics Department at the University of California-Berkeley), mentioned by Congressman Shuster. Dr. Ames was merely talking about sodium azide as it is exposed to human contact. He is not talking about sodium azide as it is solidified in pellets, and contained in sealed containers, etc. He does not have any information on that.
>
> The point I want to make is that sodium azide, if it is exposed to acidic contact, will under certain extraordinary circumstances, given the fact that it is a solid pellet, emit a hydrozoic acid gas which is an intolerably pungent gas. If anybody has ever taken the slightest whiff of this gas, they would know it.
>
> In all the crashes which involve air bag equipped cars on the highways, and sodium azide as the inflator, there has been no such reaction.
>
> I don't say that by way of saying that sodium azide should be the inflator. Undoubtedly it is likely that most of the cars with air bags in the '80s will not have sodium azide.
>
> But I do point out that the attempt to sensationalize this product in ways that are not shared by EPA, the Department of Health, Education and Welfare, or OSHA, who know how sodium azide has been used for years in medical laboratories, for example — your attempt to sensationalize it does not receive much credibility given the source of the persons who are doing the sensationalizing.[19]

The irony of Nader's effective defense of sodium azide is that the consumer and environmental movements in which Nader is influential have attacked many other substances and conditions in the same way that sodium azide and air bags were attacked; and now the same consumerists are suffering from irresponsible attacks on their own pet safety project, the air bag.

WASTE POLLUTION

Perhaps the silliest of pollution threats — but one that was nonetheless taken very seriously about ten years ago — was the fear of being overcome by our own wastes. We were asked to flush our toilets less frequently and to recycle all kinds of things. (See chapter 10 on conservation.) In the course of less than a decade, however, engineers found a myriad of new ways not only to get rid of wastes but also to get value from them. "From their one-time reputation as major pollutants, garbage and sewage now seem to be acquiring the status of national resources.[20] Within a year after Connecticut set up a Resources Recovery Authority "to manage a collection and re-use program for the entire state,"the authorities could judge that "there are no technological problems with garbage any more. All that is needed is initiative."[21]

The pollution of our living space by trash and discarded goods, especially junk cars, is a particularly interesting case. Not only can this problem be solved by the expenditure of resources for cleanup, but it also illustrates how resource scarcity is decreasing. Improved iron supplies and steel-making processes have now gotten iron and steel to the point of cheapness at which junked cars are no longer worth recycling. The old cars — if they could be stored out of sight — would be a newly created reservoir of "raw" materials for the future. In this important sense, iron is not being used up but is simply being stored in a different form for possible future use, until iron prices rise or better methods of salvage are developed. Much the same is true with many other discarded materials. But there is also an important difference from resources. The amount of junked cars and similar pollutants produced, and the price of polluting, are not automatically regulated by public demand, either by ballot vote or by dollar voting, as are market-produced-and-mediated goods. And there are strong private interests that militate against remedial actions. The outcome of this sort of pollution, like others, will therefore depend largely on the social will and on political power.

SUMMARY

Pollution is a bad thing — by definition. There are many different sorts of pollution. Some have lessened over the years — for example, filth in the streets of our cities, and the pollutants that cause contagious diseases. Others have worsened — for example, gasoline fumes in the air, noise in' many places, and atomic wastes. The long-run course of yet others, such as crime in the streets, is unknown. To summarize the direction of such a varied collection of trends is difficult, and can easily be misleading. If one has to choose a single measure of the state of pollution, the most plausible one, because the most inclusive, is life expectancy. And the expected length of a newborn's life has increased greatly in past centuries, and is still increasing.

Economists think about the reduction of pollution as a social good that can be achieved technologically, but that costs resources. This is the question before us: What is the optimal level of pollution, in light of our tastes for a cleaner environment relative to our desire for other goods?

Biologists, engineers, and environmentalists who have warned us of pollution problems and have then developed methods of abating those problems have performed a great service to mankind. And warnings about the possible dangers from coal, nuclear energy, medicines, mercury, carbon dioxide, and the like can serve a similar valuable purpose, especially in connection with ill effects that do not appear immediately but only after many years. We must keep in mind, however, that it is not possible to create a civilization that is free of such risks. The best we can do is to be alert and prudent. And exaggerated warnings can be counter-productive and dangerous.

10.

Should We Conserve Resources for Others' Sakes? What Kinds of Resources Need Conservation?

Should we try to conserve our resources? It depends. Should we avoid all waste? Certainly not. Are the Sierra Club, Friends of the Earth, and other conservationist groups barking up the wrong tree? Yes and no.

We can clarify conservation issues by distinguishing among (1) unique resources, which are one of a kind or close to it and which we value for aesthetic purposes — examples include the Mona Lisa, endangered species of animals, and Muhammad Ali; (2) one-of-a-kind resources that we value as historical artifacts — examples include the U.S. Declaration of Independence, the Dead Sea Scrolls, Abraham Lincoln's first log cabin (if it existed), and perhaps the Mona Lisa; (3) resources that can be reproduced or recycled or substituted for and that we value for their material uses — examples include wood pulp, trees, copper, oil, and food.

This chapter deals mainly with category (3), resources that we value primarily for the use we make of them. These are the resources whose quantities we can positively influence. That is, these are the resources for which we can calculate whether it is cheaper to conserve them for future use, or use them now and get the services that they give us in some other way in the future. The benefits we get from the resources in the other categories — the Mona Lisa or Lincoln's log cabin — cannot be adequately replaced, and hence the economist cannot determine whether conservation is economically worthwhile. The value of a Mona Lisa or a disappearing breed of snail must be what we as a society decide is the value, a decision upon which market prices may or may not shed some light.

The cost and scarcity of resources in category (3) — energy and extractive materials — is likely to decline continuously in the future, according to the analyses in chapters 1–3. But this chapter asks a different question: It asks whether as individuals and as a society we should try to use less of these materials than we are willing to pay for. That is, should we make special efforts to refrain from using these natural resources, and hence treat them differently from the consumption of pencils, haircuts, and Hula-Hoops? The answer is that, apart from considerations of national security and international bargaining power, we need not make special efforts to avoid using the resources.

Conservationists perform an invaluable service when they alert us to dangers to our unique treasures, and when they remind us of the values of these treasures to ourselves and to coming generations. But when they move from this role to suggesting that pulp trees or deer should be conserved beyond what we are willing to pay to set aside the trees or the deer's habitat, they are either expressing their own personal aesthetic tastes and religious values, or else they are talking misguided nonsense. And when some famous conservationist tells us that there should be fewer people so that it is easier for him to find a deserted stretch of beach or mountain range or forest, he is simply saying "gimme" — that is, "I want it, and I don't want to share it." (In chapter 16, we shall see how population growth actually leads to *more* wilderness, not less.)

CONSERVATION OF REPLACEABLE RESOURCES

Should you save old newspapers rather than throw them away? Sure you should — as long as the price that the recycling center pays is greater than the value to you of your time and energy in saving and hauling them.

Should you conserve energy by turning off lights that are burning needlessly in your house? Of course you should — just as long as the money that you save by so doing is worth the effort of shutting off the light. That is, you should turn out a light if the value of the electrical energy is greater than the cost to you of taking a few steps to the light switch and flicking your wrist. But if you are ten miles away from home and you remember that you left a 100-watt light bulb on, should you rush back to turn it off? Obviously not; the value of the gasoline spent would be far greater than the electricity saved, even if the light is on for many days. And even if you are on foot and not far away, the value of your time is surely greater to you than the cost of the electricity saved.

The appropriate rule in these cases is that we should conserve and not waste just so far as the benefits of conserving are greater than the costs if we do not conserve. That is, it is rational for us to avoid waste if the value of the resource saved is more than the cost to us of achieving the saving — a matter of pocketbook economics.

A frequent source of confusion is between *physical* conservation and *economic* conservation. For example, some have urged us not to flush our toilets each time we use them, but rather to use other rules of thumb that we need not take up here. The aim is to "save water." But almost all of us would rather pay the cost of obtaining the additional water from ground-water supplies or from cleaning the water; hence, to "save water" by not flushing is not rational economics. It *is* rational economics to systematically replace light bulbs before they burn out, so that all the bulbs can be changed at once; this is not a waste of light-bulb capacity. To do otherwise is to commit yourself to a lower level of material living.

Though a "simpler way of life" has an appeal for some, it can have a surprisingly high economic cost. One student calculated what would happen if U.S. farmers used 1918 agricultural technology instead of contemporary technology, forswearing tractors and fertilizers in order to "save energy" and natural resources: "We'd need 61 million horses and mules . . . it would take 180 million acres of cropland to feed these animals or about one-half of the cropland now in production. We'd need 26 or 27 million additional agricultural workers to achieve 1976 production levels with 1918 technology."[1]

Conservation of ordinary resources is not a moral matter but an economic matter, just like all other decisions about production and consumption. It is a misunderstanding of this point that leads us to suggest and do foolish things, actions that — though they have expressive value for us — accomplish nothing, and may even have harmful effects for others. For example, there is no discernible benefit for the food supply of people in poor countries of your not eating meat. In fact, the opposite may be true: Heavy meat eating in the U.S. stimulates grain planting and harvesting in order to feed cattle; this increased capacity represents an increased ability to handle an unexpected massive need for food. As D. Gale Johnson put it,

> Suppose that the United States and the other industrial countries had held their direct and indirect per capita use of grain to half of the actual levels for the past several decades. Would this have made more food available to India or Pakistan in 1973 and 1974? The answer is clearly no. The United States, and the other industrial countries as well, would have produced much less grain than has been produced. Reserve stocks would have been much smaller than they have been. If U.S. grain production in 1972 had been 125 million metric tons instead of 200 million or more, it would not have been politically possible to have had 70 million metric tons of grain reserves. . . .
>
> If the industrial countries had had much lower total grain consumption in the past, the institutions required to handle the grain exports to the developing countries in the mid-1960s or in 1972/73 and 1973/74 would not have been able to do so. International trade in grains would have virtually disappeared. . . .[2]

Nor would the research have been done that led to production breakthroughs if industrial countries had consumed less.

Yet experts and laymen alike espouse the "obvious" (though incorrect) short-run view that if we consume less, others in need will have more. Testifying before several Senate subcommittees sitting jointly, Lester Brown said that "it might be wise to reduce consumption of meat a few pounds per capita within affluent, overnourished societies such as the United States."[3] And concerned citizens say, "Millions of people are dying. . . . It sickens me to think of the money spent in America on food that is unnecessary for our basic nutritional needs. Would a sacrifice be so difficult?"[4] And "We . . . serve tens of millions of pets vast quantities of food that could be used to feed millions of starving people in Asia, Africa, and Latin America — if we would only practice birth control for our pets!"[5]

Would it be sound charity to eat less food or eat cheaper food and send the money saved to poor countries? It would indeed be kind for each of us to send money. But why take the money from our food budgets? Why not from our incomes as wholes — that is, while reducing other expenditures as is most convenient, rather than just reducing our expenditures on food? That would make better economic sense (though it might have less ritualistic meaning to us, which could be a persuasive argument for "saving food").

Energy conservation is another favorite target. We are urged not to eat lobsters because it takes 117 times as much energy to catch a lobster as it does to catch enough herring to yield an equal amount of protein.[6] One of the co-authors of the study that reached this conclusion is Jean Mayer, adviser to presidents, president of Tufts University, and perhaps the best-known student of nutrition in the world (but not a student of energy or economics). Marvelous disputes arise in Washington because everyone is trying to get into the energy-saving act. Any one group's panacea is another group's problem. "Transportation officials are 'outraged' by a Congressional report suggesting that buses, van pools, and car pools may use less energy than mass transit rail systems."[7] And the U.S. Post Office in 1978 issued a postage stamp entitled "Energy Conservation," picturing a light bulb, a gas can, and the sun with an inscrutable face.

Apparently it is an inbred moral intuition that makes us feel that non-conservation is wrong.

Bishop Edward O'Rourke, head of the Peoria diocese of the Catholic Church, and Bruce Hannon, environmentalist and energy researcher in the UI Center for Advanced Computation, attempted to raise the "level of consciousness" of church leaders and laymembers. . . .

One solution they cited for the growing problem is for everyone to lead lives that are simpler, more spiritual and less resource consuming. . . .

Even buying a tube of toothpaste is energy wasting. . . . The toothpaste is encased in a cardboard box, which must then be put in a paper bag, with a paper sales receipt — all of these products use wood pulp, and all are usually thrown away and destroyed. . . .

"We are custodians and stewards of God's gifts. The more precious the gifts, such as energy, the more urgent the need to protect them," Bishop O'Rourke reminded.[8]

A Louis Harris poll reveals that

a substantial, 61-23 percent majority thinks it is "morally wrong" for Americans — 6 percent of the world's population — to consume an estimated 40 percent of the world's output of energy and raw materials. And, the public indicates it is ready for a number of drastic cutbacks. . . . A 91-7 percent majority is willing to "have one meatless day a week. . . ." A 73-22 percent majority would agree to "wear old clothes, even if they shine, until they wear out. . . ." By 92-5 percent the public reports it would be willing to "reduce the amount of paper towels, bags, tissues, napkins, cups and other disposables to save energy and to cut pollution."[9]

I share this moral impulse. I take a back seat to no one in hating waste — unnecessary lights, avoidable errands, trivial conferences. But I try to restrict my waste fighting to matters where the benefit is worth the cost (though my children have a different view of my behavior). I try to remember not to waste more additional valuable resources in fighting the original waste than the original waste is worth.

This anti-waste, pro-conservation moral impulse may be used to flimflam the public. Consider The Hunger Project, an offshoot of the est organization. Under the headline "The End of Starvation," a shiny fourcolor brochure recites a few figures (uncorroborated) about the numbers of children who die of hunger each year, then asks people to (a) fast for a day, and (b) contribute money to The Hunger Project. No explanations are given about how the fast or the money will affect anyone else's hunger. The stated purpose of the fast is "To express and experience my alignment with having the end of starvation be a reality in the world. To express and experience that I am the source of The Hunger Project."[10] Whether this and the rest of the brochure is a masterpiece of communication or of non-communcation I leave for the reader to judge. But I offer six pieces of bubble gum to anyone who will explain just how The

Hunger Project (as of 1977) would end anyone's hunger except the sponsors'.[11]

After the first spurt of enthusiasm for conservation and recycling, some people began to calculate that the costs of recommended recycling projects can often exceed the savings.

[A high-school student in Los Angeles] for 18 weeks . . . collected bottles from a restaurant to raise money for a favorite organization. At the end of that time, he had collected 10,180 pounds of glass, driven 817 miles, consumed 54 gallons of gas . . . and used up 153 man-hours of work. It is difficult to estimate the amount of pollution his car threw into the air.[12]

Why do conservationists think people must be pushed to conserve more than what they "naturally" would? Apparently, they do not believe that people will react rationally to changes in resource availabilities and prices. But the slowdown in growth of electricity consumption since 1973 — enough to cause many utilities to drop plans to build new generating plants[13] — should be powerful evidence of consumers' sensitivities to cost and scarcity. Another striking example has been the drop far below the trend in gasoline use in the late 1970s, as gasoline prices rose sharply.

RESOURCES AND FUTURE GENERATIONS

Conservationists and technologists tend to focus discussion on the future, and often properly so. They suggest conserving so that there will be "enough" for future generations. We should conserve, they say, even if the value we get from the resource saved is less than what it costs us to achieve the saving.

When we use resources, then, we ought to ask whether our present use is at the expense of future generations. The answer is a straightforward no. If the relative prices of natural resources can be expected to be lower for future generations than for us now — and this seems to be a reasonable expectation for most natural resources, as we have seen earlier — this implies that future generations will be faced by no greater economic scarcity than we are, but instead will have just as large or larger supplies of resources to tap, despite our present use of them. Hence our present use of resources, considered in sum, has little if any negative effect upon future generations. And our descendants may well be better off if we use the resources in question right now to build a higher standard of living. So we need make no ethical judgments for our descendants.

Furthermore, the market tends to guard against overuse of materials that may become scarcer in the future. The current price of a material reflects expected future supply and demand as well as current conditions, and therefore current prices make an automatic allowance for future generations. If there is a reasonable basis to expect prices to rise in the future, investors will now buy up oil wells, coal mines, and copper-mining companies; such purchases raise the current prices of oil, coal, and copper, and discourage their use. Paradoxically, normal market speculation "cannot prevent an unduly *low* rate of consumption, which would leave future generations with more reserves than they need—just the opposite of what conservationists worry about!"[14]

But what if the investors are wrong? you may ask. In return I ask you: Are you prepared to believe that your understanding of the matter is better than that of speculators who study the facts full time, who are aware of the information you are aware of, and who earn their livings by not being wrong?

The storage of fresh fruits throughout the year serves as a simple illustration of how markets and businesses ensure a yearlong supply and prevent future scarcity. The example also shows how present price reflects future scarcity, and why it would not make sense to buy oranges in the summer to "conserve" for winter or for future years.

Oranges are harvested in the spring and early summer in various countries such as Italy, Israel, Algeria, and Spain. Naturally the price to consumers is cheapest at harvest time. But fruit dealers also buy at harvest time, and store the fruit in warehouses for later sale. The price throughout the winter is roughly the cost at harvest plus the cost of storage (including the cost of the capital tied up in the oranges). The price in the winter therefore is not much higher than at harvest, and there is no reason for consumers to worry about scarcity.

The force that ensures that prices will not rise precipitously at harvest time is the desire of merchants to make a profit by buying cheap at harvest and selling dear later. And the force that prevents them from pushing the price very high in the winter is the competition of other merchants, who have the same desire. Of course any consumer who worries that winter prices will be unbearably high can stockpile oranges and pay the storage price. Likewise, these forces work to prevent scarcity or a fast price run-up in natural resources. Merchants who believe—on the basis of a very full investigation, because their economic lives depend upon it—that future scarcity is not yet fully reflected in present prices will buy raw materials now for future resale. They will do our conserving for us, and we will pay them only if they were right. And the argument is even stronger with respect to metals because they do not require a refrigerated warehouse:

The fact that there will be another orange harvest next year does not make the orange situation different from the copper situation discussed earlier. New discoveries of copper, and new technological developments in the mining and use of copper, are also expected to occur, though the timing of the events is less certain with copper than with oranges. But that just means a wider market for speculating merchants. Hence we need not worry that the needs of future generations are being injured by our present consumption patterns. And please notice that orange prices at harvest time, and present copper prices, too, reflect expected population growth. If consumption is expected to rise due to increased population, foresighted merchants will take that into account (and non-foresighted merchants are not able to remain in business for very long).

If the economic situation were different than it really is—if technology were fixed and costs of resources were therefore expected to be higher in the future than now, indicating greater scarcity to come—it might be appropriate to make ethical judgments that would differ from the results that a free market can produce for us. It might then be appropriate to worry that our consumption and fertility (if influenced only by market prices) might have such adverse effects on future generations that a prudent government might intervene to reduce present use of the mineral natural resources. But such intervention is not now necessary or appropriate, because, as Barnett and Morse put it, "By devoting itself to improving the lot of the living . . . each generation . . . transmits a more productive world to those who follow."[15] It does so by accumulating real capital to increase current income, by adding to the stock of useful knowledge, by making its own generation healthier and better educated, and by improving economic institutions. This is why the standard of living has been rising with successive generations.

Because we can expect future generations to be richer than we are, no matter what we do about resources, asking us to refrain from using resources now so that future generations can have them later is like asking the poor to make gifts to the rich.

CONSERVATION OF ANIMALS OR PEOPLE?

Some say that the human population should be stabilized or reduced because it threatens some species of animals. This raises interesting questions. If we assume there is a trade-off between more people and more of species X, then which species should we favor? Buffalo or golden eagles over Homo sapiens? If yes, does the same logic hold for rats and cockroaches? And how many people do we want to trade for more buffalo? Should the whole Midwest be made a buffalo preserve, or do we want only to maintain the species just this side of extinction? If the latter, why not just put them in a few big zoos? And do we want to protect malaria-carrying mosquitoes from extinction?

We ought also consider the species of animals whose numbers are increased when the human population increases: chickens, goats, cattle, minks, dogs, cats, and canaries. Is this a justification for increasing our population? (This also is a problem for those who are against killing animals for food or clothing. Without humans to consume these products there would be fewer chickens and minks to be killed.) Which way does one prefer to have it from the viewpoint of animal welfare?

My point: Where costs are not the issue, the decision about what is conserved, and how much, is a matter of tastes and values. Once we recognize this, the arguments are easier to resolve.

PRICE AND VALUE

The most complex and confusing conservation issues are those that seem as if they are matters of only dollars and cents to some people, but to other people are matters of aesthetics and basic values. Consider the matter of saving old newspapers. Some large institutions save and recycle paper because the money obtained for the waste paper makes the effort profitable. In World War II the price of waste paper rose high enough to make the effort worthwhile for many householders. And now that shredded newspapers can be used as insulation after treatment with fire-retardant chemicals, paper collection is a fund-raising device for community groups such as Boy Scout troops.[16] But nowadays, for most of us the cost of saving and delivering the waste paper seems greater than the amount we would get for it.

Here we must consider, What is the economic meaning of the price paid for waste paper? That price will roughly equal the sum of what it costs to grow a tree, cut the tree, and then transport and convert the wood to paper. If the cost of growing new trees rises, so will the cost of paper. But if the cost of growing trees goes down, or if good substitutes for trees are developed, the price of used and of new paper, and of wood, will fall. And that is what is happening right now. The total quantity of growing trees has been increasing, and the newspapers report the successful development of kenaf as a substitute for paper (see chapter 5). So why bother to recycle newspapers?

Environmentalists, however, feel that there is more to be said on this matter. They feel that trees should be saved for reasons other than the dollars-and-cents value of pulp or lumber. They argue that it is inherently right to try to avoid cutting down a tree "unnecessarily." I believe that it is fair to characterize this argument as based on aesthetic or even religious values other than those relating to use by future generations. The environmentalists believe that stands of trees are unique national or international treasures just as Westminster Abbey is for Englishmen and as the Mosque of the Golden Dome is for Muslims. Perhaps we can express this by saying that in these cases even the believer who does not directly use the treasure is willing to pay, in money or in effort, so that other people — now and in the future — can enjoy it without paying the full price of creating it. (Additionally, there is the argument that, even if future generations will be willing to pay the price, they will be unable to do so if we don't preserve it for them.) Some people even impute feelings to nature, to trees or to animals, and they aim to prevent pain to those feelings.

There is no economic argument against these aesthetic points of view. All that the economist can do is to note a curiosity that needs explaining: Why is the word "Earth" capitalized in the Council on Environmental Quality's report (1976) whereas "people" is not capitalized? Neither is capitalized in my Merriam-Webster dictionary.

There is also conservation for the purposes of national security and international bargaining. It may well make sense for a country to stockpile enough oil and other strategically sensitive resources for months or even years of consumption. But these political matters are beyond the scope of this chapter and of the usual discussions of conservation. Furthermore, there is almost no connection between population growth and such strategic stockpiling. Hence the topic needs no further attention here.

RESOURCES AND INTERNATIONAL RAPE

Is there need for ethical judgments to supersede market decisions when rich countries buy raw materials from poor countries?

The idea that the rich countries are "raping" the poor countries and "pirating" their bauxite, copper, and oil does not rest on a solid intellectual foundation. These resources have little value for home use in a country with little industry. But when sold to an industrial country, the resources provide revenue that can aid in development — and, in fact, this revenue may represent a poor country's very best chance of development. What if the "exploiters" stop buying? This is what happened in 1974 in Indonesia:

Many of those Indonesians who took to the streets only eight months ago to protest alleged Japanese exploitation of their natural resources are now beginning to complain that the Japanese are not exploiting them enough. Because of setbacks in their own economy, Japanese importing companies have had to cut their monthly purchases of 760,000 cubic yards of Indonesian timber by as much as 40%. As a result, Indonesian lumber prices have dropped some 60% and . . . 30 firms have already gone bankrupt, causing widespread unemployment in . . . timber-dependent areas. . . .[17]

Nor are contemporary poor-country people who sell their resources benefiting at the expense of their own future generations. "Saving" the materials for the poor country's future population runs the grave risk that the resources will drop in relative value in the future, just as coal has become less valuable in the past century; a country that hoarded its coal starting a hundred years ago would be a loser on all accounts.

Please remember, too, that the U.S. and other rich countries export large amounts of primary products that poor countries need, especially food. The primary products that the poorer countries produce enable them to trade for the rich countries' primary products, an exchange from which both parties gain. Of course, nothing in this paragraph suggests that the prices at which rich countries buy these resources from poor countries are "fair" prices. The terms of trade are indeed an ethical matter, but one that is likely to be resolved by the hard facts of supply, demand, market power, and political power.

SUMMARY

A public policy of conservation implicitly assumes that the "true" value of the raw material, or other product to be conserved, is greater than its price to consumers. But in a well-operating free market, the price of a commodity reflects its full social cost. Hence if an individual or firm refrains from using the product even though its value to the firm or individual is greater than the price being asked, there is an economic loss, without benefit to anyone directly involved (except perhaps the producers of products that compete with the product being "conserved"). For example, saving old newspapers when their market value is far below the cost of your time and trouble to do so may make you feel good, but it lowers the overall productivity of the economy without any long-run benefit to the supply of timber.

Nor is conservation needed to protect future generations in ordinary situations. Market forces and present prices take into account expected future developments, and thereby automatically "conserve" scarce resources for future consumption. Perhaps more important, present consumption stimulates production and thereby increases productivity, which benefits future generations; the use of newprint today causes forests to be grown for future consumption, and encourages research into how to grow and harvest trees. Only if you suffer pain for the tree itself when it is cut does it make sense for you to save newsprint.

Nor is conservation by the rich good for the poor, domestically or internationally. What the poor need is economic growth. And "economic growth means *using* the world's resources of minerals, fuels, capital, manpower and land. There can be no return to Walden Pond without mass poverty."[18]

PART TWO

POPULATION GROWTH'S EFFECT UPON OUR RESOURCES AND LIVING STANDARD

As for the Arts of Delight and Ornament, they are best promoted by the greatest number of emulators. And it is more likely that one ingenious curious man may rather be found among 4 million than among 400 persons. . . .

WILLIAM PETTY, *Another Essay in Political Arithmetic*, 1682

11.

Standing Room Only?
The Demographic Facts

Every schoolchild seems to "know" that the world's environment and food situation have been getting worse. And the children's books leave no doubt that population size and growth are the villains. As the *Golden Stamp Book of Earth and Ecology* says, "Can the earth survive this many people? . . . If the population continues to explode, many people will starve. About half of the world's population is underfed now, with many approaching starvation. . . . All of the major environmental problems can be traced to people — more specifically, to too many people."[1] This text distills into simplest form the popular adults' books and articles about population and resources.

But there is a fly in this ointment. These propositions that are given to children with so much assurance are either unproven or wrong. This chapter deals instead with the demographic facts, and the following chapter examines the dynamics of the birthrate and of population growth in order to lay the foundation for the discussion in the rest of Part II.

POPULATION GROWTH RATES

The demographic facts, to the extent that they are known scientifically, can indeed seem frightening — at first glance. Figure 11-1 is the kind of diagram that, back in 1965, impressed and scared me enough to convince me that helping stop population growth should be my life's work. What we seem to see here is runaway population growth; the human population seems to be expanding with self-generated natural force at an exponential rate, a juggernaut chained only by starvation and disease. This suggests that unless something unusual comes along to check this geometric growth, there will soon be "standing room only."

It may be instructive that people have long been doing arithmetic that leads to the prediction of one or another version of "standing room only." In fact, the phrase "standing room only," used so often in recent discus-

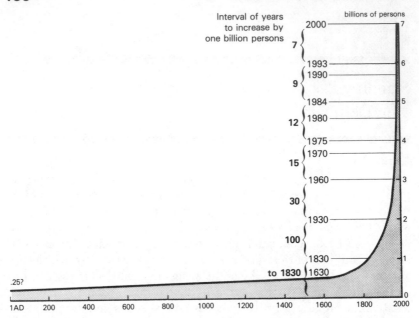

FIGURE 11-1. How the U.S. State Department Saw the World's Population Growth

sions of population growth, was the title of a book by Ross in 1927, and the notion is found explicitly in both Malthus and Godwin (whose conclusions differed completely, however). Just one among many such colorful calculations is that of Harrison Brown, who worried that humanity might continue increasing "until the earth is covered completely and to a considerable depth with a writhing mass of human beings, much as a dead cow is covered with a pulsating mass of maggots."[2]

People have worried about population growth since the beginning of recorded time. The Bible gives us this early story of population exceeding the "carrying capacity" of a particular area: "And the land was not able to carry them . . . and Abram said to Lot: . . . Is not the whole land before thee? . . . If thou will take the left hand, then I will take the right; or if thou take the right hand, then I will go to the left."[3] Euripides wrote that the Trojan War was due to "an insolent abundance of people."[4] And many classical philosophers and historians such as Polybius, Plato, and Tertullian worried about population growth, food shortages, and environmental degradation.[5] In 1802, when Java had a population of 4 million, a Dutch colonial offical wrote that Java was "overcrowded with unemployed."[6] Now Java has most of Indonesia's 125 million people, and again it is said to be overcrowded.

Just because people have worried about population growth in the past does not imply that we should not be worried now, of course. If a monster really has been on the loose for a while, the fact that it has not yet done us in is hardly reason to stop worrying. Therefore we must ask: Is population growth an unchecked monster, on the loose since the beginning of time but likely to destroy us in the foreseeable future?

Contrary to the impression given by figure 11-1, population growth has not been constant or steady over the long sweep of time. Even the broadest picture of the past million years shows momentous sudden changes. Figure 11-2 indicates that population growth has three times taken off at "explosive" rates.

Another common misleading impression about world population is that a large proportion of all the people who have ever lived are alive now. This is very far from the truth. A well-thought-out estimate is that 77 billion human beings were born from 600,000 B.C. to 1962 A.D.: 12 billion up to 6000 B.C., 42 billion from 6000 B.C. to 1650 A.D., and 23 billion from 1650 A.D. to 1962 A.D.[7] Compare this to the 4–5 billion who may be alive now. Of course many of the people born in earlier years died at young ages. But even so, the number of years of human life lived on earth in the past was large relative to the present.

It was the tool-using and tool-making revolution that kicked off the rapid rise in population around 1 million B.C., according to Edward Deevey. The aid of various tools "gave the food gatherer and hunter

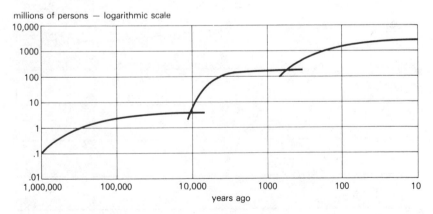

FIGURE 11-2. Deevey's Logarithmic Population Curve

access to the widest range of environments."[8] But when the new power from the use of primitive tools had been exploited, the rate of population growth fell, and population size again settled down near a plateau.

The next rapid jump in population started perhaps 10,000 years ago, when men began to keep herds, and to plow and plant the earth, rather than simply foraging for the plants and game that grew naturally. Once again the rate of population growth abated after the initial productivity gains from the new technology had been exploited, and once again population size settled down to a near-plateau, as compared with the rapid growth previously experienced. It is reasonable to think that the near-plateau was reached because the known methods of making a living constituted a constraint to further population growth once the world's population reached a certain size.

These two previous episodes of a sharp rise and a subsequent fall in the rate of population growth suggest that the present rapid growth—which began perhaps 300 or 350 years ago, in the 1600s—may well settle down again, when, or if, the gains from the new industrial and agricultural knowledge that followed the "industrial revolution" begin to peter out. And population size may again reach a near-plateau and remain there until another "revolution" due to another breakthrough of knowledge again suddenly increases the productive capacity of mankind. Of course, the current knowledge-revolution may continue without foreseeable end, and population growth may or may not continue as long as the revolution does. Either way, in this long-term view, population size

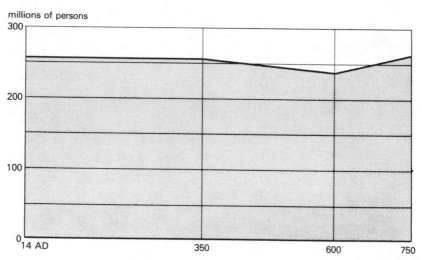

FIGURE 11-3. The Population of the World, 14 AD–750 AD

millions of persons

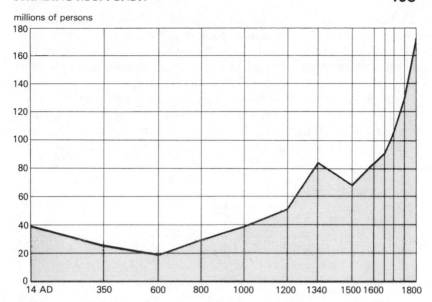

FIGURE 11-4. The Population of Europe, 14 AD–1800 AD

adjusts to productive conditions rather than being an uncontrolled monster.

To put the matter another way: This long-run view of demographic history suggests that, contrary to Malthus, constant geometric growth does not correctly characterize the human population. Rather, a major improvement of economic and health conditions produces a sudden increase in population, which gradually moderates as the major productive advances and concomitant health improvements are assimilated. Then, after the initial surge, the rate of growth slows down until the next big surge. (It was the very large increase in life expectancy that led to the recent population growth in poor countries. Throughout history, life expectancy has hardly changed, compared with the sudden jump during the past few hundred years.) In this view, population growth represents economic success and human triumph, rather than social failure.

Deevey's picture of population history (figure 11-2) still leaves us with the image of population growth as having an irresistible, self-reinforcing logic of its own, though subject to (very rare) changes in conditions. That view is so broad, however, that it can be misleading. The entire world, for example, had a stable population over the seven centuries prior to 750 A.D., as seen in figure 11-3. And if we look more closely, as in figure 11-4, we see that even for as large an area as Europe, where local ups and downs tend to cancel out, population growth did not proceed at a constant rate, nor was there always positive growth. Instead, there were advances and reverses. Figure 11-4 shows that population change is a complex phenomenon affected by a variety of forces; it is not an inexorable force checked only by famine and epidemic.

Now let us move to an even greater level of detail—the individual country or region. In figures 11-5, 11-6, and 11-7 we see three places where a decline in population has been more than a temporary episode. In Egypt, the breakdown of the Roman Empire led to a series of popu-

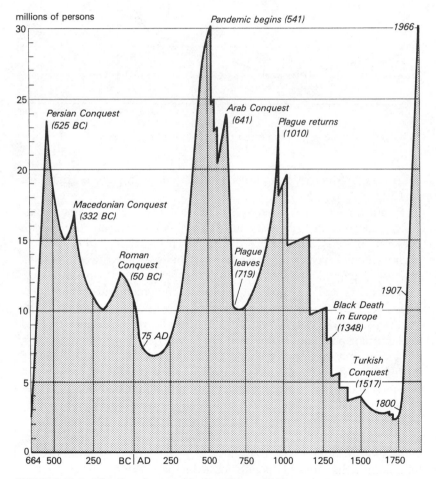

FIGURE 11-5. The Population of Egypt, 664 BC–1966 AD

NOTE: McEvedy and Jones (1978, pp. 226–229) persuasively suggest that Egypt's population was nowhere near so high as Hollingsworth shows it to be.

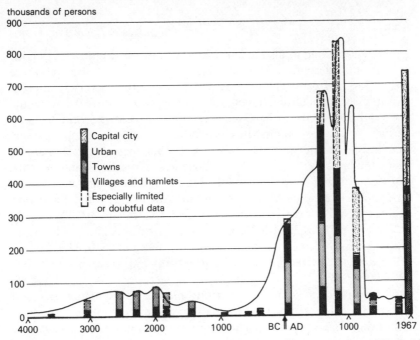

FIGURE 11-6. The Population of Baghdad (Lower Diyala, Iraq) Region, 4000 BC–1967 AD

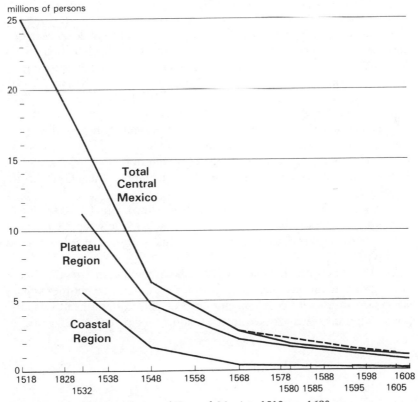

FIGURE 11-7. The Population of Central Mexico, 1518 AD–1608 AD

lation declines due to disease and bad government, declines that ended only in the last century. In Iraq's Dyala region (around Baghdad) there were a series of political-economic perturbations that adversely affected irrigation and agriculture. It took years of population growth to overcome such setbacks—only to have another such breakdown occur. And in Mexico, it was the conquest by Cortez that set off a remarkable population decline. In the Spaniards' wake came wars, massacres, political and economic breakdowns among the indigenous civilizations, and new diseases, all of which caused death, desolation, and depopulation.

A shocking example close to home, for Americans, is the population decline of Native Americans in California from perhaps 310,000 in 1769 to a low of perhaps 20,000–25,000 between 1880 and 1900. "The population decline became catastrophic between 1848 and 1860. The number of Indians fell *in twenty years* from 200,000 or 250,000 to merely 25,000 or 30,000."[9]

These historical examples are strong proof that population size and growth are influenced by political and economic and cultural forces, and not only by starvation and plague. But even contemporary data show us that the rate of population growth can go down as well as up. In many poor countries—though, of course, not all—fertility has been falling (see Appendix, figure A-18). Many of the countries with the fastest-falling birthrates are small islands, which seem especially quick to respond to new conditions and currents of thought, and which may do so because they have the best communication systems, due to their high population density. But China is no island, and it supports a quarter of all humanity; yet fertility there too has apparently dropped sharply in the last decade or two.

These recent drops in fertility make it credible that countries that are now poor and have high fertility rates will sooner or later follow the pattern of the richer countries, whose mortality rate fell years ago and whose fertility rate then likewise fell. This pattern may be seen in figure 11-8, which shows the well-known "demographic transition" as it actually occurred in Sweden.

In the more-developed countries, fertility is low by anyone's standard. In figure 11-9 we see that the birthrate is now far below replacement—that is, below zero population growth—for many of the largest countries in Europe.

Let us now summarize the key facts about population growth. Population grows at various rates under various conditions. Sometimes population size shrinks for centuries due to poor political and health conditions. The doomsday myth of "standing room only" suggests a

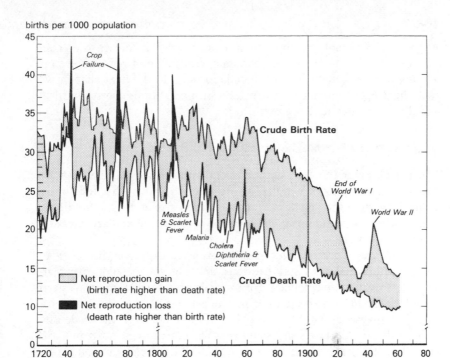

FIGURE 11-8. Birth and Death Rates in Sweden, 1720–1962

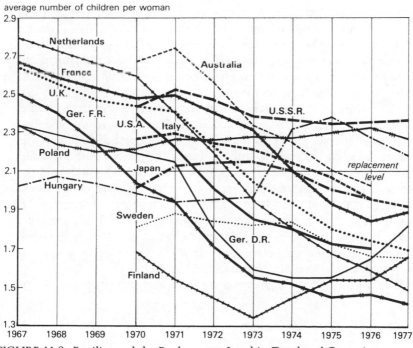

FIGURE 11-9. Fertility and the Replacement Level in Developed Countries

juggernaut inexorably bearing down upon the world, subject to no control. But the data suggest that economic, cultural, and political events, and not just catastrophe, control population size. In the next chapter we shall dig deeper to understand just *how* such conditions control fertility and the rate of population growth.

WHAT WILL THE FUTURE GROWTH RATE BE?

When looking at the demographic facts with an eye to judging what ought to be done about population, we want to know what the future holds, how great the "pressures" of population size and growth will be. This is why population forecasts are made by governmental agencies and academic researchers.

The history of demographic predictions gives us reason, however, to feel some humility and stay cautious, and not go hogwild with fear-motivated overreactive policies. For example, in the 1930s most Western countries feared an expected decline in population growth. The most extensive investigation of the "problem" was undertaken in Sweden by some of the world's best social scientists. The dotted lines in figure 11-10 show how the future looked to them then. But all of their dotted-line hypotheses about the future — intended to bracket all of the conceivable possibilities — turned out to be far below the actual course of population growth, as shown by the solid line; that is, the future turned out far better, from the point of view of those scientists, than any of them guessed it might. And had they successfully induced fertility-increasing programs, as they recommended, the results would have been contrary to what they *now* want. It may well be that we are now at an analogous point in history, except that now population growth is popularly thought to be too fast rather than too slow.

The Swedes were not alone in making inaccurate "pessimistic" forecasts. A U.S. Presidential Research Committee of eminent scientists reported to Herbert Hoover in 1933 that "we shall probably attain a population between 145 and 150 million during the present century."[10] Figure 11-11 shows a variety of forecasts made in the 1930s and 1940s by America's greatest demographic experts. For the year 2000, none of them forecast a population even as large as 200 million people; in fact, the U.S. reached 200 million people sometime around the year 1969, and is far beyond that already. A good many of the forecasters actually predicted a decline in population before the year 2000, which we now know is impossible unless there is a holocaust.

Even within the last eight years we have seen some astonishing flip-

millions of persons

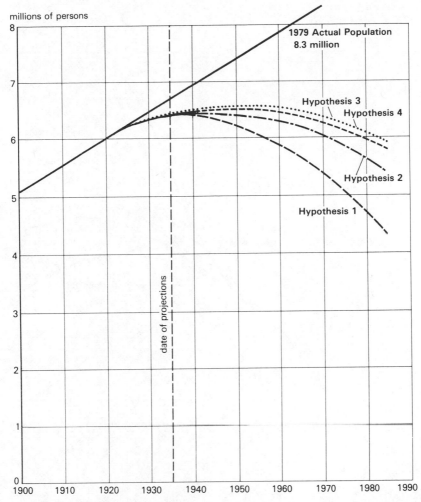

FIGURE 11-10. The Population of Sweden According to Four Hypotheses Made in 1935, and the Actual Population in 1979

flops in world population forecasts. As of 1969, the U.S. *Department of State Bulletin* forecast 7.5 billion people for the year 2000, echoing the original UN source.[11] By 1974, the figure quoted in the media was 7.2 billion.[12] By 1976, Raphael Salas, the executive director of the UN Fund for Population Activities (UNFPA) was forecasting "nearly 7 billion."[13] Soon Salas was all the way down to "at least 5.8 billion."[14] And as early as 1977, Lester Brown and the Worldwatch Institute (which the UN is

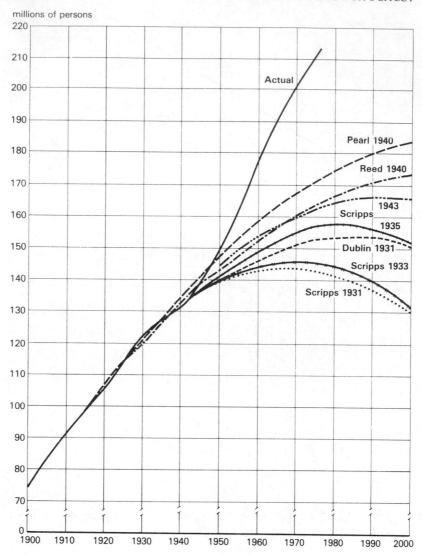

FIGURE 11-11. U.S. Population Forecasts Made 1931–43, and the Actual Population

supporting) dropped it down again, forecasting 5.4 billion people for the year 2000. This change must be astonishing to laymen — to wit, that the forecast for a date then only twenty-three years away, when a majority of the people who will then be living were already living, could be off by 2 billion people, a change of more than a third of the total current forecast. Does this example of forecasting "science" give us any reason to be impressed by population predictions?

Nor is there reason to believe that contemporary forecasting methods are better than older ones. As recently as 1972, the President's Commission on Population Growth forecast that "even if the family size drops gradually — to the two-child average — there will be no year in the next two decades in which the absolute number of births will be less than in 1970."[15] How did it turn out? In 1971 — the year *before* this forecast by the august President's Commission was transmitted to the President and then published — the absolute number of births (not the birthrate) was *already* less than in 1970. By 1975, the absolute number of births was barely higher than in 1920, and the number of white births was actually lower than in most years between 1914 and 1924 (see Appendix, figure A-15).

This episode shows once again how flimsy are the demographic forecasts upon which arguments about growth policy are based. In this case the commission did not even *backcast* correctly, let alone *forecast* well. In short, this history of population forecasts should make us think twice — or thrice — before attaching a great deal of weight to doomsday forecasts of population growth.

What population size or rate of growth does the long-run future hold in store? No one knows. One frequently hears it said that zero population growth (ZPG) "obviously" is the only viable state of affairs in the long run. But why? Why shouldn't population get *smaller* instead of staying level if it already is too large? What is sacred about the present population size, or the size that will be attained if it levels off soon? As David Wolfers puts it, the concept of ZPG is "a careless example of round number preference."[16] As to whether a larger stationary population or a larger and still growing population is plausible or desirable in the long run — the whole of Part II of this book addresses that topic.

Making forecasts of population size requires making assumptions about the fertility of future couples and also about the fertility of present couples who have begun but not finished bearing children. Such assumptions have proven wildly wrong in the past, as we have seen. Yet it is interesting to imagine the implications of assuming that childbearing patterns like those practiced at present will continue.

The trends shown in figure 11-9 contain such an implicit forecast. For example, using a sophisticated but sensible method[17] of extrapolating the partial fertility to the total fertility of women now in the childbearing ages, Colin Clark estimated the relationship of current fertility to the number of births needed for replacement, and only replacement, of the present population (that is, for ZPG). He thereby arrived at the perhaps-surprising conclusion that present fertility is far below replacement, and heading toward population decline, in the major Western countries; for example, he estimates that in 1976 the U.S. had only 81 percent of the number of births necessary for its population to remain at the present level. It must be repeated that such fertility patterns are subject to change, with a consequent change in the implied size of the future population. But this extrapolation of current fertility is at least provocative.

As to the long-run future — no one *knows* what will happen, of course. We can expect that people's incomes will rise indefinitely. But how much of that income will people feel an additional child requires? And what other activities will compete with bringing up children for parents' interest and time? These factors are likely to be the main determinants of population growth, and no one knows precisely how they will operate. We can at least say, however, that an extrapolation of the last few centuries' population growth straight upward toward infinity and doom has no warrant in the facts.

WHO WILL SUPPORT WHOM? THE DEPENDENCY BURDENS

A fast-growing population contains a large proportion of children. And children are an economic burden until they are old enough to earn their keep (just like capital investments while they are being constructed).

The difference in the child-dependency burden from one country to another can be enormous. Here are several examples: In 1955–56, 44 percent of the population of Costa Rica was younger than 15 years old, comparared with 24 percent in Sweden;[18] age-distributional differences between Mexico and Sweden in 1970 are shown in Figure 11-12; the proportions of the male population within the prime labor-force years of 15 and 64 were 70 percent in Sweden in 1940, and 53 percent in Brazil in 1900[19] (that is, there were 132 male workers in Sweden for each 100 in Brazil, relative to the total population); as of 1970, each 100 persons aged 20–59 in Mexico must support 120 persons aged 0–14, whereas in Sweden each 100 persons aged 20–59 need support only 39 persons aged 0–14.[20] Clearly, the economic effect of such differences is not trivial.

The obvious conclusion one might draw from these data is that the standard of living will be higher if the birthrate is lower. For the immediate future this is undeniable; the proposition can be demonstrated by the simplest kind of arithmetic. If income per capita is our measure of economic well-being, then we have only to divide gross national produc-

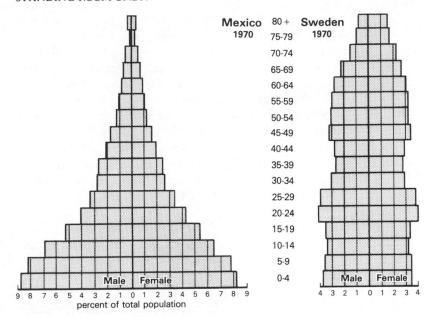

FIGURE 11-12. Age Distributions in Mexico and Sweden

tion by population (GNP/population) to calculate income per person. Adding a non-producing baby to the population immediately reduces the calculated income per capita; it is that simple.

The implications of this simple arithmetic are more complex, however. Another baby means there is less of everything to go around — for the time being. But the squeezes in schooling, feeding, and housing (the extent of which will be discussed later) may bring forth additional efforts on the part of individuals and institutions to mitigate the squeezes. Also very important in assessing the impact of an additional child is the issue of who assumes which part of the burden — the parents or the public. (Later we'll talk more about this, too.)

But the story of dependency burdens does not end here. A modern low-mortality society, with a low birthrate, supports few children. But each person in the labor force also has a great many old people to support. For example, in 1900 in the U.S., 4.1 percent of the population was over 65. But extrapolations suggest that 11.7 percent of the population will be over 65 in 2000, and 16.1 percent in the year 2050.[21]

The cost of supporting a retired person is much greater than the cost of supporting a child in the U.S. Least important in a society such as ours is the difference in food consumption. Consider: Old people may travel for twelve months a year in trailers on public roads, whereas children cannot. And old people need much more expensive health care than do children. Except for schooling, old people consume much more than do children in almost every category of expensive goods and services.

This pattern of old-age dependency is already causing perturbations in the U.S. Social Security program. In the future, the burden of Social Security payments will take up a much larger proportion of a U.S. worker's pay, and of the production of the economy as a whole, even without increases in the level of payments. In fact, the Social Security system is already in severe funding trouble as of 1980, and financing the payments is a serious economic and political problem for the federal government.

So we see that a reduction of the birthrate means that you, the working person, have fewer people who look to you now for support. But the same reduction means that there will be fewer people to support you when you get older, and you will then be a relatively greater burden on others irrespective of the saving that you do now.

This two-edged sword marks the first appearance of one of the major themes of this book: The short-run effect of a given demographic factor is often the opposite of its effect in the long run. Deciding which demographic pattern is better — faster or slower population growth — requires that you put relative values upon the long-run and short-run effects. And this, of course, requires that you decide who is to pay and who is to benefit.

SUMMARY

This chapter discussed some of the pertinent historical and contemporary facts about population growth. It showed that population growth is neither constant nor inexorable; it is not smoothly geometric, as Malthus thought it to be. And not only starvation and disease act to control population size; rather, a variety of economic, political, and social forces are also important. But this chapter did not seek to understand these forces. That is the task of the following chapter, which will show how such an understanding can help us predict what the future holds in store if we adopt one or another policy toward population growth.

12.

Do Humans Breed Like Flies?
Or Like Norwegian Rats?

"UNTRAMMELED COPULATION"

The common view of population growth—especially of population growth in poor countries—is that people breed "naturally." That is, poor people are assumed to have sexual intercourse without taking thought or doing anything about the possible consequences.

In the words of environmentalist William Vogt, whose book *Road to Survival* sold millions of copies, population growth in Asia is due to "untrammeled copulation" by Moslems, Sikhs, Hindus, and the rest of "the backward billion."[1] Biologist Karl Sax asserted that "nearly two-thirds of the world's people still rely largely on positive checks [death by starvation and disease] to control excessive growth of populations."[2] Or as Robert C. Cook, the long-time population activist and editor of *Population Bulletin*, put it more politely, "Over a billion adults in less developed countries live outside the realm of decision-making on this matter" of family size.[3] And in the words of a well-known physician in the official *Journal of the American Medical Association*, "If we breed like rabbits, in the long run we have to live and die like rabbits."[4] This idea goes hand in hand with the view that population growth will increase geometrically until starvation or famines halt it, in the ever-ascending curve shown in figure 11-1.

This view of "natural breeding," "natural fertility," and "untrammeled copulation" has been buttressed by the animal-ecology experiments that some biologists offer as analogies to human population growth. Their models include John B. Calhoun's famous Norwegian rats in a pen,[5] hypothetical flies in a bottle or germs in a bucket,[6] and meadow mice or cotton rats,[7] which will indeed keep multiplying until they die for lack of sustenance. Daniel O. Price, in *The 99th Hour*, gives a typical example of this view.

> Assume there are two germs in the bottom of a bucket, and they double in number every hour. (If the reader does not wish to assume that

it takes two germs to reproduce, he may start with one germ, one hour earlier.) If it takes one-hundred hours for the bucket to be full of germs, at what point is the bucket one-half full of germs? A moment's thought will show that after ninety-nine hours the bucket is only half full. The title of this volume is not intended to imply that the United States is half full of people but to emphasize that it is possible to have "plenty of space left" and still be precariously near the upper limit.[8]

It is interesting that a similar analogy was suggested by Benjamin Franklin two centuries ago. In Malthus's words,

> It is observed by Dr. Franklin: that there is no bound to the prolific nature of plants or animals, but what is made by their crowding and interfering with each others' means of substinence. . . . This is incontrovertibly true. . . . In plants and animals the view of the subject is simple. They are all impelled by a powerful instinct to the increase of their species; and this instinct is interrupted by no reasoning or doubts about providing for their offspring . . . the superabundant effects are repressed afterwards by want of room and nourishment . . . and among animals, by their becoming the prey of each other.[9]

Perhaps the ugliest of the biological analogies was dreamed up by Alan Gregg, the emeritus director of the Rockefeller Foundation's Medical Division: "There is an alarming parallel between the growth of a cancer in the body of an organism and the growth of human population in the earth's ecological economy."[10] Gregg then asserts that "cancerous growths demand food; but so far as I know, they have never been cured by getting it. . . . The analogies can be found in our plundered planet." And the policy implications of this analogy are quite clear. Gregg then goes on, in his paper invited by the most eminent scientific journal in the U.S., to observe "how nearly the slums of our great cities resemble the necrosis of tumors." And this "raises the whimsical query: Which is the more offensive to decency and beauty, slums or the fetid detritus of a growing tumor?"[11]

One set of demographic facts seems to confirm the view that humans will have as many children as conditions permit: After food supplies and living conditions began to improve in European countries several centuries ago, the birthrate rose. And the same effect has been observed in the poor countries in the twentieth century: "While the data are not so good as to give decisive evidence, it seems very likely that natality has risen over the past generation — certainly in the West Indies, very likely in tropical America, and probably in a number of countries of Africa and Asia."[12]

But we must recognize what Malthus came to recognize. After he published the short simplistic theory in the first edition of his *Essay on Population* and after he had the time and inclination to consider the facts as well as the theory, he concluded that human beings are very different from flies or rats. When faced with the limits of a bottle-like situation, people can alter their behavior so as to accommodate to that limit. Unlike plants and animals, people are capable of foresight and may abstain from having children from "fear of misery." That is, people can choose a level of fertility that fits the resources that will be available. And people can alter the limit — expand the "bottle" — by consciously increasing the resources available. As Malthus put it, "Impelled to the increase of his species by an equally powerful instinct, reason interrupts his career, and asks him whether he may not bring beings into the world, for whom he cannot provide the means of support."[13]

Malthus came to stress the difference between the breeding of animals and of humans, and he decisively rejected Benjamin Franklin's animal analogy: "The effects of this [preventive] check on man are more complicated. . . . The preventive check is peculiar to man, and arises from that distinctive superiority in his reasoning faculties, which enables him to calculate distant consequences."[14] Human beings are different from the animals in that we have much more capacity to alter our behavior — including our fertility — to meet the demands of our environment.

If people are to control their fertility in response to the conditions facing them, they must be capable of rational, self-conscious forethought that affects the course of sexual passion — the kind of planning capability that animals apparently do not possess. Therefore we must briefly ponder the extent to which reason and reasoning have guided the reproductive behavior of individual persons in various societies at different periods in their histories. To put the matter bluntly, we must inquire into the notion — often held by the well educated — that uneducated people in poor countries tend to breed without foresight or conscious control.

For most couples in most parts of the world, marriage precedes childbearing. It is therefore relevant to a judgment about the amount of reasoning involved in "breeding" that marriages are contracted, in most "primitive" and poor societies, only after a great deal of careful thought, especially with reference to the economic effects of the marriage. How a marriage match is made in rural Ireland shows the importance of such calculations.

The young lady's father asks the speaker what fortune do he want. He asks him the place of how many cows, sheep, and horses is it? He asks what makings of a garden are in it; is there plenty of water or spring wells? Is it far from the road, he won't take it. Backward places don't grow big fortunes. And he asks, too, is it near a chapel and the school or near town?"

The Inagh countryman could pause here; he had summarized a very long and important negotiation.

"Well," he went on, getting to the heart of the matter, "if it is a nice place, near the road, and the place of eight cows, they are sure to ask 350 fortune [pounds downy]. Then the young lady's father offers 250. Then maybe the boy's father throws off 50. If the young lad's father still has 250 on it, the speaker divides the 50 between them. So now it's 275. Then the young man says he is not willing to marry without 300 — but if she's a nice girl and a good housekeeper, he'll think of it. So there's another drink by the young man, and then another by the young lady's father, and so on with every second drink till they're near drunk. The speaker gets plenty and has a good day.[15]

An astute weighing of economic conditions is also seen to affect marriage in a Southern Italian town that was "as poor as any place in the western world."[16] The young man whose account is given lived in a family of four whose total yearly cash and computed income amounted to $482 in 1955, not much higher than the income of a peasant family in India. Edward Banfield described the courtship and marriage decision.

In 1935 I was old enough to marry. My sisters wanted me to take a wife because they had no time to do services for me.

At that time there was a law that anyone who was 25 years old and not married had to pay a "celibacy" tax of 125 lire. That amount was much, if we recall that to earn it you had to work 25 days. I thought it over and finally decided to marry.

My present wife was at that time working with relatives of my employer. Once I stopped her and asked her to marry me, and she liked the idea too, but I had to tell it before her father. He was happy to accept me, and we talked about what she had to bring as dowry and what I had to do.

He asked me to bring my mother to call so that everything would be fine. The next time I brought my mother, and we had a nice feast. When I wanted to meet my fiancee I had to ask the boss' permission.

In 1937 I asked the girl and her family to hasten the marriage before I was 25 years old. The father told me that she was not ready with the dowry. I asked him if at least we couldn't have the civil ceremony on February 6, 1938, two months late, so that I had to pay the tax for that year.

Once my mother and I went to Addo to visit my father-in-law in order to discuss and establish definitely what they were going to give us [in the dowry]. My mother wanted everything to be conveyed through a notary. My father-in-law gave us one tomolo of land and my mother gave the little house, but she reserved for herself the right to use it. Everything was written on official taxstamp paper by the notary. As soon as my wife was ready with the dowry the church marriage was set for August 25, 1938.[17]

As to reason and self-control *after* marriage, even among the most "primitive" and "backward" of people, fertility is subject to both personal and social constraints. One example is the "primitive" (as of 1936) Polynesian island of Tikopia, where "strong social conventions enforce celibacy upon some people and cause others to limit the number of their offspring,"[18] and "the motive of a married pair is the avoidance of the extra economic liability which a child brings."[19] Another example is the effect of harvests on marriages in Sweden in the eighteenth century (a backward agricultural country then, but one that happened to keep good vital statistics). When the harvest was poor, people did not marry, as figure 12-1 shows. Birthrates were also responsive to the harvest, and even unmarried procreation was affected by objective economic conditions. This is clear evidence that poor people's sexual behavior is sensibly responsive to objective circumstances.

After an extensive study of the anthropological literature, A. M. Carr-Saunders concluded, "The mechanism whereby numbers may be kept near to the desirable level is everywhere present,"[20] the particular mechanisms being "prolonged abstention from intercourse, abortion, and infanticide."[21] And as a result of a study of "data on 200 societies from all over the world . . . from tropic to arctic . . . from sea level to altitudes of more than 10,000 feet," Clellan S. Ford concluded that "both abortion and infanticide are universally known. . . . It is extremely common . . . to find a taboo on sexual intercourse during the period when the mother is nursing. . . . In nearly every instance, the justification for this abstinence is the prevention of conception."[22] He also found instances of many kinds of contraceptive practices. Some are "clearly magical." Others "are relatively effective mechanical devices [for example] inserting a pad of bark cloth or a rag in the vagina . . . [and] attempts to flush out the seminal fluid with water after intercourse. . . ."[23]

Physical evidence to confirm the anthropologists' findings that customs and norms inhibit fertility comes from actual birth statistics. In virtually no observed society (except, paradoxically, the very modern Hutterites in the U.S. and Canada, and a few other such groups) does

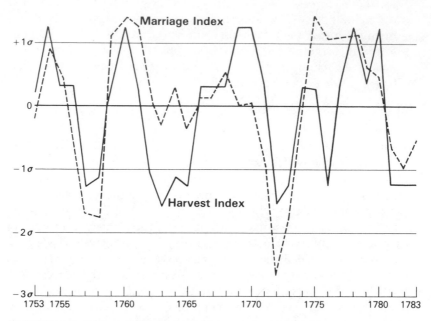

FIGURE 12-1. Harvest Index and Marriage Rates in Sweden

actual fertility approach women's fecundity (potential fertility). And in many "primitive" societies, fertility is quite low.[24]

Compare the facts with the vulgar error made by writers on this subject who have done no research or who use discredited anthropological accounts. Some say that poor people do not know how babies are made. For example, "not only are animals ignorant of the relation between mating and offspring, but even modern man until the last few thousand years was probably equally ignorant. In fact, there were recent reports of primitive tribes in Australia who are similarly unenlightened today."[25] More to be believed are such stories as the one about a "primitive" tribesman who said to a second: "Do you know what I told that white man? I told him I don't know how to make a baby. And—get this—he believed it!"

Clear evidence that poor people consider their incomes and economic circumstances when thinking about having children is found in their answers to questions about the disadvantages and advantages of large families. A variety of such surveys in various parts of Africa reveal that economic motivations are indeed important.

I could go on citing study after study. The central point is that poor peoples do indeed think about economic circumstances in relationship to fertility. They do not practice "untrammeled copulation" or "breed without limit."

People in developed countries also are accustomed to think about how family size fits their incomes.

GRENOBLE, France — a 29-year-old grade school teacher gave birth yesterday to quintuplets, three boys and two girls. . . . The children's grandfather, a tailor, said, "This certainly creates a lot of problems and you can't say it's really a joyous event because you've got to think about raising the little wolves."[26]

Lee Rainwater interviewed 409 Americans about "their family design." In representative interviews with three pairs of husbands and wives, all mentioned economic factors predominantly, though many other factors were also mentioned, of course.

Husband 1: Would [I] prefer two or four children? I guess two because you can give two more than four. You can send them to college. The average family could not give four very much. . . . Two is all we can support adequately.

Wife 1: Two, but if I had loads of money I would want loads of kids. . . . If I had lots of money, enough for fulltime help, and plenty of room I would like half-a-dozen or more.

Husband 2: I think two is ideal for the average American family based on an average income of $5,000 [1950 dollars]. I don't see how they could properly provide for more children. Personally I'd take a dozen if I could afford them. I wanted four when we got married, or as many as the family income could support.

Wife 3: I think three is ideal because I feel this is all most people are equipped to raise, to give a good education and send them through college.[27]

And in another study, a sample of U.S. wives was asked why their intended family size was not bigger. The first reason given by more than half was economic.[28]

In brief, even though income in rich countries is ample to provide a bare subsistence for many more children than the average family chooses to have, people say that their incomes constrain their family size. In all societies, rich or poor, people give much thought to sex, marriage, and childbearing. Fertility is everywhere subject to some rational control, though the degree to which achieved family sizes match the desired size varies from group to group. Couples in some countries plan their family size more carefully and are better able to carry such plans to fruition than are couples in other countries because of differences in contraceptive technology, infant mortality, and communication between husband and wife. But certainly there is strong evidence that people everywhere think rationally about fertility; and hence income and other objective forces influence fertility behavior to a significant degree, everywhere and always.

The fact that large families are often found in some poor countries does not prove the absence of rational planning in matters of fertility. Behavior that is reasonable in London or Tokyo may well be unreasonable in a Tibetan or African village. The costs of rearing children are relatively less, and the economic benefits of having children are relatively greater, in poor agricultural communities than in well-off urban places. Therefore, even though the primary motive for having children — in Nigeria as in France — surely is that couples want children for the satisfactions they give, the economic conditions may differ in such a manner that the same desire for children that sensibly implies a two- or three-child family in a city may imply a five- or six-child family in a poor rural area. The economics of child rearing depend upon the amounts of time and money that people spend on children, on the one hand, and the amounts of work that children perform and the old-age support they render after they grow up, on the other hand. It costs more time and money to rear children in urban than in rural areas, and children in rural areas of poor countries perform more work than children elsewhere.[29] Hence the larger average size of rural families reflects sound economic planning. We see this vividly in the following accounts.

BABARPUR, India, May 24, 1976 — Munshi Ram, an illiterate laborer who lives in a crude mud hut in this village 60 miles north of New Delhi, has no land and very little money. But he has eight children, and he regards them as his greatest wealth.

"It's good to have a big family," Mr. Ram explained as he stood in the shade of a leafy neem tree, in a hard dry courtyard crowded with children, chickens and a dozing cow.

"They don't cost much, and when they get old enough to work they bring in money. And when I am old, they will take care of me. . . . "

Mr. Ram, who says he is not likely to have more children, is aware that the Government is now campaigning hard with the birth-control slogan, "Stop at two." But he has no regrets.

"Children are the gods' gift," he said, as several of his own clustered around him. "Who are we to say they should not be born?"[30]

Here are two more examples, this time through the eyes of an Indian writer.

Let us take a few examples. Fakir Singh is a traditional water carrier. After he lost his job, he remained as a messenger for those Jat families which used to be his Jajmans, barely earning a subsistence living. He has eleven children, ranging in age from twenty-five to four. . . . Fakir Singh maintains that every one of his sons is an asset. The youngest one — aged five or six — collects hay for the cattle; the older ones tend to those same cattle. Between the ages of six and sixteen, they earn 150 to 200 rupees a year, plus all their meals and necessary clothing. Those sons over sixteen earn 2,000 rupees and meals every year. Fakir Singh smiles and adds: "To raise children may be difficult, but once they are older it is a sea of happiness."

Another water carrier is Thaman Singh. . . . He welcomed me inside his home, gave me a cup of tea (with milk and "market" sugar, as he proudly pointed out later), and said: "You were trying to convince me in 1960 that I shouldn't have any more sons. Now, you see, I have six sons and two daughters and I sit at home in leisure. They are grown up and they bring me money. One even works outside the village as a laborer. You told me I was a poor man and couldn't support a large family. Now, you see, because of my large family, I am a rich man."[31]

Hand in hand with the short-run reduction in fertility when times worsen in a poor country is the short-run increase in fertility that accompanies a betterment of conditions. Consider, for example, this report about an Indian village:

In the early 1950's, conditions were distinctly unfavorable. The large influx of refugees from Pakistan was accompanied by severe disruption of economic and social stability. We were repeatedly told by village leaders on the panchayat, or elected village council, that important as all of their other problems were, "the biggest problem is that there are just too many of us." By the end of the study period in 1960, a remarkable change had occurred. With the introduction of more irrigation canals and with rural electrification from the Bhakra Nangal Dam, and with better roads to transport produce to market, improved seed and other benefits of community development, and especially because there were increasing employment opportunities for Punjabi boys in the cities, a general feeling of optimism had developed. A common response of the same village leaders now was, "Why should we limit our families? India needs all the Punjabis she can get." During this transitional period an important reason for the failure of education in family planning was the favorable pace of economic development. Children were no longer a handicap.[32]

Infant mortality is another influence that uneducated villagers take into account in a very rational fashion. I asked a few men in Indian villages why they have as many or as few children as they do. A common answer came from a man with five children: "Two, maybe three, will die, and I want to have at least two that live to become adults."

Malthus's theory of population asserts that, because fertility goes up as income goes up, the extra population eats up the extra income — that is, there is a tendency for mankind to be squeezed down to a long-run equilibrium of living at bare subsistence. This is Malthus's "dismal theorem." But when we examine the facts about fertility and economic development (as Malthus himself finally did, after he dashed off his first edition) we find that the story does not end with the short-run increase in the birthrate as income begins to rise. If income continues to rise, fertility goes down.

There are two main reasons for this long-run decline in fertility. First, as income rises in poor countries, child mortality falls because of better nutrition, better sanitation, and better health care (though, in the twentieth century, mortality may decline in poor countries even without a rise in income.) As people see that fewer births are necessary to achieve a given family size, they adjust fertility downward. Evidence on the way individual families respond to the death of a child buttresses the overall historical data; several careful researchers have shown that there is a strong relationship between the death of a child and subsequent births in a family.[33] That is, couples produce additional children to "make up for" children who die. If we also consider that families decide to have additional children to allow for deaths that might occur in the future, the relationship between child mortality and fertility shows that childbearing is responsive to the family's circumstances.

The second way a rise in income reduces fertility in the long run is through a cluster of forces set in motion by increased income, including (a) increased education, which improves contraception, makes children more expensive to raise, and perhaps alters people's tastes about having children; and (b) a trend to city living, where children cost more and produce less income for the family than they do in the country.

The decline in mortality and the other forces set in motion by economic development reduce fertility in the long run. This process is the famous "demographic transition." We see it very clearly in the excellent historical data for Sweden shown in figure 11-8; notice how the death rate began to fall *before* the birthrate fell. And we can see the same relationship between income and birthrate in a cross-sectional look at various countries of the world (figure 12-2).

A few decades ago demographers were sure that the demographic transition would take place in developing countries in the twentieth century, just as it had earlier happened in Europe, North America, Japan, and elsewhere. But in the 1960s demographers began to worry that fertility would not fall in poor countries even after mortality fell. Then, in the 1970s, evidence showed that fertility is indeed falling in at least some developing countries. So by now we can be reasonably sure that the European pattern of demographic transition will also appear in other parts of the world as mortality falls and income rises.

So the props are knocked right out from under Malthus's grand theory and his dismal theorem. At the heart of Malthus's theory — I am quoting from his last edition — is the following: "(1) Population is necessarily limited by the means of subsistence. (2) Population always increases when the means of subsistence increases."[34] The history of the demographic transition disproves the second proposition. The first is shown to be false in chapters 4–6. We have seen that people respond to the two major influences on fertility — mortality and level of income — in an economically appropriate fashion. Of course, there are delays, especially in the

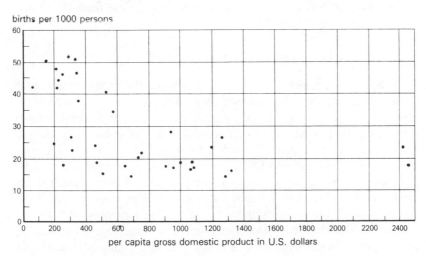

FIGURE 12-2. Per Capita Gross Domestic Product Plotted Against the Crude Birthrate for Selected Nations

response of society as a whole to changes in the cost to other people of a family's children. But overall, the fertility-adjustment system works in such a fashion that it leads to an optimistic view rather than the "dismal" view described by Malthus in the famous first edition of his book, before he changed his view in the second edition.[35]

How many children would families have if material resources presented no constraints at all? That is, what would fertility be if child mortality were extremely low — at, say, the Swedish level — and if income were very high — say, ten times the level in the U.S. now? We have little basis for predicting whether population would tend to increase, decrease, or stabilize. It is clear, however, that where the material conditions of income and child mortality are rigorous, fertility adjusts to meet those conditions, even among poor and uneducated people.

But what about the costs that big families impose on society as a whole? Certainly this is a reasonable and important question, because any child does impose some monetary and non-monetary costs on persons other than the parents. But we must also remember that a child produces some benefits for the people around her or him, in a variety of ways that we shall discuss later. In preview, the central question may be expressed quantitatively: Which are greater in various years following a child's birth, the costs or the benefits to others? Once we know whether these "external" effects are positive or negative in any given year, we must next ask, Are the external effects large or small compared with other costs and benefits in the social economy? These matters are discussed in chapters 19 and 20.

SUMMARY

At the heart of much of contemporary theorizing about population growth is the belief that, as one widely read author put it, "The Malthusian laws of population are as valid today as when they were formulated"[36] (in the first edition of his *Essay*). The core of those "laws" is that population increases faster than does the means of sustenance and continues until the standard of living has fallen to bare subsistence. This assertion is supported by analogies drawn between other forms of life and humankind. "The germs of existence contained in this earth, if they could freely develop themselves, would fill millions of worlds in the course of a few thousand years. Necessity, that imperious, all-pervading law of nature, restrains them within the prescribed bounds. The race of plants and the race of animals shrink under this great restrictive law; and men cannot by any efforts of reason escape from it."[37]

Implicit in this statement, and quite explicit in Malthus's first edition and in the writings of many writers today, is the assumption that people — or at least poor people — breed "naturally" and "without limit," due to "untrammeled copulation." But as Malthus came to accept in his subsequent editions, and as is shown with a variety of evidence in this chapter, people everywhere give much thought to marriage, sex, and procreation. The notion of "untrammeled copulation" represents either ignorance or arrogant untruth.

Income affects fertility everywhere. In poor countries, an increase in income leads in the short run to an increase in fertility. But in the longer run, in poor countries as elsewhere, a sustained increase in income leads eventually to a decrease in fertility. Decreased child mortality, increased education, and movement from country to city all contribute to this lowering of the birthrate. This process is known as the "demographic transition." Malthus's early — but still popularly accepted — theorizing does not fit the facts.

13.

Population Growth and the Stock of Capital

The amount of capital available to a worker influences his or her output and income. The education, skill, and dedication of the worker — whether at a machine or at a desk — are very important, too, and we shall discuss them shortly. But the availability of machinery, buildings, and other physical capital certainly has a strong effect on the amount of goods and services that a person can produce.

People must save some part of their income in order to build a stock of capital. Therefore, the amount we save from our present incomes influences our future incomes and consumption. And population growth and size may influence the amount of saving. How will it affect our stock of capital? There is bad news and there is good news. On balance, this chapter will not keep you from sleeping tonight, unless you have a stake in showing that population growth is bad for humanity.

SIMPLE THEORY AND DATA

Let us start with a given population of workers and a given supply of capital — a given farm acreage, a given number of factories, and a given number of machines. If the number of workers increases, then the supply of capital will be diluted; that is, if there are more workers, there is less capital available for each worker to use. If there is less capital per worker, output (and income) per worker will fall. This diluting effect is one of the main liabilities of additional population. The extent of the loss can be calculated easily: Twice as many workers with the same capital implies half as much capital per worker. In a typical modern economy this would reduce each worker's output (and hence income) by about one third.

Population growth may reduce the available capital per worker in still another way. To build and maintain a stock of capital, people must save part of their incomes. Savings can come directly from individuals and businesses, and some of the money extracted as taxes can also be saved by the government. We shall focus on individual saving, however.

A higher birthrate may reduce the rate of individual saving simply because an additional child is a burden on the family's income. This line of argument assumes that additional children induce parents to give a higher priority to immediate consumption (baby shoes now) than to later consumption (a trip around the world after retirement). Parents' "marginal utility" for money is assumed to be greater with five hungry children than with three; hence parents are assumed to spend more and save less if they have more children. The basis for this assumption is simply the psychological guess that more children mean more pleas, requests, and demands, and that this pressure shifts the parents' preferences in such a way that they spend more of their income sooner than they would otherwise. But there may also be an opposing effect. With more children, parents may forgo some luxuries in order to save for the children's future needs — for example, a college education.

This line of argument implicitly assumes that earning opportunities are fixed, so that a greater number of children cannot induce parents to go out and work more. But to assume that income is fixed, rather than variable in response to the number of children, also may be unrealistic. It is well documented that men work more if they have more children — and so do women, after their children are no longer young. The assumption of a fixed income is particularly inappropriate for subsistence agriculture. A large portion of agricultural saving — especially the clearing of new land and the construction of irrigation systems — is accomplished through the farmer's own labor, and this is usually added to the labor he expends in raising his crops. Population growth stimulates this extra labor, and hence adds to the community's stock of capital.

The effects of more children on governmental saving may also be important. It is often assumed that, in poor countries, governments have less power to tax if people have more children, because the competition in the family between feeding children and paying taxes is then more acute. We can also reason in the opposite direction, however. If there are more children, governments may be able to extract more in taxes, because people recognize a greater need for taxes to buy additional schools and other facilities. The number of children may also affect the kinds of investments that governments make. For example, an increase in children may induce a government to invest more, but much of this might be in housing and other "demographic" investment at the expense of the sort of capital investment that will immediately increase the production of goods.

The statistical evidence about the effect of population growth upon the savings rate is as mixed and inconclusive as the theorizing. Taken

together, the data suggest that a population increase may slightly reduce
the formation of industrial capital, but that this is probably not an important effect.

The efficiency of capital, as well as the quantity, is also important.
And there has recently developed a strong body of evidence showing that
capital is used more efficiently in larger communities. For example, less
capital is needed for a given amount of productivity per person in larger
cities.[1] This jibes with the fact that wages are higher in bigger cities, as
a recent survey of various countries showed.[2] Further, interest rates are
lower in bigger cities, which implies that capital is cheaper.[3] In sum, the
evidence suggests that one can get more output from a given capital
investment where there are more people.

When we think about the effect of additional children on the supply
of capital, it is crucial that we remember farm capital and social-overhead
capital as well as industrial capital. In chapter 16 we shall see that the
supply of farm capital — especially arable land — increases when population increases, because people respond to the demand for additional food
with increased investment, much of which is additional labor to clear
trees and stones, dig ditches, and build barns.

The effect of additional persons on the supply of capital is most
marked with respect to social-overhead capital such as roads, which are
crucial for the economic development of all countries and especially poor
countries. Here the effect of population is sharply positive, especially in
less-developed countries.

The Transportation Connection

If there is a single key to economic development, other than culture and
institutions and psychological makeup, that key is the transportation and
communication system. Transportation obviously includes roads and
railways and airlines, which carry agricultural and industrial products as
well as persons and messages. It also includes irrigation and electrical
systems, which transport water and power. There is abundant testimony
by the best students of contemporary and historical economic development that "the one sure generalization about the underdeveloped countries is that investment in transport and communications is a vital
factor."[4]

There are many reasons why transportation is so important in economic development. The increased ability of farmers and businesses to
sell in organized markets, and to deliver and obtain delivery at reasonable

cost, is fundamental to a developing economy. A comparison of the costs of transportation by various methods explains why. Canal transportation cost only 25–50 percent as much as land transportation between cities in England about 1790.[5] And carrying loads on human backs averages seventeen times as expensive as by ship or train.[6] Such cost differences have a great effect on the amounts of merchandise transported, and on prices at various distances from the producer.

A poor transportation system presents an enormous barrier to development. In the early nineteenth-century U.S., for example, farm products could be transported only where there were natural waterways. As for overland transport, "the cost . . . was so high that even if corn had cost nothing to produce, it could not have been marketed twenty miles from where it was grown. It was cheaper to move a ton of iron across the Atlantic than to carry it ten miles through Pennsylvania." But the Erie Canal reduced freight rates from New York City to the Great Lakes from $100 to $15 per ton.[7] Similarly, in eighteenth-century France, "food would not normally be transported more than 15 kilometers from its place of origin."[8] Such inability to transport food from farms to large markets resulted in a large difference between at-the-farm prices and market prices and was responsible for frequent local famines even when food was plentiful a short distance away. My 1977 book gives a variety of other historical and contemporary examples of how improved transportation systems have stimulated agriculture and improved the efficiency of industry in various countries.

Transportation is also important in the flow of information — technical agricultural know-how, birth control, health services, modernizing ideas, and so forth. It makes an enormous difference if a particular village in India can be reached with a truck, or even a jeep or a bicycle, rather than just by a bullock, with which a trip to the big city is out of the question. Most villages in countries like India and Iran cannot easily be reached by motor transportation. When transportation is improved, radical changes will occur.

There is great room for improvement in transportation systems, especially local rural transportation, in poor countries. This may be seen by a comparison of countries with well-developed agriculture with countries where agriculture is less developed.

In agriculturally advanced Western countries, there are from 3 to 4 miles of farm to market roads per square mile of cultivated land. . . . In India there is only about 0.7 of a mile of road per square mile of cultivated land. In Malaya it is about 0.8 mile and in the Philippines about 1 mile. None of the developing countries that are dependent on agriculture has sufficient rural access roads.[9]

And in industrial areas, too, the low transportation and communication costs in larger cities lead to their higher productivity compared with smaller cities.[10]

THE EFFECT OF POPULATION ON TRANSPORTATION SYSTEMS

There is an intimate connection between population density and the system of transporting goods, people, and information. It works in both directions. On the one hand, a dense population makes a good transportation system both more necessary and more economical. Having twice as many people in a village implies that twice as many people will use a wagon path if it is built, and that twice as many hands can contribute to building the path. This is what happened on the Continent and in England, where "the growth of population made it worthwhile to improve and create transport facilities."[11] On the other hand, a better transportation system brings an increased population,[12] and probably leads first to higher birthrates because of a higher standard of living. (But later the birthrates drop, as we have seen in chapter 12.) Furthermore, good transportation connections are likely to reduce a village's death rate, because the village is less vulnerable to famine.

The opposite condition, population sparsity, makes traveling slow and difficult. This is how it was near Springfield, Illinois, when Abraham Lincoln was a lawyer "riding the circuit" of courts.

> ... Traveling was a real hardship—so real that the words of old lawyers, describing early days, become fresh and vivid when the circuit is the subject. "Between Fancy Creek and Postville, near Lincoln," wrote James C. Conkling, "there were only two or three houses. Beyond Postville, for thirteen miles was a stretch of unbroken prairie, flat and wet, covered with gopher hills, and apparently incapable of being cultivated for generations. For fifteen or eighteen miles this side of Carlinville, the country was of a similar character, without a house or improvement along the road. For about eighteen miles between South Fork and Shelbyville, there was only one clearing. I have travelled between Decatur and Shelbyville from nine o'clock in the morning until after dark over a country covered with water, from recent rains, without finding a house for shelter or refreshment."[13]

Donald Glover and I made a cross-national study of the relationship between road density and population density, and we found that relationship to be very strong.[14] Population growth clearly leads to an improved transportation system, which in turn stimulates economic development and further population growth. (Now, I realize that this unexciting but important statistical finding cannot match the dramatic appeal of the photographs that are frequently shown by those who urge that population growth is an unmitigated evil. A picture of an emaciated, starving child is surely tragic and compelling, but it conveys no verifiable information as to why that child is suffering — as likely for the lack of a good road as for any other reason. The statistical fact is less exciting, but it reveals an irrefutable story — the enormous social benefits of population growth. Yet it is the picture of the emaciated child that appears in the popular press and remains in people's minds.)

Population density brings a similar increase in the efficiency of communications, easily seen in a comparison of cities of very different sizes. For the same price to the reader, the daily newspaper is much larger, and supplies much more information, in a big city like Chicago than in smaller Illinois cities like Champaign-Urbana. There are generally more radio and television programs available to people in larger cities. And the price charged an advertiser — whether a department store or an individual seeking employment — is much lower per 1,000 readers reached in a large city than in a small city, a clear benefit of a larger population (see Appendix, figure A-22).

SUMMARY

Population growth is responsible for great improvements in the social infrastructure, especially in transportation and communications, which are crucial to economic development. It also gives a boost to agricultural saving. Population growth also may reduce non-agricultural saving, but this is a matter of scientific controversy. For readers who wish more detail, chapters 2, 3, 10, 11, and 12 in my technical book cover the effects of population growth on capital.

AFTERNOTE

A Parable of Population Growth, Racquetball, and Squash

There are twenty-three wonderful handball-racquetball courts on the Urbana campus of the University of Illinois, and seven excellent squash courts, in addition to a batch of old courts. The new racquetball courts are frequently crowded nowadays, though not so badly that people complain a lot. From time to time, however, players worry about the future growth of the university, saying that it is going to be tough to get a racquetball court. And I have heard people argue against increasing the number of students for that reason.

The racquetball court situation exemplifies the country's situation with respect to population growth and the supply of capital. If there come to be more people there will immediately be an increased demand for the courts. It will also be harder to find parking space, and perhaps a job. That is, the immediate effect of an increase in population is an increase in congestion. The individual suffers because of the greater competition for the good things that are available and because of the greater out-of-pocket costs of providing more of these good things to take care of the added population. This increase in costs is inevitable and undeniable.

But now let us take a slightly longer view. Why are we so lucky as to have twenty-three wonderful racquetball courts and seven squash courts at the University of Illinois? Years ago there were sixteen dingy, wrong-sized courts to be used for both sports together. But then came a rapid population growth at the university. Our superb new facilities were built in response to that population growth—though at a considerable cost to the taxpayers and students at that time.

So we are now reaping the benefits of the rapid population growth in the past and at the same time talking against further population growth so that we do not have to share this stock of capital—the benefits of past population growth—with more people, and so that we do not have to cough up the investment necessary for additional population growth. There is nothing illogical about this point of view. As the sage Hillel put it, "If I am not for myself, who will be for me?" But if we see ourselves as part of a longer historical process than this instant of our own consciousness, and if we take into account the welfare of ourselves and our children in the years to come—as people before us took *our* welfare into account—then we will see that we ought to cooperate and put back as well as take from the pot. As Hillel added, "But if I am for myself alone, what am I?"

Our children may well have more racquetball courts in the future — and better ones — if more children are born year after year than if fewer are born. That is, if the population does grow at the university, more courts and better courts will be built, whereas if the population stabilizes at its present size, no more facilities will be built.

More generally, if farmers had not come to Illinois and developed the land and built up the state so that it could support a university, there would certainly be no racquetball courts at all for us to enjoy now. Central Illinois, with its remarkably productive cornfields, would still be a malarial and unproductive swamp.

Let's consider the squash courts too. I can get into a squash court at any time of the day, except very occasionally at 5:00 in the afternoon, when there are one or two courts too few for all those who would like to play. Most of the day the squash courts are used hardly at all. From one point of view, this is paradise for squash players like me. On the other hand, there are often too few people to play with. Furthermore, there is a slightly depressing air about the squash courts. It seems a bit like a home for the aged, because most of the players are thirty-five and up except for those who have come from England or South Africa. Few young students or faculty members have taken up the game, which is why there is no problem in getting a court. In contrast, there is a vitality around the racquetball courts. There are always people watching and giving advice and jostling a bit and checking out the challenge court to see the newest rising star. The racquetball courts have produced some national-level competitors in a short time. Around the squash courts it is all very dignified and peaceful.[1] But as I said, it is also a bit depressing.

What about the future? If the population of the university grows, there is a good chance that we shall still have plenty of squash courts fifteen years from now — except that the players will be doddering incompetents. And by that time the squash courts will be in rundown condition, whereas chances are that there will be a whole new battery of racquetball courts. The run-down squash courts (and players) will be the cost of having no growth in the population of squash players.

So which do you want? Will you choose the genteel, run-down, peaceful, and slightly depressing no-growth policy, as with the squash courts? Or do you prefer the less-peaceful, slightly jostling population growth that costs you capital for awhile, as with the racquetball courts?

14.

Population's Effects on Technology, Productivity, and Education

It is your mind that matters economically, as much or more than your mouth or hands. In the long run, the most important economic effect of population size and growth is the contribution of additional people to our stock of useful knowledge. And this contribution is large enough in the long run to overcome all the costs of population growth. This is a strong statement, but the evidence for it seems very strong.

Let us begin with a question: Why is the standard of living so much higher in the U.S. or Sweden than in India or Mali? And why is the standard of living so much higher in the U.S. or Sweden now than it was 200 years ago? The proximate cause is that the average worker in the U.S. or Sweden now produces X times as much goods and services per day as does the average worker in India or Mali, or as did the average worker in the U.S. or Sweden 200 years ago, where X is the ratio of the standard of living now in the U.S. or Sweden to the standard in India or Mali now or in the U.S. or Sweden then.

Though the answer is almost definitional,[1] it points us to the important next question: Just why does the average worker in Sweden now produce so much more? Part of the answer is that he or she has available a much larger and better supply of capital equipment to work with — more buildings and tools, and more efficient transportation. But that is only a minor factor; as proof, notice how fast West Germany and Japan were able to regain a high standard of living even after much of their capital was destroyed in World War II. (They had some help from the U.S., however, and the benefit of being restrained from spending on the military.)

Part of the difference between then and now (and between rich and poor countries) is due to economies of scale — the straightforward advantages of industry and market size — which we shall consider in the latter part of this chapter. But the most important difference is that there is a much greater stock of technological know-how available now, which people are educated to learn and use. The technology and the schooling are intertwined; in India now, unlike the U.S. 200 years ago, the knowledge is available in books in the library, but without schooling it cannot be adapted to local needs and put to work. The stock of industrial capital is also intertwined with knowledge and with education; the value of many of our capital goods such as computers and jet airplanes consists largely of the new knowledge that is built into them. And without educated workers, these chunks of capital could not be operated and hence would be worthless.

The importance of technological knowledge has clearly emerged in two famous studies, one by Robert Solow (1957) and the other by Edward F. Denison (1962). Using different methods, each calculated the extent to which the growth of physical capital and of the labor force could account for economic growth in the U.S. (Solow and Denison) and Europe (Denison). Both found that even after capital and labor are allowed for, much of the economic growth — the "residual" — cannot reasonably be explained by any factor other than an improvement in the level of technological practice (including improved organizational methods). Economies of scale due to larger factory size do not appear to be very important in this context, though in larger and faster-growing industries the level of technology improves more rapidly than in smaller and slower-growing ones (more about this shortly). Of course, this improvement in productivity does not come for free; much of it is bought with investments in research and development (R & D). But that does not alter the importance of the gains in technological knowledge.

How do population size and growth come into the picture? It is a simple fact that the source of improvements in productivity is the human mind, and a human mind is seldom found apart from a human body. And because improvements — their invention and their adoption — come from people, it seems reasonable to assume that the amount of improvement depends on the number of people available to use their minds.

This is an old idea, going back at least as far as William Petty in 1682.

> As for the Arts of Delight and Ornament, they are best promoted by the greatest number of emulators. And it is more likely that one ingenious curious man may rather be found among 4 million than 400 persons. . . . And for the progagation and improvement of useful learning, the same may be said concerning it as above-said concerning . . . the Arts of Delight and Ornaments. . . . [2]

More recently, this benefit of population size has been urged upon us by Simon Kuznets.[3]

In contrast, many of the doomsday writers completely omit from consideration the possibility that, all else equal, more people implies more knowledge and greater productivity. For example: "It is difficult to see how any further growth in world population could enhance the quality of human existence. On the other hand, one can readily envisage ways in which further population increments will diminish our well-being."[4]

It cannot be emphasized too strongly that "technological advance" does not only mean "science," and scientific geniuses are just one part of the knowledge process. Much technological advance comes from people who are neither well educated nor well paid — the dispatcher who develops a slightly better way of deploying the taxis in his ten-taxi fleet, the shipper who discovers that garbage cans make excellent cheap containers, the supermarket manager who finds a way to display more merchandise in a given space, the supermarket clerk who finds a quicker way to stamp prices on cans, the market researcher in the supermarket chain who experiments and finds more efficient and cheaper means of advertising the store's prices and sale items, and so on.

Here is an example, from our local paper, of inventions coming from "ordinary" people.

BETTER IDEA RESULTS IN DRYWALL INSTALLER

Two area men have combined their respective good ideas to come up with a better idea.

William Vircks of Villa Grove and Harold Propst of 2802 E. California Ave., U, have developed an electric motor-driven drywall installer called "Board Ease."

Vircks received the original patent on the machine in 1969, but the model was hand-cranked, not motorized. He said the original machine, which was designed to lift the drywall or ceiling material up and hold it there, was built by his father.

Vircks said his father built the first model, but it "stood for years in the corner" until he began tinkering with it.

He sold about 100 machines throughout the Midwest, and one of the buyers was Propst, a professional drywaller.

Propst bought the machine several years ago and developed the motor and electric controls for his own machine.

The two men got together last spring through a mutual friend and combined their ideas, and they now hope to market the machine through a national company.

Vircks, who works at Tuscola's USI plant, says he's been working on the machine for 12 to 13 years and hopes he'll soon be getting a return on his investment.[5]

The lack of additional producers of knowledge, and of their potential contribution to resources and the economy, also is manifest. Nobel prize winner Hans Bethe tells us that the future cost and availability of nuclear power—and hence the cost and availability of energy gener-ally—would be a rosier prospect if the population of scientific workers were larger. Talking specifically about nuclear fusion, Bethe said, "Money is not the limiting factor. . . . Progress is limited rather by the availability of highly trained workers."[6]

Students of organizational behavior also tell us that, all else being equal, the larger an organization's resources in numbers of people and amounts of money, the more innovations it will come up with. "If any one group of variables may be said to stand out among all others as empirically determined correlates of innovation, it is the group of inter-related factors indicating size, wealth, or the availability of resources." A variety of investigators "all conclude that organizational size and wealth are among the strongest predictors of innovation in the sense of readiness to adopt new patterns of behavior."[7]

And even a casual inspection of the historical record shows that there have been many more discoveries and a faster rate of productivity growth in the past century, say, than in previous centuries, when there were fewer people alive. True, 10,000 years ago there wasn't much knowledge to build new ideas upon. But seen differently, it should have been all the easier 10,000 years ago to find important improvements, because so much still lay undiscovered. Progress surely was agonizingly slow in prehis-tory, however; for example, whereas we develop new materials (metal and plastic) almost every day, it was centuries or millennia between the discovery and use of, say, copper and iron. It makes sense that if there had been a larger population in earlier times, the pace of increase in tech-nological practice would have been faster.

Population growth spurs the *adoption* of existing technology as well as the invention of new technology. This has been well documented in agriculture,[8] where people turn to successively more "advanced" but more laborious methods of getting food as population density increases—methods that were previously known but that were not used because they were not needed earlier. This scheme well describes the passage from hunting and gathering—which we now know requires extraordi-narily few hours of work a week to provide a full diet—to migratory slash-and-burn agriculture, and thence to settled long-fallow agriculture, to short-fallow agriculture, and eventually to the use of fertilizer, irri-gation, and multiple cropping. Though each stage initially requires more labor than the previous one, the endpoint is a more efficient and produc-

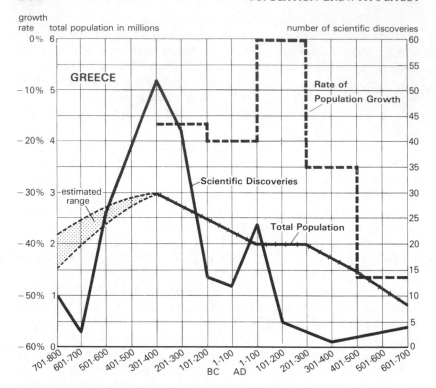

FIGURE 14-1a. Population and Scientific Discoveries in Ancient Greece

tive system that requires much less labor, as we see in chapters 4 and 16.

This phenomenon also throws light on why the advance of civilization is not a "race" between technology and population advancing independently of each other. Contrary to the Malthusian view, there is no immediate linkage between each food-increasing invention and increased production of food. Some inventions — the "invention-pull" type, such as a better calendar — may be adopted as soon as they are proven successful, because they will increase production with no more labor (or will enable less labor to produce the same amount of food). But other inventions — the "population push" type, such as settled agriculture or irrigated multicropping — require more labor, and hence will not be adopted until demand from additional population warrants the adoption.[9] The Malthusian invention-pull innovation is indeed in a sort of race between population and technology. But the adoption of the popu-

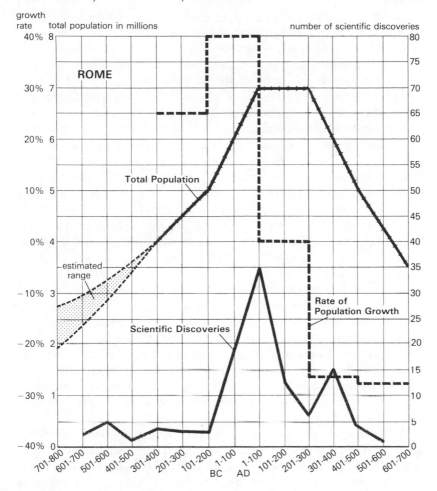

FIGURE 14-1b. Population and Scientific Discoveries in Ancient Rome

lation-push inventions is not in a race at all; rather, it is the sort of process discussed at length in the chapters on natural resources.

If a larger labor force causes a faster rate of productivity increase, one would expect to find that productivity has advanced faster and faster as population has grown. Ancient Greece and Rome have been offered as counter-examples to this line of reasoning. Therefore I plotted the numbers of great discoveries, as recorded by historians of science who have made such lists, against population size in various centuries. Figure 14-1 shows that population growth or size, or both, were associated with an increase in scientific activity, and population decline with a decrease. (Of course other factors come to bear, too, and I am exploring the matter in more detail for the whole history of Europe.)

As for the contemporary scene and better data, Solow concludes that the yearly rate of increase of productivity doubled, from 1 to 2 percent, between the periods 1909–29 and 1929–49;[10] and the populations and labor forces of the U.S. and of the developed world were larger in the latter period than in the earlier period. William Fellner found these rates of productivity increase (using two methods of calculation): *1900–29* – 1.8 (or 1.5) percent; *1929–48* – 2.3 (or 2.0) percent; *1948–66* – 2.8 percent.[11] These results are consistent with the assumption that productivity indeed increases faster when population is larger — though of course other factors could explain part of the acceleration[12]

Here an important caution is needed: Because of the economic inter-relatedness of all modern countries, we should think about the population and productivity growth of the developed world — or indeed of the world as a whole — rather than think about any particular country. One country can, to some extent, ride on the coattails of the developed world as a whole, but this is less likely than is often thought, because local research and development is needed to adapt international knowledge to local conditions. For example, high-yielding seeds cannot simply be imported and planted successfully without extensive adaptation to the local sunlight angle, temperature, water and soil conditions, and so on. So, though our data refers to individual countries, or to cross-sections of countries, the unit to which our discussion applies best is the developed world as a whole.

But is it certain that the recent acceleration of productivity would *not* have occurred if population had been smaller? The connections between numbers of scientists, inventors and ideas, and the adoption and use of new discoveries are difficult to delineate clearly. But the links needed to confirm this effect seem very obvious and strong. For example, the data show clearly that the bigger the population of a country, the greater the number of scientists and the larger the amount of scientific knowledge produced; more specifically, scientific output is proportional to population size, in countries at the same level of income.[13] The U.S. is much larger than Sweden, and it produces much more scientific knowledge. Sweden benefits from the larger U.S. population because it "imports" much more knowledge from the U.S. than the U.S. imports from Sweden; this can be seen in the references used in Swedish and U.S. scientific writings, and in the number of patented processes licensed from each other.

Then why aren't populous China and India the most advanced countries of all? Quite obviously, China and India do not produce as much new knowledge as the U.S. or the U.S.S.R. because China and India are relatively poor, and hence they are able to educate relatively fewer people. But it is instructive that despite its poverty, India has one of the largest scientific communities in the world, just because it has such a large population. Put differently, would you bet on Sweden or Holland, against Great Britain and the U.S.S.R., to produce the great discoveries that will make nuclear fusion practical? (I have omitted the U.S. from this bet because of its higher per capita income than Britain or the U.S.S.R.).

Additional evidence that more people mean a faster rate of technological advance comes from comparisons of productivity gains in various industries. This evidence is quite compelling, in my judgment. A given industry grows faster in some countries than in other countries, or than other industries in the same country. Comparisons of faster-growing and slower-growing industries show that, in the faster-growing industries, the rate of increase of productivity and technological practice is highest. This indicates that faster population growth — which causes faster-growing industries — leads to faster growth of productivity. We shall examine this in more detail in the next section. But once more the caution: Our subject is the effect of population upon productivity increase in the developed world as a whole. The discussion of particular countries is only a device to increase the size of the sample.

ECONOMIES OF SCALE: THE THEORY

The phenomenon called "economies of scale" — the greater efficiency of larger-scale production — stems from (1) the ability to use larger and more efficient machinery, (2) the greater division of labor in situations where the market is larger, (3) knowledge creation and technological change, and (4) improved transportation and communication. We shall take up each of these factors briefly, then in more detail. Please keep in mind as we proceed that there is no easy and neat distinction between increases in productivity due to increased knowledge and increases in productivity due to economies of scale. They are interdependent, and both are accelerated by population growth.

(1) A bigger population implies a bigger market, all else equal. A bigger market promotes bigger manufacturing plants that likely are more efficient than smaller ones, as well as longer production runs and hence lower setup costs per unit of output.

(2) A larger market also makes possible a greater division of labor and hence an increase in the skill with which goods and services are made. Adam Smith emphasized the importance of the division of labor and used the example of pinmaking; his predecessor William Petty made the same point when talking of the advantages of a large city like London over a small city, and he used a more vivid example than did Smith:

> ... the Gain which is made by *Manufactures*, will be greater, as the Manufacture it self is greater and better ... cach *Manufacture* will be divided into as many parts as possible, whereby the Work of each *Artisan* will be simple and easie; As for Example. In the making of a *Watch*, If one Man shall make the *Wheels*, another the *Spring*, another shall Engrave the *Dial-plate*, and another shall make the *Cases*, then the *Watch* will be better and cheaper, than if the whole Work be put upon any one Man. And we also see that in *Towns*, and in the *Streets* of a great *Town*, where all the *Inhabitants* are almost of one Trade, the Commodity peculiar to those places is made better and cheaper than elsewhere. . . . [14]

Specialization can also occur with respect to machinery. If the market for its goods is small, a firm will buy multipurpose machines that can be used in the production of several kinds of products. If its market is larger, the firm can afford to buy more efficient specialized machines for each operation.

Larger markets also support a wider variety of services. If population is too small, there may be too few people to constitute a profitable market for a given product or service. In such a case there will be no seller, and people who need the product or service will suffer by not being able to obtain it.

Increased population must be accompanied by an increase in total income for there to be a bigger market, and more babies do not automatically mean a bigger total income, especially in the short run. But under almost any reasonable set of assumptions, when the increment of population reaches the age at which it begins to work, total income and total demand will be larger than before.

(3) Economies of scale also stem from learning. The more television sets or bridges or airplanes that a group of people produces, the more chances they have to improve their skills with "learning by doing"—a very important factor in increasing productivity, as many studies show. The bigger the population, the more of everything that is produced, which promotes learning by doing.

(4) A bigger population makes profitable many major social investments that would not otherwise be profitable — for example, railroads, irrigation systems, and ports. The amount of such construction often depends upon the population density per given land area, as is discussed in chapter 13 on population and capital. For example, if an Australian farmer were to clear a piece of land very far from the nearest neighboring farm, he might have no way to ship his produce to market and will have difficulty in obtaining labor and supplies. But when more farms are established nearby, roads will be built that will link him with markets and supplies. Such reasoning lay behind Australia's desire for more immigrants and a larger population; this was also the case for the American West in the last century. Public services such as fire protection are other social activities that can often be carried on at lower cost per person when the population is larger.

There may also be diseconomies of increased scale, however, such as congestion. As the number of sellers and activity in, say, a city's wholesale fruit-and-vegetable market increases, transacting one's business may become more difficult because of crowding and confusion. Each additional person imposes some costs on other people by decreasing the space in which the other person can move around and by inflicting his pollution (soot, noise) on other people. Therefore, the more people there are, the less space each person has and the more pollution each suffers from, all else equal. These effects would be felt both in a decreased ease and joy of living and in higher prices due to the higher costs of production caused by congestion. This sort of diseconomy is very much like the concept of diminishing returns from a given acre of land that is at the heart of Malthusian reasoning. It ultimately must occur as long as there is some factor of production that remains fixed in size, be it land for the farmer or the market area for the wholesaler. But if that factor can be increased rather than remaining fixed — by building a bigger market or by bringing new land into cultivation — then the diseconomies of scale, especially congestion, can be avoided or reduced.

ECONOMIES OF SCALE: THE STATISTICAL EVIDENCE

Because there are a variety of forces associated with economic scale that affect activity in opposite directions, and because these factors cannot readily be studied separately, we shall here look at the overall net effect of greater population and larger markets upon productivity and technological change.

Let's begin with an estimate of the overall effects of population size on productivity in less-developed countries (LDCs). Hollis B. Chenery compared the manufacturing sectors in a variety of countries and found that, all else being equal, if one country is twice as populous as another, output per worker is 20 percent larger. This is a very large positive effect of population size no matter how you look at it.

Now let us move from the national level down to the industry level, and let us shift from LDCs to more-developed countries (MDCs) because most of the available information pertains to MDCs.

In every industry, there is some minimum size of factory that must be attained to reach a reasonable operating efficiency. But though this is the sort of economy of scale that has been most studied in the past (because of its industrial applications), it is not the economy of scale that is most relevant to population questions.

More relevant are studies of industries as wholes. As mentioned above, it is an important and well-established phenomenon that the faster an industry grows, the faster its efficiency increases — even compared with the same industry in other countries. The most recent and complete analysis is shown in figure 14-2. There we see comparisons of the productivity of U.S. industries in 1950 and 1963, and of U.K. industries in 1963, with U.K. industries in 1950 — and also comparisons of U.S. industries in 1963 with those of Canada in the same year. The larger the industry relative to the U.K. or Canada base, the higher its productivity. This effect is very large: Productivity goes up roughly with the square root of output. That is, if you quadruple the size of an industry, you may expect to double the output per worker and per unit of capital employed.[15]

The effect Chenery saw in economies as wholes, together with the effects seen in individual industries, are strong evidence that a larger and faster-growing population produces a greater rate of increase in economic efficiency.

The phenomenon called learning by doing[16] is surely a key factor in the improvement of productivity in particular industries and in the economy as a whole. The idea is a simple one: The more units produced in a plant or an industry, the more efficiently they are produced, as people learn and develop better methods. Industrial engineers have understood learning by doing for many decades, but economists first grasped its importance for the production of airplanes in World War II, when it was referred to as the "80 percent curve": A doubling in the cumulative production of a particular airplane led to a 20 percent reduction in labor per plane. That is, if the first airplane required 1,000 units of labor, the second would require 80 percent of 1,000 or 800 units, the fourth would

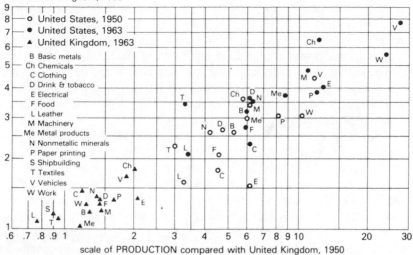

scale of PRODUCTIVITY compared
with United Kingdom, 1950

FIGURE 14-2a. The Effect of Industrial Scale upon Productivity, U.S. vs. U.K.

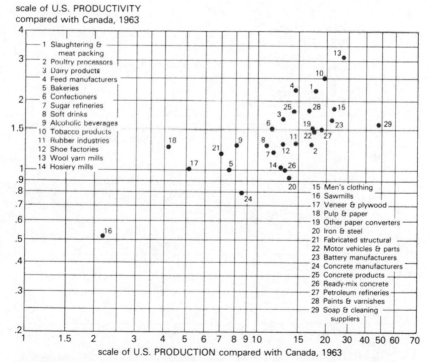

scale of U.S. PRODUCTIVITY
compared with Canada, 1963

FIGURE 14-2b. The Effect of Industrial Scale upon Productivity, Canada vs. the
U.S.

require 80 percent of 800, or 640 units, and so on, though after some time the rate of learning probably slows up. Similar "progress ratios" have been found for lathes, machine tools, textile machines, and ships. The economic importance of learning by doing clearly is great.

The effect of learning by doing can also be seen in the progressive reduction in price of new consumer devices in the years following their introduction to the market. The examples of room air conditioners and color television sets are shown in figure 14-3.

The studies discussed above automatically subtract any costs of congestion from the positive effects of scale. But it should be interesting to many readers to see how large congestion costs are by themselves. If there really are important congestion problems in bigger cities, for example, one would expect them to be reflected in the cost-of-living data for cities of different sizes. But no strong relationship between size of city and cost of living is apparent. More detailed statistical studies of this evidence reveal that at most there is a tiny effect: The largest estimate is

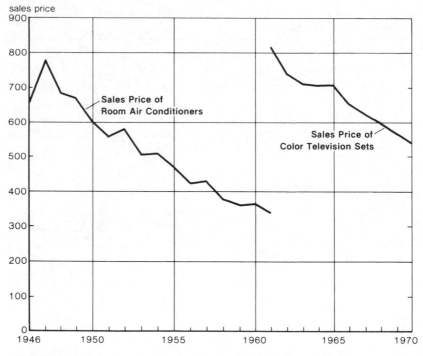

FIGURE 14-3. Sales Prices of Room Air Conditioners and Color Television Sets

a 1 percent increase in the cost of living for each additional million people, for people living on a high budget; other estimates range downward
to no effect at all.[17] (See Appendix, figure A-21.)

A study of the relationship of city size to the prices of over 200 individual goods and services found that although more prices go up with
increasing city size than go down, for almost every good or service workers are more productive in the larger cities after the higher wage in bigger cities is allowed for. And the higher incomes in larger cities more
than make up for the higher prices, so that the overall purchasing power
of a person's labor is greater in the bigger cities.[18] This suggests that the
disadvantages of congestion are less than the positive effects of greater
population, including better communications and more competition, on
the standard of living in larger cities.

QUANTITY AND QUALITY OF EDUCATION

A reduction in the quality or amount of education that children receive
is another possible negative effect of population growth upon the growth
of knowledge. Human capital as well as physical capital is crucial in the
productivity of an economy. And people might not wish to provide (or
authorities might not demand) enough additional tax revenues to maintain an equivalent level of schooling in the face of population growth. If
so, a larger population, with its larger proportion of children, might lead
to less education on the average, and thus less potential to increase the
stock of knowledge, than a smaller population.

The conventional theory of population growth's effect upon the
amount of education per child is straightforward Malthus: A fixed educational budget of money and resources divided among more students
implies less education per student. But as we know from a host of evidence, people and institutions often respond to population growth by
altering the apparently fixed conditions. In agricultural countries, for
example, having more children causes parents to increase their labor on
the land. And in industrial countries, when there are additional profitable opportunities for investment, people will shift some resources from
consumption to investment; additional children constitute such an
opportunity. Therefore, we must allow for responses contrary to the simple Malthusian pie-sharing theory.

There is no way of knowing from theory alone which of the two
effects—dilution of resources or increase of work—will dominate.
Therefore we must turn to empirical data. A comparison of rates of pop-

ulation growth in LDCs with the amounts of education given to children shows that an increase in the birthrate reduces educational expenditures per child and secondary enrollment, but not primary or postsecondary enrollment.[19] Perhaps the most meaningful result of that study is that the negative effect is nowhere near as great as the simple Malthusian theory would suggest, and in general the effect does not seem to be large.

This chapter has discussed children as if they are a homogeneous lot, making equal contributions to society. The reader may wonder, however, whether some classes of children, particularly the poor, may be a drain upon the economy even if most children make a positive contribution. There seems to be no evidence for this view, however.[20]

SUMMARY

A larger population implies a larger amount of knowledge being created, all else being equal. This is the straightforward result of there being more people to have new ideas. The data on scientific productivity compared across countries bear out this obvious proposition.

A larger population also achieves economies of scale: A larger population implies a larger total demand for goods; with larger demand and higher production come division of labor and specialization, larger plants, larger industries, more learning by doing, and other related economies of scale. Congestion is a cost of this greater efficiency, but it does not seem to present a dominating difficulty in this context.

Population growth may reduce the amount of education that children receive, but the effect is not nearly as great as simple Malthusian reasoning suggests, and not great enough to have much effect on the economy.

Babies don't create knowledge and improve productivity while still in their cradles, of course. And though the family bears most of the cost, society must also shell out to bring the baby to productive adulthood. This means that if you do not look as far as the next 25 years, the knowledge benefits of someone else's baby born today do not interest you, and that baby is therefore a poor social investment for your taxes. But if you feel some interest and obligation to the longer-run future, perhaps because you yourself are today enjoying the fruits of educational expenses that someone paid 25 or 50 or 100 years ago, then you will view the knowledge that will be produced by today's children as a great benefit. In the next chapter we shall see just how great the benefit is, and how it overwhelms the social cost of the additional children.

AFTERNOTE

On the Importance and Origins
of Productive Knowledge

This section involves a bit more economic theory than does the rest of
the book, which is why it comes after the chapter. It is labeled an "afternote" instead of an "appendix" because people seldom read appendixes
unless their need to do so is desperate. And this section should be read
by anyone with a serious desire to understand the effects of population
growth.

THE GAINS FROM KNOWLEDGE CREATION

Some understanding of the processes that govern the creation and utilization of productive knowledge can help us understand the effect of population growth upon economic growth in the industrialized world. And
the size of the population is interwoven with the creation of knowledge
on both the supply side (supply of goods through the supply of knowledge) and on the demand side (demand for industrial goods, extractive
products, services, and total output).

The main difficulty in understanding the economics of knowledge creation is the "externality" of the benefits from advances in knowledge
with respect to the producer of knowledge, that is, the difference
between the producer's private benefits from the creation of knowledge
and the benefits to the economy and society as a whole. It is this externality that distinguishes the creation of knowledge capital from investment in physical capital.

Aside from the physical wealth that people bequeath to their descendants — which clearly is only a small part of total savings, though we do
not know how much the bequests total in our society — all of people's
physical wealth created as savings is used up within their lifetimes.
Hence it follows that (aside from other complications within the systems) an additional person lowers the average income of the community
by diluting its supply of capital — which is the basic Malthusian population proposition.

The benefits of knowledge are not fully exploited by its creators, however, even if it is created as an investment whose profit is realized. Advances in knowledge spill over from the individual creator to other individuals, from the firm that invests in creating new knowledge to other firms, and from one generation to another. And the firm that creates knowledge usually is not fully able to squeeze out from consumers all the value of the new knowledge to consumers. Of course the spillover phenomenon can also interfere with knowledge creation, because the smaller the inventor's benefits and the greater the costs to him alone, the less likely is the inventor (or the firm) to invest in the knowledge.

Before going further, we shall have to distinguish between two types of knowledge. The first type is "spontaneous" knowlege; the other is "incentive-responsive" knowledge.

Spontaneous Knowledge

It is obviously true that not all knowledge creation is influenced by short-term or even long-term economic incentives. Much basic knowledge is created in universities and only distantly influenced by economic needs and priorities. Other knowledge is created with the aim of increasing efficiency but yet is uninfluenced by any profit calculations, and is produced without explicit expenditure on R & D; this is the sort of improvement in production, marketing, financing, or other aspect of a business that arises from an idea of a line executive about how to operate more efficiently — for example, Alfred Sloan's idea of decentralizing General Motors, or the idea of using cut-down old detergent boxes as magazine storage units, or a host of developments by ingenious farmers.

Incentive-Responsive Knowledge

This sort of knowledge is partly produced in universities, but to a considerable degree is the result of R & D programs in industry. Much applied knowledge and technical progress is the result of casual on-the-job discovery by workers of all kinds at all levels, in response to an opportunity to make an enterprise more efficient and more profitable.

THE BENEFICIARIES OF GAINS IN KNOWLEDGE

The Economy as a Whole

If a firm creates knowledge, invests in it, and realizes profits from the project at a 30 percent yearly rate of return, whereas the economywide return to invested capital is 20 percent and the break-even project returns

10 percent, then the economy as a whole benefits from this new project paying back at 30 percent because the resources used in it are producing returns in excess of what they would produce in alternative uses. True, the "profit" goes to the firm, at least at first. But the owners of the firm are part of the economy, and if they are better off, *ceteris paribus*, then the society is better off. If everyone owned a firm in such circumstances, then everyone would be made better off by such profits even though the profits are "private."

Furthermore, the benefits from a high-return project that utilizes resources productively go to many other parties in addition to the owners of the firm — to employees as job creation and higher wages; to suppliers; and to the fisc as taxes. So again, even without externalities in the form of knowledge, a high-yielding knowledge project is good for society.

Externalities Realized by Other Firms

The benefit realized by other firms in the same industry from the knowledge created by the knowledge-producing firm is a key element of this system. And the benefits external to the innovating firm certainly must be large, even relative to the discount-factor effect mentioned above. That is, the main social benefit from profitable R & D probably derives from effects external to the firm investing in the R & D. Firms are able to reduce costs and introduce new products more easily because of research done by others in the industry and in other industries.

Consumer Benefits from the Externalities

There is still another channel through which R & D has positive social effects. At the break-even point on the R & D opportunity ladder, the increased revenue to the firm doing the R & D only balances the added inputs to produce the new knowledge, so there is no net gain. But when competitors acquire some of the knowledge (almost) free, there will be a lowering of cost and then price throughout the industry, which will be a windfall gain to consumers and to society as a whole.

Furthermore, except under most unusual conditions a firm cannot charge consumers for all of the knowledge benefits they receive. So even if the firm can control its new knowledge so that competitors cannot acquire it, there will still be a net social benefit in the "consumer surplus."

Process and Product Research

About the size of the knowledge-creation externalities: Given that year-to-year growth in per-worker output as recorded in the national income accounts is something less than 3 percent per year on the average, and given that a sizable proportion of this growth is accounted for by inputs of labor and capital (just how sizable depends upon the researcher and upon how you are thinking about and classifying inputs),[1] you may wonder how much "residual" there really is that might show the effect of increases in technical progress. But our national income accounts do not directly show the benefits of a very large part of knowledge creation — new and improved products. If a pharmaceutical firm introduces a new drug that allows people to leave mental hospitals quickly, thereby saving large sums of money and improving health and life enjoyment, the first impact on the economy is a reduction in GNP, because some hospital workers will be out of work until they find new jobs. If a firm finds a new soup recipe that increases the pleasure people get from soup, there is no effect at all on GNP unless sales of the soup change. If a firm invents a contraceptive that is more reliable and pleasant than existing products, there is no effect on GNP unless total expenditures on contraceptives change, and if the price of the new product is the same as the price of old products (per unit of use) there will be no change.

Yet such new and improved products constitute a large part of the increase in economic welfare from year to year, accounting for increases in life expectancy, physical appearance, sense of well-being, range of activities available to us, and so on.

The proportion of expenditures on R & D that goes into new products is very large relative to the proportion that goes into new processes. In a survey of industrial firms, 45 percent said that their "main object" in R & D is to "develop new products," and another 41 percent said they concentrated on "improving existing products" — a total of 86 percent for product research — compared with 14 percent whose R & D aims at "finding new processes" to be used in manufacturing.[2] Of course these figures are sketchy and suggestive at best. And one firm's new products may change another firm's production process, of course. But no matter how unsatisfactory these figures may be, we can certainly rely on them to show that consumer product research is a large proportion of total research — let us say 50 percent in the simulation (raising process research from the observed 14 percent all the way to 50 percent for "conservatism"). Even at that, there would be much more impact on consumer welfare than is shown in any audit of GNP.

Government-supported R & D is another important category of knowledge production that contributes to technical progress. But it is exceedingly difficult to make a reasonable guess about how much of the government's total expenditure on knowledge creation affects productivity.

Probably we wish to exclude weapons research, though there is some byproduct knowledge that contributes to productivity. And probably we wish to exclude "pure" or "basic" research, though it influences technical progress in a variety of ways. Agricultural research is the best example of the relevant sort of government-supported research. An interesting estimate of "at least 700 percent per year" return on investment in hybrid corn research was arrived at by Zvi Griliches.[3]

15.

Population Growth, Natural Resources, Future Generations, and International Rape

How will the supplies of natural resources be affected by different rates of population growth? Part I discussed the supply of natural resources without reference to population growth. Now I shall consider the effects of different rates of population growth, concentrating in this chapter on mineral resources for simplicity.

Let's go back to the Crusoe story in chapter 3 and now ask, How are the situations different if both Alpha and Gamma Crusoe are on the island, or if Alpha is alone? We saw that the cost of copper to Alpha will probably be higher if Gamma is there too, unless or until one of them discovers an improved production method (perhaps a method that requires two workers) or a product that can substitute for copper. And Alpha's offspring, Beta, also probably would be better off if Gamma had never shown up. But we of later generations are almost surely better off if Gamma does appear on the scene and (a) increases the population size, (b) increases the demand for copper, (c) increases the cost of getting it, and then (d) invents improved methods of getting it and using it, and discovers substitute products.

A larger population due to Gamma and other persons influences later costs in two beneficial ways: First, the increased demand for copper leads to increased pressure for new discoveries. Second, and perhaps even more important, a larger population implies more people to think and imagine, be ingenious, and finally make these discoveries.

The Family Analogy

The analogy of the family is sometimes a satisfactory intuitive shortcut toward understanding the effects of population growth. For example, if a family decides to have an additional child, there is less income available for expenditure on each of the original family members; and just so with a country as a whole. The family may respond to the additional "need" by having the parents work more hours for additional pay, and so it is with a nation. The family may choose to save less, to pay for the additional expenses, or to save more to pay for expenses such as education that are expected later; and so it is for a nation as a whole. The additional child has no immediate economic advantages to the family, but later it may contribute to the parents and other relatives; and just so for society as a whole. And like a nation, the family must balance off the immediate non-economic psychic benefits plus the later economic benefits against the immediate cost of the child. The main way that the family analogy diverges from the situation of a nation as a whole is that an additional person in the nation contributes to the stock of knowledge and to the scale of the market for the society as a whole, which benefits the entire economy, whereas an individual family is not likely to benefit much from its own discoveries.

The family model goes wrong, however, when it directs attention away from the possibility of creating new resources. If one thinks of a family on a desert island with a limited supply of pencils and paper, then more people on the island will lead to a pencil-and-paper scarcity sooner than otherwise. But for a society as a whole, there is practically no resource that is not either growable (such as trees for paper) or replaceable (except energy). And the supply of energy should present no problems, as will be discussed shortly.

If the family starts with a given plot of land and an additional child is born, it would seem as if the result would be less land per child to be inherited. But the family can increase its "effective" land by irrigation and multiple cropping, and some families respond by opening up whole new tracts of previously uncultivated land. Hence an additional child need not increase the scarcity of land and other natural resources, as appears to be inevitable when one looks at the earth as a closed resource system; instead, there is an increase in total resources.

But, you ask, how long can this go on? Surely it can't go on forever, can it? In fact there is no logical or physical reason why the process cannot do just that, go on forever. Let's return to copper as an example. Given substitute materials, development of improved methods of extraction, and discoveries of new lodes in the U.S. and in other countries and in the sea and perhaps on other planets, there is no *logical* reason why additional people should not have a positive effect on the availability of copper or copper equivalents indefinitely.

To make the logical case more binding, the possibility of recycling copper at a faster rate due to population growth also improves the supply of the services we now get from it. To illustrate, consider a copper jug that one rubs to obtain the services of a genie. If only the single jug exists, and there are two families at opposite ends of the earth, each of them can obtain the genie very infrequently. But if the earth is populated densely, the jug can be passed rapidly from hand to hand, and all families might then have a chance to obtain the recycled jug and its genie more often than with a less dense population So it could be with copper pots, or whatever. The apparent reason that this process cannot continue — the seeming finitude of copper in the solid earth — is not a solid reason, as we have seen in chapter 3.

Of course, it is logically possible that the cost of the services we get now from copper and other minerals will be relatively higher in the future than now if there are more people in the future. But all past history suggests that the better guess is that cost and price will fall, just as scarcity historically has diminished along with the increase in population. Either way, however, the concept of mineral resources as "finite" is unnecessary, confusing, and misleading. And the notion of our planet as "spaceship earth," launched with a countable amount of each resource and hence having less minerals per passenger as the number of passengers is greater, is dramatic but irrelevant.

To repeat, we cannot know *for sure* whether the cost of the services we get from copper and other minerals will be cheaper in either year t + 50 or year t + 500 if population becomes 1 thillion rather than 2 thillion in year t. The historical data, however, show that the costs of minerals have declined faster in recent centuries, when population was larger than in earlier centuries. This is not conclusive evidence that a bigger population implies lower costs. But there is much less evidence — in fact, none at all — that a higher population in year t means a higher cost and greater scarcity of minerals in year t + 50 or t + 500.

Do you still doubt that the cost of mineral resources will be lower in the future than now? Do you still doubt that higher population growth now will eventually mean lower mineral costs? If so, I suggest as a mental exercise that you ask yourself. Would we be better off if people in the past had used less copper or coal? How great would our technological capacities to extract, process, and use these materials now be if we were just discovering these materials today?[1]

Jokes don't always go over well in serious books. But a joke that I have long been fond of seems appropriate here. Seventy-year-old Zeke's girl-friend has just left him after thirty years, and Zeke is in despair. His friends try hard to console him, and they especially point out again and again that in time he'll get over it, and might well meet another woman. Finally Zeke turns his tear-stained face to them and says, "But you don't understand. What am I going to do *tonight?*"

Similarly, you may well ask about the near-term effect of population growth on resources, after all this talk about the long run. There is more comfort for you than for Zeke, however. True, over the short period there is little chance for the natural-resource supply to accomodate to different rates of population growth. Yet, according to the President's Commission on Population Growth and the American Future in 1972, "Substitution of the lower for the higher population growth assumption generally results in a reduction of cumulative United States demand [for minerals] by only one to eight percent by the year 2000, and no more than 14 percent by 2020. Most of these modest savings would occur late in the period."[2] And the forecasting methods used in that study seem to be appropriate for their conclusions about the period in question.

THE "ENERGY CRISIS" AND POPULATION POLICY

It is standard wisdom that population growth worsens the energy situation. Here is the offical view of ERDA, predecessor of the U.S. Department of Energy, in a brochure written for the public at large.

> In other parts of the world, particularly in the developing areas, populations are growing rapidly and each new baby further strains already inadequate energy resources. Thus, if developing areas are to grow economically, it seems clear that they must first deal with the population problem. But the rich nations, too, must control population growth. If not, there simply will not be enough energy to go around, unless per capita energy consumption is held steady or reduced — and that seems unlikely. . . .
>
> We must learn to conserve energy and use it more wisely or we're going to be in serious trouble.[3]

Therefore, we must inquire into the effects of population upon the supply of energy. We want to know: What effect will more or fewer people have upon the future scarcity and prices of energy?

This much we can say with some certainty. (1) With respect to the short-run future — within say thirty years — this year's population growth rate can have almost no effect on the demand for energy or on its supply. (2) In the longer run, energy demand is likely to be proportional to population, all else equal; and hence additional people require additional energy. (3) For the longer run, whether additional population will increase scarcity, reduce scarcity, or have no effect on scarcity cannot be known theoretically. The result will depend on the net effect of the potential supply as of a given moment, together with increases in the potential supply through increased discoveries and technological advances that will be induced by the increase in demand. In the past, increased demand for energy has been associated with reduced scarcity and cost. There is no statistical reason to doubt the continuation of this trend. More particularly, there seems to be no reason to believe that we are now at a turning point in energy history, and no such turning point is visible in the future. This implies a trend toward lower energy prices and increased supplies.

It is important to recognize that in the context of population policy, who is "right" about the present state of energy supplies really does not matter. True, it matters a great deal to those of us alive today whether in the year 2000 there will be large or small supplies of oil and gas and coal at prices relatively high or low compared to now, and whether we have to wait in line at the gas station. And it matters to the State Department and the Department of Defense whether our national policies about energy pricing and development lead to large or small proportions of our energy supply being imported from abroad. But from the standpoint of our national standard of living it will matter very little even if energy prices are at the highest end of the range of possibilities as a result of relatively unfruitful technological progress and of maximum increases in demand due to maximum rises in GNP and population. At a price of energy equivalent to, say, $20–$35 per barrel of oil (1980 prices) there should be enough energy from coal, shale oil, solar power, gas, and oil — buttressed by a virtually inexhaustible supply of nuclear power — to last so many hundreds of years into the future, or thousands of years if we include nuclear energy, that it simply does not matter enough to estimate how many hundreds or thousands of years.

From this we may conclude that whatever the impact of population growth might be upon the energy situation — negative effects through increased demand, positive effects through new discoveries, with a net effect that may be positive or negative — the long-run effect of population growth on the standard of living through its effect on energy costs is quite unimportant. And refined calculations of its magnitude are of no interest in this context.

NATURAL RESOURCES AND THE RISK OF RUNNING OUT

You might wonder, Even if the prospect of running out of energy and minerals is small, is it safe to depend on the continuation of technical progress? Would it not be prudent to avoid even a small possibility of a major scarcity disaster? Would it not be less risky to curb population growth to avoid the mere possibility of natural-resource scarcities even if the chances really are good that higher population will lead to lower costs? That is, a reasonable person may be "risk averse."

The matter of risk aversion was considered at length in the discussion of nuclear energy in chapter 8; it will also be considered in the context of population and pollution in chapter 17, where risk is more crucial to the argument and to policy decisions. The reader interested in this topic should turn to those discussions. Risk aversion is not, however, very relevant for natural resources, for several reasons. First, the consequences of a growing shortage of any mineral — that is, of a rise in relative price — are not dangerous to life. Second, a relative scarcity of one material engenders the substitution of other materials — say, aluminum for steel — and hence mitigates the scarcity. Third, and perhaps most important, a scarcity of any mineral would manifest itself only very slowly, giving plenty of opportunity to alter social and economic policies appropriately. (Of course these remarks do not touch the matter of military security, but that is outside the scope of this book.) Fourth, and last, just as greater affluence and larger population contribute to the demand for more natural resources, they also contribute to our capacity to alleviate shortages and broaden our technological and economic capacity, which makes any particular material ever less crucial.

SUMMARY: THE KEY RESOURCE IS THE HUMAN IMAGINATION

There is no persuasive reason to believe that the relatively larger use of natural resources that would occur with a larger population would have any special deleterious effects upon the economy in the future. For the foreseeable future, even if the extrapolation of past trends is badly in error, the cost of energy is not an important consideration in evaluating the impact of population growth. Other natural resources may be treated in a manner just like any other physical capital when considering the economic effect of different rates of population growth. Depletion of mineral resources is not a special danger for the long run or the short run. Rather, the availability of mineral resources, as measured by their prices, may be expected to increase — that is, costs may be expected to decrease — despite all notions about "finiteness."

Sound appraisal of the impact of additional people upon the "scarcity" (cost) of a natural resource must take into account the feedback from increased demand to the discovery of new deposits, new ways of extracting the resource, and new substitutes for the resource. And we must take into account the relationship between demand now and supply in various future years, rather than consider only the effect on supply now of greater or lesser demand now. And the more people, the more minds there are to discover new deposits and increase productivity, with raw materials as with all other goods, all else equal.

This point of view is not limited to economists. A technologist writing on minerals put it this way: "In effect, technology keeps creating new resources."[4] So the major constraint upon the human capacity to enjoy unlimited minerals, energy, and other raw materials at acceptable prices is knowledge. And the source of knowledge is the human mind. Ultimately, then, the key constraint is human imagination acting together with educated skills. This is why an increase of human beings, along with causing an additional consumption of resources, constitutes a crucial addition to the stock of natural resources.

16.

Population Growth and Land

Population growth raises the specter of increased pressure on the land. More people apparently imply smaller farms per farmer, and hence a harder struggle to produce enough to eat, until each of us is nightmarishly scratching out three skimpy meals from eighteen hours' work a day, on a plot the size of a window box. "More people, less land," in the words of the Environmental Fund. This tendency toward smaller farms is seen in figure 16-1.

Along with this specter hovers another: additional people using up and ruining land, especially in arid areas. The U.S. government's *Smithsonian Magazine* editorializes that, in the desert, "traditional, more primitive agricultural techniques using natural ecological cycles are all that will work . . . and *that means small populations*."[1] The head of the Population/Food Fund, Charles M. Cargille, M.D., writes that "overpopulation contributes to . . . deforestation and agricultural practices damaging to soil fertility."[2] And according to the *Christian Science Monitor*, "The will may be needed more to control population than to deal with the more obvious aspects of desertification."[3]

Yet historically, population growth has not led to these apparently logical consequences for agriculture. The world eats as well or better now than in earlier centuries, even in present-day poor countries. How can we explain this paradox?

Here is one part of the explanation: Though more land per person was available in the past than at present, people did not farm all the land available to them, for two good reasons. (1) People were physically unable to farm larger areas than they actually farmed. There is considerable data showing that the amount of land peasant farmers can handle without modern machinery is quite limited by the availability of human strength and time.[4] (2) More important but even less understood — farmers in the past had little motive for farming more land. In the absence of markets, farmers grow only as much as they expect to eat, as was discussed at length in chapter 4.

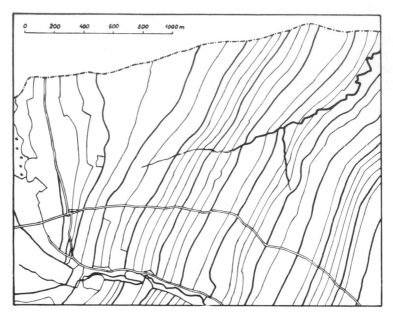

Individual peasant farms in 1787

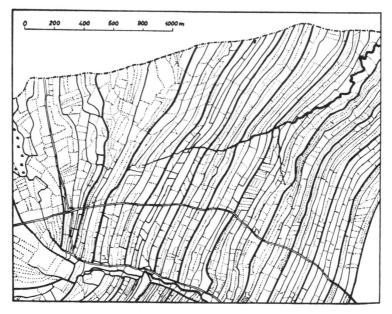

Peasant farms in 1937 (dotted lines represent divisions after 1883)
FIGURE 16-1. A Polish Village's Farm Boundaries
Note: This figure shows how farm sizes decline as population grows in LDCs before the turn-around point. Afterwards, the absolute size of the agricultural population begins to fall and farm sizes begin to get larger again, as seen in MDCs.

Why *would* a subsistence farmer grow more than his family can eat? Does an urban housewife buy so many vegetables for the week that they spoil? Malthus well understood this "natural want of will on the part of mankind to make efforts for the increase of food beyond what they could possibly consume."[5] It is no more a miracle that output increases when population increases than it is a miracle that you, the reader, have enough vegetables to last the week even when guests are staying with you.

Reduction in the amount of land available to the farmer causes little hardship if previously he was not farming all that was available (though he may have to change his farming practices so as to cultivate the same land more intensively). The other side of the coin is that when farmers need more land they make more land, as we have seen in chapter 6. The notion of a fixed supply of farmland is as misleading as is the notion of a fixed supply of copper or energy. That is, people create land — agricultural land — by investing their sweat, blood, money, and ingenuity in it.[6]

But what will happen to the supply of land as income rises and people demand more food luxuries such as meat, which requires large quantities of grain as feed? Or even more strongly, how about the effect of a rise in income combined with an increase in population?

The answer given to this question by the statistical data is so astounding that it seems weird: The absolute number of acres per farmer rises when income becomes high, *despite* increases in population. When we look at data for the U.S., Great Britain, and other more-developed countries given in table 16-1, we see that the absolute number of farm workers is going down, and that the absolute amount of land per farm worker is going up, despite the fact that the total population is going up.

Please re-read the preceding sentence carefully. It does not say that the *proportion* of the population working in agriculture is going down in the richer countries. Rather, it says something much stronger: The *absolute* number of farm workers is going down, and consequently the absolute amount of land per farm worker is going up in these countries. This fact makes it very clear that the combined increases of income and population do *not* increase "pressure" on the land, in contrast to popular theory and to the state of affairs in poor countries that have not yet been able to adopt modern farming methods.

The extrapolations of this trend for the future are extraordinarily optimistic: As the poor countries get richer, and as their rate of population growth falls, they will reach a point at which the number of people needed to work in agriculture to feed the rest of the population will begin to fall — even though the population gets bigger and richer. So

TABLE 16-1. Changes in Agricultural Labor Force, Agricultural Production, and Total Male Labor Force in Developed Countries, 1950–1960

	Agricultural Labor Force (thousands)		Cultivated Area (square kilometers)		Index of Agricultural Production		Total Male Labor Force	
	1950	1960	1950	1960	1950	1960	1950	1960
U.S.A.	6,537	4,747	1,408	1,248	93.3	109.7	43,754	47,468
Canada	983	711	252	253	101.2	99.7	4,067	4,665
Denmark	386	336	26.7	27.5	91.5	115.7	1,356	1,447
Finland	539	458	23.7	26.1	88.3	121.3	1,173	1,229
Ireland	452	359	NA	NA	92.5	108.7	951	832
Norway	224	260	8.1	8.4	97.3	101.3	1,060	1,085
Sweden	580	401	35.1	31.0	100.8	100.7	2,296	2,278
U.K.	1,153	975	50.5	44.5	88.8	117.0	15,567	16,547
Austria	536	371	17.7	16.4	86.4	118.9	2,061	2,015
Belgium	332	227	NA	9.0	92.9	109.0	2,662	2,587
France	3,695	2,802	NA	NA	90.2	116.7	12,183	12,996
Germany, F.R.	2,316	1,678	NA	NA	92.1	112.3	14,125	16,617
Netherlands	520	407	10.5	10.1	90.8	117.7	2,990	3,225
Switzerland	333	263	NA	NA	95.8	108.7	1,515	1,756
Germany, D.R.	868	772	52.4	50.6	NA?	NA?	4,541	4,475
Hungary	1,200	969	57.5	55.8	NA	NA	2,298	3,165
Poland	3,295	3,009	NA	NA	NA	NA	6,858	7,753
Greece	1,099	1,128	23.2	31.3	80.8	126.7	2,246	2,358
Italy	6,111	4,191	NA	NA	91.6	113.0	15,175	14,905
Portugal	1,258	1,238	NA?	41.3	97.6	101.7	2,453	2,580
Spain	4,828	4,268	142.4	145.5	89.1	119.0	9,084	9,514
Yugoslavia	2,737	2,645	NA	NA	76.6	143.3	4,477	5.211
Australia	440	432	79.3	101.3	85.0	123.0	2,603	3,102
New Zealand	130	121	3.8	4.1	85.8	122.3	560	659
Japan	8,623	6,853	NA	NA	86.5	118.7	21,831	26,822

SOURCE: Kumar, 1973, Appendixes.

NOTE: For a definition of the Index of Agricultural Production, see Kumar, 1973, p. 201. Includes all European countries for which there are data.

much for a long-run crisis in agricultural land caused by population growth!

Let us push this idea even further, both to see how a simple-minded extension of trends can lead to absurd conclusions and to illuminate an interesting phenomenon: A continuation of the present trend in the U.S., carried to the same absurdity as the nightmare described earlier, would eventually have just one person farming all the land in the U.S. and feeding everyone else.

Where will this benign trend stop? No one knows. But as long as agriculture is pointed in this economically desirable direction, we need not be concerned about how long it can go on — especially as there are no obvious technological forces to stop it.

While countries are still poor they cannot embark on a course of mechanization sufficiently intense to increase total output and at the same time reduce the total number of workers in agriculture. But at least the proportion of workers in agriculture falls, as is already happening in almost every developing country despite population growth. And eventually the total number of farm workers is likely to start falling, too. This is not happening yet, but the poorer countries can expect eventually to experience the same trend that was at work in the past in the now-rich countries.

Before we look at the historical examples, it is useful to look at figure 16-2 and to note this observation by Gunnar Myrdal about South Asia, the area that people most frequently point to as dangerously overpopulated:

> . . . contrary to what is often assumed, the man/land ratio in South Asia is not strikingly high in comparison with that in other parts of the world. The number of inhabitants per unit of cultivated land is comparable to the European average; it is half that of China; and, of course, much lower than in Japan, about one-sixth of the Japanese average. . . . What really distinguishes South Asia is the very low output per unit of agricultural land and per unit of labor. Per hectare, South Asia as a whole produces only about half as much as China or Europe and only about one fifth as much as Japan. . . . [7]

HISTORICAL EXAMPLES

The increase in agricultural output as population rises (with or without an accompanying rise in income) has been accomplished, in most countries, largely by increases in the amount of land that has been farmed. This accounts for the land statistics that we saw in chapter 6. As population increases, people build more land in response to the increased demand for food.

Ireland. In the late eighteenth century and the first half of the nineteenth century in Ireland — a period of very rapid population growth — peasants invested a great amount of labor in new lands, even though they did not own the land.

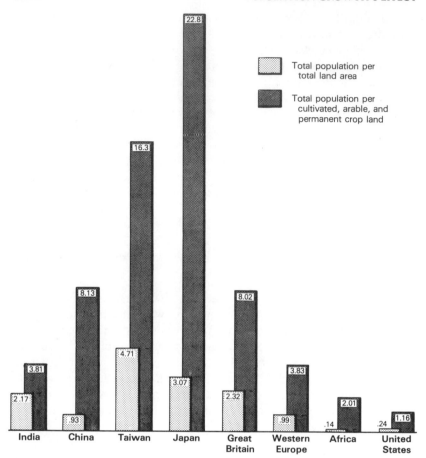

FIGURE 16-2. Population Densities for Selected Areas of the World

Every new holding marked out in mountain or bog made possible the creation of a new family. . . . The state, for all the advice of government committees and private investigators, played no significant part in works of drainage and clearance until the time of the Famine. The landlords, with outstanding exceptions, were hardly more active. The main agent of reclamation was the peasant himself. In spite of the immense discouragement of tenurial relationships which increased rent in proportion, or more than in proportion, to the increase in the value of his holding, he steadily added an acre or two a year to his cultivated area; or his sons established themselves on land hitherto unused. The peasant and his children were driven to such arduous and unrewarding work by the two forces which give their distinctive character to many of the institutions of the Irish countryside, the pressure of population and the landlords' demand for ever increasing rents.[8]

Evidence for the rapidity of land expansion is clear. Over the decade 1841-51 the amount of cultivated land increased by 10 percent, though even in the previous decade — when population growth was at its fastest before the famine that started in 1845 — population only increased at a decadal rate of 5.3 percent, from 7,767,000 to 8,175,000.[9] This suggests that rural investment was enough to account for all, and even more, of the increase in food required by the population growth during those years.

China. From 1400 to 1957 the cultivated acreage in China expanded fourfold-plus, from 25 million hectares to 112 million hectares.[10] This increase in cultivated land accounted for more than half the increase in grain output that sustained the living standard of the eightfold-plus increase in population over the same period; and investment in water-control systems and terracing accounted for much of the rest of the increase in output. "Only a small share of the rise in yields can be explained by improvements in the 'traditional' technology."[11] In this context, where the "rural technology in China was nearly stagnant after 1400,"[12] growth in output had to be accomplished either with increases in capital (including land) or in labor per person, and it is clear that additional investment was very largely, if not almost completely, responsible. Furthermore, this capital formation seems to have been caused by population growth.

This landbuilding process continues into the present. As an explanation of the last of the ten years of good harvests the Chinese had enjoyed as of 1971, the New China News Agency said that the Chinese people "worked hard at irrigation, drainage and fertilizer production last year and this should show good results in 1972 provided the weather holds up."[13]

Europe. Slicher van Bath documents the close relationship between population, food prices, and land reclamation in Europe from 1500 to 1900.[14] When population grew at a fast rate, food prices were high; and land creation increased. "The higher cereal prices after 1756 stimulated agricultural development. . . . Around Poitiers the area of reclaimed land was usually either 30 or 35 acres or about 2 hectares. In the former case the reclamation was the work of a day-labourer for a whole winter, in the latter that of a farmer with a team of oxen."[15]

Other countries. Data for Japan show that arable land increased steadily from 1877 until World War II, even though the number of agricultural workers was decreasing steadily.[16] The amounts of livestock, trees, and equipment also rose at rapid rates. These increases in agricultural capital were in response to the increase in Japanese population together with the increase in the level of income in Japan.

In Burma, the amount of land in cultivation rose at an astonishing rate starting in the middle of the nineteenth century. The cultivated area in acres was fifteen times as great in 1922–23 as in 1852–53.[17] Over the same period population increased by a factor of almost five.[18] In addition to the increase in population, the opening of the Suez Canal (1869) enabled Burma to sell its rice to Europe. Both these forces gave Burmese farmers an incentive to reclaim land, and they did so with extraordinary rapidity until World War II, when millions of acres were again overrun by jungle.

The aforegoing examples show that in the poorer agricultural countries the creation of new land has been the source of most of the long-run increase in agricultural output, which has kept up with population growth. But what will happen when there is no more "wasteland" to be converted into agricultural land? To begin with, we can be quite sure this will never happen. As the available land for crops becomes more and more costly to transform into cropland, farmers will instead crop their existing land more intensively; this practice becomes more profitable than dipping into the pool of undeveloped land, because the unused land is relatively inefficient.

Evidence for this process can be seen in the international statistics showing that, when population density is higher, the proportion of land irrigated is higher too.[19] This may be seen particularly clearly in Taiwan and India, where, after farmers exploited a large proportion (but by no means all) of the unused land, irrigation began in earnest.

Let's look closer at India, because people worry about it. The total area of all cultivated land increased about 20 percent from 1951 to 1971.[20] Even more impressive is the 25 percent increase in irrigated land from 1949–50 to 1960–61,[21] and then another 27 percent increase from 1961–65 to 1975.[22] Nor has India reached a high population density even now. Japan and Taiwan are about five times as densely populated, and China

is twice as densely populated, as India, measured by the number of persons per hectare of arable land, as seen in figure 16-2. But the yield of
rice per hectare is almost four times as great in Japan as in India; vastly
more fertilizer is used in Japan, and three times as large a proportion of
the agricultural land is irrigated (55 percent versus 17 percent).[23]

Excellent data from Taiwan show how land creation and improvement responded to population growth. During the period from 1900 to
1930 much new land was developed, along with an increase in the
amount of irrigated land. Then, from 1930 to 1960, when there was less
new land left to develop, more land was irrigated. At the same time, the
effective crop area was increased by multiple cropping, and the use of
fertilizers allowed total productivity to continue rising at a very rapid
rate. This continues a process that begins in more "primitive" and
sparsely populated areas where the pattern of farming still is to farm a
patch for a year or two, then leave it fallow for several years to regain its
natural fertility while other patches are farmed. There the response to
population growth is to shorten the fallow period and to improve land
fertility with labor-intensive methods.[24]

How much capacity still exists for enhancing land through irrigation,
new seeds, fertilizer, and new farming methods? In chapter 6 we saw
that the capacity is vast, much much greater than would be required to
handle any presently conceivable population growth. And of course the
capacity is not limited to what we now know how to do, but it will
certainly increase greatly as we make new technological discoveries. No
matter how it occurs, however, the key element in developing and har-
nessing the capacity to replace land with technology is an increased
demand for food — which arises from an increased world income, an
increased population growth, and improved markets so that farm produce can be bought and sold without the prohibitive transportation costs
still found in most very poor countries.

But what about "ultimately"? There is always at least one person in
the crowd — and often the entire crowd — who worries that the resource-
creating process "cannot go on forever."

In the chapters on national resources and energy, I argued that it
makes sense to discuss the future that we can presently foresee — 20
years, 100 years, even 500 years from now. To give much weight to an
even more distant time, so far in the future that we do not even give it
a date except that it is a figure with several zeros in it, is not sensible
decision-making. Furthermore, there is strong reason to believe that
"ultimately" — whatever that terms means — natural resources will be
less scarce rather than more scarce. And there is no reason to think that
land is different in this respect.

LOSS OF LAND TO "URBAN SPRAWL"

Many well-intentioned people worry that population growth produces urban sprawl, and that highways pave over "prime farmland" and recreational land. We shall now examine these claims, which turn out to be empty slogans.

First, the dimensions of the "sprawl": As we see in figure 16-3, there are 2.3 billion acres in the U.S., as of 1974. All the land taken up by cities, highways, non-agricultural roads, railroads, and airports amounts to only 61 million acres—just 2.7 percent of the total. Clearly there is very little competition between agriculture on the one side and cities and roads on the other. The notion that the U.S. is being "paved over" is a ridiculous, though frightening, exaggeration.

How about the trends? From 1920 to 1974, land in urban and transportation uses rose from 29 million acres to 61 million acres—a change of 1.42 percent out of the 2,266 million acres in the U.S. During those fifty-four years, population increased from 106 million to 211 million people. Even if this trend were to continue (population growth is clearly slowing down) there would be an almost insignificant impact on U.S. agriculture (see figure 16-4).

Lest you have lingering doubts, here is the opening sentence from the U.S. Department of Agriculture's 1974 study, *Our Land and Water Resources:* "Although thousands of acres of farmland are converted annually to other uses—urbanization, roads, wildlife, and recreation—and population has risen a third in 20 years, we are in no danger of running out of farmland." Increasingly efficient production methods are the major factor enabling the U.S. to "ensure our domestic food and fiber needs"[25] and yet use less land for crops—not because land is being "taken" for other purposes, but because it is now more efficient to raise more food on fewer acres than it was in the past.

But what about the fertility of the land used for human habitation and transportation? Even if the total *quantity* of land used by additional urban people is small, perhaps the new urban land has special agricultural quality. One often hears this charge, as made in my own home town in the 1977 City Council election: The mayor "is opposed to urban sprawl because 'it eats up prime agricultural land.'"[26]

New cropland is created, and some old cropland goes out of use, as we have seen. The overall effect, in the judgment of the U.S. Department of Agriculture, is that between 1967 and 1975 "the quality of cropland has been improved by shifts in land use . . . better land makes up a higher proportion of the remaining cropland."[27]

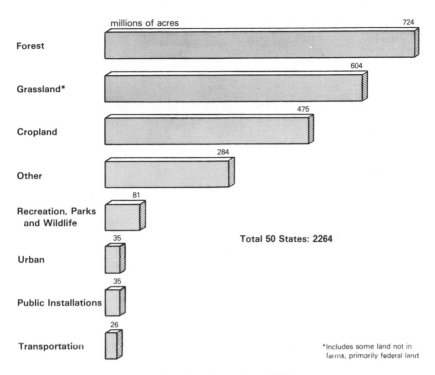

millions of acres

Forest 724

Grassland* 604

Cropland 475

Other 284

Recreation, Parks and Wildlife 81

Urban 35

Total 50 States: **2264**

Public Installations 35

Transportation 26

*Includes some land not in farms, primarily federal land

FIGURE 16-3. Major Uses of Land in the U.S. in 1969

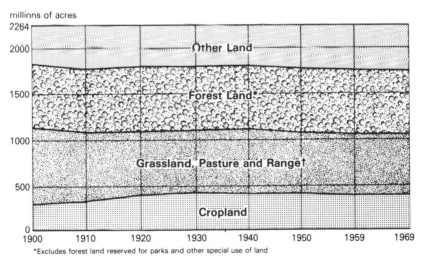

millions of acres

2264
2000 — Other Land
1500 — Forest Land*
1000
Grassland, Pasture and Range†
500
Cropland
0

1900   1910   1920   1930   1940   1950   1959   1969

*Excludes forest land reserved for parks and other special use of land
†Includes cropland used only for pasture level of hydrocarbons emitted

FIGURE 16-4. Trends in Land Use in the U.S.

The idea that cities devour "prime land" is a particularly clear example of the failure to grasp economic principles. Let's take the concrete (asphalt?) case of a new shopping mall on the outskirts of Champaign-Urbana, Illinois. The key economic idea is that the mall land has greater value to the economy as a shopping center than it does as a farm, wonderful though this Illinois land is for growing corn and soybeans. That's why the mall investors could pay the farmer enough to make it worthwhile for him or her to sell. A series of corn-y examples should bring out the point.

If, instead of a shopping mall, the corn-and-soybean farmer sold the land to a person who would raise a new exotic crop called, say, "whornseat," and who would sell the whornseat abroad at a high price, everyone would consider it just dandy. The land clearly would be more productive raising whornseat than corn, as shown by the the higher profits the whornseat farmer would make as compared with the corn-and-soybean farmer, and as also shown by the amount that the whornseat farmer is willing to pay for the land.

A shopping mall is similar to a whornseat farm. It seems different only because the mall does not use the land for agriculture. Yet economically there is no real difference between the mall and a whornseat farm.

The person who objects to the shopping mall says, "Why not put the mall on inferior wasteland that cannot be used for corn and soybeans?" The mall owners would love to find and buy such land — as long as it would be equally convenient for shoppers. But there is no such wasteland close to town. And "wasteland" far away from Champaign-Urbana is like land that will not raise whornseat — because of its remoteness it will not raise a good "crop" of shoppers or whornseat or corn. The same reasoning explains why all of us put our lawns in front of our homes instead of raising corn out front and putting the lawn miles away on "inferior" land.

Of course, the transaction between the mall investors and the farmer does not take into account the "external disutility" to people who live nearby and who hate the sight of the mall. On the other hand, the transaction also does not take account of the added external "utility" to shoppers who enjoy the mall. Some of this externality is reflected in changes in property values: Some individuals will suffer and others benefit. But neither a market system nor any other system guarantees that everyone is made better off by every transaction. Furthermore, this consideration is a long way from our original concern about the "loss" of "prime agricultural land."

EFFECTS OF POPULATION GROWTH ON LAND
AVAILABLE FOR RECREATION AND ENJOYMENT

The availability of recreational land and wilderness is another facet of
the land supply that conerns us. People worry that an increasing use of
land for cities, roads, and agriculture will reduce the amount of recreational land.

It would seem obvious that a larger number of people must imply less
recreational land and the disappearance of wilderness. But like many
intuitively obvious statements about resources, this one is not correct.

The facts: Recreational and wilderness land area has been growing by
leaps and bounds during the period for which data are available. Land
dedicated to wildlife areas, national and state parks and forests, and recreational uses has risen from 8 million acres in 1920 to 61 million acres
in 1974. And the President's Commission in 1972 foresaw a further rise
of about 37 percent from 1964 to 1980 in "pure recreation land outside
towns."[28]

Even more important than the number of acres of land given over to
recreation is the accessibility of recreational land and wilderness to the
potential user. Because of the better means of transportation and the
increased level of income — to which population growth has contributed
over the centuries — the average person in a well-off country now has far
greater access to many more types of recreational land than in any earlier
time. The average American is now richer in ability to enjoy resort areas,
recreational areas, and the wildest of wilderness than was a king 200 or
100 years ago.

To put it in economists' terms, the cost of a day in the wilderness has
steadily gone down, and the income available to pay for it has gone up,
owing in part to population growth. And there is no reason to expect a
change in this trend in the future. (On the other hand, the *value* of a
day in the wilderness may have decreased as the number of people sharing it has gone up. This tempers somewhat the generally positive conclusion reached above, but not enough to invalidate it).

The benefits to the individual American can be seen in the increasing
numbers of visits to principal recreation areas, as seen in figure 16-5. Of
course, one may look upon the increased numbers of visits as an indica-
tion that the wilderness is not so isolated anymore, and hence that it is
less desirable. But that is the point of view of an eighteenth-century
prince who wished to enjoy the entire forest all alone and could afford
to do so. That imperial view differs from the basic democratic view that

thousands of visits yearly

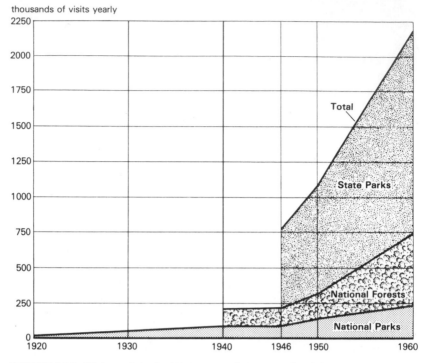

FIGURE 16-5. Visits to Principal Recreational Areas in the U.S.

more people sharing in the enjoyment of something is a good thing even if the experience is not perfect for any one of them.

This section on recreational land has regrettably been limited to the U.S. because I have not been able to assemble data for other parts of the world. And the complexities of the analysis also would be greater if we were to try to make economic and ethical sense of the conflict between, on the one hand, recreational land in foreign countries, and, on the other hand, agricultural land devoted to larger and smaller rates of population growth in those countries. It is worth pointing out, however, that despite its very high population density, China has for some time been engaged in an extensive effort to restore the forests that earlier had been cut down to push agriculture higher up the mountain slopes.[29] The purpose of the Chinese reforestation is mainly to preserve the land from erosion. But the outcome will also be a boon for recreation. So high population density is seen to be consistent with increasing forest areas even in China.

Given that agricultural productivity per acre in presently developed countries is increasing faster than population growth (as well as faster than the growth in total crop production) and given that we can expect all countries to eventually reach this productivity level and go far beyond, it follows that the total amount of land used for crops in poor countries will eventually decline, as it has been declining in the U.S. (This decline is occurring even as U.S. exports of grain are increasing, and therefore the trend of less land feeding more people holds even more strongly if we consider only domestic U.S. food consumption.) This suggests that in the future there will be a larger amount of land available for recreation because less will be used for crops.

For those interested in investment tips: The foregoing implies that agriculture may not be a good investment for the very long run, in comparison with recreational land. This contrasts with a perception that has existed since the beginning of agricultural history, to wit, that flat land accessible to markets is more desirable than hard-to-reach hilly or mountainous land — that Illinois land is more valuable than Tennessee land. The land of the Canaanites was said to be desirable in the Bible because it was "spacious," and good for agriculture. But in the future, land will be desirable because it is interesting for recreation. (Don't rush out today and sink the family fortune into hilly land, however. The long run I am talking about may be a hundred or more years into the future.)

Are these statements that agricultural land is becoming less scarce and recreational land more available just science fiction? It seems to me that a fair-minded person who examines agricultural history must conclude that the facts are more consistent with the view that a greater demand for food leads eventually to a higher output per person than with the common view that it leads to a lower output per person. The simple Malthusian speculation about population growth leading to diminishing returns is the fiction; the induced increase in productivity is the scientific fact.

Do additional people increase the scarcity of land? In the short run, before adjustments are made — of course they do. It is true with land just as with all resources. The instantaneous effect of adding people to a fixed stock of land is less land to go around. But — and this is a main theme of this book — after some time, adjustments are made; new resources (new lands in this case) are created to augment the original stock. And in the longer run the additional people provide the impetus and the knowledge that leave us better off than we were when we started. How you weigh the short-run costs against the intermediate-run and longer-run benefits is a matter of values, of course.

THE FUTURE BENEFITS OF "BLIGHT"

One expects that the constructive activities of man will constitute some saving for later years — harbors, buildings, and land clearing. But I believe that a case can be made that even activities that are not intentionally constructive tend to leave a positive legacy to subsequent generations. That is, even the unintended aspects of man's use of land (and of other raw materials) tend to be profitable for those who come afterward.

Take as an example the "borrow pits" by the sides of roadways. The pits are simply a byproduct of taking material elsewhere. One may first think of the pits as a despoliation of nature, an ugly scar on the land. But it turns out that borrow pits are useful for fishing lakes and reservoirs. Another example is a garbage dump: Later generations may find dumps profitable sources of recyclable materials. Even a pumped-out oil well — that is, the empty hole — probably has value to a subsequent generation. It may be used as a storage place for oil or other fluids, or for some as yet unknown purposes. And the casing that is left in there might be reclaimed profitably by future generations.

The reason for this general phenomenon is that man's activities tend to increase the order and decrease the homogeneity of nature. Man tends to bring like elements together, to concentrate them. This can always be taken advantage of by subsequent generations. Furthermore, man perceives order, and creates it. One can see this from the air if one looks for the signs of human habitation. Where man is, there will be straight lines and smooth curves.

One sees evidence of this delayed benefit in the Middle East. Over the last hundred years, Turks and Arabs have occupied structures originally built by the Romans 2,000 years ago. The ancient buildings save the later comers the trouble of doing their own construction. Another example is the use of dressed stones in locations far away from where they were dressed. One finds the lintels of doorways from ancient Palestinian synagogues in contemporary homes in Syria.

In sum, many acts that we tend to think of as despoiling the land actually leave increased wealth for subsequent generations. Of course this proposition is hard to test. But perhaps a mental comparison will help. Ask yourself which areas in central Illinois will seem more valuable to subsequent generations — the places where cities now are, or the places where farmlands are? I think the former (and not simply because my town's location was selected because it was the best spot to build upon; in fact Champaign-Urbana was built here for a purely accidental-historical reason, not because this spot is any better than the surrounding area).

CONCLUSION

Is the stock of agricultural land being depleted? Just the opposite: The world's total stock of agricultural land is increasing. Will farmers be farming ever-smaller plots of land as population and income grow? Just the opposite: Despite population growth, increased productivity leads to larger farms per farmer. Does population growth in the U.S. mean that too much good agricultural and recreational land is being paved over, at the expense of agriculture and recreation? Flatly no: The amount of recreational land is increasing at a rapid clip, and new agricultural land is being made as some older land goes out of cultivation, leaving a very satisfactory net result for our agricultural future.

17.

Are People an Environmental Pollution?

Human beings have been getting a bad press from writers on environmental matters. You and I and our neighbors are accused of polluting this world and making it a worse place to live. We have been characterized as emitters of such poisonous substances as lead, sulfur dioxide, and carbon monoxide, and as producers of noise, garbage, and congestion. More people, more pollution, runs the charge. Even more ugly, you and I and our neighbors, together with our children, have been referred to as "people pollution" and the "population plague." That is, our very existence is the core of the problem, in that view.

It has come to seem as if one must be against population growth if one is to be for pollution control. And pollution control in itself appeals to everyone, for good reason. A full-length *New York Times Magazine* piece on pollution ended, "The long-term relief is perfectly obvious: Fewer 'capita'."[1] And figure 17-1 appeared as a fullpage advertisement in leading newspapers. Clearly we must inquire how various rates of population growth would affect the amount of pollution.

The sober question we wish to answer here is, What is the effect of human population growth upon pollution levels? The general answer this chapter offers is that, although there may be some short-run increase in pollution due to population increases, the additional pollution is relatively small. And in the long run, pollution is likely to be significantly *less* due to population growth.

We shall also analyze how prudent risk-avoidance fits with our conclusions about population growth's effect on pollution. Though values enter strongly into any such analysis, we shall see that, on the basis of most commonly held values, the desire to avoid risk to humanity from a pollution catastrophe does not lead to the conclusion that population growth should be limited by social policy.

INCOME, GROWTH, POPULATION, AND POLLUTION

The more developed an economy, the more pollutants it produces; this story has been well and truly told by Barry Commoner in *The Closing Circle*, and elsewhere.[2] The total amounts of most kinds of pollutants depend upon the total scale of industry, and this scale may be roughly gauged by a country's GNP (except that, beyond some per capita income, the proportion of industrial products in the GNP begins to decline as the proportion of services increases). A less-known story is that along with higher income and its consequent greater supply of pollutants comes a greater demand for cleanup, plus an increased capacity to pay for it. As we saw in chapter 9, the technology for cleaning up exists in virtually every case, and waits only for our will to expend the time and money to put it to work.

For many years governments did not control the flow of industrial pollutants very well. But in recent years there has come a change in the rules of the game due to a combination of rising incomes and consciousness raising by environmentalists. And this has caused the favorable trends in air and water quality that we saw in chapter 9. The *New York Times* can now headline a story, "Industry is finally cleaning up after itself: with major exceptions, pollution controls are working."[3] Furthermore, before the U.S. Clean Air Act of 1970 and the Water Pollution Control Act of 1972 were passed, there were warnings of catastrophic impacts on business. Yet, "since 1970, the environmental agency has tallied only 81 plant closings attributable to pollution requirements, involving 17,600 jobs."[4] And West Germany's biggest strip-mining firm, Rheinbraun, has moved whole villages so carefully that it was given an international prize because its operations restored the countryside "to greater beauty and usefulness than it had before."[5]

If you have any lingering doubts that increases in income are associated with a decrease in pollution, examine the levels of street cleanliness in the richer versus the poorer countries of the world, the mortality rates of richer versus poorer countries, and the mortality rates of richer versus poorer people within particular countries.[6]

As to population growth and total pollution, some writers have claimed that there is only a slight relationship. They point out that pollution in the U.S. grows at a putative 9 percent a year, while population grows at perhaps 1 percent a year, and they adduce the facts that in Australia's rather affluent cities there is much pollution despite the country's low population, and that the communist countries fall afoul of pollution

We can't lick the pollution this little fellow.

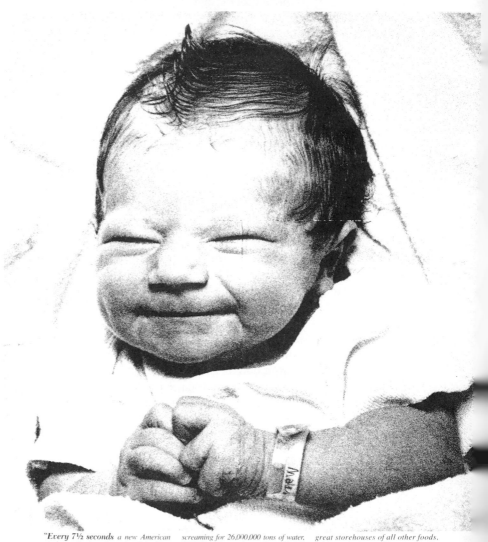

"*Every 7½ seconds* a new American is born. He is a disarming little thing, but he begins to scream loudly in a voice that can be heard for seventy years. He is screaming for 26,000,000 tons of water, 21,000 gallons of gasoline, 10,150 pounds of meat, 28,000 pounds of milk and cream, 9,000 pounds of wheat, and great storehouses of all other foods, drinks, and tobaccos. These are his life time demands of his country and its economy." Robert and Leona Train Rienow in *Moment in the Sun*

FIGURE 17-1. Propaganda on Pollution and Population Growth

problem without considering

Population stabilization is essential.

105 Billion Dollars to Clean Up Pollution

The White House Council on Environmental Quality in its second annual report recently sent to the Congress totalled up the cost of cleaning up our environment. *The price tag for the next five years is 105 billion dollars.*

The cost of cleaning up our air — 23.7 billion dollars.

The cost of cleaning up our water — 38 billion dollars.

The cost of taking care of solid waste — 43.5 billion dollars.

The cost for each man, woman, and child in the United States is $525!

President Nixon, in commenting on the report, said it will not be cheap or easy to realize this goal. "The cost," he said, "will have to be borne by every citizen, consumer, and taxpayer."

Even this vast expenditure, however, will not stop pollution unless we check the rapid growth of our population. For, let's face it, *people pollute!*

U.S. Population Explosion

Let's take a look at the growth of population in the United States:

1. We had 100 million people as recently as 1915 and never worried about pollution.

2. However, we have added another 100 million people in the brief period since 1915.

3. And *at the present rate of increase* we shall add another 100 million in the next 30 years or so, *bringing the total up to 300 million* — and a fourth 100 million after that will *bring the total up to 400 million!*

Today, with only about 200 million, the water we drink may be contaminated and the air dangerous to breathe. Noises deafen us. Our cities are packed with youngsters — many of them idle and victims of drug addiction. And millions more will pour into our streets in the years immediately ahead.

President Nixon made a ringing pledge in July 1969 to provide leadership in the population field. He said, "When future generations evaluate . . . our time . . . one of the most important factors . . . will be the way we respond to population growth. Let us act

in such a way that those who come after us . . . can do so with pride in the planet . . . with gratitude to those who lived on it in the past and with confidence in its future . . . This Administration does accept a clear responsibility to provide essential leadership."

In December of last year Congress responded by passing and sending to President Nixon the Family Planning Services and Population Research Act — which he signed.

How Pollution Control Costs Will Grow

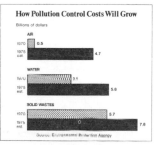

Billions of dollars

AIR
1970 0.5
1975 est. 4.7

WATER
1970 3.1
1975 est. 5.8

SOLID WASTES
1970 5.7
1975 est. 7.8

Source: Environmental Protection Agency

Landmark Legislation — But Far Too Little

The President termed it *landmark legislation,* aimed as it is at one of the twin clouds threatening mankind's survival on earth — the *population bomb* and the *atom bomb.*

Congress appropriates annually *over 75 billion dollars* for defense — of which a considerable amount is for the atom bomb to keep us on a parity with Russia. *This is over 75,000 million dollars!*

The amount now authorized to defuse the *population bomb* is less than $200 million annually. You will see that this is but a tiny fraction of the amount we spend annually for the atom bomb.

Not since Hiroshima and Nagasaki 26 years ago has the atom bomb been used in warfare. But the population bomb is ticking right along, adding over 75,000,000 human beings annually to the earth's population — most of them hungry.

Meantime, the Executive Agencies of our

government, out of additional funds made available by the above legislation, in their wisdom have asked for fiscal 1972 *only $10 million* of the $50 million authorized for population research — and only *$47 million* of the $79 million authorized for contraceptive services for women desiring them.

YOU Can Do Something About This Matter

I. Wire or write President Nixon reminding him that our present steadily increasing population is degrading the quality of life in the United States, and that the flood of people now engulfing the earth is a threat to future peace in the world. Urge him to *implement at once and to the fullest* the authority given him by Congress.

II. Wire or write your senators and your representative in Congress asking them to support Senate Joint Resolution 108, introduced by Senators Alan Cranston and Robert Taft and 31 other senators. This resolution would put Congress on record as favoring zero population growth in the United States "through public policies to reduce the birth rate voluntarily in a manner consistent with human life and individual conscience."

III. Wire or write the Commission on Population Growth and the American Future (John D. Rockefeller 3rd, Chairman), 726 Jackson Place, N.W., Washington, D.C. 20506. Urge the Commission in its next report to President Nixon to recommend a policy of population stabilization for the United States.

There is no question that population stabilization must be a part of any forward-looking program to control pollution. Population growth "is an *intensifier,*" the Commission on Population Growth has already said, "or *multiplier* of many of the problems impairing the quality of life in the United States."

when industrial production goes up, just as capitalist countries. The slight short-run relationship between population growth and pollution may be seen in figure 17-2. The solid rectangles show the (very small) differences in emitted-hydrocarbon pollution between the two-child and the three-child average family projections for the year 2000, under both high-economic-growth and low-economic-growth projections. Likewise, the pollution differences between high and low economic growth are small. The largest differences are seen to arise from different social choices among pollution-treatment policies. And the general conclusions of the President's Commission on Population Growth "are similar for other pollutants" to these conclusions about hydrocarbons.[7] In brief, population growth has a relatively unimportant effect on pollution levels in the short run, thirty years or less. And growth in GNP has a greater positive influence on pollution than population growth has negative influence, in the short run — before the additional children under discussion join the labor force.

In the long run, however, the total pollution output will be more or less proportional to the labor force, for a given level of technology. A population twice as big implies twice as much total pollution, all else being equal. If the increased population results in a proportional increase

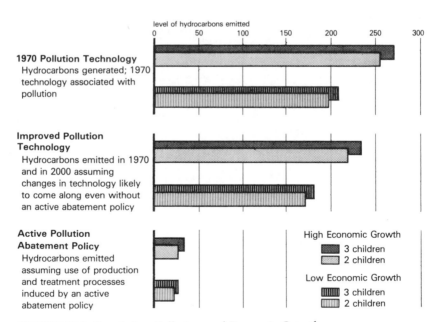

FIGURE 17-2. Population, Pollution, and Economic Growth

in population density, each person will be exposed to twice as much pollution, again all else being equal.

It is not reasonable, however, to assume that all else is equal. When pollution increases, political forces arise to fight it. Once this process begins, the result may be less pollution than ever — or, of course, nothing may happen except an even worse level of pollution. The outcome simply cannot be known in advance; there seems to be nothing in economic logic or political history that can help us predict with confidence whether the long-run result of the larger population and of the initially higher pollution would be a situation better or worse than if the population had now grown so large. Yet we must keep in mind the empirical fact that over the longest sweep of human history, while population has grown enormously, total pollution — as measured by life expectancy, and by the rate of deaths due to socially transmitted and socially caused diseases — has fallen markedly.

AESTHETICS, POLLUTION, AND POPULATION GROWTH

Aesthetics obviously are a matter of taste, and especially here it is not sensible to dispute about tastes. For some people, to be alone in a virgin forest is the ideal, and other visitors would constitute "people pollution"; for others, seeing lots of people at play is the best sight of all.

Of those who praise a reduction of population in the name of making the world more beautiful, I ask these questions: (1) Have you not seen much beauty on this earth that comes from the hand of man — gardens, statues, skyscrapers, graceful bridges? (2) The population of Athens was only 6,000 persons in 1823. Do you think Athens was more beautiful in 1823 or two millennia earlier, when it was more crowded? (3) If the world's population now were a hundredth of what it actually is, would there be a transportation system to get you to Yosemite, the Grand Canyon, the Antarctic, Kenya's wildlife preserves, or Lake Victoria?

POLLUTION, POPULATION, AND RISK OF CATASTROPHE

A safety-minded person might say, "Perhaps the additional risk of the particular pollutant X that is induced by more population is a small one. But would it not be prudent to avoid even this small possibility?" This question is related to the issue of risk aversion discussed in the section on nuclear energy in chapter 8. To state the problem at its worst: In an advanced technological society there is always the possibility that a totally new form of pollution will emerge and finish us all before we can do anything about it.

Though the incidence of general catastrophes to the human race has decreased from the time of the Black Death forward, the risk *may* have begun to increase in recent decades — from atomic bombs or from some unknown but powerful pollution. But the present risk of catastrophe will only be known in the future, with hindsight. The arguments in Part I about natural resources are not a counterpart to this explosive unknown, and there is no logical answer to this threat except to note that life with perfect security is not possible — and probably would not be meaningful.

It might make sense to control population growth if the issue were simply the increased risk of catastrophe due to population growth, and if only the number of deaths mattered, rather than the number of healthy lives lived. One flaw in this line of reasoning is revealed, however, by pushing it to its absurd endpoint: One may reduce the risk of pollution catastrophe to zero by reducing to zero the number of persons who are alive. But such a policy obviously is unacceptable to all but a few persons who have values quite different from the rest of us. Therefore we must dig deeper to learn how pollution ought to influence our views about population size and growth.

The argument that population growth is a bad thing because it may bring about new and possibly catastrophic forms of pollution is a special case of a more general argument: Avoid any change because it may bring about some devastating technological destruction as yet unknown. There is an irrefutable logic in this argument. In its own terms, adding a few not-too-unreasonable assumptions, it cannot be proven wrong, as follows. Assume that any alteration in technology may have some unexpected ill effects. Assume also that the system is acceptably safe right now. Additional people increase the need for change, and this makes a prima facie case against population growth. And the same argument can be applied to economic growth: Economic growth brings about change, which can bring dangers. Hence economic growth is to be avoided.

Of course, this sit-tight, leave-well-enough-alone posture is only possible for us 1980s humans, because economic and population growth in the past produced the changes that brought many of us to the "well enough" state that might now be "left alone."[8] That is, the high life expectancy and high living standard of middle-class people in developed countries could not have come about if people in the past had not produced the changes that got the most fortunate of us here — and if they had not suffered some consequences in doing so. We are living off our inheritance from past generations the way children may live off the inheritance of parents who worked hard and saved.

There is nothing logically wrong with living off an inheritance without in turn increasing the heritage of knowledge and high living standards that will be left to subsequent generations. But you should at least be clear that this is what you are doing if you opt for "zero growth" — if zero growth really were possible. (In fact, upon close examination, the concept of zero economic growth, unlike zero population growth, turns out to be either so vague as to be undefinable, or just plain nonsense; and it offers benefits to the well-off that are withheld from the poor.)[9]

Proponents of zero growth argue that future generations will benefit from fewer changes now. That is conceivable, of course. But the historical evidence quite clearly runs the other way: If our ancestors had, at any time in the past, opted for zero population growth or for a frozen economic system, we would certainly be less well-off than we now are. Hence it seems reasonable to project the same trend into the future. Most specifically, a larger economic capability and a larger population of knowledge creators has put into our hands a wider variety of more powerful tools for preventing and controlling threats to our lives and environment — especially communicable diseases and hunger — than society could have bequeathed to us if its size had been frozen at any time in the past.

Furthermore, additional people can also improve the chances of reducing pollution even in their own generation, because additional people create new *solutions* for problems, as well as create new problems. Let's consider a poor-country example: Higher population density may increase the chance of communicable disease. But higher population density also is the only force that really gets rid of malaria, because the swamps that breed malaria-carrying mosquitoes do not co-exist with settled fields and habitation. And of course, if population growth had never occurred, there would not likely have been the growth of civilization and science that led to pharmaceutical weapons against malaria and improved methods of fighting mosquitoes.

On balance, then, we must put onto the scales not only the increased chance of a pollution catastrophe induced by more people; we must also weigh the new knowledge for an increased control of pollutants, and of their ill consequences, that additional people contribute. So it is not at all clear whether the chance of catastrophe (involving 10,000 or 1 million people) is greater with a world population of 4 trillion or of 6 billion, or with a growth rate of 2 percent or 1 percent yearly.

It would be an error to assume that all (or even most) indirect environmental effects of economic and population growth are negative. Happy accidents sometimes arise due to growth. If more genetic changes occur (they occur naturally, or we would not be here at all), some of the mutants will be "undesirable," but others will be "desirable." And some environmental changes also affect species for the good:

SEAFOOD INDUSTRY FINDS FISH THRIVE IN WATER DISCHARGED BY POWER COMPANIES.

The water, used as a coolant in generating plants, is about 20 degrees warmer when it leaves a plant than when it entered. Cultivating catfish, oysters, shrimp, trout and other marine life in this warm water often cuts in half the length of time it takes them to mature. Cultured Catfish Co. of Colorado City, Texas, says its catfish grow to 1½ pounds in three to four months in the warm water flowing from a Texas Electric Service plant. It usually takes catfish, considered a delicacy in some parts of the U.S., 18 months to grow that big in a natural pond.[10]

Still — there is our natural aversion to risk and uncertainty. We should keep in mind, however, that risk and uncertainty are not all in one direction, and that the major social and cultural changes that would be needed to prevent growth are also fraught with uncertainty, and possible catastrophe. For example, what would be the social and political implications of freezing the present pattern of income distribution among the poor and the rich due to reduced economic growth? What would be the effects on incentive if people were told that they could not increase their incomes or have more children? What would be the psychological implications of a stationary economy and society? And which legal sanctions would be imposed to enforce these decisions? Certainly none of these matters is of small importance compared with the likely dangers from catastrophic pollution. Hence there is no prima facie case for ceasing economic or population growth due to fear of pollution.

SUMMARY

More people mean higher total output, and this implies more pollution in the short run, all else being equal. But more people need not imply more pollution, and they may well imply less pollution; this has been the trend in human history as indicated by the most important general index of pollution — increasing life expectancy. Additional people have created new ways of reducing pollution, and contributed additional resources with which to fight pollution. There is no reason to expect a different course of events in the future.

Population Density Does Not Damage Health, or Psychological and Social Well-Being

For years people have thought that high population density is dangerous to health. It was, in some earlier years. For example, during the industrial revolution, the death rate was generally higher in cities than in the country. But whatever the explanation of that phenomenon, there seems no evidence that an increase in population density is unhealthy nowadays. We'll tackle this first; the effect of population density on psychological and social well-being will occupy the second part of the chapter.

POPULATION DENSITY AND PHYSICAL HEALTH

Health is obviously a central concern to everyone. Feeling and being healthy is as valuable as anything else an economy can provide. Moreover, health is a central issue in the functioning of the economy — healthy people can and do work harder and better than sick people, and prevalent illness surely is a crucial barrier to the economic development of many poor countries.

Life expectancy is the key measure of a country's health situation, as discussed in chapter 9, on pollution. There it was shown that population density and growth have no apparent negative effects on life expectancy; rather, there are reasons to believe that the effects are positive.

In earlier times, living in areas of high population density — cities — reduced one's life expectancy. In the seventeenth century, when William Petty wrote about London, the death rate was so much higher in urban than in rural areas (and probably the birthrate was so much lower) that cities like London depended on migration from the country to maintain their populations. In 1841 the life expectancy for males was 35 years in London but 40 years in the rest of Great Britian.[1] And life expectancy in the U.S. was still much lower in urban places than in rural areas from 1900 until 1940: for white males, 44.0 versus 54.0 *(1900)*; 47.3 versus 55.1 *(1910)*; 56.7 versus 62.1 *(1930)*; and 61.6 versus 64.1 *(1939)*.[2]

In more recent times in developed nations, however, as communicable diseases have been controlled with sanitation and other public health measures, this disadvantage of population density has disappeared. By 1950–52 life expectancy in London was 67.3 years compared with 66.4 years in the rest of Great Britain.[3]

More generally, the historical picture in the West during the last half-millennium, and in most countries in the world during the last few decades, has shown related growth in all three key factors — population density, income, and life expectancy. This suggests that increased density and increased income — either individually or in combination — benefit people's life expectancy and health, as well as vice versa.

Why should people enjoy better health by living where there is a higher population density? Let's make a negative point first. There is nowadays no reason why population density should worsen health, now that the important infectious diseases, excepting malaria, have been conquered. And malaria — which many medical historians consider to have been the most important of mankind's diseases — flourishes where population is sparse and where large tracts of moist land are therefore left uncultivated; in these areas increased population density removes the mosquitoes' breeding grounds.[4]

The Case of Malaria

As Pierre Gourou puts it,

> Malaria is the most widespread of tropical diseases. . . . It attacks (or did until recently) something like one-third of the human race, but in practice all the inhabitants of the hot, wet belt may be considered to be more or less infected. Malaria weakens those whom it attacks, for the bouts of fever sap their physical strength and make them unfit for sustained effort. Hence agriculture does not receive all the care it needs, and the food supply is thereby affected. In this way a vicious circle is formed. Weakened by insufficient nourishment, the [infected person's] system offers small resistance to infection and cannot provide the effort required to produce an adequate supply of food. The malarial patient knows quite well that a bout of fever may be the unpleasant reward for hard work. . . .
>
> Undoubtedly, malaria is largely responsible for the poor health, small numbers, and absence of enthusiasm for work of tropical peoples. . . .
>
> In the pre-scientific age, men kept the most serious infectious diseases in check by organizing the total occupation of the land, thus eliminating the breeding places of the mosquito. Such occupation

demanded a high density of population and a complete control of land use, and hence the interdependence of a highly organized agricultural system (itself a function of soil quality, reliable climate and a certain degree of technical competence), a dense population and an advanced political organization. . . . It is also difficult to improve sanitation and health in sparsely peopled areas; anti-malarial campaigns stand but small chance of lasting success, whilst the tsetse fly finds such areas very much to its liking, for it is impossible for a population of ten or a dozen persons to the square mile to keep down the vegetation to a level unfavourable to this insect. Health services are difficult to maintain, and doctors and hospitals are inevitably far removed from patients; whilst education is almost impossible.[5]

The data on Ceylon in table 18-1 support Gourou's argument, showing that a low population is associated with a high incidence of malaria. Of course one might wonder whether population is low in malarial areas because people simply chose to move away from malaria. But the history of Ceylon suggests otherwise.[6]

The ancient civilization of Ceylon had centered in the area with hyperendemic malaria. The ruins of 10,000 dams testify to the level and magnitude of this civilization in successive stages of history. Decay of the ancient order was associated with collapse of the irrigation systems, emergence of conditions that favored transmission of malaria, and retreat of the Singhalese to the nonmalarious area of the island.[7]

Likewise, some historians have suggested that the decline of the Roman Empire was in large part due to the spread of malaria after political

TABLE 18-1. Population, Area, and Population Density of Districts of Ceylon (Sri Lanka) Grouped by the Endemicity of Malaria in the Districts

| Endemicity of Malaria | Spleen Rates* (%) | Population** | | Area | | Population Density per Square Mile |
		Number	(%)	Square Miles	(%)	
Not endemic	(0–9)	4,142,889	(62)	5,113	(20)	810
Moderately endemic	(10–24)	1,207,569	(18)	5,271	(21)	229
Highly endemic	(25–49)	994,495	(15)	8,460	(33)	118
Hyperendemic	(50–74)	312,466	(5)	6,489	(26)	48

SOURCE: Frederiksen, 1968, in Heer, 1968, p. 70.

*Average of surveys in 1939 and 1941.

**1946 census.

upheaval and decreased population density interfered with the mainte-
nance of the drainage system.[8]

Looking to examples of improvement rather than retrogression, now,
the history of England was heavily affected by the decline of malaria
induced by population growth. In London, "Westminster was paved in
1762 and the City in 1766 . . . and the marshes near London were drained
about the same time." This led a writer to observe in 1781 that "very
few die now of Ague [malaria] in London." [9]

The history of the U.S. also reveals the interplay between malaria,
population, and economic development:

> . . . a mighty influence buoying up wages paid to the men building
> canals during the 1820's and 1830's was the danger of yellow fever and
> malaria. Built through marsh and swamps (in many instances) to
> reduce construction problems, the canals were known as killers. . . .
> As the country was settled, the marshy land where malaria was bred
> was filled in. Buildings covered the waste spaces where [disease car-
> riers] could survive.[10]

Because of DDT and other synthetic pesticides, medical technologists
thought for a time that population density was no longer necessary to
prevent malaria. Malaria was considered beaten. But throughout the
world, the disease has bounced back.[11] India went from 75 million suf-
ferers in 1953 to "total control" in 1968, but in the 1971 epidemic there
were 1.3 million reported cases, rising to 5.8 million cases reported in
1976.[12] Due to the evolution of pesticide-resistant strains of carrier insects
and the concomitant damage to the insects' natural predators, pesticides
soon lose their effectiveness. Barry Commoner gives this example:

> In Guatemala, some twelve years after the start of a malaria "erad-
> ication program" based on intensive use of insecticides, the malarial
> mosquitoes have become resistant and the incidence of the disease is
> higher than it was before the campaign. The levels of DDT in the
> milk of Guatemalan women are by far the highest reported anywhere
> in the world thus far.[13]

Other public health experts also are grim about the prospects of fighting
malaria with chemicals.

> Asked whether we are winning or losing the battle against tropical
> diseases, some experts, among them Dr. B. H. Kean of Cornell Uni-
> versity Medical College, answer promptly that we are losing. He notes
> that malaria, for example, seemed almost conquered in the decade or

so after World War II. But since then mosquitoes have become resistant to pesticides, and the malaria parasite has learned to cope with some of the more widely used drugs.[14]

Once again the only sure weapon against malaria may turn out to be increased population density.

Some Other Health Examples

Not only is the infectious-disease drawback of population density a thing of the past, but higher density also has many positive effects on health, even aside from control of insects that carry malaria, sleeping sickness (the tsetse fly in Africa), and other diseases. For example, cities in the modern world have safer water supplies than rural areas have. Medical care is better in cities, too, and medical help arrives quicker, or is easier to reach, where there is a good transport system — which is the result of population density (see chapter 13).

We must also remember the additional knowledge, created by more people, that contributes to health. Item: Emergency medical systems, springing up in the U.S., are saving lives after auto accidents and in other emergencies. The population-induced road network of the U.S. is a key to the success of such systems. A country with a much sparser population would find such emergency service much more expensive. And last, it takes imagination and skill — human minds and hands — to invent and develop such medical systems. Item: Electrical wiring is safer than it used to be. Many old houses have been rewired more safely since wiring ideas were developed by "additional" people — that is, by people who may not have been born if population growth were lower. And new houses are built, with safer wiring, because population growth (together with increased income) creates new demand for houses. (In Ireland, where population has not grown much in the past century, one seldom sees a new building. I shudder at the electrical monstrosities that must lie within some of the larger older buildings.)

The Psychological and Sociological Effects of Crowding

You have probably heard many times that high population density has bad psychological and sociological effects. This is sheer myth. High population density has indeed been shown to harm animals — but not humans. Rather, it is too much isolation that harms humans. The belief that crowding harms people is supported only by analogies to animals, analogies that are patently misplaced.

For hundreds of years biologists have observed that, when animals are confined to a given area with given resources, "unhappy" events occur. An increased death rate was noted by such observers as Benjamin Franklin. Modern students such as Konrad Lorenz and John B. Calhoun have focused on "anti-social" and "pathological" behavior in fish, geese, and Norwegian rats. For example, the title of Calhoun's famous article is "Population Density and Social Pathology." These biologists simply assumed that the same processes necessarily occur with humans.

The earliest — and still most crushing — rebuttal is that given to Benjamin Franklin by, of all people, the old master Malthus himself after he learned some facts and smartened up subsequent to publishing his first edition. (This episode is described in chapter 12.) Biologist Julian Huxley explains how we go wrong in reasoning from animals to people.

> We begin by minimizing the difference between animals and ourselves by unconsciously projecting our own qualities into them: this is the way of children and of primitive peoples. Though early scientific thinkers, like Descartes, tried to make the difference absolute, later applications of the method of scientific analysis to man have, until quite recently, tended to reduce it again. This is partly because we have often been guilty of the fallacy of mistaking origins for explanations — what we may call the "nothing but" fallacy: if sexual impulse is at the base of love, then love is to be regarded as nothing but sex; if it can be shown that man originated from an animal, then in all essentials he is nothing but an animal. This, I repeat, is a dangerous fallacy.
>
> We have tended to misunderstand the nature of the difference between ourselves and animals. We have a way of thinking that if there is continuity in time there must be continuity in quality. A little reflection would show that this is not the case. When we boil water there is a continuity of substance between water as a liquid and water as steam; but there is a critical point at which the substance H_2O changes its properties. This emergence of new properties is even more obvious when the process involves change in organization, as in all cases when chemical elements combine to produce a chemical compound.
>
> The critical point in the evolution of man — the change of state when wholly new properties emerged in evolving life — was when he acquired the use of verbal concepts and could organize his experience in a common pool. It was this which made human life different from that of all other organisms.[15]

And thus human organization is different from animal organization, especially in man's capacity to create new modes of organization.

Here is a similar critique of Lorenz's analogies:

> [Lorenz has a] regrettable tendency to describe animal behavior in human terms — "married love" in monogamous geese, for example. This cannot be dismissed as harmless anthropomorphism in the service of popularization, for it promotes the very misuse of analogy that lies at the heart of Lorenz's problems. A curious twist of logic to be sure — impose a human concept by dubious metaphor upon an animal, then re-derive it for humans as obviously "natural." Thus, a drake that tried to copulate with Lorenz's boot is a fetishist by "exact analogy," and a mob of geese frightening off a coati-mundi play the same role as a human picket line.[16]

So much for the animals. In an authoritative survey in his presidential address to the Population Association of America, Amos Hawley concluded that human population density has no general ill effects on such measures of welfare as longevity, crime rates, mental illness rates, and recreational facilities. The most recent surveys, such as that by Harvey M. Choldin, agree.[17]

After it became apparent that city density is not necessarily connected to pathology, those who worry about these matters turned to crowding at home and work. But experiments show that people are not affected by crowding as animals are. For example, a recent study of "the effect of household and neighborhood crowding on the relations between urban family members" showed that "crowding is found to have little or no effect."[18] Furthermore, density and crowding are not necessarily found together.[19] Slums at urban fringes often have low density, and "these areas have more pathology than high-density slums."[20] The most ambitious experimental tests, conducted by psychologist Jonathan Freedman (once an associate of Paul Ehrlich and a believer that density is pathological) led to the conclusions that

> intuitions, speculations, political and philosophical theory appear to be wrong in this respect. . . . People who live under crowded conditions do not suffer from being crowded. Other things being equal, they are no worse off than other people. . . . It took me and other psychologists working in this area many years to be convinced, but eventually the weight of the evidence overcame our doubts and preconceptions."[21]

No matter what the effects of crowding really are, the amount of crowding has been going down in the U.S. even as population has been rising. The percentage of households living in "crowded conditions" (more than one person per room) has been: *1940,* 20 percent; *1950,* 16 percent; *1960,* 12 percent; *1970,* 8 percent.[22] (Would those who worry about crowding offer population growth as a salutary prescription?)

Once I had a conversation with a woman who was worried about the ill effects of crowding — as we sat haunch to haunch in a football stadium packed with 75,000 people! She saw no humor in my pointing out that she seemed to be enjoying herself tolerably well under the circumstances.

War is perhaps the most grisly outcome that population density is said to threaten. "At the present rate of world population increase, overpopulation may become *the* major cause of social and political instability. Indeed, the closer man approaches the limits of ultimate density or 'carrying capacity,' the more probable is nuclear warfare."[23] The simple fact, however, is that there is zero evidence connecting population density with the propensity to engage in war, or even fist fights.

As to the effect of size of family on children's intelligence, the evidence is so mixed that it defies summary. The well-known recent study of IQ scores by R. B. Zajonc interprets the data in a manner favorable to smaller families.[24] But even in the Zajonc survey it is crystal clear that whatever real IQ differences exist among children in families with one, two, or three children are small by any meaningful measure.[25] Other reviews offer conflicting points of view; the interested reader may consult Terhune, Kunz and Peterson, and Lindert.[26] There is, however, little doubt that only children do *worse* than children with one or two siblings. On balance there is little reason to believe that, all else equal, a larger family lessens a child's intelligence or chances in life. And the long-run trend is toward smaller families anyway, as populations grow and countries develop — so all else is *not* equal.

There are many other ill effects of population density that one may imagine. But we've covered the main ones that people have written about. So let's stop here.

CONCLUSIONS

Regarding the purported ill effects of population density, the charges are many and imaginative. But the verdict must be "Innocent." And this is not for lack of evidence. As the most recent extensive review sums up, "It is reasonable to conclude that the density-pathology hypothesis fails to be confirmed within urban areas. When social structural differences among neighborhoods are considered (held constant) population density appears to make a trivial difference in predicting pathology rates."[27]

19.

The Big Economic Picture: Population Growth and Living Standards in MDCs

The conventional economic theory of population growth says one thing. The data say something else entirely. This chapter discusses the theory, presents the facts, and then reconciles theory and fact for the more-developed countries (MDCs). Chapter 20 does the same for the less-developed countries (LDCs). This chapter and the next are tougher reading than most of the others, but I hope you will bear with them. (Read them when your mind is fresh, perhaps.)

THE THEORY OF POPULATION AND INCOME

Classical economic theory apparently shows irrefutably that population growth must reduce the standard of living. The heart of all economic theory of population, from Malthus to *The Limits to Growth*, can be stated in a single sentence: The more people using a stock of resources, the lower the income per person, if all else remains equal. This proposition derives from the "law" of diminishing returns: Two men cannot use the same tool at the same time, or farm the same piece of land, without reducing the output per worker. A related idea is that two people cannot nourish themselves as well as one person can from a given stock of food. And when one considers the age distribution resulting from a higher birthrate, the effect is reinforced by a larger proportion of children, and thus a lower proportion of workers, in the larger population. Let us spell out these Malthusian ideas.

The Consumption Effect

Simply adding more people to a population affects consumption directly. If there is only one pie, the pieces will be smaller if it is divided among more eaters. The experience of hippies in San Francisco in 1967 illustrates this problem.

> Most hippies take the question of survival for granted, but it's becoming increasingly obvious as the neighborhood fills with penni-

less heads, that there is simply not enough food and lodging to go around. A partial solution may come from a group called the "Diggers," who have been called the "worker-priests" of the hippy movement and the "invisible government" of the Hashbury. The Diggers are young and aggressively pragmatic: they have set up free lodging centers, free soup kitchens and free clothing distribution centers. They comb the neighborhood soliciting donations of everything from money to stale bread to camping equipment.

For a while, the Diggers were able to serve three meals, however meager, each afternoon in Golden Gate Park. But as the word got around, more and more hippies showed up to eat, and the Diggers were forced to roam far afield to get food. Occasionally there were problems, as when Digger Chieftain Emmett Grogan, 23, called a local butcher a "Fascist pig and a coward" when he refused to donate meat scraps. The butcher whacked Grogan with the flat side of his meat cleaver.[1]

This consumption effect occurs most sharply within a family. When there are more children, each one gets a smaller part of the family's earnings, if earnings remain the same. We see the effect in Hardy's *Mayor of Casterbridge*.

[Mr. Longways]: True; your mother was a very good woman — I can mind her. She were rewarded by the Agricultural Society for having begot the greatest number of healthy children without parish assistance, and other virtuous marvels.

[Mrs. Cuxsom]: 'Twas that that kept us so low upon ground — that great hungry family.

[Mr. Longways]: 'Ay. Where the pigs be many the wash runs thin.[2]

The Production Effect

Adding people also affects consumption indirectly, through the effect on production per worker. Consider a country that possesses a given amount of land and a given quantity of factories and other industrial capital at a given time. If the country has a larger labor force, the production per worker will be lower because each worker has, on the average, less land or tools to work with. Hence average production per worker will be lower with a larger labor force and fixed capital. This is the classical argument of diminishing returns.

The Public Facilities Effect

If a given population is instantly enlarged by, say, 10 percent in all age groups, there will be 10 percent more people wanting to use the village well or the city hospital or the public beach. An increase in the demand for such freely provided public services inevitably results in an increase in the number of people who are denied service, a decrease in the amount of service per person, or an additional expenditure by the government to increase the amount of public facilities. If the 10 percent population increase also results in a 10 percent increase in the number of people working, and if the productivity of the added people is as great, on the average, as that of the original population, then the added population will have no effect on per capita income. But such a compensating increase in production is not likely. If more children are born, the demand for public facilities—especially schools—will occur before the children grow up, find work, and become productive; and even immigrating adults use at least the customhouse before starting work. And after the additional children join the labor force, they are likely to lower the average worker's productivity at first because of the "law" of diminishing returns discussed earlier, and hence the added workers will not be able to contribute as much in taxes to support public facilities as the average person formerly did. These effects were discussed in chapter 13 (as were the data that called into question these theoretical propositions).

As a result of the increased demand, the average level of public services received is likely to be lower; the average person will receive less education and less health care than if the population remains fixed. And some tax moneys that might have gone into harbors or communication systems may go instead to the education and health care of the added people.

In classical theory, then, sheer numbers of people depress per capita income in two ways: More consumers divide any given amount of output; and each worker produces less because there is less capital, private and public, per worker.

Age-Distribution Effects

As we saw in chapter 11, a faster-growing population implies a larger proportion of children, which means that a larger proportion of the population is too young to work. This smaller proportion of workers must mean a smaller output per capita, all else equal. Therefore, the effect of sheer numbers of people, and the age distribution that occurs in the process of getting to the higher numbers, both work in the same direction, causing a smaller per capita product. (Chapter 11 discussed the age distributions in greater detail.)

When one also takes women's labor into account, the effect of having a higher proportion of children is even greater. The more children that are born per woman, the less chance she has to work outside the home.

For example, in the 1920s and 1930s, when most Israeli kibbutzim were near bare subsistence, strong pressure was often brought upon couples not to have more than two children, in order to enable women to do more "productive" work.[3] And the same is true in China now. (But in the U.S., at least, this effect is not as great as one might expect. Calculations show that each baby after the first keeps an average woman out the labor force for only about half a year.)[4]

There is a counterbalancing effect from the father's work. A wide variety of studies show that an additional child causes fathers to work additional hours, the equivalent of two to six extra weeks of work a year. In the long run this yearly 4–10 percent increase in work for an additional child may fully (or more than fully) balance the temporary loss of labor-force time by the mother. (One might say that an additional child "forces" a father to work — a "bad" outcome. But if he chooses to have the additional child at the cost of working more, it is reasonable to say that he prefers that alternative of having more children and more work to fewer children and less work. This is quite the same as working more hours to have a nicer home or to pay for additional education. Who is to say which choice is "bad" or "wrong"?)

Age distribution affects income distribution, too. In the discussion of social security and saving in chapter 11, we saw that a larger proportion of younger persons implies that more earners will one day support each retired person, which means a better pension for each retired person and a smaller burden on each working-age person.

Other Theoretical Effects

The dilution of capital through reduced saving, and through reduced education per person, are other elements of the standard economic theory of population growth (though chapter 13 shows them to be far smaller drawbacks than commonly thought, and perhaps no drawbacks at all). The only positive theoretical effect is that of larger markets and larger-scale production, known to economists as "economies of scale," which chapter 14 discussed.

THE EVIDENCE VERSUS THE MALTHUSIAN THEORY

The Malthusian supply-side effect of diminishing output from additional workers and the demand-side effect of less to go around among a larger number of consumers have dominated the conventional economic theory of population growth. And their implication is clear: Additional people must reduce the standard of living, all else equal.

But the evidence does not confirm the conventional theory. It suggests that, at least in MDCs, population growth almost certainly does not hinder, and perhaps helps, economic growth. One piece of historical evidence is the concurrent explosion of both population and economic development in Europe from 1650 onward. Other evidence is found in the rates of population growth and output per capita as compared in figure 19-1, which includes contemporary MDCs for which data is available for the last century. No strong relationship appears. Studies of the most recent rates of population growth and economic growth are another source of evidence. Many comparisons have been made among various countries by now, and there is agreement among them that population growth does not hinder economic growth.[5]

These overlapping empirical studies do *not* show, however, that fast population growth in MDCs *increases* per capita income. But they certainly imply that one should not confidently assert that population growth *decreases* economic growth.

These data, which contradict the simple Malthusian theory, have naturally provoked explanations. One such explanation is that population growth is a "challenge" that evokes the "response" of increased efforts from individuals and societies. There certainly is evidence that people make special efforts when they perceive a special need. The other side of this coin is that people can slack off when population growth slows and demand lessens, as we see now in education. One typical newspaper

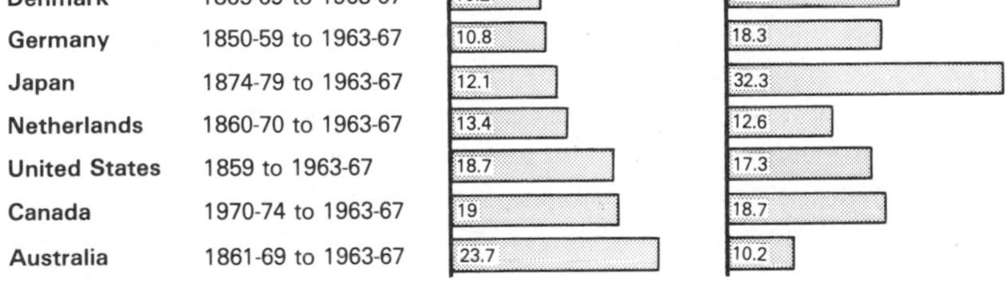

		Population Growth Rate per Decade	Output per Capita Growth Rate per Decade
France	1861-70 to 1963-66	3	17
Sweden	1861-69 to 1963-67	6.6	28.9
Great Britain	1855-64 to 1963-67	8.2	13.4
Norway	1865-69 to 1963-67	8.3	21.3
Denmark	1865-69 to 1963-67	10.2	20.2
Germany	1850-59 to 1963-67	10.8	18.3
Japan	1874-79 to 1963-67	12.1	32.3
Netherlands	1860-70 to 1963-67	13.4	12.6
United States	1859 to 1963-67	18.7	17.3
Canada	1970-74 to 1963-67	19	18.7
Australia	1861-69 to 1963-67	23.7	10.2

FIGURE 19-1. The Non-Relationship between Population Growth and the Growth of Living Standards

story is headlined "Empty-Desk Blues."[6] And another story complains
that

> books run short, classes get big, sports are dropped; teachers decry cut-
> backs. . . . The Detroit schools this year are operating on what one
> official calls a "suicide" budget — even tighter than last year's "sur-
> vival" budget and far below the spending level needed for what
> administrators consider normal operations.
>
> That means shortages of everything from textbooks and filmstrips
> to such mundane items as paper and duplicating fluid. It means big
> cuts in art, music and sports programs and bigger classes. And, educa-
> tors here claim, it means further deterioration in the quality of edu-
> cation in the nation's fifth-largest school system. . . .
>
> Public school systems all over the country are having problems with
> rising costs and voter opposition to higher tax rates, of course. [7]

It is illogical and peculiar that less demographic pressure should be associated with budget squeezes in the schools, but a clear fact it nevertheless
is.

Another explanation why population growth does not retard economic
growth focuses on the advantages of proportionately more *youth* in the
labor force. (1) A younger worker produces relatively more than he consumes, in contrast to an older worker, largely because of increases in pay
with seniority whether or not there is increased productivity with
seniority. (2) Each generation enters the labor force with more education
than the previous generation; hence a larger proportion of youth implies
an increase in the average education of the labor force, all else being
equal. (3) Younger workers save a larger proportion of their income than
do older workers.

Another possible explanation is that population growth creates additional opportunities and facilitates adaptive changes in the economic and
social structures of MDCs. This has several aspects. (1) A necessary
reduction in the size of an organization or work force is always painful.
But when the population and the economy are growing, a facility or
work force that needs reduction can be reduced in relative size by leaving it the same absolute size. (2) Cessation of population growth makes
it more difficult to staff new departments to adjust to changing conditions. In universities, for example, when there is an overall growth in
enrollments, new fields can be staffed by new faculty without cutting
back on existing faculty; when there is no overall growth, new fields
cannot be staffed without fighting the entrenched faculty, who do not
wish to give up the positions they hold.[8] (3) Cessation of growth also

means that there are fewer new appointments to be made overall. In U.S. universities since the 1970s this strikes particularly hard at the numbers of young professors who can be appointed, which is demoralizing to aspirants for the Ph.D. And it is causing screams of anguish from senior professors who can no longer easily obtain offers elsewhere, which they can use as levers to get their salaries raised. (4) Where new occupational needs arise, they can be filled more easily if there are more youths who might learn these occupations. Hence, population growth facilitates adjustments in the sizes of industries and in occupational structure. (5) When the total economy is growing relatively fast, savings can more easily be found for new investments without having to shift investment out of old capital. This is the physical counterpart to the human-capital phenomena discussed in points (1) and (2) above. (6) Investment is less risky when population is growing more rapidly. If housing is overbuilt or excess capacity is created in an industry, a growing population will take up the slack and remedy the error, whereas without population growth there is no source of remedy for the miscalculation. Hence a growing population makes expansion investment and new entrepreneurial ventures more attractive by reducing risk—as well as by increasing total demand, of course.

Still another possible explanation is that a faster-growing population increases the internal mobility of the labor force. The greater mobility is caused by a larger number of job opportunities, and by a larger number of people in the young age groups, which tend to be more mobile. Internal mobility greatly enhances the efficient allocation of resources—that is, the best matching of people to jobs. As Kuznets wrote, "We cannot exaggerate the importance of internal mobility and of the underlying conditions . . . in the modern economy to allocate and channel human resources."[9] But when population growth is declining, the economy can get stuck with a hard-to-adjust oversupply of people in various occupations; this is currently the case with elementary and secondary schoolteachers.

A More Realistic Model for MDCs

We have seen that population size and growth have a variety of economic effects, some negative and others positive. Economists worth their keep must take account of the size and importance of the relevant forces. Furthermore, if several influences operate concurrently, we must concern ourselves with the overall effect rather than with only a single effect of any one variable at a time. In such a case we can only obtain a satisfactory overall assessment by constructing an integrated model of the economy, and then comparing the incomes produced under various conditions of population growth.

When building such a dynamic model, we must compromise between the greater complexity of a more realistic model and the greater distortion of a more abstract one. Furthermore, different models are required for countries with different economic and demographic conditions. More specifically, we must have separate models for MDCs and LDCs. The model that follows is for MDCs;[10] a model for LDCs is presented in the next chapter.

Whether mathematical or verbal, simple or complex, computerized or not, conventional models of the effect of additional people on the standard of living in MDCs — including those from Malthus to *The Limits to Growth* — share the common root of first-edition Malthus: Adding people who must work and live with the original fixed supply of land and capital implies less income for each person.

If, however, we add to the simple Malthusian model another fundamental fact of economic growth — the increase in productivity due to additional people's inventive and adaptive capacities — we arrive at a very different result. The analysis whose results are presented below does just that. This model is outlined in figure 19-2, where the elements of the usual neo-Malthusian model for MDCs are shown in solid lines and where the novel knowledge-creation elements are shown in dotted lines. That is, this model embodies not only the standard capital-dilution effects but also the contribution of additional people to technological advance through the creation of knowledge and through economies of larger scale. The latter elements have been omitted from population models in the past, but they are crucial to a balanced understanding of the problem.

Three factors may be seen as acting upon the creation of new technological knowledge: (1) the total number of persons in the labor force (or in research and development), who may produce valuable improvements; (2) the total production in a year — the gross national income — with which improvements may be financed; and (3) the per capita income level, which influences the average amount of education a worker receives and hence affects the individual's capacities to make technological discoveries.

The time horizon is roughly 50 to 150 years, short enough to rule out major changes in the natural resources situation. But it is sufficiently long so that the delayed effects of knowledge are able to play their role.

Though the model refers to the U.S., it is more appropriate to think

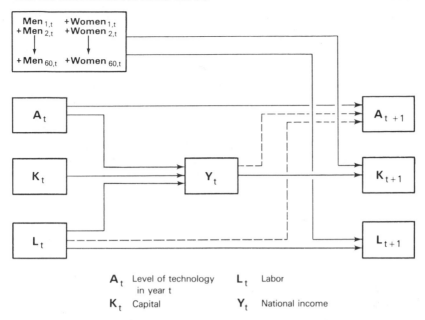

FIGURE 19-2. Model of Population and Economic Growth

of this analysis as applying to the developed world as a whole, because of the scientific and technological interdependence among the MDCs. This wider point of view skirts the possibility that one country might try to take a ride on the coattails of technological advance created by other countries (which cannot be done well anyway).

You may feel uneasy with the lack of precision in our understanding of how population size and growth affect the creation of new technological knowledge, as discussed in chapter 14. But to simply leave out the effect altogether is to implicitly (and unreasonably) estimate that the effect is zero (which is what the conventional models do). Certainly the effect of population size on knowledge is greater than zero. Where else but from people's minds, past and present, can advances in knowledge come from? Physical capital alone cannot generate ideas, though it enhances "learning by doing."

To put it differently, additional workers certainly are not the only cause of increased productivity. But over any period longer than the business cycle, the size of the labor force is a major influence upon total output. And if we hold constant the physical capital endowment and the original level of technological practice, then population size is the only influence upon total output. Hence, the appropriate argument is about how to estimate this factor, and which estimates to use, rather than whether to include it at all.

This model does not treat human beings only as "human capital," a commodity that is essentially plastic and inert like physical capital. Rather, it treats people *as people* — responding to their economic needs with physical and mental efforts up to and including the creative spark. Imagination and creativity are not concepts commonly included in economic models, nor are they ever above the surface even here. But let us recognize their importance unselfconsciously, and be willing to give them their due.

The Model's Projections

Streams of per-worker income were compared for a wide variety of population-growth structures, including both one-time increases in population size and different rates of population growth such as zero, 1 percent, and 2 percent yearly. And the comparisons were made under a variety of economic assumptions about savings rates and about the ways that additional people and various income levels affect changes in productivity. The most important result is that, under every set of conditions, demographic structures with more rapid population growth come to have higher per-worker income than less rapid population-growth structures, within 30 to 80 years after the birth of the additional child. Most often this happens after about 35 years — that is, about 15 years after the additional person enters the labor force (see figure 19-3).

It is true that 30 to 80 years is a long way off, and therefore may seem less important than the shorter run. But we should remember that our long run will be someone else's short run, just as our short run was someone else's long run. Some measure of unselfishness should impel us to keep this in mind as we make our decisions about population policy. And it may help to know that the cost differences will be quite small: The short-run differences between the various demographic structures are not important by any absolute measure, and relatively small compared to other variables that are subject to governmental policies. As Harvey Leibenstein notes, "The economic implications of the difference between the U.S. and the Japanese saving rates are much greater than the differences between the demographic structures. A modest decrease in the unemployment rate could more than offset any likely short-run drop in per-worker income due to higher fertility."[11]

For purposes of population policy, however, we can reduce the comparisons of the different population-growth structures to a simpler

output per worker

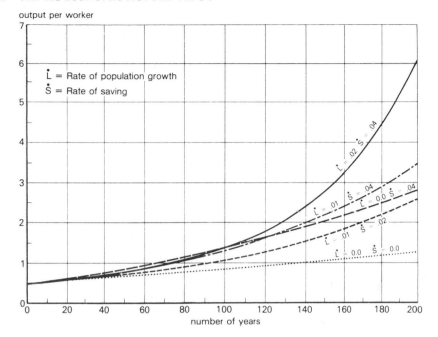

FIGURE 19-3. Output per Worker with Various Rates of Population Growth

form — the tradeoff between present and future consumption. This simple tradeoff applies to population just as to such long-lived social projects as dams and environmental changes. That is, a key issue in any overall judgment about population growth is the relative importance we attach to consuming something now versus investing part of it so as to consume more later.

The effect of additional children upon the standard of living (putting aside the pleasure that children give to their parents) is clearly negative in the short run. In the years while children consume but do not produce, additional children mean less food and less education for each person, or additional effort on the part of the parental generation to fulfill the needs of the additional children. During this early period, then, children are an investment; their effect upon the standard of living is negative. And if attention is confined to this early period, then additional children are seen as a negative economic force.

But if, on the other hand, we give weight to the more distant future, then the overall effect of the additional child may be positive. The positive effects will last much longer then the negative effects — indefinitely, in fact — and hence can outweigh the short-run effects even though it is natural to care less about a given period of time in the far future than about an equal period beginning now.

The device used by economists to summarize this stream of future effects is the "discount rate." A low discount rate indicates that one gives relatively more weight to the future than does a high discount rate, though a future benefit or cost always gets *somewhat* less weight than a present benefit or cost. The futurity discount is very similar in concept to an interest rate, and the choice of appropriate discount rate is similar to the decision about the rate of interest one would be willing to accept in borrowing or lending money. If, for example, we set a discount rate of 5 percent per year we mean that, for every year longer we have to wait for a payoff, we require the payoff to be at least 5 percent more than the amount we invested the year before, or else we would not make the investment. If we invest $1.00 now, we would require $1.05 a year from now. If investing does not look that promising, we would rather spend our dollar now than forgo a dollar's worth of consumption until later. If we expect more than $1.05 back, the deal seems worthwile — if the appropriate discount rate is 5 percent.

The model indicates that even up to substantial rates of discount — 5 percent at a minimum, to be contrasted with the real inflation-adjusted discount rate of 2-3 percent that seems to prevail in Western society over the long run — faster population growth has a higher "present value" than slower population growth. That is, social investment in population growth would be far more profitable than the marginal social invest-ments of other kinds. This finding may be contrasted with the standard conclusion that a lower rate of population growth is better at all rates of discount.

You might check the conclusions drawn from this model with your intuition about whether all the people in the U.S. would be better off today if there had been half as many people in 1830 or 1880 or 1930 as there actually were. To me it seems reasonably plain that our ancestors bestowed benefits upon us through the knowledge they created and the economies of scale they left us, and if there had been fewer of those ancestors the legacy would have been smaller. It is worth keeping this in mind when speculating about whether life today and in the future would be better if there were fewer people alive *today*.

Population models such as the one presented here would have had little chance of being accepted ten or twenty years ago, because of the pre-eminence of physical capital in the thinking of economists until then. But with the recognition in recent years of the fundamental impor-tance of knowledge, education, and the quality of the labor force in the productive process, models that allow for the contribution of additional people to technology and human capital should be more congenial.

If you continue to wonder whether population growth has a negative effect on the standard of living, you may find instructive the outcome of the recent President's Commission on Population Growth and the American Future. That commission was urged upon us by such persons as John D. Rockeffeller III, who became chairman. Rockefeller had a long record of concern about the dangers of population growth, and he and the commission's other creators clearly hoped and expected that it would bring in a report that called strongly for fertility reduction. As President Nixon put it in a message to Congress, "Population growth is a world problem which no country can ignore."[12]

Despite its anti-natalist origin, the strongest anti-population recommendation the commission gave was, "We have looked for and have not found any convincing economic argument for continued national population growth."[13] And when one considers that almost no child born during the 1972–2000 period covered by the report could have a positive effect on production, because few children born after 1972 would reach the labor force before 2000, it takes no analysis to see that additional children could not possibly benefit the standard of living during that period of time. But in years after 2000, when the 1972–2000 generation could join the labor force and create and innovate, they would have a positive impact.

It is also interesting to note the changes in views of the economists on the President's Commission. Allen Kelley was responsible for the central review-paper on economic aspects of population change, and Richard Easterlin had the task of evaluating Kelley's study. This was the evolution of their views, as described by Easterlin:

> It is instructive, I think, to note Kelley's own statement on the change in his views as a result of this research. Whereas he started out in the expectation that an anti-natal government policy was justifiable on economic and ecological grounds, he ended up in a much more neutral position. In this respect, Kelley's experience is representative, I think, of that of many of us who have tried to look into the arguments and evidence about the "population problem."[14]

By 1980 many people in the U.S. and Europe — school administrators, university teachers, social security planners, and publishing houses, for example — have seen the face of zero population growth, and many do not like what they see. ZPG means a cut in real salaries for many, and a lack of the excitement that growth usually brings. And the result is as

Adam Smith had it: "The progressive state is in reality the cheerful and the hearty state to all the different orders of the society; the stationary is dull; the declining melancholy." But there is no economic need for ZPG; there are no necessary "limits" on our growth. So let us have done with this ZPG idea.

Can it be that the increase in the MDC standard of living as a result of population growth comes at the expense of the poorer countries? Many assert that a country is "overpopulated" if it is not self-sufficient in food and other raw materials, and this shades over into the idea that poor countries are being exploited. Consider these paragraphs, for example, by Paul Ehrlich.

> Few Europeans seem to realize that they must draw heavily on the rest of the world for the resources necessary to maintain their affluence. Few also seem to realize that, with a few exceptions, European nations could not feed themselves without importing food (or fertilizer, or the petroleum to run farm machinery, etc.). A Dane once bragged to me about his nation's position as a food exporter, sending dairy products, eggs, and meat to other nations. He was not aware that, in order to do so, Denmark has to import vast amounts of protein, much of it in the form of oilseed cakes and grain to be fed to livestock. More protein is imported, per person, by Denmark than by any other nation in the world. For each Danish man, woman, and child, 240 pounds of protein enter the country, nearly three times the average protein consumption of each Dane. The Netherlands is the second largest per capita importer at 170 pounds.
>
> Even an island nation like Great Britain seems relatively oblivious to her extreme degree of overpopulation. At a recent conference on "Optimum Population in Britain," one distinguished participant pointed out that only a small percentage of England was used by man (the significance of the green fields of England's countryside was lost on him — after all, people weren't standing in them, *ergo* they were not "used"!) The fact of Great Britain's almost total dependence on the rest of the world is only dimly perceived, and the continuance of today's world trade system is simply taken for granted.[15]

But Ehrlich himself (in his own sort of rhetoric) "fails to realize" that exchange is a fundamental and necessary element of human civilization, and that it is quite misleading to think of one trade partner "supporting" another. Saudi Arabia no more "supports" the Netherlands by exporting oil than the Netherlands "supports" Saudi Arabia by exporting electronic goods. If you are a white-collar worker, you support a farmer with what you produce just as much as the famer supports you. To divide the exchange in half and call one direction "supportive" while the other is "exploitive" can only be misleading.

There is yet another misleading idea underlying this notion that the so-called dependence of densely settled on sparsely settled areas is a sign of overpopulation: This view implicitly assumes that national borders are the only ones that matter. If we are thinking of war, that certainly is true. But in the peacetime that I assume we are discussing, Chicago is at least as "dependent" on downstate Illinois for soybeans as is Tokyo, yet no one thinks that Chicago is overpopulated because it is not self-sufficent in soybeans. To make the sort of distinction Erhlich makes between the U.S. and Japan — to call the latter "overpopulated" because it gets its soybeans from abroad — is an archaic nationalistic theory of economics called "mercantilism," a theory that was discussed and discarded by Adam Smith in 1776. The more general charge that MDCs "exploit" the LDCs and "rape" them of the resources that they should be saving for their own use was dispatched in chapter 15.

SUMMARY

The conventional theoretical models of population growth's effects — all founded on the Malthusian idea of diminishing returns — are directly contradicted by the empirical data. The conventional models say that adding more people causes a lower standard of living; the data show no such thing. This chapter describes a different sort of theoretical model, one that is more consistent with the facts.

The increases in productivity that result from the larger scale of industry, and from the additional knowledge contributed by additional people, are here added to a simple conventional model of a more-developed country. The model works with a range of assumptions that I trust are realistic. The results indicate that demographic structures with faster rates of population growth initially fall behind in per capita income, but only very slightly. Later they overtake the structures with lower rates of population growth, usually in 30 to 80 years. That is, for the first 30 to 80 years after the birth of an additional child — 35 years is perhaps the most common period in the models — per capita income is very slightly lower because of the additional child. But after that period, per capita income is higher with the additional child, and the advantage of the faster population growth comes to be very considerable. Thus, though an increment of population initially has a small negative effect upon economic welfare, after a few decades the effect becomes positive, and large.

Most telling of all, computations that weight and combine the longer-term and the shorter-term population effects in a standard present-value framework of investment analysis indicate that, even at costs of capital that are quite high relative to the social cost of capital, faster population growth has a higher present value than slower population growth in almost all model variations. That is, higher population growth in MDCs is an attractive social investment as compared with other social-investment possibilities.

To achieve a reasonable understanding of the effects of population growth, we must extend our horizon beyond the near-term years and weigh the effects of the long run and the short run together. When this is done, population growth in the MDC world is seen to be beneficial, rather than being the burden it seems to be in standard Malthusian models, which have only a short-run perspective.

AFTERNOTE

How Immigrants Affect Our Standard of Living

Immigration, illegal and legal, regularly touches a sore spot in American public opinion and has done so for 100 years and more, the Irish having been the object of perhaps the most hostility. The reasons opponents of immigration give are mostly economic — jobs, welfare, and housing. But in fact, American citizens can do well while doing good by admitting refugees. Rather than being a matter of charity, we can expect our incomes to be higher rather that lower in future years if we admit more Cubans, Haitians, Indo-Chinese, Mexicans, Italians, Filipinos, and other ethnic immigrants.

Before beginning, let's examine the demographic scope of the illegal-alien problem, because this comes up in every discussion of immigration. For a long time the Immigration and Naturalization Service (INS) said there were 4–12 million illegals in the country; no supporting evidence was given. Then the INS shifted to 8.2 million, as of mid-1975. This estimate came from a Lesko Associates study commissioned by INS.[1] The basis for the estimate was the "Delphi Technique," a fancy name for asking a small group of people for a series of opinions. On the initial round the panel's opinions ranged from 2.5 million to 25.1 million illegals in the country; when successively revised in light of the opinions of others on the panel, the estimates averaged 8.2 million. Samuel Johnson said that a compendium of gossip is still gossip, and the INS-Lesko estimate is simply a compendium of opinions. Even Lesko called the estimate "not analytically defensible." Yet they reported it, and the INS publicized it, and it has been the basis for much of the political debate on the subject since then.

Ingenious statisticians have recently tackled the problem in a variety of interesting ways, including analysis of alien deaths in the U.S.,[2] changes in the Mexican population from census to census, and comparisons of data (such as Social Security and income tax records) in which illegal aliens are pretty sure to be counted.[3] There is consensus among these investigations that there are around 4 million illegals or less, a fair proportion of them not Mexican, and a large proportion intending to leave after some months. Korns' study of illegal-alien employment even suggests that there has been no increase in the total number of illegals since the 1964–69 expansion period.[4]

Most immigrants who enter illegally leave when their job runs out or when they have earned what they came to earn. They then return to the families they left behind, usually after half a year or less.[5] This explains how there can be a constant inflow and yet little or no increase in the total number resident.

Now about the economic impact: Immigrants affect the average standard of living, and the standard of living of particular groups of citizens, in a variety of ways. One key issue is how much the immigrants work, which is largely determined by their age and sex. Data on the Cubans coming now are lacking, but there is sound reason to believe that they are like other migrants in this respect: On average, it is the young, strong, and single who make the move. Of the illegal Mexicans, more than 80 percent are male, half are single (most of the married men leave their wives and children in Mexico), and most are youthful — less than 20 percent of the workers are over 35, and they average perhaps 27. Among the Vietnam refugees, only 12 percent are 45 or over, compared to 32 percent for the 45-and-over age group in the U.S. population as a whole. There is, however, a larger proportion of young children among the Vietnam refugees than in the citizen population.

As to actual employment, a large survey showed that 47 percent of the

Vietnamese males 14 years or older were working within three months of entry.[6] This rapid job-finding jibes with the results of studies of immigrant employment in Canada,[7] Israel (Russian immigrants),[8] and the United Kingdom (New Commonwealth immigrants).[9]

Labor unions worry that immigrants displace citizens from jobs. It is difficult to get a fair reading on this phenomenon, because the jobs created by immigrants are less obvious than the existing jobs that they fill. Some Americans certainly will suffer from the competition of additional workers, and it does little good to tell them that adjustment is just a matter of time. But luckily the Cubans and the Indo-Chinese apparently are a heterogeneous lot, and their immediate labor-force effect is spread widely. Hence no occupation will suffer much, even in the short run, whereas in the long run many citizens will benefit. As to the Mexicans, experiments by the INS and San Diego County showed that U.S. citizens could not be found to fill jobs that illegals were removed from.[10] Smith and Newman found that adjusted wages are 8 percent lower in the Texas border cities where the proportion of Mexicans is relatively high, a relatively small differential in their judgment (but perhaps relatively large as seen by others).[11] And as shown by studies in other countries and historically in the U.S., migrants come in good times and leave in bad times, thereby buffering unemployment for citizens.

About immigrants and the public coffers: I have just completed a study[12] of a large survey of immigrants and natives conducted by the Bureau of the Census in 1976, which provides a wealth of data on the services used by individual families — public welfare, Aid to Dependent children, unemployment compensation, Social Security, schools, Medicare, Medicaid, and so on. It also provides excellent data on family earnings, which allows us to infer the amounts of taxes paid. The conclusions of the analysis are as follows.

Immigrant families use substantially less public services (largely due to Social Security) than do native families from the time of entry until about twelve years later, when their usage becomes roughly equal to natives. After about two to six years immigrant families come to pay as much, and then substantially more, in taxes than do native families. And the net effect of these two forces in every year favors the natives; that is, immigrants contribute more to the public coffers than they take.

About illegals and public revenues: North and Houstoun[13] found that 73 percent of illegal aliens had federal income tax withheld, and 77 percent paid Social Security tax — even though they can never collect on it. On the other hand, the proportions who use welfare services are small: medical, 27 percent; unemployment insurance, 4 percent; child schooling, 4 percent; federal job training, 1 percent; food stamps, 1 percent; welfare payments, 1 percent. And practically no illegals are in a position to avail themselves of the most expensive welfare programs of all: Social Security and other aid to the elderly.

On balance, then, immigrants — and to an indecent extent, the illegals — contribute more in taxes than they use in services, even in the first few years. And later on they will alleviate our impending Social Security problem.

In the long run the economic effect of any group of immigrants is likely to be greatest through its contribution to technological change. The evidence on learning by doing, and from comparisons in rates of productivity increase in industries of various sizes and growth rates in various countries, suggests that additional people — and the larger markets that result from additional people — have a very positive effect on productivity, and hence on the standard of living.

The economist worth his or her salt should offer a cost-benefit assessment for policy analysis. Therefore, I combined the most important elements pertaining to legal immigrants like the Cubans or Indo-Chinese with a simple macroeconomic model, making reasonable assumptions about the returns to indigenous capital that new immigrants manage to capture. The net effect is slightly negative in the early years, but after four or five years the balance turns positive and large. And when we value the streams of future costs and benefits the way we compute the present value of any other investment, the rate of return from immigrants to the citizen public is of the order of 20 percent per annum, a remarkably good investment for anyone's portfolio.[14] The return from illegals must be even greater, of course, because the public services they receive out of the taxes they pay are almost non-existent.

On balance, then, admitting immigrants improves our standard of living. If we just plain don't want any more "foreigners," let's say so, but let's not justify our xenophobia or our desire to avoid new competition with unsound economic arguments.

The Big Picture II: LDCs

During the past decades, economic models of the effect of population growth upon the standard of living in less-developed countries (LDCs) have had considerable influence on governmental policies, as well as on the thinking of social scientists and the public. Phyllis Piotrow's historical account attributes enormous impact to the Coale-Hoover book of 1958, which concluded that population growth hampers LDC economic growth: "The Coale-Hoover thesis eventually provided the justification for birth control as a part of U.S. foreign aid policy."[1] Piotrow traces much of this impact through Philander Claxton, Jr., who, as the highest-ranking State Department official involved in population matters, had considerable influence on U.S. foreign aid policies and expenditures. Immediately after his appointment in 1966, Claxton prepared an extensive position paper.

> Adopting completely the Coale-Hoover thesis. . . . Claxton argued that the U.S. government must move from reaction and response to initiation and persuasion. . . . By the time the paper reached the Secretary of State's desk, it had already achieved part of its purpose. All the appropriate State Department and Aid bureaus had reviewed, revised, commented, added to, and finally cleared the document. The rest of its purpose was accomplished when Rusk agreed to every single one of Claxton's ten recommendations.[2]

This histroy makes clear the importance of having a sound economic-demographic model for LDCs.

The Conventional Theoretical Models

The now-standard population model of Coale and Hoover has two main elements: (1) an increase in the number of consumers, and (2) a decrease in saving due to population growth (a proposition whose validity was discussed in chapter 13, with ambiguous results). Their famous conclusion is that, whereas in India income per consumer over 1956–86 could be expected to rise from an index of 100 to 138 with continued high fertility, it could be expected to rise from 100 to 195 with declining fertility — some 2½ times as fast.

It is crucial to notice that the main Coale-Hoover model simply *assumed* that the total national product in an LDC would not be increased by population growth for the first thrity years, either by a larger labor force or by additional productive efforts. Therefore, their model boils down to the ratio of output divided by consumers; an increase in the number of consumers decreases the per capita consumption, by simple arithmetic. In their own words, "The inauspicious showing of the high-fertility case in terms of improvement in levels of living is traceable entirely to the accelerated growth in the number of consumers that high fertility produces."[3] To repeat: The main mechanism producing their result is simply an increase in the denominator of the output/consumer ratio, where output is the same *by assumption* for the first thirty years for all rates of population growth.

Subsequent LDC models (including a variant by Coale and Hoover) took into account that a faster-growing population produces a larger labor force, which in turn implies a larger total output. But this modification still implies Malthusian capital dilution, and, while slightly altering the main Coale-Hoover result, such a model still necessarily indicates that a faster-growing population leads to a lower output per worker and lower per capita income.

In sum, the conventional theory suggests that a larger population retards the growth of output per worker in LDCs. The overwhelming element in the conventional theory is the Malthusian concept of diminishing returns to labor, operating with the assumption that the stock of capital (including land) does not increase in the same proportion as labor.

Another important theoretical element is the dependency effect, which suggests that saving is more difficult for households where there are more children, and that higher fertility causes social investment funds to be diverted away from industrial production. Combined in simulation models, these conventional elements imply that a relatively high fertility and population growth diminish the output per worker (and even more the income per consumer, because the proportion of consumers to workers is higher when the birthrate is higher).

AGAIN — THE DATA CONTRADICT THE CONVENTIONAL MODELS

But the empirical data do not support this a priori reasoning. The data — inadequate though they may be — do not show that a higher rate of population growth decreases the rate of economic growth, for either LDCs or MDCs. These data include the historical study of Simon Kuznets shown in figure 19-1. Also relevant are cross-sectional studies that relate the rate of population growth to the growth rate of per capita income in various LDCs; no correlation between the two variables is found.[4]

Another sort of study plots the growth rate of per capita income as a function of population density. Roy Gobin and I studied the separate and combined effects of population density and population growth on economic growth. We found that population growth does not show a negative effect, but that population density shows a *positive* effect on the rate of economic growth, as seen in figure 20-1.[5] And a study by J. Dirck Stryker found that, among the French-speaking African peoples, lower population density is associated with lower economic growth — that is, higher population density implies a higher standard of living.[6]

There may be some confusion because many have an incorrect impression of the current rate of economic growth in the poorer countries. Contrary to common belief, per capita income in LDCs has been growing as fast as or faster than in the MDCs from 1950 to 1975.[7] And "during the period 1970 through 1975, the largest figures available, per-capita production of the developing countries grew at a 3% annual rate while the developed countries gained only 1.9% yearly,"[8] despite the fact that population growth in LDCs has been much faster than in MDCs. This is prima facie evidence that population growth does not have a negative effect on economic growth.

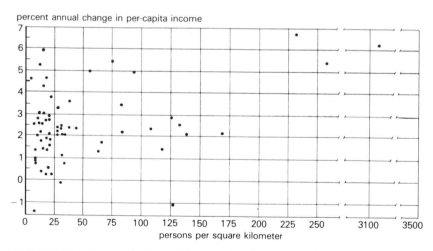

FIGURE 20-1. Economic Growth Rates Related to Population Density in LDCs, 1960–65

A MODEL THAT RECONCILES THEORY AND EVIDENCE FOR LDCs

When the theory and the data do not jibe, either (or both) may require re-examination. The available raw data have been re-examined several times, always with the same result. Let us therefore turn to a re-examination of the theory as embodied in the simulation models.

The model whose results are presented below includes the standard economic elements of the well-known earlier models. But it also includes some of the additional effects discussed in earlier chapters. These newly added elements include, among others (1) the positive effect of increased demand (coming from a larger population) upon business and agricultural investment; (2) the propensity of people to devote more hours to work and fewer to leisure when family size increases; (3) the shift in labor from agriculture to industry as economic development proceeds; and (4) economies of scale in the use of social infrastructure and other sources. All of these elements are well documented.

Further, if we are to understand the effect of population growth upon income and the standard of living, we must know the effect of income on population size and growth. All else being equal, income raises fertility and reduces mortality. But other factors do not remain the same as income changes, except in the very short run. In the long run, an increase in income in a poor country with a high fertility rate reduces the fertility rate. (This is the demographic transition described in chapter 11, which results from income-induced changes in mortality, urbanization, child cost, and so on.) And mortality no longer falls significantly with additional income after some point. Hence the long-run effect of an increase in income is a decrease in the rate of population growth. These effects also must be added to a realistic simulation.

When these important economic elements are included rather than excluded, as they are from earlier economic-demographic models of LDCs, and when reasonable assumptions are made about the various dimensions of the LDC economy, the results are very different than they were with past models: The simulation indicates that a moderate population growth produces considerably better economic performance in the long run (120 to 180 years) than does a slower-growing population, though in the shorter run (up to 60 years) the slower-growing population performs slightly better. A declining population does very badly in the long run. And in the experiments with the "best" estimates of the parameters for a representative Asian LDC (the "base run"), moderate population growth has better long-run performance than either fast population growth (doubling over 35 years or less) or slow population growth.

Experiments with one variable at a time reveal that the difference between these results and the opposite results generated by previous models is produced, not by any single variable, but by the combination of the novel elements — the leisure-versus-work decision with extra children in the family, economies of scale, the investment function, and depreciation; no single factor is predominant. And over the range of positive population growth, different parameters lead to different positive rates of population growth as "optimum." This means that no simple qualitative theory of population growth of the classical Malthusian sort can be very helful, and that a more complex, quantitatively based theory such as this one is necessary.

For the interested technical readers, a fuller statement of the findings follows. Others may skip ahead.

(1) Using those parameters that seem most descriptive of LDCs today, the model suggests that very high birthrates and very low birthrates both result in lower long-run per-worker outputs (hereafter referred to as "economic performance") than do birthrates in between. It will surprise no one in this decade that very high birthrates are not best. But the outcome that moderate birthrates produce higher income in the long run than do low birthrates runs very much against the conventional wisdom. The same result appears with quite different levels of the various parameters. The moderate-fertility populations also enjoy more leisure in the long run than do the low-fertility and high-fertility populations.

(2) In a variety of conditions, over quite a wide range of moderate to high birthrates, the effect of fertility upon income is not spectacularly large — seldom as much as 25 percent even after 180 years (though the difference in results produced by low and moderate birthrates is great). This is extremely surprising at first thought. But it is what Kuznets anticipated:

> . . . given the political and social contest, it does not follow that the high birth rates in the underdeveloped countries, per se, are a major cause of the low per capita income; nor does it follow that a reduction of these birth rates, without a change in the political and social context (if this is possible), will raise per capita product or accelerate its rate of growth. We stress the point that *the source of the association between demographic patterns and per capita product is a common set of political and social institutions and other factors behind both* to indi-

cate that any direct causal relations between the demographic movements and economic growth may be quite limited; and that we cannot
easily interpret the association for policy purposes as assurance that a
modification of one of the variables would necessarily change the
other and in the directions indicated by the association.[9]

These results suggest a population "trap" — but a benevolent and very
different sort of trap from the Malthusian one: If population growth
declines too fast as a result of increasing income, total output fails to rise
enough to stimulate investment; depreciation is then greater than investment, and income falls. In the model, this results in a return to higher
fertility and then another cycle. Hence the ill results follow from population decline in this model, rather than from population increase as in
the Malthusian trap.

(3) The advantage of moderate birthrates over low birthrates generally
appears only after quite a while, say, 75–100 years. This is another reason
why the results found here differ from those of the Coale-Hoover and
similar models in which the time horizon is only 25–30 years (55 years
in the Coale-Hoover minor extension), whereas the time horizon here is
180 years (or longer in some cases). This points up the grave danger of
using short-horizon models in the study of population growth. The population effects take a long time to begin and a much longer time to
accumulate.

(4) Perhaps the most important result of this simulation is that it
shows there are some reasonable sets of conditions under which fairly
high fertility has better economic performance at some times than does
low fertility, but there are also other reasonable sets of conditions under
which the opposite is true. There are even sets of conditions well within
the bounds of possibility under which extremely high fertility offers the
highest income per capita and output per worker in the long run. That
is, the results depend upon the choice of parameters within ranges that
seem quite acceptable. This implies that any model of population that
concludes that any one fertility structure is unconditionally better or
worse than another must be wrong, either because that model's construction is too simple or for some other reasons. The sole exception to this
generalization is fertility below replacement. Such a low-fertility structure does poorly under every set of conditions simulated here, largely
because a reasonable increase in total demand is necessary to produce
enough investment to overcome the drag of depreciation.

In sum, the differences between the results produced by this method
and the results obtained by Coale and Hoover are due to the inclusion

in this model of several factors omitted from the Coale-Hoover model: (a) the capacity of people to vary their work input in response to their varying income aspirations and family-size needs; (b) an economies-of-scale social-capital factor; (c) an industrial investment function (and an industrial technology function) that is responsive to differences in demand (output); and (d) an agricultural savings function that is responsive to the agricultural capital/output ratio. These factors together, at reasonable parameter settings, are enough to offset the capital dilution diminishing-returns effect as well as the effect of dependency on saving found in the Coale-Hoover model. The difference in overall conclusions between this model and others, however, is also due to the much longer time horizon used in this model.

Our judgment about the overall effect of an additional child depends upon the discount rate we choose as appropriate for weighing the costs and benefits in immediate periods versus periods further into the future (on the assumption that an additional child will eventually make a positive contribution to the stock of capital), as was discussed in the context of the MDC model in chapter 19. If we give little or no weight to society's welfare in the far future, but rather pay attention only to the present and the near future, then additional children are a burden. But if we weigh the welfare of future generations almost as heavily as the welfare of present generations, then additional children now are a positive economic force. In between, there is some discount rate that, depending upon the circumstances of each country, marks the point at which additional children now are at the borderline of having a negative or positive effect. The choice of that discount rate is ultimately a matter of personal values, which we shall take up in chapter 23.

In brief, whether we assess the effect of additional children now as being negative or positive depends largely upon our time perspective. And given the economic analysis developed here, anyone who takes a long-range view — gives considerable weight to the welfare of future generations — should prefer a growing population to a stationary or declining population.

Some Objections Considered

This and the previous chapter have reached conclusions that run contrary to prevailing popular opinion as well as to most of the professional literature since Malthus, and before. Therefore, it may be useful to consider some of the objections to these conclusions. Of course, the full text of this book and my technical book, including both the analysis and the empirical data, constitute the basic rebuttal to these objections. The following paragraphs take up the objections in a lighter and more casual fashion.

Objection 1. But population growth must stop at *some* point. There is *some* population size at which the world's resources must run out, some moment at which there will be "standing room only."

When someone questions the notion that we need to immediately check population growth in the U.S. or in the world, the standard response ever since Malthus has been a series of calculations showing how, after population doubles a number of times, there will be standing room only, a solid mass of human bodies on the earth or in the U.S. This apparently shows that population growth ought to stop *sometime* — well before "standing room only," of course. But even if we stipulate that population growth must sometime stop, by what reasoning do people get from "sometime" to "now"? At least two aspects of such reasoning can be identified.

First, the stop-now argument assumes that if humans behave in a certain way now they will inevitably continue to behave the same way in the future. But one need not assume that, if people decide to have more children now, their descendants will continue to have them at the same rate indefinitely. By analogy, because you decide to have another drink today, you will automatically drink yourself to death. But if you are like most people, you will stop after you recognize a reasonable limit. But many seem to have a "drunkard" model of fertility and society; if you take one drink, you're down the road to hell.

Another line of reasoning that leads people away from the conclusion that mankind will respond adaptively to population growth follows the mathematics of exponential growth, the "geometric increase" of Malthus. The usual argument that population will "explode" to a doomsday point is based on the crudest sort of curve fitting, a kind of hypnotism by mathematics. Starkly, the argument is that population will grow exponentially in the future because so it has always grown in the past. Certainly this proposition is not even true historically, as we saw in chapter 11. Population has remained stationary or gotten smaller in large parts of the world for long periods of time (for example, in Europe after the Roman Empire, and among aborigine tribes in Australia). And many other sorts of trends have been reversed in the past before being forced to stop by physical limits (the length of women's skirts, and the spread of Christianity and Islam).

If you are attracted to the sort of curve fitting that underlies most arguments about the need to control population growth, you might do well to consider other long trends that we have discussed earlier. For example, the *proportion* of people who die each year from famine has probably been decreasing since the beginning of mankind, and even the *absolute number* of people who die of famine has been decreasing despite the large increases in total population (see chapter 4). An even more reliable and important statistical trend is the steady increase in life expectancy over recorded history. Why not focus on these documented trends rather than on the hypothetical total-population trend?

An absurd counter-speculation is instructive. The exponential increase of university buildings in the past decades, and perhaps in the past 100 years, has been much faster than the rate of population growth. Simple-minded curve fitting will show that the space occupied by university buildings will overtake and pass the amount of space in which people stand long before there is "standing room only." This apparently makes university growth the juggernaut to worry about, not population growth!

Some will reply that the analogy is not relevant because universities are built by reasonable people who will stop when there are enough buildings, whereas children are produced by people who are acting only out of passion and are not subject to the control of reason. This latter assertion is, however, empirically false, as we saw in chapter 12. Every tribe known to anthropologists, no matter how "primitive," has some effective social scheme for controlling the birthrate. People choose to have children.

Even the proposition that population growth must stop *sometime* may not be very meaningful (see chapter 3 on "finitude"). The length of time required to reach any absolute physical limits of space or energy is long in the future, and many unforeseeable things could happen between now and then that could change those apparent limits.

Objection 2. But do we have a right to live high on the hog — consume all we want, have as large families as we want — and let later generations suffer?

The facts seem to be the opposite: If population growth is higher in earlier generations, later generations benefit rather than suffer. During the Industrial Revolution in England the standard of living might (or might not) have been higher for a while if population had not grown so quickly. But we today clearly benefit from that high growth rate and consequent high economic growth of that period, just as the LDC model suggests.

Objection 3. Your models emphasize the long-run positive effects of population growth. But as Keynes said, in the long-run we're all dead.

Yes, but in the long run others will be alive. And as emphasized earlier, your overall judgment about population growth depends upon your discount rate — how you weigh the immediate and the future effects against each other.

SUMMARY

History since the Industrial Revolution does not support the simple Malthusian model. No negative relationship between population growth and economic growth is revealed in anecdotal history, in time-series studies over the past 100 years, or in contemporary cross-sections. Rather, the data suggest that there is no simple relationship at all, for either LDCs or for MDCs (as discussed in the previous chapter).

Various explanations of this discrepancy between theory and evidence have been offered. For MDCs, the most general and most appealing explanation is the nexus of economies of scale, the creation and adaptation of new knowledge by additional people, and the creation of new resources from new knowledge. Therefore the MDC model in chapter 19 incorporates this fundamental element of economic progress that has previously been left out of population models. And that model — more complete than Malthusian and neo-Malthusian models such as *The Limits to Growth* — indicates that, after a few years during which a representative additional child has a net negative effect, the net effect upon per capita income comes to be positive. And these positive long-run effects are large compared with the added costs to the community until the child reaches full productivity. A present-value weighting of the short and long run at reasonable costs of capital reveals that the on-balance effect of additional persons is positive, an attractive "investment" compared to other social investments.

In LDCs the scenario is different, but the outcome is similar. Additional children influence the LDC economy by inducing people to work longer hours and invest more, as well as by causing an improvement in the social infrastructure, such as better roads and communication systems. Additional population also induces economies of scale in other ways. The upshot is that, although additional children cause additional costs in the short run, a moderate rate of population growth in LDCs is more likely to lead to a higher standard of living in the long run than either zero population growth or a high rate of population growth.

AFTERNOTE

The Limits to Growth

The *Limits to Growth* simulation, which has us breeding to the exhaustion of resources, is not worth detailed discussion or criticism. But it is a fascinating example of how scientific work can be outrageously bad and yet be very influential.

The Limits to Growth has been blasted as foolishness or fraud by almost every economist who has read it closely and reviewed it in print, for its silly methods as well as for disclosing so little of what the authors did, which makes close inspection impossible. To use their sort of language, the whole *Limits to Growth* caper is a public-relations hype, kicked off with a press conference organized by Charles Kytle Associates (a public-relations firm) and financed by the Xerox Corporation; this whole story, along with devastating commentary, was told in detail in *Science* the week following the book's appearance in 1972. (The public-relations campaign may not be a bad thing in itself, but it certainly shows how the authors and the sponsoring Club of Rome intended to have their material make its way in the world of ideas.)

One strong reason not to put stock in the *Limits to Growth* predictions is that the model was quickly shown to produce *rosy* forecasts with minor and realistic changes in the assumptions.[1] The most compelling criticism of the *Limits to Growth* simulation, however, was made by the sponsoring Club of Rome itself. Just four years after the foofaraw created by the book's publication and huge circulation — an incredible 4 million copies were sold — the Club of Rome "reversed its position" and "came out for more growth." But this about-face has gotten relatively little attention, even though it was written up in such places as *Time* and the *New York Times*.[2] And so the original message is the one that remains with most people.

The explanation of this reversal, as reported in *Time*, is a masterpiece of face-saving double talk.

> The Club's founder, Italian industrialist Aurelio Peccei, says that *Limits* was intended to jolt people from the comfortable idea that present growth trends could continue indefinitely. That done, he says, the Club could then seek ways to close the widening gap between rich and poor nations — inequities that, if they continue, could all too easily lead to famine, pollution and war. The Club's startling shift, Peccei says, is thus not so much a turnabout as part of an evolving strategy.[3]

In other words, the Club of Rome sponsored and disseminated untruths in an attempt to scare us. Having scared many people with these lies, the club can now tell people the *real* truth.

But it is possible that the Club of Rome did not really practice the deceitful strategy that it now says it did. Maybe the members have simply realized that the 1972 *Limits to Growth* study was scientifically worthless. If so, the Club of Pome is *now* lying about what it originally did, in order to save face. From the outside, we have no way of knowing which of these ugly possibilities is the "truth."

Is my summary of the reported facts not fair? Perhaps I should use quieter language, because I know that some will find the use of words like "lie" sufficient reason to reject what I am saying. But I have no public-relations firm to magnify my message a millionfold in the media, nor do I have a message that people are waiting breathlessly to hear. So I must use strong language to get this point across. And — is there really anything wrong with calling a documented and self-confessed lie a lie?

Surely this is one of the more curious scientific episodes of recent years. The *Limits to Growth* authors have not recanted, to my knowledge, even though their sponsors have. But neither did the authors confront and contradict their sponsors when the sponsors recanted. The whole matter seems to have passed with little notice, and *The Limits to Growth* continues to be cited in the popular press as authoritative. If the shoe were on the other foot, I would surely hear plenty from such organizations as Zero Population Growth and the Environmental Fund.

The *Global 2000 Study Report*, done for the Council on Environmental Quality and the Department of State, was published too late for discussion in this book. It is very much in the *Limits to Growth* tradition, done by people associated with that group and with the environmental organizations à la Ehrlich. I discuss this report at length in *The Public Interest* (Winter, 1980–81). Here I shall say only that I find the conclusions of *Global 2000* almost wholly without merit and the method shoddy, largely because of the absence of the very trend data that the authors say is the proper basis for such a study. Yet this study is being heavily ballyhooed, and will surely form the basis for many policy decisions in coming years.

PART THREE

BEYOND THE DATA

The liberal reward of labour, therefore, as it is the effect of increasing wealth, so it is the cause of increasing population. To complain of it, is to lament over the necessary effect and cause of the greatest public prosperity . . . it is in the progressive state, while the society is advancing to the further acquisition . . . of riches, that the condition of the labouring poor, of the great body of people, seems to be the happiest and the most comfortable. It is hard in the stationary, and miserable in the declining state. The progressive state is in reality the cheerful and the hearty state to all the different orders of the society. The stationary is dull; the declining melancholy.

ADAM SMITH, *The Wealth of Nations*, 1776

21.

The Politics and Finances of Population Control

THE ISSUE at STAKE

Should U.S. government funds — and UN funds, a large chunk of which are contributed by the U.S. — be used to finance propaganda and propaganda organizations dedicated to reducing fertility in the U.S. and abroad? An important sub-question is whether some very dubious rhetorical and organizational practices are acceptable simply because the people involved are sincerely convinced that the end is so important that such undesirable means are justified.

Let us be very clear: The issue in Part III is *not* whether governments and organizations should make birth-control methods available as freely as possible. There is a wide consensus — in which I enthusiastically share — that birth control is simply a human right. Disseminating birth-control methods and information helps people attain the kind of life they wish by helping them control their family size; it is one of the great social works of our time. Rather, the issue here is whether the power and funds of the government should be used — successfully or unsuccessfully — to pay for campaigns that attempt to change people's desires for children, and their childbearing behavior.

Not many decades ago, Margaret Sanger was thrown into jail for disseminating information about birth control to women in the U.S. Now there are tens of organizations, funded with tens of millions of dollars annually, employing hundreds of skilled people to prepare information and propaganda showing that population growth in the world ought to be reduced. In little more than one decade the anti-natalists have won power in the U.S. government and in such international organizations as the UN Fund for Population Activities (UNFPA) and the World Bank. There is no visible organized opposition to them except on the special issue of abortion. This chapter gives some details on these organizations, their politics, and how they are supported with your tax dollars. Chapter 22 discusses the rhetoric they use.

WHERE DOES THE BIG MONEY COME FROM?

The big money for world population activities comes from the U.S., as seen in table 21-1. Most of it is taxpayers' money, channeled from the U.S. State Department's Agency for International Development (AID) either directly to the recipients or through a wide variety of non-governmental agencies, some of which are discussed below.

After a slow start in 1965, AID has worked up to well over $100 million a year in this activity. As seen in figure 21-1, the money spent on population control has exceeded the worldwide health-related AID expenditures in total since 1969. And in such years as 1973, expenditures on fertility reduction have been almost three times the expenditures on health assistance! (That's worth an exclamation point in my book.) Additional funds come from the World Bank, which is largely funded by the U.S., and from UNFPA, which also is heavily bankrolled by the

TABLE 21-1. Primary Sources of International Population Assistance Funds (in thousands of U.S. dollars), 1965–76

Source	1965–69	1970	1971	1972	1973	1974	1975	1976	Total Through 1976
Australia	—	—	—	424	595	—	545	NA	1,564
Belgium	—	010	147	018	102	637	424	1,050	2,388
Canada	—	1,000	3,911	4,682	6,223	4,730	5,700	7,600	33,846
Denmark	297	1,350	1,916	1,953	3,990	2,432	3,985	3,510	19,433
Fed. Rep. of Germany	250	1,530	1,660	2,392	4,286	5,900	7,494	NA	23,512
Japan	199	1,500	2,089	2,196	2,812	5,367	7,899	NA	22,062
Netherlands	338	1,410	1,539	3,041	5,744	6,040	7,159	8,119	33,390
Norway	225	990	3,870	5,539	12,542	12,727	13,636	23,091	72,620
OPEC countries	—	300	078	265	123	136	180	1,471	2,553
Sweden	12,786	6,520	9,200	12,700	13,676	18,272	29,374	31,963	134,491
United Kingdom	261	971	2,520	6,680	4,225	3,000	3,415	4,100	25,172
United States	90,665	74,527	95,868	123,265	125,554	112,445	109,975	135,235	867,534
All other countries	076	605	1,205	1,327	1,624	2,189	1,660	2,347	11,033
Total government	105,097	90,713	124,003	164,482	181,496	173,875	191,446	218,486	1,249,598
Ford Foundation	86,550	15,096	15,222	13,673	12,016	14,000	10,700	10,500	177,757
Rockefeller Foundation	21,248	15,125	2,791	6,563	5,911	6,131	6,198	4,700	68,667
Total nongovernment	107,798	30,221	18,013	20,236	17,927	20,131	16,898	15,200	246,424
Total government and private aid	212,895	120,934	142,016	184,718	199,423	194,006	208,344	233,686	1,496,022
Total U.S.	198,463	104,748	113,881	143,501	143,481	132,576	126,873	150,435	1,113,958

SOURCE: Bradshaw et al., 1977, p.] 278

millions of U.S. dollars

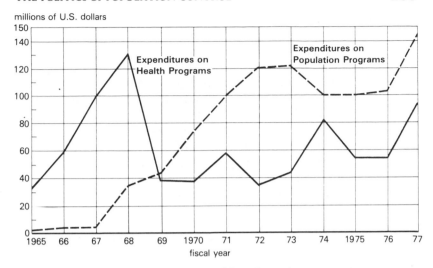

FIGURE 21-1. AID Expenditures on Health and Population Programs

U.S. Other sources of big money are the Ford Foundation and the Rock-efeller Foundation, which have given almost $250 million from 1965 through 1976 and which have worked closely with government agencies in this activity. The only close competitor is the Swedish government, which has provided $134 million over that period.

In 1978 the comptroller general made a report to Congress on AID's present and future activities, which may be considered an official state-ment of U.S. and AID policies. Lest there be doubt that the official U.S. position is to actively attempt to reduce world population growth for its own self-interest, consider these excerpts: The short summary on the front cover says that AID programs aim to "slow rapid population growth in developing countries" in order "to achieve an acceptable stabilized world population." And elsewhere, "AID ... views efforts to contain population growth as a part of its congressional mandate."[1] The reasons given for these aims are the supposed consequences of population growth.

> Rapid population growth in developing countries seriously impedes the already difficult task of improving the lives of millions who live at or near subsistence levels. Population growth often:
> — Places additional burdens on food production.
> — Increases unemployment and migration to urban areas.

— Places additional demands on inadequate health and educational services.
— *Encourages political and civil disorders.*
— *Accelerates the use of natural resources.*
— *Threatens the Earth's ability to support life.*

Population increases can also necessitate increased food imports and related debt increases. In parts of the developing world, declining agricultural productivity due to widespread slash-and-burn farming, overgrazing, overcropping, excessive cutting of forests to provide firewood and ground to cultivate, and the expansion of desert areas have also been attributed to population pressures. One recent report concluded that, unless there is some check on population growth, "there ultimately is no solution to the world food problem."[2]

My earlier chapters argue that there is no factual basis whatsoever for most of these AID assertions. And the U.S. clearly has gone far beyond simply offering other countries material and informational assistance in its euphemistically labeled "family planning programs." Though recent official pronouncements have tried for political reasons to avoid heavy-handed language, we can still read that our official policy is to "contain population growth" in other countries by "motivational programs," which include programs that "would make families want fewer children."[3] That is, the U.S. aims to bring people in other countries to want the lower fertility that we think they ought to want. Consider, for example, this statement: "Since large numbers of children may be desired for a variety of reasons, including help in agriculture, support in old age, and status, elements of the socioeconomic milieu which encourage large families need to be changed."[4] And this about Ivory Coast: AID informed the comptroller general that it planned to assign a full-time "population officer" to Abidjan in order to "help create awareness of the impact of population growth and foster greater private and government involvement in supplying family planning services."[5] Translated from bureaucratese, AID intends to tell the Africans that they had better get cracking or else. And in many countries we have made our other development assistance contingent on their efforts to reduce population growth, by requiring a "development project population impact statement" before funding.[6] In other words, if you want our help, you've got to have fewer children. And AID even has a mechanism to "influence fertility through development in countries where it has no bilateral assistance programs."[7] The device is to give money to international "private" organizations such as the International Planned Parenthood Foundation (IPPF) and UNFPA and have them do the job.

A bizarre but revealing episode began with a speech by R. T. Ravenholt (the number-one man in AID's population program since its beginning) concerning a program for foreign doctors at Washington University in St. Louis. The news story was headlined "Population Control of Third World Planned: Sterilization Storm in U.S.," in a Dublin (Ireland) newspaper where I saw it; the account went as follows.

> In what must be this year's prize-winning entry for reckless candour in public places, a senior State Department official has said the U.S. is seeking to provide the means to sterilize a quarter of all Third World women, in part to·protect the interests of American business overseas.
>
> The official is Dr. R. T. Ravenholt, Director of the U.S. Office of Population. . . .
>
> Population control, said Dr. Ravenholt in an interview, is needed to maintain the normal operation of U.S. commercial interests around the world.
>
> "Without our trying to help these countries with their economic and social development, the world would rebel against the strong U.S. commercial presence. The self-interest thing is a compelling element."
>
> If the population explosion proceeds unchecked, said Dr. Ravenholt, it will cause such terrible economic conditions abroad that revolutions will ensue. And revolutions, he suggested, are scarcely ever beneficial to the interests of the United States.
>
> The centre of the storm now raging over U.S. population policy is at Washington University in St. Louis, where about 70 foreign doctors are being trained in "advanced fertility management" under a 2.8 million dollar grant from AID. Each doctor is presented with a free $5,000 laparascope, a lighted tube which is inserted into the stomach under local anaesthetic to cauterise or clip the fallopian tube.
>
> William Danforth, the Chancellor of the University, who only a few days ago was describing the programme as "a broad brush up course in new obstetrical techniques" is now complaining he was misled as to the real purpose of a course which has existed on his own campus since 1973.
>
> In a sharply worded letter to Cyrus Vance, the U.S. Secretary of State, Danforth suggests Vance consider how he would feel if a foreign country took upon itself the lofty task of reducing the population of the United States for its own economic benefit.[8]

I am mystified as to the true meaning of Ravenholt's remarks, or of similar views that I often hear in private conversations about population. But as an economist I am sure that this "self-interest" motivation makes

TABLE 21-2. Recipients of AID Population Program Assistance Funding Allocations in Thousands of Dollars

				Fiscal Year 1965 through Transition Quarter, 1976						Transition Quarter	Total 1965–76 TQ
	1965–68	1969	1970	1971	1972	1973	1974	1975	1976		
Private Voluntary Organizations											
IPPF[a]	4,478	5,964	7,300	5,000	8,000	12,104	12,747	12,437	7,794	3,134	78,958
Pathfinder	1,494	4,359	–	3,066	4,350	6,735	4,001	3,660	3,622	394	31,681
Population Council	3,104	7,487	2,435	4,247	5,525	7,280	–	750	800	–	31,628
AVS[b]	–	–	–	–	876	1,000	1,250	1,850	1,000	–	5,976
FPIA[c]	–	–	–	3,800	4,000	–	3,730	4,424	6,329	1,352	23,635
Other	421	458	6,868	6,241	13,542	9,469	6,654	8,204	7,897	3,095	62,849
Subtotal	9,497	18,268	16,603	22,354	36,293	36,588	28,382	31,325	27,442	7,975	234,727
Universities	8,014	3,797	6,494	23,559	14,741	14,100	11,430	10,672	15,036	4,098	111,941
Participating Agency Service Agreements	419	2,585	1,301	1,883	2,911	3,767	3,667	3,772	3,086	659	24,050
Bilateral Programs	22,942	13,778	39,635	25,287	34,230	47,588	33,617	30,319	37,800	14,358	299,554
UNFPA[d]	500	2,500	4,000	14,000	29,040	9,000	18,000	20,000	16,000	4,000	117,040
Other	2,890	3,432	5,070	6,892	3,636	10,582	5,049	3,887	3,628	1,378	46,444
AID Operational Expenses	959	1,084	1,469	1,893	2,414	3,929	12,300	10,000	–	–	34,048
Total	45,221	45,444	74,572	95,868	123,265	125,554	112,445	109,975	102,992	32,468	867,804

SOURCE: U.S. General Accounting Office, 1978, Appendix I, table 21-3, and Association for Voluntary Sterilization Annual Statement for 1979.

[a]International Planned Parenthood Federation
[b]Association for Voluntary Sterilization
[c]Family Planning International Assistance
[d]UN Fund for Population Activities

no economic sense in this case. Of course Ravenholt is a physician and not an economist — but he is also the fellow who controls those big bucks at AID.

The recipients of AID population-program assistance are shown in table 21-2. Please note the large chunk that went to private U.S. and international organizations, to universities, and to UNFPA, which in turn also funds private organizations and universities.

THE U.S. POLITICS OF BIRTH CONTROL

The politics of population in the U.S. have been well and extensively analyzed by Piotrow, Bachrach and Bergman, and Littlewood.[9] In brief, for many years until the late 1960s, U.S. federal policy was to avoid any involvement in birth control, and even to oppose it with laws against mailing contraceptives and birth-control information. Then the political climate began to change. And once the change began, it continued with such speed and intensity that it seems to have gotten beyond the control of the normal political process. More specifically, public funds are being spent to implement the values and beliefs of a sub-group of the U.S. population that believes population control in the U.S. and abroad is a good thing. And this is apparently being done without the knowledge and approval of the public as a whole. It is not entirely farfetched to compare this operation to the CIA attempts to assassinate leaders and other persons in countries with which the U.S. is at peace, without explicit approval of the American voters and taxpayers.

Three key facts emerge from Piotrow's well-told history. First, U.S. national policy as executed by AID aims to induce *all* people in other countries to use contraceptives whether or not they initially wish to. Second, in 1969–70 AID was able to exert pressure on U.S. universities, private U.S. foundations, and international organizations to move "toward greater activism." This move was facilitated by the sudden big-bang join-up of population activists and environmentalists. Third, in order to avoid charges of interfering with foreign governments, AID gives U.S. taxpayers' money to private organizations to persuade foreign governments to alter their population policies. AID was not merely trying to help other countries achieve their own aims, but was (and still is) trying to pressure foreign governments to do what the U.S. population activists want to see done abroad.[10]

WHO IS ORGANIZED TO PUT PRESSURE ON WHOM?

The National Organization for Non-Parents (NON) claims that it is not against people having children; it only wants people to make responsible choices. But NON and related organizations claim that it is necessary to "balance the pro-natal pressure" brought upon people in the U.S. It is interesting, then, to enumerate the organizations on various sides of the issue, to see where the balance of pressure is.

Let us consider the list of "private organizations in the population field" as compiled by the Population Crisis Committee, as of September 1976.[11] This list does not include any organization working in favor of

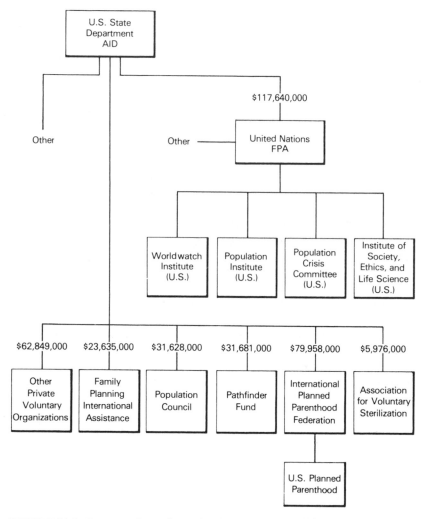

FIGURE 21-2. Patterns of Population-Program Funding by the U.S., 1965-1976

more births. (If there were any such organization, we can be sure that the Population Crisis Committee would not have missed it.) The year for which I have most information is 1975, but the picture has not changed markedly since then (though many of the personnel have changed). Unfortunately I have not had the resources to gather up-to-date information comprehensively, and it is not easy to find out what's what. For example, the Alan Guttmacher Institute, which spends in the millions for "publications" and "policy analysis and public education," lists $1,314,689 in 1979 "grants from non-government agencies." But this includes agencies that themselves get much of their money from the federal government. (In a different context this might seem like money laundering.)

The Planned Parenthood group includes the International Planned Parenthood Federation (IPPF); the Western Hemisphere regional office; Planned Parenthood Federation of America, which also is called Planned Parenthood/World Population; and the Alan Guttmacher Institute.

The total of the budgets for the Planned Parenthood groups was $121 million in 1975, of which $12.4 million was funded by the U.S. government through AID, whose aim is fertility control and reduction. Planned Parenthood also gets money from the Draper Fund (formerly the Victor/Bostrum Fund), which is completely committed to fertility reduction. Details will be provided shortly about Planned Parenthood's evolution from an organization whose aim was simply to help families and individuals get the number of children they want to an organization that aims to reduce population growth on grounds of pollution, crime in the streets, parking problems, and so forth.

Next is the tightly interrelated group of organizations that are frankly committed to the view that population growth is a bad thing and that reduction in the number of births is a good thing. These organizations differ in their dominant motivations and in the means they consider acceptable in the pursuit of that goal. (For example, they differ about whether coercion of potential parents not to have children is acceptable.) But they are all clearly anti-natalist in the sense that they cheer when a birthrate goes down. These organizations include (a) The Population Crisis Committee, which "works ... to promote population awareness among policy makers and to encourage high-level support for a wide range of population policies and programs, particularly in the developing countries"; (b) The Population Reference Bureau, which "prepares and distributes *Population Bulletins* on demographic and population-related topics; *Intercom*, a monthly newsletter; *Interchange*, a periodic review of population education; an annual *Population Data Sheet* with current demographic data for 106 countries; and occasional special reports and books. It also provides library services and workshops for teachers. The 1975 budget was $642,000, supported by USAID, foundations, individuals and memberships"; and (c) The Draper World Population Fund, which aims to "encourage and expand innovative private sector programs promising the greatest impact on population growth."

In addition, there are a variety of influential independent organizations. The Pathfinder Fund (a), which helps "initiate local family planning activities," says that "the 1975 budget of $3.5 million was provided by USAID, individuals, and foundations." But AID says that $3.66 million was given to the Pathfinder Fund in 1975 (table 21-2), and there must have been other sources of funds as well. Also there are (b) Zero Population Growth (ZPG); (c) Negative Population Growth (NPG);[12] (d) the National Organization for Non-Parents (NON);[13] (e) Population Services International; (f) the International Fertility Research Program "established with funds from USAID . . . with a 1976 budget of over $3 million"; and (g) the Association for Voluntary Sterilization, "organized in 1972 with funds from USAID to encourage and assist voluntary sterilization activities throughout the world . . . [with] a 1976 budget of $2.3 million." AID says that it gave $1.85 million to them in 1975, and $1.0 million in 1976 (table 21-2). Pathfinder's 1979 Annual Report says $4,918,779 came in from AID, for total expenses of $5,761,490. Finally, in this category are (h) Planned Parenthood/Church World Service; (i) the Population Department, United Methodist Church; and (j) Projects for Population Action.

Then there are the Sierra Club, the Environmental Fund, and other environmental organizations that espouse reduction in population growth as part of their environmental programs.

As a recent example of how much clout the population lobby can muster, consider this list of organizations — with many millions of members — that are on record as supporting H.R. 5062, a bill now (July 1980) before Congress that would create an Office of Population Policy with the aim of achieving zero population growth: the Arizona Family Planning Council; the American Public Health Association; Concern; the Conservation Foundation; Defenders of Wildlife; Environmental Action; the Environmental Fund; the Hawaii State Commission on Population and the Hawaiian Future; the Izaak Walton League of America; the Los Angeles Regional Family Planning Council; the National Alliance for Optional Parenthood; the National Audubon Society; the National Family Planning and Reproductive Health Association; the National Parks and Conservation Association; the National Wildlife Federation; the Natural Resources Defense Council; the Population Action Council; the Population Crisis Committee; the Population Institute; the Population Reference Bureau; the Sierra Club; the Texas Family Planning Association; the World Population Society; Zero Population Growth.

WHERE ARE THE PRO-NATALISTS?

On the other side are — who? I do not know of a single organization on the national scene that tries to persuade people to have more children. If one exists, it must be operating underground. Some readers will say that the Catholic church is such an organization, but in recent decades it has not been outspoken on the issue of family size, even for Catholic families. And it is even an open question whether the Catholic hierarchy and priesthood are now in favor of U.S. population growth.

The only nationally organized group that might be considered pronatal is Right to Life, because it is anti-abortion. But one can be against freely available abortion and also against population growth (for example, Richard Nixon); or pro-abortion-freedom and pro-population-growth (for example, the writer of this book); or anti and pro; or pro and anti. Certainly many members of Right to Life are not in favor of population growth. In any case, Right to Life has made no propaganda in favor of population growth; it does not, for example, run full-page ads in national newspapers, as anti-natal organizations do. And, perhaps most important in this context, Right to Life gets no government funds.

So where is the balance of public-relations pressure — for or against natality?

PLANNED PARENTHOOD/WORLD POPULATION

Among all the population organizations, Planned Parenthood requires special mention. From the date of its origin, Planned Parenthood has done the wonderful work of helping people have no more — and no fewer — children than they want, a straightforward matter of increasing people's options. But in recent years Planned Parenthood has partly changed its mission, though it waffles about saying so. It has become "Planned Parenthood/World Population" (PP/WP). As of 1980, one of the five general goals of PP/WP is stated as, "to combat the world population crisis by helping to bring about a population of stable size in an optimum environment in the United States." The reasons given for this goal are:

> Countries which cannot curb their popluation growth have little hope of achieving a decent standard of living enjoyed by the developed nations. Moreover, the monumental problems created by masses of impoverished, hungry, and unemployed or underemployed people are causing the lights of human liberty to go out and around the globe, as dictatorial regimes with draconian solutions step in and take over. Yet the problem is so overwhelming and amorphous that public interest in this country is difficult to sustain.[14]

And among the actions for which Planned Parenthood money — public and private — pays are:

Advocacy and Public Information

— Raise the level of awareness, both at home and abroad, about the magnitude of the population problem, the role that the United States must play in meeting it, the relationship between population growth and the role of women, and the need for increased support for these programs.

Education and Training

— Foster, through population education initiatives, the idea that there is an urgent need to slow population growth and conserve resources worldwide, and that these considerations should be a part of the process of personal choice regarding one's fertility.[15]

It pains me as a former contributor to document this turn of events. PP/WP's fund-raising campaign has used some of the crudest appeals to low emotions, and some of the wildest unproven claims found in American advertising. (If a commercial firm were to engage in similar promotional tactics, the Federal Trade Commission and the Postal Service might well prosecute the advertiser and maybe throw someone into jail. But, as with many non-profit organizations, PP/WP apparently feels no need to adhere even to commercial standards of promotional decency, because the principals believe that their cause is just and because they claim that such appeals are the only efficient way to raise funds.) Examples of the rhetoric and promotional devices used by PP/WP are in the Afternote to chapter 22.

UNITED NATIONS FUND FOR POPULATION ACTIVITIES

The UN Fund for Population Activities (UNFPA), which is, as we saw earlier, a major recipient of U.S. State Department AID funds ($177 million from 1965–78),[16] deserves a few words here. Rafael M. Salas, its executive director since the start, takes pains not to use inflated rhetoric, because "the concept of multilateral assistance continues to be highly appropriate in a field where sensitivities are still more acute than in other fields of development assistance."[17] But what really motivates UNFPA, and why it does not use inflammatory language, is clear from its own statements:

> Serious warnings have been issued from time to time on the population situation. But the Fund, while being constantly aware of the urgency and magnitude of the population question, particularly in third world countries whose economic resources are being rapidly overcome by population growth, has advisedly avoided making apocalyptic statements since it would be contrary to its mandate to influence Government decisions on population problems in any way.[18]

Yet UNFPA provides funds to support some thoroughly unequivocal scaremongering by organizations such as the Worldwatch Institute. Details on one such project, the book *Losing Ground*, were discussed in chapter 16. Another example is the pamphlet *Twenty-Two Dimensions of the Population Problem* by Lester Brown and others, a short propaganda broadside paid for by UNFPA; all twenty-two discussed aspects of population growth are said to be bad, simply on the basis of rhetoric and anecdotes. As Salas said in the introduction (in an uncharacteristically frank phrase), "The United Nations Funds for Population Activities has supported this research project of Worldwatch Institute to help *deepen public understanding of the population question.*"[19] In many of their recent publications UNFPA and the Worldwatch Institute perform excellent public relations for each other and for their directors, a sweetheart of a relationship.

UNFPA also funnels money back to U.S. groups that work for fertility reduction, including the Population Institute, the Population Crisis Committee, the Institute of Society, Ethics and Life Sciences in Hastings-on-Hudson, and the Worldwatch Institute. And the Worldwatch Institute's publications are advertised regularly (apparently for free) in *People*, the magazine of IPPF—another of the various channels through which Worldwatch Institute's activities are supported indirectly by U.S. taxpayers' money.

One of the interesting aspects of UNFPA is that many of its publications show high Arab dignitaries, such as the king of Saudi Arabia, who appears on page 2 of the 1975 report. Yet that same report shows only token contributions from oil-rich Arab countries from 1967 to 1975, as follows: Iraq, $500,000; Kuwait, $20,000; Libya, $20,000; Qatar, $10,000; Saudi Arabia, $60,000; Syria, $2,000. No other Arab countries were listed. And oh yes, the United States: a cool $97 million, almost half of the total UNFPA budget.

INTERLOCKING PERSONNEL

Noting how jobs shift and boards of directors interlock is useful in understanding the Washington "population community." For example, the January 1975 *Newsletter* of the World Population Society (one of the organizations most worried about population growth) said:

> Last month's Newsletter announed that Dr. Ward P. Allen had left the State Department and become the new Executive Director of the Society. Now we are happy to announce that Mr. Philander P. Claxton, Jr., since 1966 the Special Assistant to the Secretary of State for Population Matters, will, upon his year-end retirement, become a member of the Board of Directors of the Society. As "Mr. Population," Mr. Claxton was an early and initially an almost solitary voice in the councils of the Executive Branch in urging that problems of population dynamics were important factors in development of foreign policy. He has given consistent support and encouragement to the Society since its inception. His presence on our Board will bring us added strength and wisdom.

The headline of that squib could easily be understood in a manner other than was intended: "The U.S. Government's Loss Is the WPS's Gain," it said.

Another interconnection: William Gaud is the former head of AID who sparked AID's decision to strive to "reduce population growth." Now he is chairman of the Population Crisis Committee. He is also co-chairman of the Draper World Population Fund.

These job shifts remind me of the movement of people from government regulatory agencies to those private businesses that the agencies regulate — from, for example, the FTC to law firms that practice before the FTC, or from the FCC to communications firms. The same questions arise: Does this indicate that organizations with a special axe to grind — population control, in this case — have influence over the very public agencies that disburse funds to them, to which the government bureaucrats later move? Are the after-government jobs a form of reward — financial or honorary — for services rendered, and are services rendered in hope of such rewards? Of course, such job shifts may be perfectly honest and sincere. But such questions must be asked in an open society, if only to help keep the system honest.

As to interlocking directorates and other intertwinings, the names of many of the same people recur on the boards of directors of many population organizations. Many of these persons — William Draper, Hugh Moore, and Harold Bostrom, among others — clearly are or were persons who have been extraordinarily generous with their time, energy, and money, purely or largely for selfless, idealistic reasons. Yet these are men who have had very strong anti-natal views. And through their interconnections with Planned Parenthood, the Population Crisis Committee, the Association for Voluntary Sterilization, the Population Reference Bureau, and related organizations, together with their well-documented strong influence with U.S. Presidents, UN officials, and U.S. Congresses, they have managed to have the U.S. federal government commit its funds and its influence to the cause of fertility-reduction programs for which the U.S. citizenry has not expressed its approval.[20]

As to the interconnecting affiliations of organization executives and demographers, Bachrach and Bergman undertook a systematic study of the staffs, boards, panels, committees, and consultantships as of 1970 in the following institutions: The Population Council; the Ford Foundation; PP/WP; HEW; the National Institutes of Health; AID; the Bureau of the Census; and the National Academy of Sciences. They found an astonishing amount of multiple affiliations. Bachrach and Bergman discovered this interconnecting network in 1970, before the Washington–New York "population community" was nearly as well established as it has now become. All of these interconnections must have greatly intensified since then. And these interlocks help keep the "population community" a closed society with respect to dissenting views.

Pro-Natality Pressures? Tax Supported Anti-Natality Pressures?

Anti-natalist sometimes say that their aim is simply to restore a fair balance in the U.S. between pro-natalism and anti-natalism. The pro-natal incentive that the anti-natalists criticize most is the subsidy to children through the income-tax deduction.

Anti-natalists would do better to take aim at the system whereby a community pays for schools, because the income tax allowance is small relative to the public school expenditure. But even the subsidy to children through funds for schools — whereby each parent pays out less to raise a child than it actually costs — is small relative to the total parental cost of rearing a child — perhaps a fifth or a quarter of it. And the child later returns more than half of that in defense taxes (all discounted at 5 percent.)[21]

Though relatively unimportant as an influence on childbearing, because the amounts are relatively small, the issue of child subsidies in the form of free schooling has other complexities. Is free schooling an expression of the community's desire for more children? If so, the anti-natalists' criticism is misdirected. Is free schooling actually a beneficial investment for the rest of society? Entirely possible. Is free schooling a welfare payment to children rather than to parents? If so, the matter is very tangled. The entire issue of school subsidies is complex, much more complex than the anti-natalists' argument makes it out to be.

The other main "pressure" mentioned by anti-natalists is the influence that parents and friends exercise upon young couples to bear children. The issue here is simple: Should public money be spent to counter this expressed desire of potential grandparents and other well-wishers? If so, why not a publicly financed campaign for people to write more poetry and fewer detective stories? Or to use a fork rather than a spoon to eat corn? The anti-natalists argue that countering the desire of relatives and friends to see couples bear children is beneficial for the national economy and society. NON falls back on the same old arguments that "in a world in which population is outrunning food supply . . . in which every American child innocently consumes a disproportionate amount of the planet's energy and resources . . . NON parents benefit society."[22] This book shows that there is no scientific foundation for these sweeping generalizations. Furthermore, what is judged good for society is a matter of values, a matter that chapter 23 takes up. A better and truer statement of NON's real purpose is its slogan, "None is Fun."

Certainly NON and other groups are entitled in a democratic society to attempt to convince others of their views and to try to counter what they consider to be an "enormous propaganda machine — families, churches, schools, advertisements, doctors, the works — that impels every woman toward maternity."[23] But is it fair for organizations such as PP/WP along with NON, ZPG, and related groups, to use *public* funds to do so, and to help sponsor conferences on such folderol as "Pronatalism in the Arts"?[24]

CONCLUSION

Taxes paid to the U.S. federal government are being used by both public and private organizations to pressure citizens of the U.S. and of foreign countries to have fewer children. The U.S. government has embraced the aims of the population activists and is spending taxpayers' money to further those aims, at least in part out of a misguided impression that it is in the U.S. economic interest to do so. Much of this is done indirectly and under misleading labels such as "family planning" to avoid criticism by those U.S. taxpayers who may not want their money used for this purpose.

The Rhetoric of Population Control:
Does the End Justify the Means?

The ranking black lawmaker in the Illinois House and the
Republican sponsor of a bill which would offer poor persons a
chance for a free sterilization with a $100 bonus thrown in . . .
squared off and traded verbal blasts Wednesday in the House
Human Resources Committee where Rep. Webber Borchers
was presenting his free vasectomy bill.

Though observers said Borchers may have won the battle of
insults, Rep. Corneal Davis, an aging and routnd black preacher
who has spent 30 of his 70-some years in the House, relished
the satisfaction of having the bill defeated. . . .

Davis set the tone for the hearing on the bill soon after the
committee sat down.

"Where is Borchers?" the Democratic assistant minority
leader said, waving an arm at the ceiling. "He ought to take his
bill and go back to Nazi Germany."

Thirty minutes later Borchers, a Decatur landowner who
boasts of his ultraconservatism, arrived to explain his bill.

"This bill would allow persons who have an income of
$3,000 or less to get a free vasectomy and a $100 bonus . . . ,"
Borchers began.

But Davis had sprung to his feet.

"Are you sincere about this?" the Chicago Democrat asked
sarcastically.

"Sit down," Borchers yelled back.

"I am a preacher and I didn't want to lose my cool with
you," Davis said.

Why don't you listen? Sit down," Borchers said as both men's
words began to get lost in the uproar.

Rep. Louis Capuzi, R-Chicago, chairman of the Human
Resources Committee, pounded the gavel but it took several
minutes for the two men to become silent.

Davis sat down and Borchers continued speaking.

"This bill was suggested to me by a black woman in
Chicago," Borchers said.

Davis's eyes flared with rage but he remained silent.

Borchers said the bill was similar to one passed in Tennessee.

He estimated that more than 19,000 children are born to families receiving public aid each year and that the state would stand to save $20 million in welfare payments under the voluntary sterilization plan.[1]

The Davis-Borchers interchange illustrates the subject of this chapter, the passions and the rhetoric found in discussions of resources and population.

It is a truism by now that resources are getting more scarce, and that population growth exacerbates the problem. You have read numerous examples of such statements in previous chapters by persons who are supposedly experts. So well accepted have these ideas become that eminent people in other fields treat them as assumptions in their own work, on an "everyone knows" basis — the way everyone knows that without sunshine the flowers will not grow. Just a few examples of persons publicly decrying population growth that I have stumbled across in casual reading: psychologist O. H. Mowrer; Nobel agronomist Norman Borlaug; sociobiologist Edward Wilson; author Isaac Asimov; English professor Richard P. Adams; columnist Jack Anderson; Nobel physicist Murray Gell-Mann; basketball player Wilt Chamberlain; columnist Ann Landers; her sister, columnist "Dear Abby"; physician and head of the Rockefeller Foundation John H. Knowles; John D. Rockefeller III; former Secretary of HEW Robert Finch; and a bucket more including newspaper editorial writers, U.S. senators, and plain citizens who write letters to the newspaper saying that a "world without population curbs . . . would be a sickening, violent, depressing, congested hell, with the complete destruction of the human race, all animals, and the world's natural environment."[2]

These pessimistic propositions about resources and growth are so generally accepted that eminent people in other fields will sign petitions to the President and endorse full-page advertisements that run in the nation's most-read national newspapers. Even Nobel prize winners such as John Northrop, Linus Pauling, and William Shockley were willing to lend their prestige to anti-natal efforts, an example of which is shown in figure 22-1. Another may be seen in the Appendix.

The weight of doomsday opinion is indicated by the long list of such books found in any library; books by Beckerman and Kahn and Maddox are the rare exceptions of opposing voices.[3] And so deeply has the notion

Pope denounces birth control as millions starve

BLACK STAR PHOTO

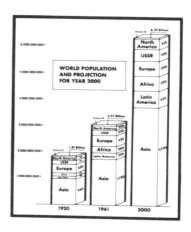

WORLD POPULATION AND PROJECTION FOR YEAR 2000

"Every marriage act must remain open to the transmission of life," said Pope Paul in his recent encyclical. He ruled out every action which proposes "to render procreation impossible."

The Pope denounced artificial contraception – the only practical means of controlling population. He held that it is not reasonable "to have recourse to artificial birth control" even though "we secure the harmony and peace of the family, and better conditions for the education of the children already born."

By his edict the Pope has struck a crushing blow against current efforts to reduce the flood of people now engulfing the earth.

In the advanced countries most couples–Catholics as well as Protestants–already practice birth control. But in the under-developed countries, such as in Latin America, the Pope's teaching may result in the birth of hordes of children who will not have enough to eat.

Famine already stalks the earth. Half of humanity goes to bed hungry every night. Ten thousand or more people are dying of starvation every day. This means that more than three and a half million starve to death every year. (The present tragic Biafra toll is *in addition* to these figures.)

As recently as 1953 there were 2½ billion people on earth. Today only 15 years later there are 3½ *billion.* A generation from now that number will approximately double at the present rate of increase, as the chart shows.

The Pope dismissed the population explosion with a few brief words, merely saying that it should be met by greater social and economic progress, rather than to resort to "utterly materialistic" measures to limit births.

The encyclical appears to millions of Catholics and Protestants as a rather incredible document, considering the eminence of the author and his access to the world's leading demographic, agricultural and other authorities. It is viewed by many as one of the most fateful blunders of modern times.

For there can be no doubt that unless population is brought under control at an early date the resulting human misery and social tensions will inevitably lead to chaos and strife—to revolutions and wars, the dimensions of which it would be hard to predict.

Nothing less than survival of the human race is at stake.

CAMPAIGN TO CHECK THE POPULATION EXPLOSION
EMERSON FOOTE, CHAIRMAN

FIGURE 22-1

of a "population explosion" sunk into the popular consciousness that the term appears in *The Living Bible*, a widely read paraphrase of the Old and New Testaments. In that version, the story of Noah begins in this manner: "Noah was 500 years old and had three sons, Shem, Ham, and Japheth. Now a population explosion took place upon the earth" (Genesis 6). And of course the flood followed.

Proof that the "population movement" has succeeded in convincing people that population growth is bad is seen in the discrepancy between people's beliefs about their own local situation and the situation of their nation as a whole. Polls in the U.S. and in Great Britain find that people do not think that their own neighborhoods — about which they have direct information from their own observations — are overpopulated. But they do say that their country as a whole — which they know mostly from reports in the media — is overpopulated.[4] What else can account for people's reaching this conclusion other than successful rhetoric?

Test this for yourself. Ask yourself, and your children, whether the country is overpopulated, or whether population is growing too fast. Then ask about your block and your neighborhood. There is a curious inconsistency here: You say your house is fine but mine is overpopulated, and I say mine is fine but yours is overpopulated. What would an impartial observer learn from this about the condition of each house?

Let's consider the rhetoric used to engender a fear of population growth and afterward speculate why this rhetoric has been so effective.

INFLAMMATORY TERMINOLOGY AND PERSUASION BY EPITHET

Fear of population growth has been inflamed by extravagant language. Examples are the terms "population explosion," "people pollution," and "population bomb." These terms are not just the catchwords of popular wordsmiths, whose rhetoric one is accustomed to discount. Rather, they have been coined and circulated by distinguished scientists and professors. One example comes from the justly famous demographer Kingsley Davis, who began a recent article in a professional journal: "In subsequent history the Twentieth Century may be called either the century of world wars or the century of the population plague."[5] Davis also has said that "Over-reproduction — that is, the bearing of more than four children — is a worse crime than most and should be outlawed."[6] Or Paul Ehrlich: "We can no longer afford merely to treat the symptoms of the cancer of population growth; the cancer itself must be cut out."[7] And it was in his Nobel Peace Prize speech, of all places, that Norman Borlaug spoke of "the population monster" and the "population octopus."

Such language is loaded, pejorative, and unscientific. It also reveals something about the feelings of contemporary anti-natalist writers. Psychiatrist Frederick Wertham pointed out that many of these terms have overtones of violence, for example, "bomb" and "explosion," and many show contempt for other human beings, such as "people pollution." Referring to expressions such as "these days of the population explosion and the hydrogen bomb" and "both nuclear weapons and population growth endanger mankind," he says: "The atomic bomb is the symbol, the incarnation, of modern mass violence. Are we justified in even speaking in the same vein of violent death and birthrate? And is it not a perverse idea to view population destruction and population growth as twin evils?"[8]

There is no campaign of counter-epithets to allay the fear of population growth, perhaps because of a Gresham's law of language: Bad terms drive out good. Reasoning by epithet may well be part of the cause of the fear of population growth in the U.S.

Not only epithets but also value-smuggling neologisms have been used against fertility. The term "childfree" is a neologism coinèd by NON — the National Organization for Non-Parents — as a replacement for "childless." Their intention is to substitute a positive word, "free," for a negarive word, "less." This neologism is an interesting example of skillful propaganda. Whereas the term "less" is only slightly pejorative — you can have less of something good (love) or of something bad (acne) — the term "free" *always* seems better than "unfree," and one can only be free of something bad. If not having children makes you "free," then this clearly implies that children are bad. In a similar vein, environmentalists now speak of "wetlands lost," a phenomenon earlier referred to as "swamps drained."

PHONY ARGUMENTS, CRUDE AND SUBTLE

Some of the anti-natalist propaganda is quite subtle. While seeming to be only straightforward birth-control information, in reality it is a persuasive appeal for having fewer children. Planned Parenthood was responsible for such a campaign on television and radio a few years ago. There would be no complaint about such a persuasive message except that it was indirectly paid for by taxpayers. The campaign was produced by the Advertising Council as a "public service" and shown on television during time given free by the broadcasters as part of their quid pro quo to the public in return for their licenses. The following is drawn from a letter written in complaint to the Advertising Council decision-makers — the only letter they said that they had ever received.

You may have seen an advertising campaign staged by Planned Parenthood that ran on radio, television, and in many national magazines. There were a number of specific ads in the campaign including one that was headlined "How Many Children Should You Have? Three? Two? One"; another that adduced "Ten Reasons for Not Having Children"; and, finally, the most offensive one was called the "Family Game": the game was staged on a great monopoly board and every time the dice of life were thrown and a child was born — rather like going to jail without passing "go" — the background audio announced the disasters that came in the wake of children — "there goes the vacation," or "there goes the family room . . . ."

One of the ads enjoins young people to "enjoy your freedom" before, by having children, you let some of that freedom go. Such a theme . . . continues the view that the contribution children make to persons and to society is a purely negative one. In this view children are a loss: they take space, constrict freedom, use income that can be invested in vacations, family rooms, and automobiles. We find no consideration here of how children enhance freedom, and of how the advantages of freedom itself are realized when shared rather than prized as a purely personal possession. Finally, one of the ads encapsulates the spirit of the entire campaign: "How many children should a couple have? Three? Two? One? None?" Such an ad belies the claim that the advertising avoids the designation of any specific number of children as "preferred." Why not 12? 11? 10? or six? five? four? In the same ad, in order to lead audience thinking, it is noted that the decision to have children "could depend on their concern for the effect population growth can have on society." The direction of the effect on society is implied, but nowhere is the effect analyzed, or even clearly stated.

In summary, the ads not only teach family planning but recommend population control. Moreover, they do this by defining the range of acceptable family size as between zero and three, by placing children as negative objects alongside the positive goods supplied by industry, by equating the bringing up of children with merely equipping them with these same goods, by viewing children as an essential constriction of human freedom, and by suppressing a view of life and children that might lead people to think that having more children is a positive and rewarding act. There are values, not just techniques embodied in those ads.[9]

Not all anti-natality rhetoric is that subtle. Some of it is crude name-calling, especially the attacks on the Catholic church and on people with

Catholic connections. An example is the bold black headline on the full-page ad that was run in national magazines by the Campaign to Check the Population Explosion: "Pope denounces birth control as millions starve." Another example is the dismissal of opposing views by referring to the happenstance that the opponent is Catholic. Consider, for example, the religion-baiting of Colin Clark—a world-respected economist who presented data showing the positive effects of population growth—by sociologists Lincoln and Alice Day: "Colin Clark, an internationally known Roman Catholic economist and leading advocate of unchecked population growth." And Jack Parsons writes, "Colin Clark, the distinguished Roman Catholic apologist . . . refrains from discussing optimization of population at all . . . an extraordinary omission." Gunnar Myrdal is not a Catholic and is a Nobel prize winner, and yet *he* called the concept of an optimum population level "one of the most sterile ideas that ever grew out of our science." But Parsons feels free to attribute religious motives to Clark's choice of technical concepts and vocabulary when Clark does not mention this "optimization" concept. And in the widely read text of Paul Ehrlich and others, *Population, Resources, and Environment*, we find a reference to Clark as an "elderly Catholic economist," an innovation in the name-calling by referring to Clark's age as well as to his religion.[10]

As a firsthand example in the same vein, my own views—which had already become those of this book—were described by Paul Silverman, a biologist, before a packed auditorium on the first and greatest Earth Day, in 1970, as "inspired by Professor Simon's contact with the Bible. . . . Indeed, a new religious doctrine has been enunciated in which murder and abstinence from sex are not distinguishable."[11]

GRABBING VIRTUE, DAUBING WITH SIN

A rhetorical device of the anti-natalists (as of all rhetoricians, I suppose) is to attribute to themselves the most virtuous and humanitarian of motives, while attributing to their opponents motives that are self-serving or worse. Biologist Silverman again: " . . . people such as Paul Ehrlich and Alan Guttmacher and presumably myself . . . out of our great concern for the future of the world and the threat to the quality of life . . . have urged that voluntary means be adopted for bringing about restraints on the overburdening of our environment by overpopulation. . . . We must, we can, and we will achieve a fine and beautiful world for ourselves and our children to inherit. . . . We can realize a new quality of life, free from avarice which characterizes our current society."[12] (A few minutes before, the same speaker had said, "If voluntary restraints on population growth are not forthcoming, we will be faced with a need to consider coercive measures" — not very different from Ehrlich's "by compulsion if voluntary methods fail.")

WHY IS POPULATION RHETORIC SO APPEALING?

Let us consider some of the reasons that anti-natality rhetoric has won the minds of so many people.

Short-run costs are inevitable, whereas long-run benefits are hard to foresee. In the very short run, the effects of increased births are negative, on the average. If your neighbor has another child your school taxes will go up, and there will be more noise in your neighborhood. And when the additional child first goes to work, per-worker income will be lower than otherwise, at least for awhile.

It is more difficult to foresee and understand the possible long-run benefits. Increased population can stimulate increases in knowledge, pressures for beneficial changes, a youthful spirit, and the "economies of scale" discussed earlier. The last means that more people constitute bigger markets, which can often be served by more efficient production facilities. And increased population density can make economical the building of transportation, communication, educational systems, and other kinds of "infrastructure" that are uneconomical for a less-dense population. But the connection between population growth and these beneficial changes is indirect and inobvious, and hence these possible benefits do not strike people's minds with the same force as do the short-run disadvantages.

The increase in knowledge created by more people is especially non-material and thus easy to overlook. Writers about population growth mention a greater number of mouths coming into the world and more pairs of hands, but never more brains arriving. This emphasis on physical consumption and production may be responsible for much unsound thinking and fear about population growth.

Even if there are long-run benefits, the benefits are less immediate than are the short-run costs of population growth. Additional public medical care is needed even before the birth of an additional child. But if the child grows up to discover a theory that will lead to a large body of scientific literature, the economic or social benefits may not be felt for 100 years. All of us tend to put less weight on events in the future compared with those in the present, just as a dollar that you will receive twenty years from now is worth less to you than is a dollar in your hand now.

The above paragraphs do not imply that, on balance, the effect of increased population will surely be positive in any longer-run period. The fact is that we do not know for sure what the effects will be, on balance, in 50 or 100 or 200 years. Rather, I am arguing that the positive effects tend to be overlooked, causing people to think — without sound basis — that the long-run effects of population growth *surely* are negative, when in fact a good argument can be made that the net effect *may* be positive.

Now let's consider some of the rhetorical devices themselves.

Apparent consensus of expert judgment. Anti-natalists make it seem that all the experts agree that population is growing too fast in the U.S. and, therefore, that it is a *fact* that population is growing too fast. An example from Lester Brown: "There are few if any informed people who any longer deny the need to stabilize world population." Other examples come from Paul Ehrlich: "Everyone agrees that at least half of the people of the world are undernourished (have too little food) or malnourished (have serious imbalances in their diet)." And, "I have yet to meet anyone familiar with the situation who thinks India will be self-sufficient in food by 1971, if ever." And from a *Newsweek* columnist and former high State Department official: "Informed men in every nation now know that, next to population growth and avoidance of nuclear war, the despoiling of nature is the biggest world problem of the next 30 years."[13]

These "everyone agrees" statements are just plain wrong. Many eminent experts do not agree with them. But such assertions that "everyone agrees" may well be effective in manipulating public opinion. Which non-specialist is likely to pit his or her own opinion against that of all the "informed people"?

Population as a cause of pollution. Fear of population growth is surely heightened by the linking of population and pollution issues. It has come to seem as if one must be against population growth if one is to be for pollution control. And pollution control in itself appeals to everyone, for very substantial reasons.

To understand why the link-up of population control and pollution control has occurred with such force, we must understand the nature of the rhetoric on both sides of the argument. One can directly demonstrate that more people increase the flow of a pollutant — for example, that more people make more trash. The argument that more people may reduce pollution is less direct and not so obvious. For example, as more people make a bigger pollution problem, forces of reaction arise that may make the situation better than ever before. Furthermore, the ill effects of people and pollution can be understood deductively: More people *must* create more trash. But whether the endpoint after a sequence of social steps will be an even cleaner environment can only be shown by an empirical survey of experiences in various places: Are city streets in the U.S. cleaner now than they were 100 years ago? Such empirical arguments are usually less compelling to the imagination than are the simplistic deductive arguments.

Population, natural resources, and common sense. With respect to natural resources, the population-control argument apparently makes perfect "common sense." If there are more people, natural resources will inevitably get used up and become more scarce. And the idealistic, generous side of young people responds to the fear that future generations will be disadvantaged by a heavy use of resources in this generation.

Perhaps such a doomsday view of natural resources is partly accounted for by the ease of demonstrating that more people will cause some particular negative effects — for example, if there are more Americans there will be less wilderness. The logic of the rebuttal must be global and much more encompassing than the logic of the charge. To show that the loss of wilderness to be enjoyed in solitude is not an argument against more people, one must show that an increase in people may ultimately lead to a general expansion of the "unspoiled" space available to each person — through easier transportation to the wilderness, high-rise buildings, trips to the moon, plus many other partial responses that would not now be possible if population had been stationary 100 years ago. It is obviously harder to show how good is the sum effect of these population-caused improvements than it is to show how bad is the partial effect of a decrease in this or that wilderness area that one may enjoy in solitude. Hence the result is a belief in the ill effects of population growth.

Judgments about people's rationality. At the bottom of people's concern about population growth often lies the belief that other people will not act rationally in the face of environmental and resource needs. Arguments about the need to stop population growth now often contain the implicit premise that individuals and societies cannot be trusted to make rational, timely decisions about fertility rates. This is the drunkard model of fertility behavior refuted in chapter 12.

One of the themes that runs through much of the population movement is that the experts and the population enthusiasts understand population economics better than other persons do. As John D. Rockefeller III put it, "The average citizen doesn't appreciate the social and economic implications of population growth."[14] It is not at all clear why a politician or businessman — even though a very rich one — should have a clearer understanding of the costs of bearing children than "an average citizen." But Rockefeller has been, and is, in a position to do much to turn his opinion into national action.

Media exposure. Anti-natality views get enormously more exposure than pro-natality or neutralist views. Paul Ehrlich has repeatedly been on the Johnny Carson show, and for an unprecedented hour, but no one who holds contrary views gets such media exposure. This is also clear from a casual analysis of the titles of articles listed in the *Reader's Guide to Periodical Literature.*

Money. The leaders of population agencies that have vast sums of money at their disposal — UNFPA and USAID — clearly see as their goal the reduction of population growth in the poorer countries. Scientists who work in population studies and who have a reasonable degree of career prudence are not likely to go out of their way to offend such powerful potential patrons. Rather, individuals and organizations hitch all kinds of research projects to this money-star. Furthermore, various agencies such as UNFAO realize that their own budgets will be larger if the public and government officials believe that there are fearsome impending dangers from population growth, environmental disaster, and starvation. Therefore, their publicity organs play up these threats.

Standards of proof and of rhetoric. The standard of proof demanded of those who oppose the popular view is much much more exacting than is the standard of proof demanded of those who share the popular view. One example: The scientific procedure of the *Limits to Growth* study has been condemned by every economist who has reviewed it, to my knowledge. Yet its findings are acclaimed and retailed by the "population community." But if I say that the world food situation has been improving year by year, you will either say "Prove it," or "I won't believe it." Now consider the advertisement run in national newspapers by the Environmental Fund (figure 22-2). No one asks for proof of the statements in that advertisement.

Furthermore, anti-doomsday people are in a double bind rhetorically: The doomsdayers speak in excited, angry, high-pitched voices, using lan-

DEPEND ON US FOR MORE FOOD *Hunger*

Increased famine in the developing world in Asia, Africa and Latin America is inevitable because:

1. Food production cannot keep pace with runaway growth in population, and

2. Population growth in those areas is out of control. It cannot, and will not, be stopped in the foreseeable future, using conventional methods now being practiced or contemplated by our foreign aid establishment.

Last year, The Environmental Fund sponsored an advertisement ("The Real Crisis Behind the Food Crisis") which elaborated on the above statement. Its publication stimulated a surprising 23,000 replies (all but 13 in agreement with the analysis). Many asked, "What can we do about it?"

Indeed, how can Americans ameliorate the impending tragedy? First, we must understand that we are being misled into believing that the United States has no problem with excessive population growth.

Second, we are being misled into thinking that many poor nations of Asia, Africa and Latin America are successfully coping with their runaway population growth.

Both assumptions are wrong.

The United States has a serious population problem; the vast majority of the hungry nations have an even more serious one. Yet nearly all nations, the United States included, lack any sort of population stabilization program. Most do not want one.

Unless people lower the birth-rate (or, as some argue, raise the death-rate) the world's population will quadruple during the lifetime of many of us now reading this page.

This insupportable growth is not the result of an increase in the birth rate. It is the result of a precipitous drop in the death rate, with no accompanying drop in the birth rate. It takes no special foresight to see that birth rates must come down, or death rates will climb to what used to be considered "normal."

The U.S. Department of Agriculture has announced that the world can no longer rely on U.S. food aid gifts or concessional sales to fill the world food gap.

This unusually candid declaration from the USDA provoked an immediate and vigorous response from various groups, organizations and individuals. Some, recognizing the wastes of an affluent society, declared that the problem was not limited capacity, but a reluctance to distribute resources fairly. Others declared that it was a moral imperative for us to become the "breadbasket of the world" today, and that the future would take care of itself. Still others are lobbying in Washington to establish food aid as "the cornerstone of our foreign policy", i.e., charity-by-law. Even granting the consent of the taxpayers and the good intentions of the lobbyists, this course of action is a prescription for disaster.

THE ADVERSE EFFECTS OF FOOD AID

Consider what food aid does.

Each piece of land has a specific carrying capacity. That capacity can be altered by fertilizer, improved management, and superior crop varieties. But there are still definite limits to how many people a given unit of land can support. Food aid violates the carrying capacity principle by artificially allowing more people to live on the land than can live from it.

Today, in order to provide large amounts of food aid, the donor country must overcultivate its own land, farming marginal acres, destroying the topsoil, and reducing its future ability to produce. When a 10,000 ton freighter loaded to the scuppers with U.S. wheat sails forth, it carries with it 200 tons of nitrogen, 41 tons of phosphorus, and 50 tons of potassium – all lost forever from the fertility of our soils.

THE INVERTED ETHICS OF FOOD AID

Food aid also enables the donor to postpone facing the grim reality which no one wants to face, which is: unless population growth is stabilized, the inescapable result of saving lives today will be an even greater number of lives lost tomorrow.

Those who ask the United States to increase its foreign aid commitment so that more food may be sent to the hungry overseas, simply misunderstand the problem: there are now too many people for the carrying capacity of the land. This year, the world's population will add 93 million people; next year, 95 million. Within eight years, 800 million people will be added to the world.

Nearly all of the 123 countries of Asia, Africa and Latin America – whether or not they have "benefited" from the U.S. foreign aid program – now have more poor, more illiterate, more hungry people than they had when this program began. Yet today, the U.S. development establishment allows recipient nations to

count on food shipments from this country or to depend on the empty promise that those shipments will continue tomorrow – no matter how large populations grow.

This is a cruel deception.

By means of promises, declarations and resolutions, the United States is assuming a role it cannot play, and responsibilities it cannot carry out. This perception of the United States as a limitless cornucopia is a dangerous delusion to all concerned. It is dangerous to Americans because it isn't true, and, like all evasions of reality, it eventually leads to disillusionment and despair.

But it is an even more dangerous disservice to the leaders of the crowded and hungry nations. Belief in those promises enables them also to evade reality, to evade the hard decisions that must be made if their mushrooming populations are to be matched by their own resources.

WHAT AMERICA CAN DO AT HOME AND ABROAD

In order to help anyone at all – at home or abroad – Americans must learn to distinguish fact (the carrying capacity of the land) from fancy ("We can feed the world, if we really want to"). We must learn to distinguish pride in our achievements from the vanity of our ambitions. America cannot control the world, but perhaps we can influence policy. We can do it better and more honestly if the United States first puts its own house in order – which means facing the American population problem (our own growth rate will double our population in 67 years).

To put our own house in order, the United States should:

A. Enact a national population stabilization program

B. Encourage smaller families

C. Stop illegal immigration, which now doubles our annual growth rate

D. Balance legal immigration with emigration

All of these are necessary steps for our own benefit; in addition, they will also enable us to face our overpopulated neighbors with a clearer conscience and increased credibility.

Obviously, our most direct opportunity to deal with the population problem abroad is in the area of foreign policy, and there we should:

E. Stop any U.S. foreign aid program which encourages population growth

One way of doing this would be for the Congress to enact a Resolution along these lines:

WHEREAS we are aware, and are rightly fearful, of the ominous consequences of the growing world food/population crisis; and

WHEREAS the consequence of continued population growth will be increased human misery; and

WHEREAS increasing food production and/or availability, which lowers the death rate without influencing the birth rate, accelerates population growth; and

WHEREAS agricultural production cannot keep pace with a world population growth rate that would double our numbers every twenty-five years;

NOW THEREFORE BE IT RESOLVED that it is the sense of Congress that a moratorium be declared on all U.S. food aid and technical assistance to any country if:

1. its population growth rate is above the world average, unless

2. it officially acknowledges that its national birth rate must be lowered and unless it adopts stringent measures to control population growth, which measures must be judged adequate by the United States as the donor nation.

What would be the value of such a moratorium?

It might awaken the leadership of the developing countries to the urgency of their population problem. For the United States, through this Resolution, to say it cannot endorse the unrestricted use of its assistance funds, because to do so will increase the sum of human suffering, would be a total reversal of what the world has been hearing for the past quarter of a century.

Why haven't the leaders of the developing world taken the necessary steps to check their population growth rates? Why are

countries with the fastest-growing populations often the least willing to acknowledge the existence of a problem?

One answer is the optimism generated by the American scientific community and development establishment. Year after year, since we initiated the foreign aid crusade, the leadership of the hungry nations has heard that the agricultural profession can solve the food problem if given enough support. It cannot.

A moratorium would not eliminate all foreign assistance. Our government should continue not only to help, but to extend its assistance to those few developing countries with population growth rates lower than the world average. But it should concentrate its assistance on those countries which clearly show through active practices, a determination to decelerate their rate of population growth. The moratorium would affect only these nations which will not do so.

Many will feel that such a moratorium is morally wrong.

Those who feel this way must weigh the morality of the moratorium against the morality of any action which contributes to overpopulation. Overpopulation today makes it impossible for half of those within the hungry nations to have the diet necessary to protect them against debilitating diseases that bring early death. Overpopulation makes whole nations dependent upon the vagaries of the weather to prevent famine in their lands. Overpopulation leads to more suffering and more deaths, to war, and to chaos.

None of this is new, but the number of people involved is new. Who, then, are the moral – those who advocate steps that will decelerate population growth, or those who advocate steps that will encourage population growth?

A moratorium on assistance will not abandon the developing world of Asia, Africa and Latin America to a future without resources. We sometimes forget that the world consists of independent nations that possess convictions of their own and the ability to order their priorities on how to spend their money. Every year they spend, for instance, $28 billion on armaments. We may not think this makes much sense, but it is their decision.

Might not declaring a moratorium on assistance be the alarm signal that would alert the leadership of such countries to the necessity for different decisions?

For too long, we have tried to solve the food crisis without trying to solve the problem which causes it. Confusing the effect with the cause, we have been told to tighten our belts, and "asceticize" our diets, so that more food could be shipped to the world's hungry. None of the variations on this theme deal with the cause of the crisis: runaway population growth.

Whether your most urgent concern is peace, freedom, the food supply, civil liberties, the environment or social justice, it's a lost cause unless the population of the world is stabilized. We share these concerns, and all are compelling reasons why population stabilization is essential.

If you have a better solution, tell us. Tell us how you would solve the problem.

The Environmental Fund does not solicit contributions or memberships. However, we would welcome your comments and if you would like to be on our mailing list, please let us know.

Mr. Justin Blackwelder, President
THE ENVIRONMENTAL FUND, INC.
1302 18th Street, N.W.
Washington, D.C. 20036

Name _____

Address _____

_____ Zip Code _____

Comments: _____

THE ENVIRONMENTAL FUND

1302 EIGHTEENTH STREET, N.W. • WASHINGTON, D.C. 20036 • 202-293-2548

Directors: JUSTIN BLACKWELDER • EMERSON FOOTE • GARRETT HARDIN • WILLIAM C. PADDOCK • BURNS W. ROPER • ADOLPH W. SCHMIDT

FIGURE 22-2.

guage such as "Famine 1975!" They say that such tactics are acceptable because "we are faced with a crisis . . . the seriousness of which cannot be exaggerated."[15] The fears they inspire generate lots of support money — from the UN, AID, and popular fund-raising campaigns in full-page advertisements.

Many anti-doomsday people, on the other hand, speak in quiet voices — as reassurance usually sounds. They tend to be careful people. And they are totally ignored. The great geologist Kirtley F. Mather wrote a book called *Enough and To Spare* in 1944; it was withdrawn from the University of Illinois library just twice — in 1945 and 1952 — prior to my 1977 withdrawal of it. But there are literally armfuls of books such as Fairfield Osborn's 1953 *Limits of the Earth* that have been read vastly more frequently. Even a book published by a vanity press and written by a retired army colonel who has Malthus's first name as "Richard" and who believes that *Overpopulation* (the title of the book) is a plot of the "Kremlin gangsters" has been withdrawn ten times since 1971, and untold more times between its 1958 publication and 1971, when the charge slip was changed.[16]

A RHETORICAL ANALOGY

An analogy may help explain the power inherent in the anti-growth rhetoric. Think how much easier it would be to argue that the automobile is detrimental to life and health than that it is beneficial. To show how terrible cars are for people, all you need are the statistics of the people killed and maimed each year, plus a few gory pictures of smash-ups. That's strong stuff. To argue that the auto is beneficial to health you would need to show a lot of relatively small, indirect benefits — the ability to get to a doctor or hospital by car, which could not be done otherwise; the therapeutic results of being able to take a trip into the countryside; the improved transportation know-how that eventually saves lives (the emergency health systems discussed in chapter 18 are an example); and so on. My point here is not to prove that cars are, in fact, beneficial on balance, but only to illustrate how much easier rhetorically it is to show their maleficence than their beneficence. Just so it is with arguments about population growth.

WHAT ARE THE UNDERLYING REASONS FOR DOOMSDAY FEARS AND RHETORIC?

Earlier chapters have suggested some reasons for doomsday fears about minerals, food, and energy — especially the seductively simple twin notions of a fixed stock of resources and the "law" of diminishing returns from that stock. Therefore, this section will focus on reasons for doomsday fears about population growth, though all doomsday fears have much in common.

The most obvious reason that doomsday fears get disproportionate attention is that bad news is newsworthy, and frightenting forecasts cause people to sit up and take notice. But why are frightening forecasts, out of kilter with the evidence, made by the forecasters in the first place? And what explains the related activist movements? Here I shall do no more than present a list of the possibilities. Certainly Thomas Littlewood is right when he says that "humanitarian and bigot can find room under the same tent."[17] There is also lots of space for many fellow-traveling motives, both generous and selfish.

Simple world-saving humanitarianism. Many people who give time and money to population activities are unmistakably humanitarian, motivated by sincere good will; the givers wish that poor people at home and abroad should have a better life. This motive gets less space in the list than do some less-pretty motives, but this does not mean it is less important in the overall picture.

Taxation fears. The haves naturally worry that there will be an increase in the number of have nots to be supported at public expense, both domestically and internationally. This theme is found in Malthus and is an underlying motive in much population activity. Where the have nots differ racially from the haves, it is difficult to separate this motive from racism.

Supposed economic and political national self-interest. The pull-up-the-ladder "lifeboat ethics" of Garrett Hardin—we are fighting for places in a small lifeboat that is the earth, and so "every life saved this year in a poor country diminishes the quality of life for subsequent generations"—is a dramatic elaboration of the self-interest motive.[18]

Fear of communism. The belief that communism will win out in the poor countries causes some people in rich countries to want to reduce population growth in the poor countries.

> ... In the cold war between the Communist bloc and the free world, in every area where the Red penetration is most successful— the Middle East, Indonesia, Japan, Guatemala, British Guiana and North Africa—population pressure is severe and increasing ... one of

the most potent factors in the success of the Reds in their campaign for world domination. . . . [19]

Dislike of business. Some people dislike business because of the self-interest profit motive. And they see among businessmen a desire for population growth because of the larger markets it brings. In reaction, they favor population reduction.

Others, Thomas Mayer suggests, charge business with polluting and wasting resources because they want to transfer control of economic activity to the government. He further suggests that this desire is a sequel to the attempt to shift control to government "experts" on the grounds of greater efficiency, the latter being an argument that few in the U.S. now find persuasive.[20]

Belief in the superiority of "natural" processes. Some people feel that the use of resources by humans is a disturbance of the natural ecological order, and that each such disturbance is likely to be damaging in the long run. For some, this reflects an assumption that natural systems are so complex that man's interference — even just his increased numbers — is bound to result in unexpected destruction. For others, a mystical or religious faith underlies this belief.

Religious antagonisms. One religious group worries that some other group's higher birthrate will make it more powerful. In the past, for example, U.S. Protestants have feared the population growth of U.S. Catholics, and Hindus in India fear the high birthrates of Moslems.

Racism. There is plenty of anecdotal evidence that racism has been a key motivation in domestic and international population activities. Some solid evidence of this is found in data showing that the opening of state-supported birth-control clinics is closely related to the concentrations of poor black people in various states.[21] As of 1965, 79 percent of the state-supported clinics in the U.S. were in the ten states of Alabama, Arkansas, Florida, Georgia, Kentucky, Mississippi, North Carolina, South Carolina, Tennessee, and Virginia, which have only 19 percent of the country's population. Analysis that holds per capita income constant shows that the proportion of blacks in a local population is closely related to the density of family-planning clinics.[22] It seems reasonable to conclude that southern society's birth-control policies are motivated, at least in part, by the desire to reduce the fertility of blacks. The motivation may be racial, or it may be that southern whites believe blacks make welfare demands upon the state in excess of their contributions, or both together.[23]

The belief of the more educated that they know what is best for the less educated. Even the most unselfish well-off persons think they know better than do poor people what is good for them and for the world. Most of us secretly harbor the notion that we know how some others should live their lives better than they themselves know. But the thought is only a matter of concern when it is hitched up with sufficient arrogance and willfulness that we are willing to compel them to do what we think they ought to do.

Lack of historical perspective. Clearly this is an important cause of doomsday fears. A bad turn in some index — say, the 1973 oil price rise, or the early 1970s bad harvests — leads people to draw graphs of a few years' experience prior to the bad turn of events, and then to extrapolate a negative trend. If one draws long-run graphs instead — the sort shown in earlier chapters on mineral resources, food, and energy — the bad turn of events usually is seen as only a blip on the line, and the overall trend may be seen to be positive rather than negative.

Fitness of the human race. Improvement of the human race — or of the genetic quality of one's own countrymen — has in the past been one of the important motives of population activists, especially with respect to immigration and sterilization policies. The roots of this motive are some compound of unproven genetic ideas about intelligence and physical health, unselfish devotion to mankind, and narrow in-group preferences.

The proponents of eugenics (which should not be confused with the scientific discipline of genetics) have been sufficiently successful over the decades so that tax moneys are being used to involuntarily sterilize poor people (often black) without medical or other justification. As a result of the eugenics movement, which has been an intertwined partner with the population-control movement for decades, there are now laws on the books of thirty states providing for the involuntary sterilization of the mentally defective.[24]

In recent famous exemplary cases, a perfectly normal young black woman was sterilized under the guise of being given a birth-control shot,[25] and a childless married woman who went to have a small uterine tumor removed was sterilized without her knowledge or consent.[26] At just one institution in Virginia — the Lynchburg Training School and Hospital — 4,000 "patients" were sterilized between 1922 and 1972 as "misfits" in order to avoid "racial degeneracy." The superintendent of the Lynchburg institution was a eugenics enthusiast who aimed to produce genetic purity.[27] The law sanctioning this practice was upheld by the U.S. Supreme Court and is still Virginia law. And in 1976, a North

Carolina law was upheld in state and federal courts that permits the sterilization of "mentally retarded" or "mentally ill" persons. Sterilization may be authorized if, "because of a physical, mental, or nervous disease or deficiency which is not likely to materially improve, the person would probably be unable to care for a child or children; or, because the person would be likely, unless sterilized, to procreate a child or children which probably would have serious physical, mental or nervous deficiencies." Furthermore, it is a "duty" of certain health officers to start the process if

(1) . . . sterilization is in the best interest of the mental, moral or physical improvement of the retarded person,

(2) . . . sterilization is in the best interest of the public at large,

(3) . . . [the retarded person] would be likely, unless sterilized, to procreate a child or children who would have a tendency to serious physical, mental, or nervous disease or deficiency; or, because of a physical, mental or nervous disease or deficiency, which is not likely to materially improve, the person would be unable to care for a child or children.

The U.S. Federal District Court said that "evidence that is clear, strong and convincing that the subject is likely to engage in sexual activity without using contraceptive devices and that either a defective child is likely to be born or a child born that cannot be cared for by its parent" is grounds for sterilization. Perhaps most frightening, the Supreme Court of North Carolina stated that the state may sterilize because "the people of North Carolina also have a right to prevent the procreation of children who will become a burden to the State." In other words, if you do poorly on an IQ test, or if an M.D. says that you are mentally ill — both of which could happen to any of us under certain circumstances, as is happening today to some anti-government activists in the USSR — then you could be forcibly sterilized.[28]

A recent resurgence of the eugenics movement: The California firm of Robert Klark Graham has obtained the sperm of five Nobel laureates, the first volunteer being William Shockley, who has argued that whites are inherently smarter than blacks.[29] Graham hopes to improve the intelligence of Americans by disseminating this sperm.

Finally — The Piper

Many of those in favor of population control are frank to admit the use of emotional language, exaggerated arguments, and political manipulation. They defend these practices by saying that the situation is very serious. The worst that might happen, they say, is that people will become concerned about the dangers of "overpopulation."

But exaggeration and untruth run up debts with the piper, who eventually gets paid. Philip Handler, president of the National Academy of Sciences, is a strong supporter of environmental and population control programs. But even he worries about the piper.

> It is imperative that we recognize that we know little and badly require scientific understanding of the nature and magnitude of our actual environmental difficulties. The current wave of public concern has been aroused in large measure by scientists who have occasionally exaggerated the all-too-genuine deterioration of the environment or have overenthusiastically made demands which, unnecessarily, exceed realistically realizable — or even desirable — expectations. . . . *The nations of the world may yet pay a dreadful price for the public behavior of scientists who depart from . . . fact to indulge . . . in hyperbole.*[30]

This leads to an open question: To what extent is the current public belief that the U.S. economy and society are on the skids related to false doomsday fears that we are running out of minerals, food, and energy, and to the unfounded belief that the U.S. is an unfair plunderer of the world's resources, the latter an "exploitation" that people believe must eventually cease, with grave consequences for the U.S.?

CONCLUSIONS

Two propositions constitute the "bottom lines" of this chapter. (1) U.S. tax money is being used to implement the aim of population-activist individuals and organizations, that is, to reduce fertility among the poorer peoples of the world, and among U.S. citizens, too, by means both fair and foul, the latter including various types of propaganda and forced sterilization. Some of this tax money is being spent to convince us that we should share the beliefs of the moving spirits of these groups, and support them. (2) Though an important motivation of many of these people surely is the simple good-will desire to help poor people get ahead, now and in the future,[31] not absent from this movement are the beliefs that (a) poor people, and especially poor non-white, non-Anglo Saxon non-Protestants, are inherently inferior; and (b) the present and future well-being of all U.S. taxpayers will be best served by reducing the birthrate among these peoples. Only such beliefs can explain the anti-immigration policies of these organizations. These latter ideas are not only dangerous but are, in the main, scientifically unfounded. And these beliefs have led to shocking prescriptions: Do not lower the death rate of poor people, and get the poor not to reproduce, even if the means used are economic pressure or physical coercion.

Having our government put pressure on others—domestically with sterilization laws and policies, and internationally by tying food aid to fertility reduction—would be bad enough even if all the scientific propositions upon which these policies are founded were objectively supported. But these policies are *not* scientifically warranted. Even less noble, some part of the motivation in population campaigns is pure selfishness, the desire to keep for ourselves what we can, against the supposed (but non-existent) drains of our resources by the children of the poor and non-whites, and by the "yellow (and brown) peril" of immigration. This is the witch's brew at its nastiest.

To the extent that the U.S. has actually had any effect in developing countries, it has increased people's family-size options—which I view as a good thing. I don't worry very much about brainwashing, because I believe that, on important matters such as these, most people—educated or not—are basically levelheaded and too wise to pay much attention to other people's views about their fertility behavior. Of course, the fertility-reduction propaganda can affect some people, and I feel badly for them. I consider it a moral outrage. But as an ex-practitioner and teacher of advertising and marketing, I doubt that the U.S. AID campaign has had much success in brainwashing. Nevertheless, this happy failure of U.S. attempts leaves me feeling uncomfortable.

AFTERNOTE

Planned Parenthood's Rhetoric

Just a few examples of Planned Parenthoods's rhetoric are given here, to document the assertions made in chapter 21 of how PP/WP has changed its course over the years. This material is far less lurid than that of the Campaign to Check the Population Explosion. But PP/WP is a very large and important organization, and many people still identify it only with its older aims and find it hard to believe that it is responsible for such activities.

I'll start with some material from 1980, to show that the practices I describe continue to the present. The only message in the donor's card is, "Yes, I will help contain runaway population growth by supporting the crucial work of Planned Parenthood," plus this assertion by Robert McNamara: "Excessive population growth is the greatest single obstacle to the economic and social advancement of most societies in the developing world."[1] Some of the statements in a 1980 fund-raising letter are,

> Thai women and millions of other women like them in India, China, Africa and throughout the developing nations control our destiny. *Their decisions—decisions of hundreds of millions of young women—about their family's size—control your future more surely, more relentlessly than the oil crisis or the nuclear arms race.*
>
> *. . .unless population growth is harnessed and slowed to meet the limited resources and human services of these nations, development of nations will be shattered. Chaos, mass famine and war will continue to increase. We will be affected for better or worse.*
>
> The great tinderbox for revolution and international anarchy is rising expectations of the world's masses *coupled with unrestrained population growth. Starvation, revolution and violent repression will fill our headlines unless human fertility is reduced to meet the finite limits* of available resources and services.
>
> International Assistance. In developing countries of the world, the population "time bomb" ticks on, putting ever-increasing strains on the scarce resources of our planet, locking large areas of the globe into self-perpetuating poverty and setting the stage for famine and war.[2]

Now let's consider a few of the more striking examples from the last decade. One of the fund-raising letters by Margaret Mead is shown in figure 22-3. Other letters by celebrities such as Mead, Mrs. Edward R. Murrow, and Cass Canfield mention famine, drought, flood, "the crush of visitors [that] forced the National Park Service to close one entrance to Yosemite National Park last summer," packed campgrounds, despoliation of fragile ecology, cars and trucks clogging expressways, people dying in the streets of starvation, and the following:

> In India entire families commit suicide to escape a lingering death from starvation. In Bangladesh famished infants are thrown into rivers to drown. Hungry hordes of abandoned children roam the cities of Latin America looting, terrorizing and scavenging for food. By conser-

MARGARET MEAD
515 MADISON AVENUE
NEW YORK, N. Y. 10022

Dear Friend:

Within today's crowded world there is a tremendous increase in suffering and brutality. Growing numbers of children are beaten or neglected. In New York City child abuse cases have risen 30% and similar increases are reported throughout this country and in other parts of the world. Children are the main victims of overpopulation. Due to the population explosion 500 million of them are chronically hungry -- living in misery and degradation. It is their generation and those still unborn who will pay the frightful penalties for our unbridled growth and for our reckless abuse of the environment.

Each day world population is increased by 190,000 and our earth is scarred by our efforts to provide for them. Mass famines have been temporarily averted but 12,000 a day still die of starvation. Irreplaceable resources are being wantonly depleted and in some countries water is sold by the glass. Our land, air and water are so toxic with chemicals and wastes that the Secretary General of the United Nations has warned that "if current trends continue, the future of life on earth could be endangered." This is not the world we want to bequeath to our children.

In America, our population is expected to climb to nearly 300 million by the end of the century and three out of four of us will be living in extremely congested cities. We are beginning to feel the congestion now -- in our crowded schools and clogged highways; in the destruction of our environment; in the erosion of the quality of life.

One of the grimmest aspects of the population explosion is the poverty it perpetuates and intensifies. In America 14,400 are hungry and 39 million are classified poor or near-poor. Half of our impoverished children come from families of five or more. Stunted by hunger, lacking in schooling and skills, they rarely break free from poverty's grip. What is true for these deprived Americans is tragically also true in many other nations.

Planned Parenthood/World Population is the only private organization through which you as an individual can work to curb population growth abroad in 101 countries and in our own. PP/WP programs of direct service, technical assistance, public education, research and training are cutting birth rates in selected areas around the globe. Most national family planning programs in other countries began as PP activities and are carried on with our continuing help. And 650 U.S. clinics run by Affiliates provide contraceptive help to almost half a million.

War, famine and plague are both unthinkable solutions and untenable ones. In World War II twenty-two million died: it takes less than four months to add that number to the world's population. Birth control is the only humane and rational answer to our population dilemma. PP/WP programs here and abroad will cost $40 million in 1971. Please send your tax-deductible gift today to help assure a worthwhile life for future generations.

Sincerely,

P.S. If you have already contributed to your local PP/WP Affiliate, please share this appeal with a friend. We are grateful for your interest and support.

FIGURE 22-3.

vative estimates 400 million people—a tenth of humanity—live on the ragged edge of starvation: 12,000 a day die of hunger as food-short nations sink deeper into crisis and anguish. Regional crop failures this year will almost certainly mean mass famine. For 10 to 30 million, the Malthusian nightmare may become reality. . . .

A family of thirteen is found living in a basement flooded with water and smelling of sewer gas. The children are cold and hungry. This is "the other America"—a land of limited opportunity, of corrosive poverty. Sixty percent of our poor live in urban centers, in enclaves of misery stretched like scars across the nation.

Last spring eleven mayors met to warn of the collapse of U.S. cities, rapidly becoming "repositories for the poor." In Boston one in five gets public assistance; in N.Y.C. one in seven; in Los Angeles one in eight. These agonizing statistics underscore today's welfare crisis. Agonizing because for each person getting aid, someone eligible is not; agonizing because welfare benefits guarantee only a life of grinding poverty, physical survival and little else. . . .

On an afternoon in N.Y. not too long ago four boys were playing in the streets when suddenly from a second story window a shot rang out and a 13-year old fell to the ground dead. The man who killed him said he couldn't bear the noise, that he was a night worker and had to get his sleep. In Paris three recent murders were attributed to noise and now studies in England and America suggest it is a cause of serious mental disorder provoking many to acts of violence.

The city dweller is constantly assailed by noise, doubling in volume every 15 years and now approaching levels which can cause permanent damage. Three out of five American men have lost some hearing and growing evidence links noise to heart disease. And still our cities swell until finally 80% of us will live in crowded and festering sinks and pollution will be a personal hazard and affront. We are hastening to what Archibald MacLeish has called "the diminishment of man. . . ."

Along with one of the Mead letters came a reprint of Paul Ehrlich's "Eco-Catastrophe," a dramatically frightening doomsday document. It predicted—for the 1970s!—"the end of the ocean," falling agricultural yields, smog disasters for New York and Los Angeles ("nearly 200,000 corpses"), "birth of the Midwestern desert"; and "both worldwide plague and thermonuclear war are made more probable as population growth continues; . . . "population control was the only possible salvation suggested."[3]

Perhaps most astonishing is Planned Parenthood's prodigal use of
money — some of it public money — and phony emotional appeals in a
twenty-eight page supplement in the *New York Times*, whose back
cover is shown in figure 22-4, sponsored by PPFA together with the Population Crisis Committee. PP/WP also was a main sponsor of the anti-
natal television campaign discussed in this chapter. All these activities
make it very clear that Planned Parenthood's goal is fewer births.

As to the rhetorical tactics used in pursuit of this goal: The arguments
used and the issues raised in connection with population growth — parking problems, famine, crime in the streets, mental disorder, and so on —
are at best simply speculations subject to the kind of counter-evidence
given elsewhere in this book, for example, with respect to famine. Or

FIGURE 22-4.

worse, they are plain untruths that fly in the face of well-established scientific evidence, for example, that population growth increases mental disorder. The best that can be said of these Planned Parenthood activities is that they are mindless actions, taken just for the sake of action by people who are motivated by the public spirit but who have never given attention to the facts or thought through to the consequences, and who simply assume that "everyone knows" that the rhetoric is true. That's the most favorable construction I can give to activities such as Planned Parenthood's bumper-sticker campaign. Example:

POPULATION NO PROBLEM?
HOW DENSE CAN YOU GET?

Support Planned Parenthood

Some Planned Parenthood people say privately that these sorts of appeals do not reflect a change in Planned Parenthood's mission from the original "children by choice — not chance," but are only used because they are effective in fund raising. If that is so, then what is the moral basis of such behavior? Either PP/WP is getting money under false pretenses, or it is simply altering its behavior to produce maximum contributions.

Ultimately—What Are Your Values?

The market for cat food in the U.S. "is two-and-a-half to three times the size" of the baby food market, says Anthony J. F. O'Reilly, president of H. J. Heinz Co., a major producer of both products. "That will tell you something about our changing tastes," the executive cracks.

Wall Street Journal, January 31, 1980, p. 1

A small number of scientists have convinced a great many politicians and laymen that rational population policies with respect to fertility, mortality, and immigration can be deduced directly from actual or supposed facts about population and economic growth. The persuaded politicians have come to believe it is "scientific truth" that countries should reduce their population growth. And the persuading scientists want the politicians to believe that such judgmental propositions really are "scientific." For example, the front page of the handbook of the population control movement in the U.S., *The Population Bomb*, says "Paul Ehrlich, a qualified scientist, clearly describes the dimensions of the crisis . . . over-population is now the dominant problem . . . population control or race to oblivion?"

But it is scientifically wrong—outrageously wrong—to say that "science shows" there is overpopulation (or underpopulation) in any given place at any given time. Science can only reveal the likely *effects* of various population levels and policies. Whether population is now too large or too small, or is growing too fast or too slowly, cannot be decided on scientific grounds alone. Such judgments depend upon our values, a matter about which science is silent.

Whether you think that it is better for a country to have a population of, say, 50 million human beings at a $4,000 per capita yearly income, or 100 million at $3,000, is strictly a matter of what you consider important. And further, please keep in mind that if the empirical studies and my theoretical analysis are correct, the world can have a larger population and *higher* per capita income. This is just as true for less-developed as for more-developed countries. But the judgment about whether this is good news or bad news, and whether population is growing too fast or too slowly, or is already too large, depends on values. This is reason enough to say that science does not show that there is overpopulation or underpopulation anywhere.

Because many writers act as if population policies can be deduced from scientific studies alone, particular values enter implicitly into policy decisions, without any explicit discussion of whether the values really are those that the decision makers and the community desire to have implemented. For a leading example, because almost all economic analyses of "optimum" rates of growth take per capita income as the criterion, this criterion implicitly becomes the community goal and the guideline for policy makers. In some cases values are smuggled in consciously, though without discussion; in other cases the values enter without any conscious recognition.

This chapter first presents a list of some important values related to population policy. Then some of these values will be discussed in more detail, and I will express some of my own views. A discussion of which values motivate the moving spirits of the population movement, by name and organization, may be found in chapter 22.

SOME VALUES RELEVANT TO POPULATION POLICY

The time discount rate. The relative importance of the nearer versus the further future must affect every investment decision, and every judgment about the costs and benefits of resource use and population growth. This was discussed in chapter 19.

Altruism versus selfishness. Our willingness to share our worldly goods—either directly or, more commonly, indirectly through taxation—affects a variety of population-related policies, as has been discussed vehemently at least since Malthus. Should additional children or immigrants be welcomed into a community if there will be an immediate tax burden upon others? Should the poor be supported by welfare rather than left to die? Each of us has some limited willingness to contribute to others, but that willingness differs from person to person, and from moment to moment. In discussion, this factor usually gets tangled up with the matter of whether the transfers are a contribution or an investment.

Racism. Almost all of us tend to favor our kinsmen, countrymen, co-religionists, and those of similar race, and this is not necessarily a bad principle. Just how far we allow this taste to affect public policy with respect to immigration, welfare, and birth-control campaigns differs among us. Certainly this value or taste often influences public policy, especially with respect to race.

Space, privacy, and isolation. This is the Daniel Boone/Sierra Club value. How much of your isolation in the forest are you prepared to give up so that others may also enjoy the experience?

The right of inheritance. Should only the blood descendants of the builders of a country be allowed to enjoy its fruits, or should others be allowed to come in and enjoy them, too? This issue is at the heart of immigration policy in the U.S., Australia, Israel, Great Britain, and every other country in which the standard of living is higher than in the country of some potential immigrants. The issue also arises internally. For example: Are Native Americans or blacks morally entitled to partake of the benefits of social investments made by whites in past years? Do whites have a responsibility to repay blacks for the profits made by exploiting slave labor in previous centuries?

The inherent value of human life. Some economists and laymen believe that some people's lives are so poor that they would have been better off had they never been born. Others believe that no life is so poor that it does not have value. Still others believe that only the individual should be allowed to decide whether his or her own life is worth living. Surprisingly to me, this value, which is one of the most influential in population discussions, is rarely mentioned explicitly.

The acceptability of various methods of preventing life. To some people, abortion or contraception or infanticide are acceptable; for others any of these may be unacceptable.

A value for numbers of people. Both the Bible, which urges people to be fruitful and multiply, and the utilitarian philosophy of "the greatest good for the greatest number" lead to a value for more people, a value that many people do not share.

Animals and plants versus people. The Bible says, "And God said, Let us make man in our image, after our likeness: . . . Be fertile and increase, fill the earth and master it; and rule the fish of the sea, the birds of the sky, and all the living things that creep on earth" (Genesis 1:26–28).

In sharp contrast is the view of some environmentalists — for example, the "Greenpeace Philosophy" of the whale-protecting group: "Ecology teaches us that humankind is not the center of life on the planet. Ecology has taught us that the whole earth is part of our "body" and that we must learn to respect it as we respect life — the whales, the seals, the forests, the seas. The tremendous beauty of ecological thought is that it shows us a pathway back to an understanding and appreciation of life itself — an understanding and appreciation that is imperative to that very way of life."[1]

Eugenics. Some have thought that the human race can be improved by selective breeding. This leads to policies encouraging fertility and immigration for some groups and discouraging them for others.

Individual freedom versus community coercion.

Now let's consider some of these values at greater length.

The Value of a Poor Person's Life

It is sometimes said that some people's lives are so poor and miserable that an economic policy does them a service if it discourages their births. It is a fundamental and unresolvable question whether the poorest person's life is worth living — that is, whether it is better for that poor person to live or to die. The view of many is that some lives are not worth living (they have "negative utility"). This implies that the sum of human happiness would be greater if people with incomes below the threshhold had never been born. My aim here is not to persuade anyone that all lives have value but only to show that the question is an open one, whose answer depends upon our values and view of the world.

The belief that very poor people's lives are not worth living comes out clearly when Paul Ehrlich writes about India.

I came to understand the population explosion emotionally one stinking hot night in Delhi. . . . The streets seemed alive with people. People eating, people washing, people sleeping, people visiting, arguing, and screaming. People thrusting their hands through the taxi window, begging. People defecating and urinating. People clinging to buses. People herding animals. People, people, people.[2]

But Ehrlich writes nothing about those people laughing, loving, or being tender to their children — all of which one also sees among those poor Indians.

There *is* misery in India. Intestinal disease and blindness are all around. A fourteen-year-old girl catches bricks on a construction job for thirty cents a day as her baby, covered with flies and crying, lies on a burlap sack on the ground below the scaffold on which the young mother works. A toothless crone of indeterminate age, with no relatives in the world and no home, begins with a cake of wet cow-dung to lay a floor for a "dwelling" of sticks and rags, by the side of the road. All this I have seen. And yet these people must think their lives are worth living, or else they would choose to stop living. (Note that to choose death does not require violent suicide. Anthropologists describe individuals — even young people — who decide they want to die and then do. People even die on their own schedules, frequently waiting until after weddings or birthdays of relatives to die.) Because people continue to live, I believe that they value their lives. And those lives therefore have value in my scheme of things. Hence I do not believe that the existence of poor people — either in poor countries or, a fortiori, in the U.S. — is a sign of "overpopulation."

THE BORN AND THE UNBORN

One hears in population discussions: "It doesn't make sense to take into account the lives of people who have not yet been born." This issue comes up in two contexts. First, it arises with respect to the long-run effects of population growth upon the economy 50 or 100 or 200 years in the future. Second, this objection arises when someone like me suggests that the level of per capita income is not necessarily the only criterion, the end-all and be-all of population policy, but that the sheer number of people alive, enjoying life, may also be relevant.

In fact, most people and all societies act in ways that show concern for people who have not yet been born, whether or not they justify these actions metaphysically. Governments often build public works to last beyond the lifetimes of the present generation of citizens, explicitly taking future generations into account. And young families take their own unborn children into account when they save money or buy a house with enough space for children. So taking unborn children into account is a basic fact of life, and it requires no further defense when we are considering the long-run as well as the short-run benefits of population growth.

But let us go further. Some people say that they cannot feel a concern for unborn children. But does this imply that it is foolish for others to feel such a concern? You can clearly feel concern for someone you do not know — and similarly for an unborn person. For example, prospective parents often imagine terrible events in which their unborn children would be injured or killed; that can arouse an emotion much stronger than an imagined (or real) scene in which a living person on another continent, of another race and nationality, is injured or killed. So again I think that it is a psychological fact that some people feel a sentimental tie to children who are not yet born, and who might not be born.

Given that people take unborn children into account, it is clear that, to various people, the importance of unborn children can vary, all the way from low to high. This is the sort of value about which economics and science generally has nothing to say. As an individual, however, I obviously place a particular value on unborn children. And since this value gets so little public expression — some people assume that it does not even exist — I will take this opportunity to say a few words about it, even at the risk of seeming preachy. Holding the standard of living constant, I think it better to have more rather than fewer people. And if the price is not too great, I would even be in favor of a somewhat lower standard of living per person if more people were alive to enjoy it (though the analysis given here suggests that in the long run a larger population implies a higher rather than a lower standard of living).

But what does it mean to like the idea of more people? To me it means that I do not mind having more people in the cities I live in, seeing more children going to school and playing in the park. I would be even more pleased if there were more cities, more people in unsettled areas — even another planet like this one.

I believe that this particular value is in the best spirit of Judeo-Christian culture, which is the foundation for much of our modern Western morality: In Biblical terms, Be fruitful and multiply. It also accords with the spirit and logic of the utilitarian philosophers, starting with Jeremy Bentham, whose thinking underlies much of our legal and social philosophy, as well as modern economic thinking. I hold this preference for more life because it is generally consistent with the rest of my values and tastes. It is a value that many other people hold, too, perhaps unconsciously. And others may come to recognize its importance to them as they come to recognize, as I did, that population growth bodes well rather than ill for civilization, in the long run.

WHAT IS TO BE LOST?

The following argument is found in Ehrlich's *Population Bomb*: If population control is undertaken and is successful in preventing births, but it turns out to be unnecessary, then what is lost?[3] It depends. If you value additional human lives, and some lives are unnecessarily prevented from being lived, that is an obvious loss. The fact that this is not a loss in Ehrlich's eyes tells us his implicit values.

THE VALUE OF PER CAPITA INCOME

Economists have long used the concept of an "optimum population" for a given country, and this sounds very scientific. But these discussions about optimum population sizes or growth rates must have some criterion of better and worse, and this criterion is usually the per capita income of the present population, including the "quality of life" as income.

No one, however, is prepared to take the income criterion to its logical conclusions. For one thing, it would mean doing away with all lower-income people. Removing the lower half of the income distribution in any country will raise the average income of the remaining people, by a purely arithmetic process. And logically we should carry this to the point at which only one person is left — the richest person at the start. Of course this is absurd, but this is the kind of absurdity that the criterion leads to.

Here is another way to raise per capita income, then: We should drive the birthrate down to ridiculously low levels, and perhaps to zero births — the particular level depending upon the weight we give the future relative to the present. For example, if the future is discounted at, say, 10 percent per year, the value of per-person income would be maximized into the infinite future if we stop having babies completely. This is because it takes a long time before babies begin to produce anything, though they consume immediately. Hence a baby born today lowers the income of everyone else, on the average, by simple arithmetic. So having no babies at all next year would be good for computed per capita income next year. But no one wants to go that far with this implication of the average-income criterion, either.

The value that I personally wish to use as a criterion for decisions about population growth is one that I think a great many other people also subscribe to, as they will find if they inspect their beliefs closely. In utilitarian terms it is "the greatest good for the greatest number." That is, my judgment about the welfare of a community depends *both* on the average income per person and on the number of people who partake of that standard of living. (My judgment also is affected by the evenness of income distribution within the community, but this issue can be left aside here.)

Other things being equal, a greater number of people is a good thing, according to this value criterion. Furthermore, by this criterion a society may even be better off with a lower average income if more people are partaking of it — though how much lower is a tricky matter, of course. Someone must decide the basis on which to trade people for material welfare. Should 10 percent fewer people be traded for 5 percent more income per person in the immediate future? Or should the trade-off be 10 percent fewer people for 1 percent more income per person, or for 20 percent more? This is an ethical choice, of course, but one that must be made either explicitly or implicitly when setting policy about the amount of pressure that will be put upon people to have small families. The important point here is that I reject average per capita income *by itself* as a criterion for judgments about population size. Under some conditions I accept that it is better to have more people and a lower per capita income in the immediate future. And I think a lot of other people share this value, especially since the income loss is only temporary. In the long run, per capita income will be higher with more people, either more children or more immigrants (and higher within your expected lifetime, if you are a young parent in a highly developed country), by my analysis.

This criterion seems to be consistent with our other values — our abhorrence of killing, and our desire to prevent disease and early death. And why not? Why should we feel so strongly that murder is bad, and that children in war-torn countries should be saved, and then not want to bring more people into the world? If life is good and worth supporting, why does preventing murder make sense, but not encouraging births? I understand well that a death causes grief to the living — but I am sure that your abhorrence of killing would also extend to the extermination of a whole group at once, under which conditions there would be no one to suffer grief. So, what are the differences between the murder of an adult, the infanticide of another's child, and the coercion of someone else not to have a child? The main difference between murder and forcing someone not to bear children is that murder threatens our *own* persons, and unregulated murder would rip up the fabric of our society — good reasons indeed to be against murder. But we also condemn murder on the moral ground that murder denies life to someone else — and in this sense it seems to me that there is no difference between murder, abortion, contraception, and abstinence from sex. I am not *equating* abortion or contraception to murder, and I am *not* branding as immoral all who do not have as many children as are biologically possible. Nor do I want to impose my own values, which come to these conclusions, upon you. Rather, I just wish us to get clear on the meaning of the moral distinctions we make.

PEOPLE AS DESTROYERS AND CREATORS

"If we have more children, when they grow up there will be more adults who can push the nuclear button and kill civilization," some say.

True. More generally, David Wolfers reduces the matter to this absurdity: "All human problems can be solved by doing away with human beings."[4] But to have more children grow up is also to have more people who can find ways to avert catastrophe.

WHEN IS COERCION JUSTIFIED?

Some people advocate forced birth control "if necessary." Again to quote Ehrlich, "We must have population control at home, hopefully through a system of incentives and penalties, but by compulsion if voluntary methods fail."[5]

The logic for having the state control the number of children we may rear has been stated as follows.

> In conditions of scarcity the civil right to have unlimited births simply does not exist. Such a claim is attention-getting and suspect. It is a favorite argument of minorities in support of their own overproduction of births. The right to have children fits into the network of other rights and duties we share and must dovetail with the rights of others. When all of us must curtail our production of children none of us has an overriding civil right of this kind. The closer we live together and the more of us there are, the fewer civil rights we can exercise before they infringe upon those of another. This adverse relation between dense population and personal freedom is easily documented around the world. It is time for people sincerely interested in civil rights to expose such special pleading, and to intervene when it is leveled against local or national programs.[6]

A briefer statement is that of Kingley Davis: "It can be argued that over-reproduction — that is, the bearing of more than two children — is a worse crime than most and should be outlawed."[7]

Many Americans have become persuaded of the necessity of such coercion, as these Roper poll results[8] show:

> Q. The population crisis is becoming so severe that people will have to be limited on the number of children they can have.
> A. Agree   47%
>   Disagree   41%

And the astonishing kinds of programs that have been suggested in the "population community" are summarized in table 23-1.

Some countries already have enacted into law coercive policies with respect to fertility. In India during the first Indira Ghandi period, in the state of Tamil Nadu, "Convicts . . . who submit to sterilization [could] have their jail term reduced"; and in the state of Uttar Pradesh, "Any government servant whose spouse is alive and who has three or more children must be sterilized within three months, pursuant to a state government order issued under the Defense of Internal Security of India Rules. Those failing to do so will cease to be entitled to any rationed article beyond the basic four units."[9] In the state of Maharastra, population 50 million, the legislature passed an act requiring compulsory sterilization for all families with three or more children (four or more if the children were all boys or all girls), but this measure did not receive the necessary consent of the President of India. And in other states in India, in Singapore,[10] and perhaps elsewhere, public housing, education, and other public services are conditioned on the number of children a family has. It is this possibility of coercion — by penalty, taxation, physical compulsion, or otherwise — that concerns me most.

I hope you share my belief that it is good for people to be able, as much as possible, to decide how to run their own lives. Such a desire for individual self-determination is quite consistent with giving people maximum information about birth control, because information increases their ability to have the number of children they want. It is also consistent with legal abortion. And it is consistent with public health and nutrition measures to keep alive all the children that people wish to bring into the world. I am unqualifiedly in favor of all these policies to increase the individual's ability to achieve the family size she or he chooses. But the same belief leads me to be against coercing people not to have children. By definition, coercion reduced people's freedom to make their own decisions about their own lives.

Though I would vote against any overall U.S. policy that would coerce people not to have children — including taxes on children greater than the social cost of the children — I do accord to a community the right to

TABLE 23-1. Examples of Proposed Measures to Reduce U.S. Fertility, by Universality or Selectivity of Impact

Universal Impact: Social Constraints	Selective Impact Depending on Socio-Economic Status		Measures Predicated on Existing Motivation to Prevent Unwanted Pregnancy
	Economic Deterrents/Incentives	Social Controls	
Restructure family:	Modify tax policies:	Compulsory abortion of out-of-wedlock pregnancies	Payments to encourage sterilization
a) Postpone or avoid marriage	a) Substantial marriage tax	Compulsory sterilization of all who have 2 children except for a few who would be allowed 3	Payments to encourage contraception
b) Alter image of ideal family size	b) Child tax		Payments to encourage abortion
Compulsory education of children	c) Tax married more than single	Confine childbearing to only a limited number of adults	Abortion and sterilization on demand
Encourage increased homosexuality	d) Remove parents' tax exemption		Allow certain contraceptives to be distributed non-medically
Educate for family limitation	e) Additional taxes on parents with more than 1 or 2 children in school	Stock certificate-type permits for children	Improve contraceptive technology
Fertility control agents in water supply		Housing Policies:	Make contraception truly available and accessible to all
Encourage women to work	Reduce/eliminate paid maternity leave or benefits	a) Discouragement of private home ownership	Improve maternal health care, with family planning as a core element
	Reduce/eliminate children's or family allowances	b) Stop awarding public housing based on family size	
	Bonuses for delayed marriage and greater child-spacing		
	Pensions for women of 45 with less than N children		
	Eliminate welfare payments after first 2 children		
	Chronic Depression		
	Require women to work and provide few child care facilities		
	Limit/eliminate public-financed medical care, scholarships, housing, loans, and subsidies to families with more than N children		

SOURCE: Reproduced from Elliott et al., 1970. Originally, Frederick S. Jaffe, "Activities Relevant to the Study of Population Policy for the U.S.," Memorandum to Bernard Berelson, March 11, 1969.

make such a decision if there is a consensus on the matter. If people recognize, however, that this decision is a matter of values, and that science cannot prove that we are overpopulated or on the road to overpopulation, people may be less likely to choose to coerce members of their own group not to have children.

Do as I Do? Or as I Say?

"How can one call upon people in poor countries to reduce their birthrates if we in rich countries go on having many children?" This pious sentiment is frequently heard.

Some countries' populations may be growing so fast that on balance a reasonable citizen *might* want to slow down the birthrate. If the citizens of Singapore decide that immediately increasing the economic welfare per person is worth the price in slowed population growth, then someone with my values can accept most programs that will help them achieve their goals. I especially sympathize with the goal of enabling poor people to feel that, for themselves and for their children, the future will be economically better than the present. It is good to be able to believe that individuals and societies have a chance to get ahead economically, in my view. I am, however, strongly against Westerners telling Indians that "science proves" that fewer Indian births are a good thing, unconditionally. That is a lie, and an abuse of science. And I am against the U.S.'s putting pressure on other countries to adopt population control programs.

Yet some have added that we cannot ethically be in favor of lower birthrates in poor countries without also supporting strict control of population growth in our own country. There are several reasons why this argument is not persuasive. First, if peoples of all countries have a right to make decisions about social and personal population policies on the basis of what *they* want and what *they* believe is good for them, why should this not hold for us, too? Second, birthrates and growth rates in the U.S. are presently lower than those in most poor countries, and hence should give us no cause for embarrassment. Third, and most important, additional people in more-developed countries may well be of benefit, on balance, to people in poor countries. The positive effects include bigger markets for poor-country products, increased development of technology that poor countries can later use, and a larger pool of potential technical aides such as agronomists and Peace Corps workers. Of course the rich countries may not pay fair prices for the raw materials they buy, or may exploit the poor countries in other ways. Unfortunately, no one has yet even begun to analyze scientifically what the net effect is.

Summary

Science alone does not, and cannot, tell us whether any population size is too large or too small, or whether the growth rate is too fast or too slow. Science can sometimes give citizens and policy makers a better understanding of the consequences of one or another decision about population; sadly, however, too often scientific work on this subject has instead only misinformed people and confused them. Social and personal decisions about childbearing, immigration, and death inevitably hinge upon values as well as upon probable consequences. And there is necessarily a moral dimension to these decisions over and beyond whatever insights science may yield.

CONCLUSION

The Ultimate Resource

If you turned first to this final chapter to get an overview, I suggest you go to the Introduction, which lists some of the more dramatic findings of the book. And each chapter ends with a summary on its particular topic. This chapter offers only a few short and general comments about our situation with respect to resources, population, and the environment, plus some general speculation about why the facts are popularly believed to be very different — and much more threatening — than they really are.

In the short run, all resources are limited — natural resources such as the pulpwood that went into making this book, created resources such as the number of pages Princeton University Press can allow me, and human resources such as the attention you will devote to what I say. In the short run, a greater use of any resource means pressure on supplies and a higher price in the market, or even rationing. Also in the short run there will always be shortage crises because of weather, war, politics, and population movements. The results that an individual notices are sudden jumps in taxes, inconveniences and disruption, and increases in pollution.

The longer run, however, is a different story. The standard of living has risen along with the size of the world's population since the beginning of recorded time. And with increases in income and population have come less severe shortages, lower costs, and an increased availability of resources, including a cleaner environment and greater access to natural recreation areas. And there is no convincing economic reason why these trends toward a better life, and toward lower prices for raw materials (including food and energy), should not continue indefinitely.

Contrary to common rhetoric, there are no meaningful limits to the continuation of this process. (Resolving this paradox entailed considerable explanation in the early chapters.) There is no physical or economic reason why human resourcefulness and enterprise cannot forever continue to respond to impending shortages and existing problems with new expedients that, after an adjustment period, leave us better off than before the problem arose. Adding more people will cause us more such problems, but at the same time there will be more people to solve these problems and leave us with the bonus of lower costs and less scarcity in the long run. The bonus applies to such desirable resources as better health, more wilderness, cheaper energy, and a cleaner environment.

This process runs directly against Malthusian reasoning and against the apparent common sense of the matter, which can be summed up as follows: The supply of any resource is fixed, and greater use means less to go around. The resolution of this paradox is not simple. Fuller understanding begins with the idea that the relevant measure of scarcity is the cost or price of a resource, not any physical measure of its calculated reserves. And the appropriate way for us to think about extracting resources is not in physical units, pounds of copper or acres of farmland, but rather in the services we get from these resources — the electrical transmission capacity of copper, or the food values and gastronomic enjoyment the farmland provides. Following on this is the fact that economic history has not gone as Malthusian reasoning suggests. The prices of all goods, and of the services they provide, have fallen in the long run, by all reasonable measures. And this irrefutable fact must be taken into account as a fundamental datum that can reasonably be projected into the future, rather than as a fortuitous chain of circumstances that cannot continue.

Resources in their raw form are useful and valuable only when found, understood, gathered together, and harnessed for human needs. The basic ingredient in the process, along with the raw elements, is human knowledge. And we develop knowledge about how to use raw elements for our benefit only in response to our needs. This includes knowledge for finding new sources of raw materials such as copper, for growing new resources such as timber, for creating new quantities of capital such as farmland, and for finding new and better ways to satisfy old needs, such as successively using iron or aluminum or plastic in place of clay or copper. Such knowledge has a special property: It yields benefits to people other than the ones who develop it, apply it, and try to capture its benefits for themselves. Taken in the large, an increased need for resources usually leaves us with a permanently greater capacity to get them, because we gain knowledge in the process. And there is no meaningful physical limit — even the commonly mentioned weight of the earth — to our capacity to keep growing forever.

Perhaps the most general matter at issue here is what Gerald Holton calls a "thema." The thema underlying the thinking of most writers who have a point of view different from mine is the concept of fixity or finiteness of resources in the relevant system of discourse. This is found in Malthus, of course. But the idea probably has always been a staple of human thinking because so much of our situation must sensibly be regarded as fixed in the short run — the bottles of beer in the refrigerator, our paycheck, the amount of energy parents have to play basketball with their kids. But the thema underlying my thinking about resources (and the thinking of a minority of others) is that the relevant system of discourse has a long enough horizon that it makes sense to treat the system as not fixed, rather than finite in any operational sense. We see the resource system as being as unlimited as the number of thoughts a person might have, or the number of variations that might ultimately be produced by biological evolution. That is, a key difference between the thinking of those who worry about impending doom, and those who see the prospects of a better life for more people in the future, apparently is whether one thinks in closed-system or open-system terms. For example, those who worry that the second law of thermodynamics dooms us to eventual decline necessarily see our world as a closed system with respect to energy and entropy; those who view the relevant universe as unbounded view the second law of thermodynamics as irrelevant to this discussion. I am among those who view the relevant part of the physical and social universe as open for most purposes. Which thema is better for thinking about resources and population is not subject to scientific test. Yet it profoundly affects our thinking. I believe that here lies the root of the key difference in thinking about population and resources.

Why do so many people think in closed-system terms? There are a variety of reasons. (1) Malthusian fixed-resources reasoning is simple and fits the isolated facts of our everyday lives, whereas the expansion of resources is complex and indirect and includes all creative human activity — it cannot be likened to our own larders or wallets. (2) There are always immediate negative effects from an increased pressure on resources, whereas the benefits only come later. It is natural to pay more attention to the present and the near future compared with the more distant future. (3) There are often special-interest groups that alert us to impending shortages of particular resources such as timber or clean air. But no one has the same stake in trying to convince us that the long-run prospects for a resource are better than we think. (4) It is easier to get people's attention (and television time and printer's ink) with frightening forecasts than with soothing forecasts. (5) Organizations that form in response to temporary or non-existent dangers, and develop the capacity to raise funds from public-spirited citizens and governments that are aroused to fight the danger, do not always disband when the danger evaporates or the problem is solved. (6) Ambition and the urge for profit are powerful elements in our successful struggle to satisfy our needs. These motives, and the markets in which they work, often are not pretty, and many people would prefer not to depend on a social system that employs these forces to make us better off. (7) Associating oneself with environmental causes is one of the quickest and easiest ways to get a wide reputation for high-minded concern; it requires no deep thinking and steps on almost no one's toes.

The apparently obvious way to deal with resource problems — have the government control the amounts and prices of what consumers consume and suppliers supply — is inevitably counter-productive in the long run because the controls and the price fixing prevent us from making the cost-efficient adjustments that we would make in response to the increased short-run costs, adjustments that eventually would more than alleviate the problem. Sometimes governments must play a crucial role to avoid short-run disruptions and disaster, and to ensure that no group consumes public goods without paying the real social cost. But the appropriate times for governments to play such roles are far fewer than the times they are called upon to do so by those inclined to turn to authority to tell others what to do, rather than allow each of us to respond with self-interest and imagination.

I do not say that all is well. Children are hungry and sick; people live out lives of physical and intellectual poverty, and lack of opportunity; war or some new pollution may do us all in. What I *am* saying is that for most of the relevant economic matters I have checked, the *trends* are positive rather than negative. And I doubt that it does the troubled people of the world any good to say that things are getting worse though they are really getting better. And false prophecies of doom can damage us in many ways.

Is a rosy future guaranteed? Of course not. There always will be temporary shortages and resource problems where there are strife, political blundering, and natural calamities — that is, where there are people. But the natural world allows, and the developed world promotes through the marketplace, responses to human needs and shortages in such manner that one backward step leads to 1.0001 steps forward, or thereabouts. That's enough to keep us headed in a life-sustaining direction. The main fuel to speed our progress is our stock of knowledge, and the brake is our lack of imagination. The ultimate resource is people — skilled, spirited, and hopeful people who will exert their wills and imaginations for their own benefit, and so, inevitably, for the benefit of us all.

Appendix

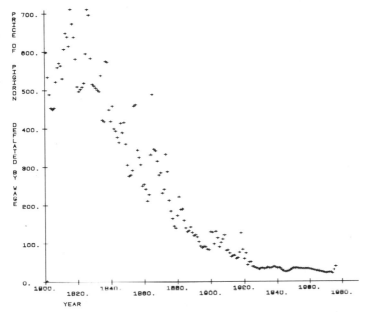

A-1. The Scarcity of Pig Iron as Measured by Its Price Relative to Wages

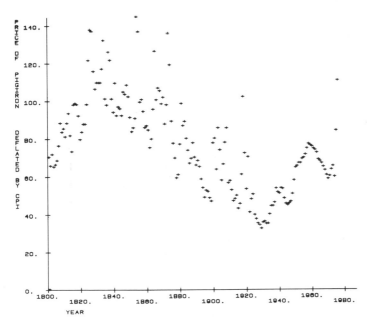

A-2. The Scarcity of Pig Iron as Measured by Its Price Relative to the Consumer Price Index

Figures A-1 through A-6, as well as figures 1-1, 5-2, 5-4, 7-2, 7-3, and others in the text, refer to the frequently heard idea that the long-run trends in resource availability do not apply, because we are now at a moment of discontinuity, of fundamental change. Indeed, one cannot logically dispute assertions about present or impending discontinuity. And one can find mathematical techniques suggesting discontinuities that will be consistent with any trend data. To illustrate this point, my

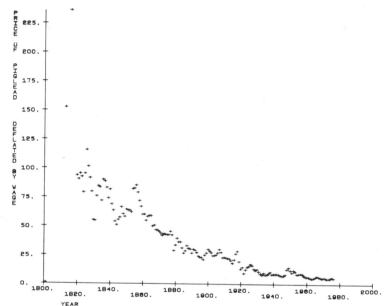

A-3. The Scarcity of Pig Lead as Measured by Its Price Relative to Wages

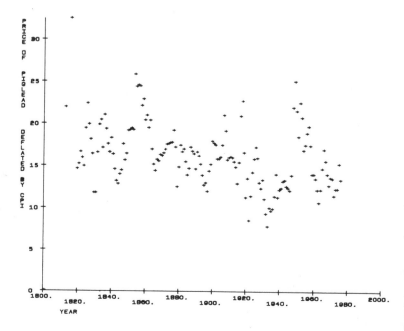

A-4. The Scarcity of Pig Lead as Measured by Its Price Relative to the Consumer Price Index

co-worker Douglas Love fitted third-degree polynomials to the price data for copper, wheat, and electricity (figure A-6). Such graphs seem to imply an upward tendency for all these prices. My own judgment, however, is that the long-run monotonic trends in resource costs are more meaningful. This is only one person's judgment, of course. Yet we can say scientifically that if in the past one had acted on the belief that the long-run price trend was upward rather than downward, one would have lost money, on the average.

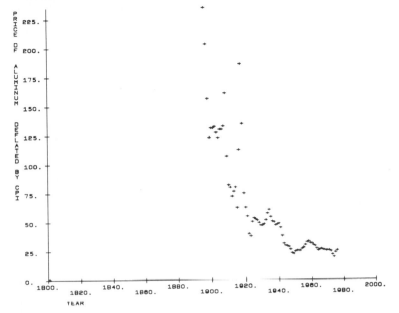

A-5. The Scarcity of Aluminum as Measured by Its Price Relative to the Consumer Price Index

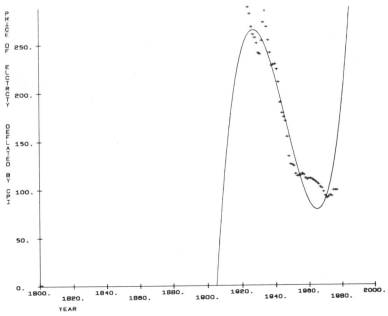

A-6. The Scarcity of Electricity as Measured by Its Price Relative to Wages, with Nonsensical Third-Degree Polynomial Fitted

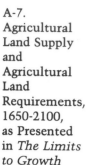

A-7.
Agricultural
Land Supply
and
Agricultural
Land
Requirements,
1650-2100,
as Presented
in *The Limits
to Growth*

This figure illustrates the kinds of unwarranted assumptions on which *The Limits to Growth* and related studies are based. Compare the supposed negative trend in "arable land available for agriculture" as shown in this figure with the facts shown in tables 6-1 and 6-2 in the text.

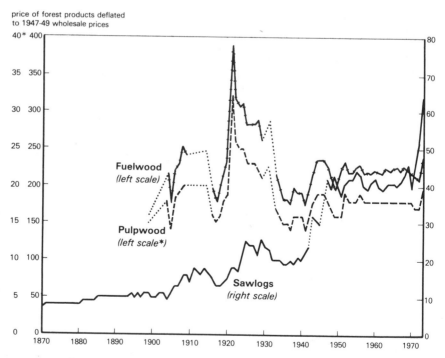

A-8. The Scarcity of Fuelwood, Pulpwood, and Lumber (Sawlogs) as Measured by Their Prices Relative to the Wholesale Price Index

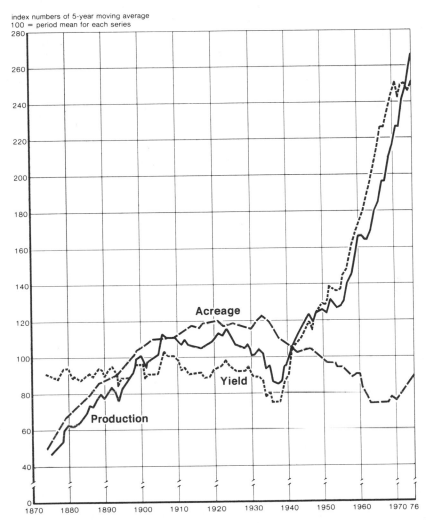

index numbers of 5-year moving average
100 = period mean for each series

A-9. U.S. Acreage, Yield, and Production of Corn, 1870-1976

This graph shows that change in acreage is no longer the main influence upon change in food production. It suggests that concern about the competition between urbanization and agriculture is misplaced. Also interesting is that corn yield per acre was stable for many years even though output per worker rose greatly with the mechanization of agriculture.

APPENDIX

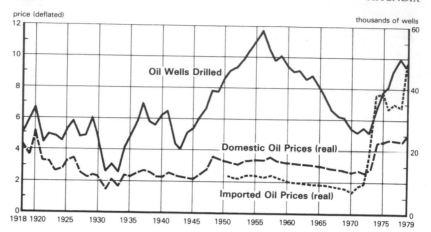

A-10. Oil Wells Drilled, Real Domestic Oil Prices, and Real Imported Oil Prices in the U.S., 1918-79

This diagram shows how the development of oil wells responds to the price of oil.

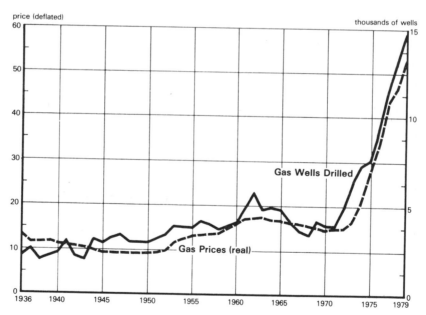

A-11. Natural Gas Drilling and Natural Gas Prices in the U.S., 1936-79

This diagram shows how the development of gas wells, like oil wells, responds to the price of gas.

energy consumed per capita
(tons oil equivalent)

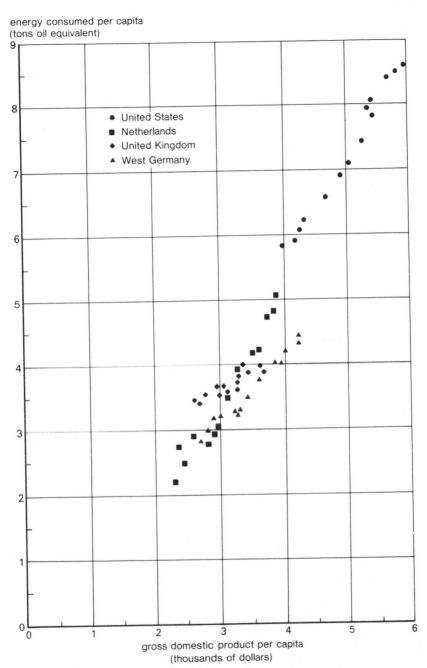

gross domestic product per capita
(thousands of dollars)

A-12. Energy Consumption per Capita vs. National Output per Capita
for Four Selected Countries, 1961-74

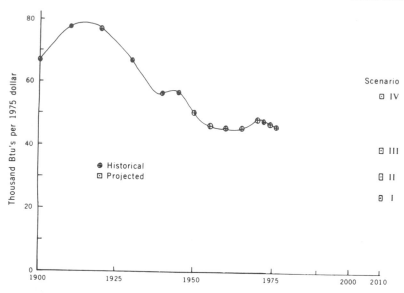

A-13. The Amount of Energy Used in the U.S. per Unit of Final Output, 1900-75

This graph shows that with the passage of time it has cost less energy to produce a constant dollar's worth of output, even with the rise in energy costs since 1973 (due to OPEC but unrelated to the cost of energy production).

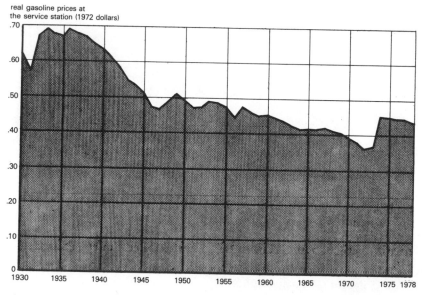

A-14. Gasoline Prices in the U.S. in Constant Dollars, 1930-78

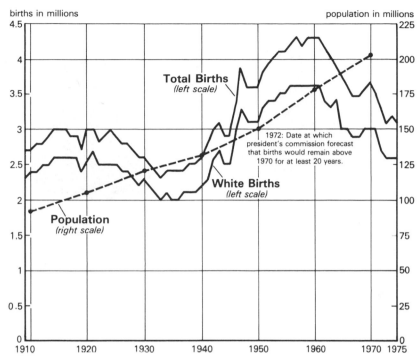

births in millions
population in millions

A-15. Total Births, White Births, and Population in the U.S., 1909-75

This graph shows that even though the total population rose markedly, total births were no higher in 1975 than in 1909. That is, there has been a huge decline in fertility.

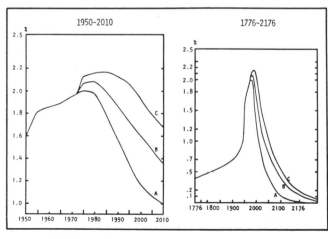

A-16. Herman Kahn's Guesstimates about the Growth Rate of the World Population

A...UN MEDIUM/HUDSON LOW
B...HUDSON MEDIUM (SURPRISE-FREE)
C...HUDSON HIGH (A FORTIORI)

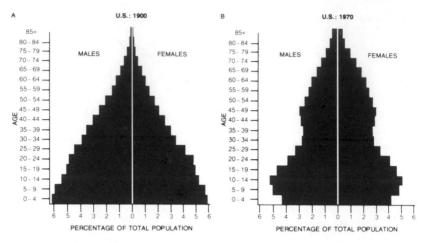

A-17. Age Distribution of the U.S. Population, 1900 and 1970

This figure shows how much the age distribution has changed in only 70 years. By 1980 it is even narrower at the bottom than shown for 1970.

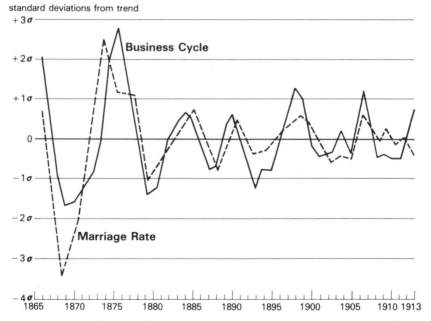

A-19. The Business Cycle and Marriage Rates in Sweden, 1865-1913

This graph, together with figure 12-1 in the text, shows that sex-related behavior is influenced heavily by economic conditions.

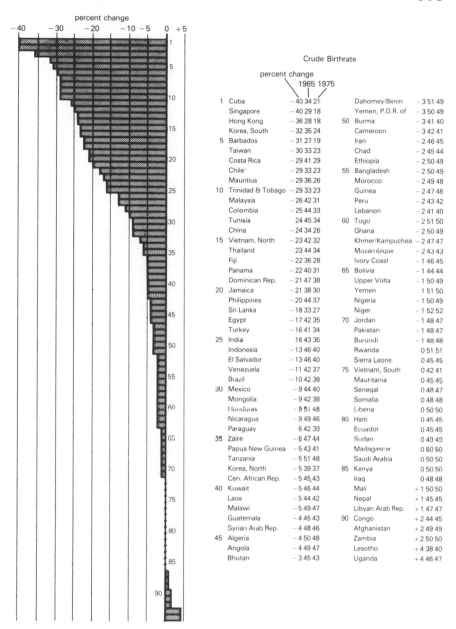

percent change

−40	−30	−20	−10 −5	0	+5

Crude Birthrate

percent change
1965 1975

1	Cuba	− 40 34 21			Dahomey/Benin	− 3 51 49
	Singapore	− 40 29 18			Yemen, P.D.R. of	− 3 50 49
	Hong Kong	− 36 28 18		50	Burma	− 3 41 40
	Korea, South	− 32 35 24			Cameroon	− 3 42 41
5	Barbados	− 31 27 19			Iran	− 2 46 45
	Taiwan	− 30 33 23			Chad	− 2 45 44
	Costa Rica	− 29 41 29			Ethiopia	− 2 50 49
	Chile	− 29 33 23		55	Bangladesh	− 2 50 49
	Mauritius	− 29 36 26			Morocco	− 2 49 48
10	Trinidad & Tobago	− 29 33 23			Guinea	− 2 47 46
	Malaysia	− 26 42 31			Peru	− 2 43 42
	Colombia	− 25 44 33			Lebanon	− 2 41 40
	Tunisia	24 45 34		60	Togo	− 2 51 50
	China	− 24 34 26			Ghana	− 2 50 49
15	Vietnam, North	− 23 42 32			Khmer/Kampuchea	− 2 47 47
	Thailand	− 23 44 34			Mozambique	− 2 43 43
	Fiji	− 22 36 28			Ivory Coast	− 1 46 45
	Panama	− 22 40 31		65	Bolivia	− 1 44 44
	Dominican Rep.	− 21 47 38			Upper Volta	− 1 50 49
20	Jamaica	− 21 38 30			Yemen	1 51 50
	Philippines	− 20 44 37			Nigeria	− 1 50 49
	Sri Lanka	− 18 33 27			Niger	− 1 52 52
	Egypt	− 17 42 35		70	Jordan	− 1 48 47
	Turkey	− 16 41 34			Pakistan	− 1 48 47
25	India	16 43 36			Burundi	− 1 48 48
	Indonesia	− 13 46 40			Rwanda	0 51 51
	El Salvador	− 13 46 40			Sierra Leone	0 45 45
	Venezuela	− 11 42 37		75	Vietnam, South	0 42 41
	Brazil	− 10 42 38			Mauritania	0 45 45
30	Mexico	− 9 44 40			Senegal	0 48 47
	Mongolia	− 9 42 38			Somalia	0 48 48
	Honduras	− 9 51 48			Liberia	0 50 50
	Nicaragua	− 9 49 46		80	Haiti	0 45 45
	Paraguay	6 42 39			Ecuador	0 45 45
35	Zaire	− 6 47 44			Sudan	0 49 49
	Papua New Guinea	− 5 43 41			Madagascar	0 60 60
	Tanzania	− 5 51 48			Saudi Arabia	0 50 50
	Korea, North	− 5 39 37		85	Kenya	0 50 50
	Cen. African Rep.	− 5 45 43			Iraq	0 48 48
40	Kuwait	− 5 46 44			Mali	+ 1 50 50
	Laos	− 5 44 42			Nepal	+ 1 45 45
	Malawi	− 5 49 47			Libyan Arab Rep.	+ 1 47 47
	Guatemala	− 4 45 43		90	Congo	+ 2 44 45
	Syrian Arab Rep.	− 4 48 46			Afghanistan	+ 2 49 49
45	Algeria	− 4 50 48			Zambia	+ 2 50 50
	Angola	− 4 49 47			Lesotho	+ 4 38 40
	Bhutan	− 3 45 43			Uganda	+ 4 46 47

A-18. Recent Changes in the Birthrate in Developing Countries

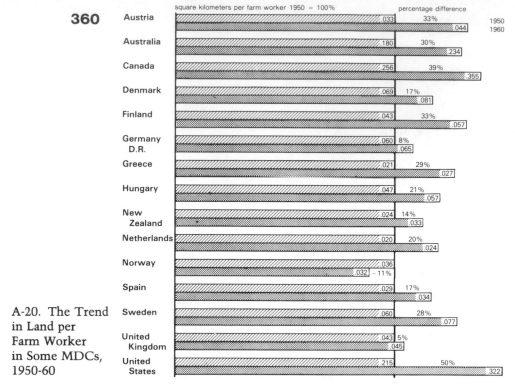

square kilometers per farm worker 1950 = 100%   percentage difference

Austria	.033	33%	.044
Australia	.180	30%	.234
Canada	.256	39%	.355
Denmark	.069	17%	.081
Finland	.043	33%	.057
Germany D.R.	.060	8%	.065
Greece	.021	29%	.027
Hungary	.047	21%	.057
New Zealand	.024	14%	.033
Netherlands	.020	20%	.024
Norway	.036	.032	−11%
Spain	.029	17%	.034
Sweden	.060	28%	.077
United Kingdom	.043	5%	.045
United States	.215	50%	.322

1950
1960

A-20. The Trend in Land per Farm Worker in Some MDCs, 1950-60

This chart shows that the average amount of farmland per farm worker increased in all but one of these industrialized countries from 1950 to 1960, a trend that has continued until the present.

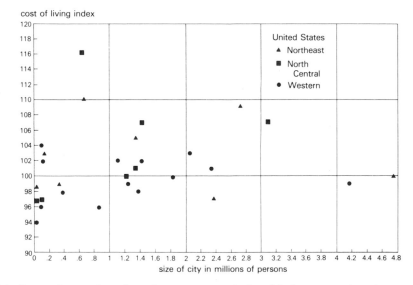

A-21. The Relationship of Cost of Living to Size of City in the U.S.

This figure shows that there is no strong relationship between city size and cost of living, even though wages are systematically higher in large cities.

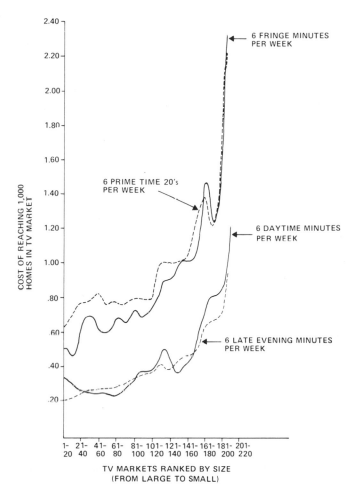

A-22. Spot TV Costs per 1,000 Homes by TV Market Size

This graph shows that communication costs can be much greater in smaller communities than in larger ones.

A-23. The Relationship of Scientific Activity to Population Size

LEGEND: A = 1 OBS , B = 2 OBS , ETC

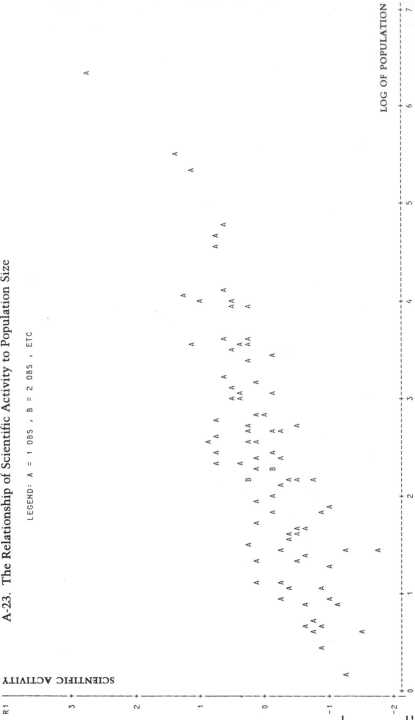

SCIENTIFIC ACTIVITY

LOG OF POPULATION

This diagram illustrates the close relationship between the total amount of scientific activity and the population of countries, after per capita income is allowed for. This fits with the idea that more people imply faster increases in technology and economic growth. Technically, this is a plot of log population versus the residuals of the model log (authors in country) = a + b log (per capita income).

A-24. Advertisement by the Campaign to Check the Population Explosion

Notes

Introduction: What Are the *Real* Population and Resource Problems?

1. *Newsweek*, March 30, 1970, p. 87.
2. *Saturday Review*, March 11, 1972, p. 49.
3. Ehrlich, 1968, p. 198.

Chapter 1: The Amazing Theory of Raw-Material Scarcity

1. Ehrlich and Ehrlich, 1974, p. 7.
2. Richard J. Barnet, "No Room in the Lifeboats," *New York Times Magazine*, April 16, 1978, pp. 32, 33.
3. Michael Parenti, quoted in *Daily Illini*, April 20, 1978, p. 7.
4. Letter from Judith Senderovitz, vice-president for public affairs, Zero Population Growth, in *New York Times Magazine*, June 3, 1974, p. 20.
5. This section draws upon Simon, 1975a, pp. 267–78.
6. Bauer, 1976, p. 63.
7. From Simon, 1978a, pp. 390-94.
8. Barnett and Morse, 1963, p. 220.
9. Fishman and Landsberg, in Ridker, 1972, p. 82; see also Ehrlich, Ehrlich, and Holdren, 1977, p. 516. The dollar cost of fuels rose sharply starting in 1973, of course, because of the OPEC increase in oil price, which affected all fuel prices.
10. *Wall Street Journal*, December 7, 1977, p. 1.
11. Peter Drucker, "A Troubled Japanese Juggernaut," *Wall Street Journal*, November 22, 1977, p. 11.
12. Two technical notes: (1) Inflation and the cost of storage are automatically allowed for in the market prices, so there is no hidden benefit to me from those sources. (2) One could not make the same sort of wager by dealing in the common stocks of firms that produce the raw materials, because those firms' stock prices are influenced by changes in their production capacities due to technological change. This is in contrast to a ton of copper at fixed market grade, which is physically the same from year to year.
13. Ehrlich, 1970, quoted by Dixon, 1973.

Afternote: The True Cost (Price) of Natural Resources

1. See Brown and Field, 1978, for an exposition of this point of view.

Chapter 2: Do Technological Forecasts and Economic Forecasts Necessarily Contradict Each Other?

1. The report of the 1952 President's Materials Policy Commission (the Paley Commission) was the first clear explanation of this paradox that I know of. The idea was also discovered by Erich W. Zimmerman (1951/1965). It was then restated by Joseph Davis

(1953) and, most important, explored at Resources for the Future, the organization that grew out of the Paley Commission. The idea was developed most fully by Barnett and Morse (1963), but despite its thorough development over almost two decades, most of the public and even some very competent economists are still not fully aware of it — probably because of its paradoxical counter-intuitive nature.

2. This discussion draws on Nordhaus, 1974, p. 23.

3. Fischman and Landsberg, 1972, p. 90.

4. *Report on the limits to growth,* 1972, p. 37, as quoted by Weber, 1977, p. 62.

5. Kuznets, quoted by Rosenberg, 1972, p. 6.

6. Cloud, quoted by Weber, 1977, p. 62.

7. Kahn et al., 1976, p. 101.

8. Mather, 1944, p. 29.

9. Brown, Bonner, and Weir, 1963, p. 92.

10. Goeller and Weinberg, 1978, p. 4.

11. Ibid., p. 10.

12. Ibid.

13. McKelvey, quoted by Weber, 1977, p. 47.

14. This paragraph draws upon Kahn et al., 1976, pp. 90–91, which the interested reader should examine for a fuller treatment of this aspect of *The Limits to Growth.* The original source of the quote is the U.S. Geological Survey, *U.S. Mineral Resources,* 1973, p. 304.

15. Sauvy, 1976, p. 251.

16. Brobst, 1979, p. 115.

CHAPTER 3: Can the Supply of Natural Resources Really Be Infinite? Yes!

1. Meadows et al., 1974, p. vii.

2. U.S., the White House, 1972, Signet ed., pp. 2-3.

3. Meadows et al., 1974, p. 265.

4. U.S., the White House, 1952, summary of vol. 1, pp. 12–13; idem, p. 1.

5. Ibid., p. 2.

6. Ibid., p. 1.

7. Fuller, 1969, p. 4, quoted by Weber, 1977, p. 45.

8. I appreciate a discussion of this point with Alvin Roth.

9. Sheldon Lambert, quoted in *Newsweek,* June 27, 1977, p. 71.

CHAPTER 4: Famine 1985? Or 1995? Or 1975?

1. Associated Press (hereafter cited as AP), February 12, 1975.

2. Edouard Souma in *Chicago Sun-Times,* November 26, 1976, p. 18.

3. Advertisement of Arno Press, 1977.

4. *Wall Street Journal,* October 30, 1975.

5. Quoted in *Time,* April 1, 1974, p. 40.

6. *Wall Street Journal,* December 13, 1976, editorial page.

7. Ehrlich, 1968, p. xi.

8. Ibid.

9. Fichter, 1972, pp. 24, 25.

10. *Newsweek,* November 11, 1974, p. 16.

11. Paddock and Paddock, 1967, p. 222.

12. Simon, 1977.

13. Johnson, 1974a.

14. Sanderson, in Abelson, 1975, p. 1.

15. Johnson, 1976, p. 3.

16. *Champaign-Urbana News Gazette*, October 13, 1977, p. 1.

17. *Champaign-Urbana News Gazette*, July 26, 1977, p. 1.

18. *New York Times*, October 2, 1977, p. 3.

19. Abercrombie and McCormack, 1976, p. 482.

20. Price, 1967, p. 5.

21. Johnson, 1974b, p. 17.

22. Johnson, 1973, pp. 6-7.

23. Fichter, 1972, p. 25.

24. This section draws heavily upon Clark, 1967, p. 124; Bennett, 1954; and Poleman, 1975.

25. *Newsweek*, September 11, 1972, p. 38.

26. AP, in *Champaign-Urbana News Gazette*, January 10, 1978, p. A-5.

27. Letter from Helen Ware, March 20, 1978.

28. *Arizona Daily Star*, July 10, 1980, p. F-1.

29. Ehrlich, 1968, pp. 40-41.

30. Don Kendall, "U.S. Ag Experts to India Shift," AP story in *Champaign-Urbana News Gazette*, September 9, 1977, p.A-3.

31. *New York Times*, August 28, 1977, p. 11.

32. Kasturi Rangan, "Indian Price Supports Lead to Bigger Grain Crops," *New York Times*, November 28, 1976.

33. *Wall Street Journal*, December 20, 1976.

34. Ibid.

35. *Wall Street Journal*, December 29, 1976, p. 1.

36. *Wall Street Journal*, December 20, 1976.

37. Ibid.

38. Poleman, in Abelson, 1975, p. 12.

39. *New York Times*, February 6, 1977, p. 24.

40. *Wall Street Journal*, June 6, 1978, p. 12.

CHAPTER 5: Food in the 1970s: From Shortage-Crisis to Glut-Crisis

1. The call by U.S. farmers for "parity prices" is really a complaint that food prices have fallen relative to other prices since the 1910 parity date.

2. *The Brookings Bulletin*, 1976, 13:1.

3. Sanderson, in Abelson, 1975, p. 3.

4. *Newsweek*, March 14, 1977, p. 85.

5. *Wall Street Journal*, July 7, 1977, p. 28.

6. *Wall Street Journal*, October 10, 1977, p. 22.

7. *Champaign-Urbana News Gazette*, February 27, 1977, p. 13–14.

8. *Newsweek*, April 11, 1977.

9. *Wall Street Journal*, August 29, 1977, pp. 1, 12.

10. Don Kendall, "Consumer and Farmer Lose Either Way," AP story in *Champaign-Urbana News Gazette*, July 17, 1977, p. 14-A.

11. *Champaign-Urbana News Gazette*, January 17, 1978, p. A-5.

12. *Newsweek,* January 30, 1978, p. 29.

13. In 1850, wood supplied 90% of U.S. energy, and 50% in 1885. Reference lost.

14. All information in this paragraph is from Sherry H. Olson, 1971, p. 2.

15. U.S. Council on Environmental Quality, 1976, p. 315.

16. *Advertising Age,* September 12, 1977, p. 78.

17. *Advertising Age,* December 24, 1977, p. 26.

CHAPTER 6: Are We Losing Ground?

1. Eckholm, 1976, p. 9.

2. *New York Times,* April 15, 1976.

3. *New York Times,* August 28, 1977, p. 1.

4. *Newsweek,* September 19, 1977.

5. Fichter, 1972, pp. 36–67.

6. Kumar, 1973, p. 112.

7. Ibid., p. 259.

8. Barlowe, 1972, p. 46.

9. *Wall Street Journal,* February 24, 1977, p. 1.

10. Eckholm, 1976, p. 19.

11. Wagret, 1968, p. vi.

12. Ibid., p. 85.

13. Ibid.

14. Malthus, 1803, p. 78.

15. Childe, 1950, pp. 138-39.

16. Robert M. Adams, 1976, p. 19.

17. U.S., the White House, 1967, 1:64.

18. Schran, 1969, pp. 75–78.

19. Epstein, 1965, p. 177.

20. University of Illinois, *Student-Staff Directory,* 1976-77, inside front cover.

21. *Champaign-Urbana News Gazette,* March 6, 1977, p. 1.

22. *Newsweek,* September 7, 1977, p. 67.

23. *Newsweek,* November 20, 1974, p. 83.

24. Shoji, 1977, p. 62ff.

25. Johnson, 1974b, p. 73.

26. *Chicago Tribune,* February 26, 1978.

CHAPTER 7: When Will We Run Out of Energy? Never!

1. *Champaign-Urbana News Gazette,* October 16, 1977, p. 2-A.

2. *Advertising Age,* September 24, 1979, p. 48.

3. Goeller and Weinberg, 1978.

4. Stan Benjamin, "U.S. Energy Use Like Spending the Family Fortune," in *Champaign-Urbana News Gazette,* May 4, 1977, p. 37-C.

5. Jevons, 1865, pp. xiv and xvi.

6. Barnett and Morse, 1963, p. 181.

7. *Wall Street Journal,* August 22, 1979, p. 6.

8. Kahn et al., 1976, pp. 94-95. Orginally from Presidential Energy Program, *Hearings before the Subcommittee on Energy and Power of the Committee on Interstate and Foreign Commerce,* House of Representatives, 1st session on the implications of the Presi-

dent's proposals in the Energy Independence Act of 1975, serial no. 94-20, p. 643 (Washington, D.C.: GPO, February 17, 18, 20, and 21, 1975).

9. *Daily Illini, April 4, 1976, p. 7.*

10. Hazel Henderson, letter to the editor of the *New York Times*, dated August 16, 1975 (italics added).

11. *Wall Street Journal*, June 4, 1977, p. 18.

12. Merklein and Hardy, 1977, p. 39; *Middle East Information Series*, 1974, p. 104.

13. Bernardo Grossling, quoted in the *Wall Street Journal*, September 14, 1977, p. 18.

14. Joseph Barnea, quoted in the *Wall Street Journal*, September 14, 1977, p. 18, from UN Pergamon Press book, suggests that the estimate would rise by a factor of 100.

15. *Wall Street Journal*, May 3, 1977, p. 1.

16. Rose, in Abelson, 1974, p. 91.

17. *New York Times*, March 18, 1979, p. E-5.

18. *Wall Street Journal*, April 27, 1977, p. 22.

19. Ibid.

20. *Wall Street Journal*, September 16, 1977, p. 14.

21. Ibid.

22. *Wall Street Journal*, December 3, 1977, p. 16.

23. *Wall Street Journal*, January 3, 1978, p. 3.

24. *Wall Street Journal*, December 5, 1977, p. 16.

25. *Wall Street Journal*, editorial, November 17, 1978, p. 20.

26. See articles in Abelson, 1974.

27. *Wall Street Journal*, August 22, 1979, p. 6.

28. Metz, in Abelson, 1974.

29. Ericsson and Morgan, 1978, p. 457.

30. Howard Benedict, "Giant Space Power Plant Urged by Boeing Study," AP story in *Champaign-Urbana News Gazette*, February 9, 1978, p. 1.

31. *Newsweek*, April 17, 1978, p. 101.

32. National Academy of Sciences, 1979, pp. 487–88.

33. Bernard L. Cohen, 1977.

34. Fred A Donath, "Deep Storage Could Solve Nuclear Waste Problem," *Champaign-Urbana News Gazette*, May 8, 1977, p. 2-A.

35. Marvin Resnikoff, "Nuclear Wastes—The Myths," *Sierra*, July/August 1980, pp. 30–35.

36. Kahn et al., 1976, pp. 58, 83.

CHAPTER 8: Today's Energy Issues

1. Shmuel Yaari, 1974, "World over a Barrel," *Jerusalem Post*, October 4, p. 4.

2. Shah of Iran, 1974, quoted in *Jerusalem Post*, September 27.

3. Mitchell, 1974, table A-3, p. 82.

4. *Near East Report*, August 28, 1974, p. 188.

5. *Newsweek*, March 3, 1975, p. 31; see also *International Economic Report of the President*, GPO, 1974; Zonis, 1976.

6. Barkai, 1977, p. 16.

7. *New York Times*, December 25, 1977, p. E-3.

8. *Wall Street Journal*, December 23, 1977, p. 2.

9. Ibid.

10. *Daily Illini*, April 27, 1978, p. 14.

11. *Wall Street Journal*, July 14, 1978, p. 1.

12. *Wall Street Journal*, July 21, 1978, p. 4.

13. *Wall Street Journal*, August 14, 1978, p. 2.

14. Walter S. Mossberg and Jerry Landauer, "Energy Agency Alleges Oil-Price Manipulation by Middleman Firms," *Wall Street Journal*, September 22, 1978, pp. 1, 26.

15. "Possible Misconduct within Energy Unit Is Charged in Study of Oil-Pricing Cases," *Wall Street Journal*, December 11, 1978, p. 10.

16. "Kerr-McGee to Settle U.S. Oil-Price Claims," *Wall Street Journal*, February 9, 1979, p. 4.

17. Margaret Gentry, "Natural Gas Company to Pay $1 Million Fine," *Champaign-Urbana News Gazette*, July 28, 1979, p. 1.

18. Rich Jaroslovsky, "U.S. Is Accusing Nine Major Oil Concerns of $1.1 Billion in Consumer Overcharges," *Wall Street Journal*, November 9, 1979, p. 2.

19. "Mobil Oil Ordered to Pay $500,000 Fine on Criminal Charges Involving Gas Sales," and "Indiana Standard Settles Price Case for $100 Million," *Wall Street Journal*, February 15, 1980, p. 3.

20. Walter S. Mossberg, "President's Price Council Plans to Report 11 Oil Concerns Violated U.S. Guidelines," *Wall Street Journal*, February 22, 1980, p. 3.

21. "The Price Is Wrong — By $716 Million," *Newsweek*, February 25, 1980, p. 60.

22. *Wall Street Journal*, August 13, 1980, p. 27.

23. Edward Mitchell, "Energy: Ideology, Not Interests," *Wall Street Journal*, July 7, 1977.

24. *Wall Street Journal*, June 3, 1977, p. 18.

25. *Wall Street Journal*, September 15, 1977, p. 19. It later failed to pass the Senate, probably because of publicity.

26. *Wall Street Journal*, August 4, 1977, p. 10.

27. This is not intended to single out Jimmy Carter for criticism, but rather to provide an example of how all kinds of special interests have a stake in government energy regulation of one sort or another.

28. *Wall Street Journal*, April 13, 1977, p. 24.

29. *Wall Street Journal*, February 29, 1980, p. 5; March 6, 1980, p. 2.

30. U.S., the White House, 1952, 1:21.

31. Jack Anderson, in *Champaign-Urbana News Gazette*, March 9, 1980, p. A-3.

32. For a full day-to-day commentary from this point of view, one need only read the editorials of the *Wall Street Journal* (which, by the way, is no friend of the oil companies' policies).

33. Donald Bauder, "Energy Program: Huge Spending," Copley News Service in *Champaign-Urbana News Gazette*, June 16, 1978, p. A-4. Originally from Supran Energy Corp.

34. Ehrlich and Ehrlich, 1970, 2nd ed., 1972, pp. 66–67. The word "considerably" was substituted for the word "massive" that was in the first edition of the book; the subsidies refer to environmental effects which Ehrlich asserts exist but does not quantify.

35. Though the cost of nuclear energy is sufficiently low that it puts a comfortable ceiling on our long-run concerns about electrical power and heat, it still leaves open the question of fuel for transportation. And transportation accounts for about a quarter of our energy consumption (Hirst and Moyers, in Abelson, 1974, p. 14.), or about 40% to 54% of oil consumption (Landsberg, in Abelson, 1974, p. 4; Mitchell, 1974, p. 27).

If U.S. consumption of oil were to be reduced sharply by a switch to nuclear fuel for electricity, and by a shift to smaller cars and lower gasoline consumption due to an increased price of gasoline, total world demand for oil would be reduced considerably (because the U.S. accounts for a large proportion of total world oil consumption, roughly 30%, calculated from the 17,300 U.S. and 58,000 world barrels per day consumption in 1973— *Middle East Information Series*, 1974, p. 103). This by itself would reduce the scarcity of oil in near-term future years and put less pressure on potential supplies.

Additionally, electricity can be used for much of our transportation needs, if necessary. In years past, many city buses and commuter trains were electrically powered. And much of our auto transportation could be battery powered if the cost of petroleum rose severely. Therefore, even though electricity from nuclear energy and coal cannot immediately be used to supply *all* energy needs, it—together with other feasible means—can indirectly remove a great deal of the need for consumption of oil from fossil deposits. (And of course oil can be generated from coal and from newly grown crops. Even more likely would be the development of shale oil; all that seems to be needed for shale to be used is that potential producers be sure that the price of crude oil would not drop so precipitously as to wipe out their investment.)

36. Bethe, 1969, p. 92.
37. *Newsweek*, November 21, 1977, p. 132.
38. Kahn et al., 1976, p. 77.
39. Bethe, 1969, p. 92.
40. Jablon and Kato, 1970; discussed in Hoyle and Hoyle, 1980, pp. 23–24.
41. Hoyle and Hoyle, 1980, pp. 59-61.

CHAPTER 9: More Pollution? Or Less?

1. Ernest Callenbach, quoted in *Daily Illini*, March 8, 1977, p. 5.
2. *Chicago Tribune*, April 19, 1970, p. 19.
3. Fichter, 1972, pp. 28–35.
4. *Statistical Bulletin* of the Metropolitan Life Insurance Company, May, 1977, p. 9.

"The expectation of life at birth in the United States improved steadily in the 1970s, and reached a new high of 72.8 years in 1975, according to preliminary data prepared by the Statistical Bureau of the Metropolitan Life Insurance Company. In the 1970-76 period, average expected life-time increased by 2.1 years, compared with a gain of only 0.8 years in the sixties. A male child born in 1976 could look forward to 68.9 years of life and a female to 76.7 years, gains of 1.9 years and 2.1 years, respectively, since the beginning of the decade."

5. *New York Times*, January 23, 1977, p. 44.
6. U.S., Council on Environmental Quality, 1976, p. 285.
7. Herfindahl and Kneese, 1965, p. 2.
8. *New York Times*, February 6, 1977, page unknown.
9. *Time*, November 30, 1979, p. 44. See also Goldman, 1970, in Dorfman and Dorfman repr., 1972, pp. 294–307.
10. H. B. Creswell, quoted by Jane Jacobs in *Architectural Review*, December, 1958, p. 19.
11. Opinion Research Corporation, quoted by Wattenberg, 1974, p. 226.
12. Herfindahl and Kneese, 1965, p. 2.
13. Quoted by Alfred Friendly, 1970.
14. Ibid.
15. *U.S. News and World Report*, December 15, 1969, p. 77.
16. *Newsweek*, November 16, 1970, p. 67.

17. *Statistical Abstract of the U.S.*, various years; the quote is from "News of the Week in Review," *New York Times*, October 10, 1976, p. 4.

18. *Wall Street Journal*, September 15, 1977, p. 1. For the classic ecologists' analysis of Lake Erie see Barry Commoner, 1972, pp. 91–108. In fairness, I must add that Commoner noted that the total fish catch had not declined in the fashion Ehrlich and others charged (p. 93).

19. Ralph Nader, quoted in *Wall Street Journal*, September 20, 1977, p. 20.

20. *Newsweek*, January 28, 1974, p. 83.

21. *Time*, December 2, 1974, p. 59.

Chapter 10: Should We Conserve Resources for Others' Sakes? What Kinds of Resources Need Conservation?

1. *Champaign-Urbana News Gazette*, October 16, 1977, p. 52-C.

2. Johnson, 1974b, pp. 35–37.

3. Ibid., p. 35, quoting from *Hearings on U.S. and World Food Situation*, 93rd Congress, 1st session, October 1973, p. 103.

4. Steven Conwin, letter to editor, *New York Times Magazine*, June 30, 1974, p. 20.

5. *The Humanist*, April 1975, p. 20.

6. Study described in *Daily Illini*, October 20, 1977, page unknown.

7. *New York Times*, October 9, 1977, p. 48.

8. *Champaign-Urbana News Gazette*, March 15, 1977, p. 2.

9. *Champaign-Urbana Caravan*, December 10, 1975, p. 3.

10. *The End of Starvation*, n.d., p. 6.

11. I have just seen an exposé of The Hunger Project and est in *Mother Jones* magazine (Suzanne Gordon, "Let Them Eat est," pp. 41–54). Gordon shows that the funds of The Hunger Project, a non-profit organization, are not kept distinct from the funds of est, the profit-making organization of Werner Erhard. This has involved tax suits and money laundering in offshore tax havens.

12. *Champaign-Urbana News Gazette*, March 18, 1973, p. 9.

13. *Wall Street Journal*, February 7, 1979, p. 38.

14. Houthakker, 1976, p. 122 (italics added).

15. Barnett and Morse, 1963, p. 249.

16. *Wall Street Journal*, November 3, 1977, p. 1.

17. *Newsweek*, September 30, 1974, p. 52.

18. *Wall Street Journal*, February 11, 1977 (?), p. 8.

CHAPTER 11: Standing Room Only? The Demographic Facts

1. Fichter, 1972, pp. 24-25.

2. Harrison Brown, 1954, p. 221, quoted in Barnett and Morse, 1963, p. 30.

3. Genesis 13:6-9.

4. Quoted by C. L. Sulzberger, *New York Times*, December 18, 1977, p. iv-19.

5. Spengler, 1978.

6. G. Mydral, 1968, p. 974.

7. Annabelle Desmond, "How Many People Have Ever Lived on Earth?" *Population Bulletin* 18:1–19. Reprinted in Kenneth C. W. Kammeyer (ed.) *Population Studies*, 2nd ed. (Chicago: Rand McNally, 1975).

8. Deevey, 1960, in Ehrlich, Holdren, and Holm, 1971, p. 42.

9. Cook and Borah, 1971, p. 199.

10. *Recent Social Trends in the United States*, vol. 1, *Report of the President's Research Committee on Social Trends*, 1933, p. xx., quoted in Price, 1967, p. 12.

11. U.S. Dept. of State, 1969, p. 2.

12. *Time*, April 1, 1974, p. 40.

13. Lester R. Brown, McGrath, and Stoker, 1976, p. 3.

14. *New York Times*, July 28, 1978.

15. Elliot R. Morss and Ritchie H. Reed, eds., *Economic Aspects of Population Change* (Washington, D.C., 1972), p. 4, as quoted by Larry Neal, *Illinois Business Review*, March 1978, vol. 35, no. 2.

16. Wolfers, 1971, p. 227.

17. Gompertz curve extrapolation, in personal communication.

18. Dorn, 1963, p. 24.

19. UN, Dept. of Economic and Social Affairs, 1956, p. 15.

20. 1975 data, courtesy of Paul Handler and PLATO, University of Illinois.

21. *New York Times*, February, 1977, p. 1.

CHAPTER 12: Do Humans Breed Like Flies? Or Like Norwegian Rats?

1. Vogt, 1948, p. 228.

2. Sax, 1960, p. 23.

3. Quoted by Howard Rusk in *New York Times*, August 4, 1968, p. 71.

4. A. J. Carlson, "Science Versus Life," *JAMA* 147:1440, quoted by Barnett and Morse, 1963, p. 31.

5. Calhoun, 1962.

6. Price, 1967, p. 4.

7. van Vleck, 1970.

8. Price, 1967, p. 4.

9. Malthus, 2nd ed., 1803, p. 203.

10. Gregg, 1955a, p. 74, quoted by Barnett and Morse, 1963, p. 31.

11. Gregg, 1955b, p. 682.

12. Kirk, 1969, p. 79.

13. Malthus, 2nd ed., 1803, p. 3.

14. Ibid., pp. 3, 9.

15. Arensberg, 1968, pp. 107–8.

16. Banfield, 1958, p. 45.

17. Ibid., pp. 111-12.

18. Firth, 1939/1965, pp. 36–37.

19. Firth, 1936, p. 491.

20. Carr-Saunders, 1922, p. 230.

21. Ibid., p. 124.

22. Ford, 1952, p. 773.

23. Ibid., pp. 765–66.

24. Krzywicki, 1934, p. 216; Nag, 1962, p. 142.

25. Stuart, 1958, p. 99.

26. *Champaign-Urbana Courier*, January 20, 1971, p. 1.

27. Rainwater, 1965, pp. 162–73.

28. Whelpton, Campbell, and Patterson, 1966, p. 55.

29. Repetto, 1976; Mueller, 1976.

30. William Borders, "Indian Sees Benefits in His 8 Children," *New York Times*, May 30, 1976, p. 18.

31. Mamdani, 1973, p. 109.

32. Carl E. Taylor, 1965, pp. 482–83.

33. Ben-Porath, 1976; Schultz, 1976; Knodel, 1968; and Knodel and Van De Walle, 1967.

34. Malthus, 5th ed., 1817/1963, p. 12.

35. For me, one of the great mysteries of the intellectual world is the continued re-publication of Malthus's first edition — even by scholars of the first rank whose intellectual honesty is beyond question, such as Kenneth Boulding, who wrote an introduction to a re-publication of the first edition — though Malthus essentially repudiated his simple first-edition theorizing in later editions.

36. Sax, 1960, p. 13.

37. Malthus, quoted ibid.

CHAPTER 13: Population Growth and the Stock of Capital

1. Alonso and Fajans, 1970, summarizing Mera, 1970, and Fuchs, 1967.

2. Alonso, 1970, p. 439.

3. Stevens, 1978, summarizes previous literature and presents an analysis of bank rates.

4. Edward K. Hawkins, in Wilson et al., 1966, p. 2.

5. L. J. Zimmerman, 1965, p. 113.

6. Clark and Hasswell, 1967, p. 189.

7. Owen, 1964, pp. 23–24.

8. Clark and Haswell, 1967, p. 179.

9. U.S., the White House, 1967, 2:582.

10. Segal, 1976, shows that this is true for the U.S.

11. Habakkuk, 1963, p. 615.

12. Wilson et al., 1966.

13. Angle, 1954, pp. 102–3.

14. Glover and Simon, 1975.

AFTERNOTE: A Parable of Population Growth, Racquetball, and Squash

1. In truth, I exaggerate for effect here. Even we middle-aged squash types get worked up and awfully — amazingly — competitive sometimes. But I hope a touch of dramatic license can be permitted to all, without damaging credibility and compromising honesty.

CHAPTER 14: Population's Effects on Technology, Productivity, and Education

1. This first answer is largely definitional because the average worker's output per day is the same as the average worker's income per day, and aside from differences in the proportion of the population that works and the number of work days per years, average output per worker arithmetically equals per capita income.

2. Petty, 1889, p. 474.

3. Kuznets, 1960. Just to make it a bit harder to criticize this basic idea by impugning its source, let us note that this general point of view has been stated by William Petty,

the 17th century English statistician who had no obvious ideological axe to grind; by Colin Clark, who is indeed a Roman Catholic as "charged" by so many anti-natalists; by Simon Kuznets, a non-Catholic non-Communist Nobel prize winner, who, economists agree, knows the broad factual outlines of economic-statistical history better than anyone who ever lived; and by Friedrich Engels, Marx's co-worker, who stated the argument most cogently and completely. If this point of view represents some sort of plot, the plotters obviously are a peculiar set of bedfellows.

4. Lester Brown, 1974, p. 149.

5. *Champaign-Urbana News Gazette*, June 17, 1978, p. A-4.

6. Bethe, 1976, p. 2.

7. Mohr, 1969, p. 112.

8. Observation of this phenomenon by economists goes back to von Thunen in the nineteenth century (1966) and was demonstrated theoretically and empirically by Chayanov (1966). But Boserup (1965) has explored this idea most thoroughly and has presented a large quantity of supporting data. In the last decade anthropologists have found that this idea fits a great many of their observations in a variety of cultures; for a valuable integration and summary, see Mark Cohen (1977).

9. Elsewhere (1977, chapter 8, and 1978) I have studied the distinction between these two types of inventions both theoretically and with historical examples.

10. Solow, 1957, p. 320.

11. Fellner, 1970, pp. 11–12.

12. Productivity measured broadly has not done so well in the 1970s in the U.S. The reasons for this are not clearly understood, nor is it clear how much of this regression is due to such one-time factors as an increase in women, and a big cohort of youths, in the labor force. In my judgment, however, based on the long-run past, this is more likely to be a pause rather than a change in trend. For more information see Denison (1962).

13. Love and Pashute, 1978.

14. Petty, 1899, p. 473.

15. The U.S.-U.K. comparisons in the same year are relatively free of the potential bias arising from the fact that those industries where world technology grew faster exogenously were also those whose scale of production therefore expanded faster, a bias which afflicts analogous time-series studies within a single country.

16. The basic paper on learning by doing by an economist is that of Alchian, 1963. In it he refers to the Rand Study he did just after World War II, and to the earlier engineering literature. More general data and discussion is found in Hirsch, 1956. Since then the theoretical and empirical literature on the subject is large, but to my knowledge has not been well summarized.

17. Sheffer, 1970; Alonso and Fajans, 1970; Haworth and Rasmussen, 1973. Of course clean air is not included in these comparisons of cities of different sizes. But then, neither is the wider variety of cultural and entertainment opportunities in larger cities, and a whole host of other negative and positive factors.

18. Love, 1978.

19. Simon and Pilarski, 1979. See also Winegarden, 1975.

20. The data presented in this chapter should be qualified by the observation that they mostly do not pertain to "socialist" countries. And another qualification: The effect of a country's population on its productive efficiency depends, of course, on its physical and political circumstances. One such factor is the extent to which a country is economically integrated with its neighboring countries. If the borders do not much restrict the flow of trade and if transportation is good and cheap, then the size of the country itself is less

important. Monaco does not suffer from lack of division of labor, because it is so well integrated with its region; Israel's situation is quite different. Another factor affecting the absolute size of population required for efficiency is the stage of economic development. The less advanced is a society, the fewer specialities at which different people can work. That is, smallness may have less of a depressing effect on a very backward country than on a country further along in industrialization, all else equal (or it may *not* have; we don't have evidence).

AFTERNOTE: On the Importance and Origins of Productive Knowledge

1. Jorgensen and Griliches, 1967.
2. *Business Week*, May 7, 1966, pp. 164–65; see also Scherer, 1970, p. 349.
3. Griliches, 1958, p. 419. For a summary of other studies, all of which also arrive at estimates of a very high rate of return to society on investment in agricultural research, see Hayami and Ruttan, 1971.

CHAPTER 15: Population Growth, Natural Resources, Future Generations, and International Rape

1. After Fischman and Landsberg, in Ridker, 1972, p. 81.
2. Ibid., p. 95.
3. U.S. ERDA, 1976.
4. Feiss, 1963–65, p. 117.

CHAPTER 16: Population Growth and Land

1. *Smithsonian Magazine*, December 1976, quoted in *The Other Side*, April 1977, p. 1, italics in original.
2. Letter in *The Other Side*, ibid.
3. Takashi Oka, "Can the Spread of Deserts Be Halted?" *Christian Science Monitor*, November 12, 1976, p. 16, quoted in *The Other Side*, ibid.
4. Clark and Haswell, 1967, chapter 7.
5. Malthus, 1830/1960, p. 15.
6. Compare the view of a conservationist: "Every grain of wheat and rye, every sugar beet, every egg, and piece of wheat, every spoonful of olive oil, every glass of wine, depends on an irreducible minimum of earth to produce it. The earth is not made of rubber; it cannot be stretched. As the number of human beings increases, the relative amount of productive earth decreases by the amount" (William Vogt in *Reader's Digest*, January 1949, p. 141. Quoted by Zimmermann, 1951/1965, p. 815).
7. G. Myrdal, 1968, p. 415.
8. Connell, 1965, pp. 430–31.
9. Ibid, p. 423.
10. Perkins, 1969, p. 240.
11. Ibid., p. 77.
12. Ibid.
13. See in Simon, 1977, p. 248.
14. Slicher van Bath, 1963, pp. 195–239.
15. Ibid, p. 231.

16. Ohkawa, 1970, pp. 11, 18, 22.

17. Furnivall, 1957, p. 48.

18. Andrus, 1948, p. 235.

19. Simon, 1975b.

20. Revelle, 1974, p. 170.

21. Lele and Mellor, 1964, p. 20.

22. UN, Food and Agriculture Organization, 1975, p. 24.

23. William Preter, AP story in *Champaign-Urbana News Gazette*, March 21, 1977, p. 5-A.

24. This is the pattern described by von Thunen, 1966; Slicher van Bath, 1963; and especially recently by Boserup, 1965. See Simon, 1977, chapter 8, and 1978c.

25. U.S. Dept. of Agriculture, 1974, p. vi.

26. *Daily Illini*, March 30, 1977, p. 7.

27. "USDA Says Quality of Cropland on Rise," *Champaign-Urbana News Gazette*, March 5, 1978, p. V 7.

28. Ridker, 1972, chapter 8.

29. Reference lost.

CHAPTER 17: Are People an Environmental Pollution?

1. Edwin L. Dale, Jr., "The Economics of Pollution," *New York Times Magazine*, April 19, 1970 pp. 29ff.

2. Commoner, 1972.

3. See note 18 of chapter 9; compare with headline cited in note 5 of that chapter.

4. Gladwin Hill in "News of the Week in Review," *New York Times*, October 17, 1974, p. 4.

5. *Newsweek*, December 1, 1975, p. 86.

6. The difference in mortality by income is not merely a matter of higher incomes buying better nutrition. The poorest person in the U.S. can buy a nutritious diet of soybeans, milk, and dog food. The fact that poor people do not eat such diets speaks to the complexity of the income-health relationship.

7. Ridker, 1972, p. 25.

8. An interesting account of the logic of sit-tight is found in Nathan Leopold's description of prison (1958):

> Penitentiaries are hidebound institutions, regulated down to their tiniest detail by tradition. There is tremendous inertia to overcome in effecting any change. A compelling reason for doing anything in a given way is that it has always been done that way. Obvious improvements, easier ways of doing something are rejected simply because they are new. In the management of the prison itself, especially with regard to custodial matters, there is a certain amount of justification for this conservatism. The smallest change in routine may involve angles not immediately apparent — not thought of by the administration. But you can bank on it that there are always three thousand active brains engaged in watching attentively for the slightest loophole. And in such matters one mistake is one mistake too many. It is often better, as it is always safer, to stick by the tried and true.

9. For information on that subject, which is beyond our scope here, see *The No-Growth Society*, edited by M. Olson and H. Lansberg (1973).

10. *Wall Street Journal*, December 22, 1977, p. 1.

CHAPTER 18: Population Density Does Not Damage Health, or
Psychological and Social Well-Being.

1. Glass, 1964, quoted in Bogue, 1969, p. 606.

2. Dublin et al., 1949, p. 73. A peculiarity of the data, however (p. 342): 1939 U.S. life expectancy for white females was 54.6 for "cities of 100,000 or more" but only 51.1 for "other urban places." This does not jibe with lower life expectancy being associated with higher density. But it may be due to selective migration.

3. Glass, 1964, in Bogue, 1969, p. 606.

4. For completeness, we should note that, at the *very lowest* population densities, there may be too few people to maintain a chain of malarial and other parasitic infections, and an increase in density may then *increase* the incidence of these diseases. But this applies only to people living at densities that were ordinarily found at much earlier stages of human history, and in a few extraordinary situations in the world today. For more information, see McNeill, 1977, chapter 2.

5. Gourou, 1966, pp. 8, 9, 14, 98.

6. Ibid., p. 10.

7. Frederikson, in Heer, 1968, pp. 70–71.

8. Gourou, 1966, p. 10.

9. Buer, 1968, p. 219.

10. Lebergott, 1964, p. 250.

11. Leonard, 1979.

12. R. B. Gupta and Dr. K. Gupta, eds., *International Institute for Population Studies*, October 1979, p. 7.

13. Commoner, 1972.

14. B. H. Kean quoted in Harold M. Schmeck, Jr., "Tropical Diseases May Be Gaining on Humanity," *New York Times*, Education Section, July 9, 1978, p. 1PE.

15. Huxley, 1953, pp. 137–38.

16. Stephen J. Gould, review of Konrad Lorenz in *New York Times Book Review*, February 27, 1977, p. 2.

17. Hawley, 1972, and Choldin, 1978.

18. Booth and Edwards, 1976, p. 308.

19. Webb, 1975, cited by Choldin, 1978, p. 110.

20. Choldin, 1978, p. 110.

21. Freedman, 1975.

22. Wattenberg, 1974, p. 175.

23. Reid and Lyon, 1972, preface. Having lived with more than two hundred other men on a Navy destroyer 390 feet long and 41 feet wide — much less surface area than on three 100 by 50 ft. home lots — I knew that sometimes one would appreciate a bit more space to oneself at sea. But the ship did not seem oppressively crowded when we were in port. And if the ship's living quarters had included the space devoted to armaments, I think it would have been quite comfortable — for bachelors.

24. Zajonc, 1976.

25. The range is 3½ points between worst and best. And interestingly, in the data that Zajonc leans on most heavily — the National Merit Scholarship Qualification Test of 1965 — only children do worse than (a) both children in two-child families, (b) the first and second children in three-child families, and (c) the first child in the largest families for which data is given. In only one of four data sets reviewed by Zajonc — a Scotch study — does the only child do best. And in the French and Scotch data, later-born chil-

dren seem to do better than earlier-born children, just the opposite of the U.S. and the Netherlands. All in all, it seems unwise to attach any meaning, or to base any policies, on data as conflicting and as small in real differences as these.

26. Terhune, 1975; Kunz and Peterson, 1972; Lindert, 1980, in Easterlin, 1980.
27. Choldin, 1978, p. 109.

CHAPTER 19: The Big Economic Picture: Population Growth and Living Standards in MDCs

1. *New York Times Magazine*, May 14, 1967, p. 121.
2. Thomas Hardy, *The Mayor of Casterbridge* (New York: New Am. Lib., Signet, 1962),.p. 89.
3. Kanovsky, 1966, p. 38.
4. Simon, 1977, p. 56. The calculation was for 1960; it may be a bit more now.
5. Kuznets, 1967; Easterlin, 1967; Chesnais and Sauvy, 1973.
6. *Newsweek*, April 24, 1978, p. 94.
7. *Wall Street Journal*, March 31, 1977, p. 1.
8. Sauvy, 1969, p. 195.
9. Kuznets, 1965, p. 16.
10. Full discussion of an earlier form of this model may be found in Simon, 1977, chapters 4-6. This model is described in Steinmann and Simon (forthcoming) and in a series of recent technical papers available from the author on request.
11. Leibenstein, 1972, p. 64.
12. Lader, 1971, p. 73.
13. U.S., the White House, 1972, p. 53.
14. Easterlin, 1972, p. 45.
15. Ehrlich and Harriman, 1971, pp. 36–67.

AFTERNOTE: How Immigrants Affect Our Standard of Living

1. Lesko Associates, 1975.
2. Robinson, 1979.
3. Lancaster and Schewen, 1977.
4. Korns, 1977.
5. North and Houstoun, 1976; Cornelius, 1977.
6. Opportunity Systems, Inc., 1975-77.
7. Manpower and Immigration (Lande), 1974.
8. Shuval et al., 1973.
9. Jones and Smith, 1970.
10. Villalpondo, 1976.
11. Smith and Newman, 1977.
12. Simon, 1980.
13. North and Houstoun, 1976.
14. Simon, forthcoming.

CHAPTER 20: The Big Picture II: LDCs

1. Piotrow, 1973, p. 15.
2. Ibid., p. 124.

3. Coale and Hoover, 1958, p. 275.

4. Kuznets, 1967; Easterlin, 1967; Chesnais and Sauvy, 1973; Simon and Gobin, 1979.

5. Simon and Gobin, 1979.

6. Stryker, 1977.

7. Morawetz, 1978.

8. World Bank 1977 Annual Report quoted in *Wall Street Journal*, September 19, 1977, p. 13.

9. Kuznets, 1965, p. 29 (italics added).

AFTERNOTE: The Limits to Growth

1. Boyd, 1972.

2. *New York Times*, April 14, 1976; *Global 2000*, II, p. 613.

3. *Time*, April 26, 1976, p. 56.

CHAPTER 21: The Politics and Finances of Population Control

1. U.S. General Accounting Office, 1978, p. 7.

2. Ibid., pp. 2–3 (italics added).

3. Ibid., pp. 7, 6, and 29.

4. Ibid., p. 38.

5. Ibid., p. 68.

6. Ibid., p. 71.

7. Ibid., p. 82.

8. "Population Control of Third World Planned: Sterilization Storm in U.S.," *Evening Press* (Dublin, Ireland), May 12, 1977, p. 9.

9. Piotrow, 1973; Bachrach and Bergman, 1973; Littlewood, 1977.

10. Another scrap of evidence of how U.S. government money permeates the population "business": Piotrow was careful that "none of the agencies referred to provided any financial support for the research and writing of this study" (1973, p. xvii). And yet her book wound up as part of a series of the Law and Population Program of the Fletcher School of Law and Diplomacy at Tufts University, and the overleaf of the title page says, "The Law and Population Program is sponsored, in part, by the Agency for International Development" (AID).

11. *Population*, September 1976.

12. Not on PCC's list.

13. Not on PCC's list.

14. Planned Parenthood Federation of America, n.d., *Federation Declaration of Principles*, p. 12.

15. Ibid., p. 13.

16. *The Other Side*, July 1978, p. 3.

17. UN, Fund for Population Activities, 1975, p. 4.

18. Ibid., p. 7.

19. In Brown et al., 1976, preface (italics added).

20. See Piotrow, 1973.

21. Friedman, 1972, p. 19.

22. Fund-raising brochure, n.d., largely a quote from Alvin Toffler.

23. *Newsweek*, November 5, 1973, p. 82.

24. *New York Times*, November 11, 1975, p. 246.

CHAPTER 22: The Rhetoric of Population Control: Does the End Justify the Means?

1. H. F. Wollenberg IV, "Davis, Borchers Clash over Vasectomies," *Champaign-Urbana News Gazette*, May 10, 1973, p. 2.

2. Mowrer, 1961, p. 6. Borlaug, 1971, pp. 8-9: "the frightening power of human reproduction must also be curbed; otherwise, the success of the green revolution will be ephemeral only." Wilson quoted in *Time*, August 1, 1977, p. 58: "It would be foolish, he says, to rear as many healthy children as possible in today's crowded world." Asimov in *Jewish News*, September 23, 1975, p. 32: "natural resources are being haphazardly drained and the population is allowed to grow unchecked ... the population is increasing faster than the capacity to provide material and food for the growing numbers of people." Adams, 1974, p. 25. Anderson, *Newark Star Ledger*, August 27, 1977: "The final Armageddon will likely come, in the opinion of intelligence analysts, not from a nuclear holocaust but from the simple crush of people ... U.S. embassies predict rising unemployment and underemployment, with countless millions unable to eke out a living in rural areas, jamming into already overcrowded cities, where living conditions for many are appalling. This can only spawn social unrest with serious political and even potential strategic 'implications,' the study stresses." Gell-Mann, "The Population Crisis: Rising Concern at Home," *Science*, November 7, 1969, p. 723: "We are all of us appalled at man's ravaging of his environment. The problem comes about as a product of three factors: population, the propensity for each individual to destroy the environment, and his capacity to do so through being armed with technology. All of these are increasing; all must be worked on in an effort to find some way to control the trend and ultimately make it level off or reverse." Wilt Chamberlain and David Shaw, 1973, *Wilt* (New York: Warner Paperback): "I was especially hoping I would convince Richard [Nixon!] to take the lead in trying to solve the overpopulation problem — probably the biggest problem in the world today, the way I see it. I figured that if he would throw the prestige of his office and the power of this country behind some sweeping birth-control programs in the more backward countries, we might make some real progress in that area." Landers, *Chicago Sun-Times*, June 23, 1970, p. 40: "Dear Ann Landers: It is now abundantly clear to even the most empty-headed fools that something drastic must be done within the next decade to limit the size of families or we are all doomed." The writer then called for sterilization as a remedy. Landers replied, "Yes, I'm with you." "Dear Abby," *Champaign-Urbana News Gazette*, May 9, 1974, p. 34: "When the writers of the Good Book implored us to go forth and multiply, the world needed more people. Not so today. Quite the contrary." Knowles in *New York Times*, December 30, 1969, p. 26. Rockefeller in *Newsweek*, March 30, 1970, p. 87. Finch in an AP story in *Champaign-Urbana Courier*, February 19, 1970, p. 10. Letter to a newspaper on a "world without population curbs" in *Des Moines Register*, July 12, 1972, p. 8.

3. Beckerman, 1974; Kahn, 1976; Maddox, 1972.

4. Musson, 1974.

5. Kingsley Davis, 1970, p. 33.

6. Davis, 1968, quoted in Elliott et al., 1970.

7. Ehrlich, 1968, p. xi.

8. Wertham, 1969, chapter 6.

9. Carey, in Carey and Simon, 1978.

10. Day and Day, 1964, p. 134; Parsons, 1971, p. 298; Ehrlich, Ehrlich, and Holdren, 1977, p. 807.

11. Silverman, 1970.

12. Ibid.

13. L. Brown, 1974, p. 148; Ehrlich, 1968, p. 36; idem, 1968, p. 41; William P. Bundy, "Learning to Walk," *Newsweek*, February 25, 1972, p. 35.

14. *Newsweek*, March 30, 1970, p. 87.

15. Silverman, 1970.

16. I mention these facts about Stuart's publication (1958) not to dismiss the book — I think we should try to look beyond the cover of the book to evalute it — but to show that *despite* its inauspicious start in life the book could obtain so much more interest than could Mather's and the well-known Harpers publishing firm.

17. Littlewood, 1977, p. 6.

18. Hardin, 1974.

19. Stuart, 1958, p. 9.

20. Mayer, personal communication, 1980.

21. Love and Pashute [Simon], 1978. This study was originally published under a pseudonym. My purpose was not to hide these views behind the pen name, and in fact the study originally but unsuccessfully sought publication under my real name. It was published under a pseudonym to avoid the impression that the volume in which it was published, which I edited, contained too much of my own material.

22. This is similar to the finding of Kammeyer, Yetman, and McClendon, 1972, using county data.

23. I do not mean to suggest that southern family-planning clinics are bad. Rather, I think that such clinics are good because, like all aids to contraception, they help the individual achieve the kind of family and way of life that he or she wishes. Nevertheless, it seems to me that we should try to understand the motivations that lie behind such clinics, in order that we may meet truthfully and successfully with political objections to the extension of such clinics in the U.S. and elsewhere. The dedication of my 1977 technical book on population is as follows: "For my grandmother, Fanny Goodstein, who never went to school, but whose life made her family and community richer, economically and spiritually." Since I wrote that dedication I have learned (Chase, 1977) that predecessors of the leaders of today's population organizations (going back through Guy Burch, director of the Population Reference Bureau, and key intellectual adviser to the environmental movement's early best-selling writers such as Vogt and Osborn) considered people like my grandmother to be mentally incompetent; like other Jewish immigrants from eastern Europe at the turn of the century, she would have scored abysmally low on the IQ test they considered a valid measure of her mental competence; eight out of ten of her sort of immigrant were rated as "feeble-minded defectives" (Chase, 1977, p. xix). Had the eugenicists had their way about immigration policy, my grandmother could not have entered the U.S., and she and her descendants would have perished in Europe during World War II, as did her relatives who remained. Had Burch, Vogt, and Osborn had their way — which is what Zero Population Growth wants.

24. If such laws had been on the books in the past, they would have been used against the immigrant ancestors of many of us. If an IQ test indicates a score of 70 or lower the person is designated "feeble-minded or mentally retarded." Administration of the IQ test "to steerage immigrants at Ellis Island [New York] in 1912 showed that, *according to the scores they made on these tests*, more than 80 percent of all Jewish, Italian, Hungarian, Russian, Polish and other non-Nordic people tested were feeble-minded defectives" (Chase, 1977, pp. xix, 16). The results of such IQ tests were brought before Congress by the eugenics movement when lobbying to achieve the restrictive U.S. Immigration Act

of 1924. Now — my grandmother would not have procreated, and (present company aside) her very productive and socially useful offspring would not have been born to make their contribution to their society and that of their descendants. The present leaders of the population movement have cleaned up their act to a considerable extent, and eugenics seldom comes into the discussion now. But the same old restrictive-immigration and sterilization policies are still being advocated, or are already enacted into laws. As this book and my earlier technical book (1977) argue, the economic rationale for such restrictive policies does not exist. And so we have a miserable irony: Policies created for selfish economic purposes turn out not to serve the economic ends of those who advocate the policies. And the policies damage the rest of us, too; so there is not even the bittersweet taste of poetic justice.

25. Littlewood, 1977, pp. 107–8.

26. Ibid., p. 80.

27. AP, *Daily Illini*, February 23, 1980, p. 3.

28. *Annual Review of Population Law*, 1976, pp. 38–39.

29. *Newsweek*, March 10, 1980; AP, *Champaign-Urbana News Gazette*, March 1, 1980, p. 1.

30. Testimony before Congressional Subcommittee on Science, Research, and Development, July 21, 1970, quoted by Wolman, 1971, p. 97 (italics added).

31. Let me go further. Some of the people involved with these organizations are among the most unselfish and dedicated people that I have ever met. Take, for example, P, who set up a population-related private enterprise partly to diffuse contraception and partly to create a dependable source of funding for innovative fertility-reduction programs. He is almost saintly in turning over to non-profit ventures almost all the profits from the private business that, in the highest conscience, he could have divided among himself and the other stockholders.

AFTERNOTE: Planned Parenthood's Rhetoric

1. Donor card accompanying a PP/WP brochure.

2. Faye Wattleton in fund-raising letter and leaflet accompanying brochure.

3. Paul Ehrlich, "Eco-Catastrophe," *Ramparts* 7: 24–28 (1969).

CHAPTER 23: Ultimately — What Are Your Values?

1. Mailing piece received August 1980.

2. Ehrlich, 1968, p. 15.

3. Ibid., pp. 197–98.

4. Wolfers, 1971, p. 229.

5. Ehrlich, 1968, prologue.

6. Willing, 1971, p. 161.

7. Kingsley Davis, 1968, from Elliott et al., 1970, p. ix.

8. Wattenberg, 1974, p. 228.

9. International Advisory Committee on Population and Law, 1977, pp. 26, 174.

10. Salaff and Wong, 1978.

Source Notes for Figures

1-1. U.S. Dept. of Commerce, Bureau of the Census, *Historical Statistics of the United States: Colonial Times to 1970* (Washington: GPO, 1976).

2-1. Kahn et al., 1976, p. 92.

2-2. After Brobst, 1979, p. 118.

4-1. Drawn from table 4-1; USDA estimates used from 1974 on.

4-2. Reproduced from *Business Week*, June 16, 1975, p. 65.

4-3. Reproduced from the *New York Times*, April 9, 1972, p. E-5.

5-1. Reproduced from Brown, 1974, pp. 57–58.

5-2. Same as figure 1-1.

5-3. Johnson, 1980.

5-4. Same as figure 1-1.

5-5. Redrawn from U.S. Council on Environmental Quality, *Ninth Annual Report* (Washington, D.C.: GPO, 1978), p. 321.

6-1. U.S. Dept. of Agriculture, Economic Research Service, AER #291, table 2.

7-1. Jevons, 1865, frontispiece.

7-2, 7-3, 7-4. Same as figure 1-1.

7-5. Reproduced from *Newsweek*, May 24, 1976, p. 70.

7-6. Reproduced from *Newsweek*, June 27, 1977, p. 71.

7-7. Reproduced from *Newsweek*, May 23, 1977, p. 48.

9-1. U.S. Dept. of Commerce, Bureau of the Census, *Historical Statistics of the United States*, p. 55, and idem, *Statistical Abstract*, various years.

9-2. Reproduced from Abdel R. Omran, "Epidemiologic Transition in the U.S.," *Population Bulletin* 32 (May 1980): 26.

9-3. Part a: U.S. Council on Environmental Quality, 1976, p. 226. Part b: *Ninth Annual Report*, 1978.

9-4. Kahn et al., 1976, p. 160.

9-5. U.S. Council on Environmental Quality, 1975, p. 352.

11-1. After Piotrow, 1973, p. 4; originally from U.S. Dept. of State.

11-2. Deevey, 1960, in Ehrlich, Holdren, and Holm, 1971, p. 52.

11-3. Freedman and Berelson, 1974, pp. 38–39.

11-4, 11-5. Clark, 1967, p. 64.

11-6. Robert M. Adams, 1965, p. 115.

11-7. Cook and Borah, 1971, pp. viii, 82.

11-8. Bogue, 1969, p. 59.

11-9. Clark, 1967, p. 2; Institute National d'Etudes Demograp-hiques (INED), Paris, taken from *People*, vol. 7, no. 1 (1980), pp. 4, 5.

11-10. Alva Mydral, 1941/1968, p. 80 (originally, Population Commission, *Report on Demographic Investigation*, and *Population Index*).

11-11. Dorn, 1963, p. 75; and sources for figure 1-1.

11-12. Freedman and Berelson, 1974, pp. 38–39.

12-1. Thomas, 1941, p. 82.

12-2. Bogue, 1969, p. 85, and *Population Index*, various issues.

14-1. Sorokin, 1978, p. 148; Clark, 1967; McEvedy and Jones, 1978.

14-2a. Clark, 1967, p. 265.

14-2b. West, 1971, pp. 18–22.

14-3. Based on data in Bass, 1978.

16-1. Reproduced from Stys, 1957.

16-2. Taiwan: Kumar, 1973, appendix 1, and *Population Index*, spring 1980. Western Europe: UN, Food and Agriculture Organization (UNFAO), *Production Yearbook*, 1976. Other Countries: UNFAO, *Production Yearbook*, 1978.

16-3. U.S. Dept. of Agriculture, Economic Research Service, Agricultural Economic Report No. 247, H. Thomas Frey, "Major Uses of Land in the United States, Summary for 1969."

16-4. Ibid., p. 5.

16-5. Landsberg, 1964, p. 171.

17-1. *New York Times*, April 19, 1970.

17-2. Ridker, 1972.

19-1. Kuznets, 1971, pp. 11–14.

20-1. Simon and Gobin, 1979.

21-1. U.S. Dept. of Commerce, Bureau of the Census, *Population Reports*, series J (March 1977), p. J-272; U.S. General Accounting Office, 1978, p. 92.

21-2. Controller General of U.S., 1978, p. 91, and annual reports of UNFPA and other organizations.

22-1. Lader, 1971, p. 66.

22-2. *Wall Street Journal*, January 13, 1977.

22-3. Mailing piece.

22-4. *New York Times*, April 30, 1972, section 12, page 1.

A-1 through A-6. Same as figure 1-1.

A-7. Donella H. Meadows et al., 1972 *(The Limits to Growth)*.

A-8. Robert S. Manthy, *Natural Resource Commodities: A Century of Statistics* (Baltimore: John Hopkins, 1978).

A-9.   James O. Bray and Patricia Watkins, "Corn Production in the United States, 1870–1960," *Journal of Farm Economics* 46 (1964): 753.

A-10. *Twentieth Century Petroleum Statistics*, vol. 35 (Dallas: DeGolyer and MacNaughton, 1979), pp. 15 and 41; and U.S. Dept. of Energy, *Monthly Energy Review*, June 1980, pp. 48, 70–71.

A-11. *Gas Facts* (Arlington, Va.: American Gas Association, 1953), pp. 33, 42, and (1978), pp. 35, 122; U.S. Dept. of Energy, *Monthly Energy Review*, June 1980, pp. 48, 81.

A-12. Joel Darmstadter, Joy Dunkerley, and Jack Alterman, *How Industrial Societies Use Energy: A Comparative Analysis* (Baltimore: Johns Hopkins Press for Resources for the Future, 1977).

A-13. Demand and Conservation Panel of the Committee on Nuclear and Alternative Energy Systems, "U.S. Energy Demand: Some Low Energy Futures," *Science*, April 14, 1978, p. 147.

A-14. *Platt's Oil Price Handbook and Oilmanac, 1978 Prices* (New York: McGraw Hill, 1978), p. 106.

A-15. Same as figure 9-1.

A-16. Kahn et al., 1976, p. 28.

A-17. Ehrlich et al., 1977, figure 5-15.

A-18. W. Parker Mauldin and Bernard Berelson, "Conditions of Fertility Decline in Developing Countries, 1965–1975," *Studies in Family Planning* 9 (1978): 90–148.

A-19. Thomas, 1941, p. 16.

A-20. Kumar, 1973, appendix tables I and II.

A-21. U.S. Bureau of Labor Statistics, *Handbook of Labor Statistics*, no. 1630, July 1969.

A-22. *Media/Scope*, August 1964.

A-23. Love and Pashute, 1978.

A-24. *New York Times*, June 30, 1968, p. E-5.

References

Abelson, Philip H. 1972. Limits to growth (editorial). *Science* 175.

———, ed. 1974. *Energy: use, conservation and supply.* Washington, D.C.: AAAS.

———, ed. 1975. *Food: politics, economics, nutrition, and reserach.* Washington, D.C.: AAAS.

Abercrombie, Keith, and Arthur McCormack. 1976. Population growth and food supplies in different time perspectives. *Population and Development Review* (September/December). 2:479–98.

Adams, Richard P. 1974. On the necessity of literature. *AAUP Bulletin* (Spring): 24–26.

Adams, Robert M. 1965. *Land behind Baghdad.* Chicago: U. of Chicago Pr.

———. 1976. From sites to patterns. *University of Chicago Magazine* (March), vol. 19.

Adelman, Irma. 1963. An econometric analysis of population growth. *American Economic Review* 53: 314–19.

Alchian, A. A. 1963. Reliability of progress curves in airframe production. *Econometrica* 31: 679–93.

Alonso, William. 1970. The economics of urban size. Mimeo.

Alonso, William, and Michael Fajans. 1970. Cost of living and income by urban size. Mimeo.

Andrus, J. Russell. 1948. *Burmese economic life.* Stanford: Stanford U. Pr.

Angle, Paul, ed. 1954. *The Lincoln reader.* New York: Pocket Books.

Arensberg, Conrad M. 1968. *The Irish countryman.* 2nd ed. New York: Macmillan.

Bachrach, Peter, and Elihu Bergman. 1973. *Power and choice: the formulation of American population policy.* Lexington, Mass.: Lexington Bks.

Banfield, Edward. 1958. *The moral basis of a backward society.* Chicago: Free Pr.

Banks, Ferdinand E. 1976. *The economies of natural resources.* New York: Plenum Pr.

Barkai, Haim. 1977. Reflections on the political economy of energy conservation in the United States. Mimeo. Research report no. 100. Dept. of Economics, Hebrew U. of Jerusalem. January.

Barlowe, Raleigh. 1972. *Land resource economics: the economics of a real property.* 2nd ed. Englewood Cliffs, N.J.: Prentice-Hall.

Barnett, Harold J. 1971. Population problems—myths and realities. *Economic Development and Cultural Change* (July) 19.

———. 1977. Scarcity and growth: revisited. Mimeo. Dept. of Economics, Washington U., St. Louis. Printed in V. Kerry Smith, 1979.

Barnett, Harold J., and Chandler Morse. 1963. *Scarcity and growth: the economics of natural resource availability.* Baltimore: Johns Hopkins.

Barnett, Larry. 1970. Political affiliation and attitudes toward population limitation. *Social Biology* 17: 124–31.

———. 1971. Zero population growth, inc. *Biosocial Science* 21: 759–65.

Bass, Frank M. 1978. The relationship between diffusion rates, experience curves, and demand elasticities for consumer durable technological innovations. Mimeo. Paper no. 660, Institute for Research in the Behavioral, Economic and Management Schools. Purdue U., West Lafayette, Ind. March.

Bauer, Peter T. 1976. *Dissent on development.* London: Weidenfeld and Nicholson, rev. ed.

Beckerman, Wilfred. 1974. *In defence of economic growth.* London: Jonathon Cape.

Bennett, Merrill Kelley. 1954. *The world's food: a study of the interrelationships of world population, national diets, and food potentials.* New York: Harper.

Ben-Porath, Yoram. 1976. Fertility response to child mortality: microdata from Israel. *Journal of Political Economy* 84: S168–78.

———. 1980. Child mortality and fertility: issues in the demographic transition of a migrant population. In Easterlin, 1980.

Bethe, Hans. 1969. Atomic power. In Cornell U. Faculty Members, eds. *The quality of life.* Ithaca: Cornell U. Pr.

———. 1976. The necessity of fission power. *Scientific American* 234: 16ff.

Bisselle, C. A.; S. H. Lubore; and R. P. Pikul. 1972. *National environmental indices: air quality and outdoor recreation.* McLean, Va.: The Mitre Corp.

Blakeslee, Leroy L.; Earl O. Heady; and Charles F. Framingham. 1973. *World food production, demand, and trade.* Ames: Iowa St. U. Pr.

Bogue, Donald. 1969. *Principles of demography.* New York: Wiley.

Bonar, James. 1966. *Theories on population from Raleigh to Arthur Young.* New York: R. M. Kelley.

Booth, Alan, and John N. Edwards. 1976. Crowding and family relations. *American Sociological Review* 41: 308–21.

Borgstrom, Georg. 1970. *Too many: a study of earth's biological limitation.* Rev. ed. New York: Macmillan.

Borlaug, Norman E. 1971. We must expand population research now to slow world population growth. In Population Crisis Committee, *Mankind's greatest needs: population research.* Washington, D.C.: Population Crisis Committee.

Borrie, Wilfred D. 1970. *The growth and control of world population.* London: Weidenfeld & Nicolson.

Boserup, Ester. 1965. *The conditions of agricultural growth.* London: Allen & Unwin.

Boyd, Robert. 1972. World dynamics: a note. *Science* 177: 516–19.

Bradshaw, Lois E., and Cynthia P. Green. 1977. A guide to sources of family planning program assistance. *Population reports* (March) series J: J272–78.

Brobst, Donald. 1979. Fundamental concepts for the analysis of resource availability. In Vincent Kerry Smith, ed., 1979, pp. 106–42.

The Brookings Bulletin. 1976. 13: 1ff.

Brooks, D. B., and P. W. Andrews. 1974. Mineral resources, economic growth, and world population. *Science* 185: 13–19.

Brown, Gardner M., Jr., and Barry C. Field. 1978. Implications of alternative measures of natural resource scarcity. *Journal of Political Economy* 86: 229.

Brown, Harrison. 1954. *Challenge of man's future.* New York: Viking Pr.

Brown, Harrison; James Bonner; and John Weir. 1963. *The next hundred years.* New York: Viking Pr.

Brown, Lester. 1974. *In the human interest: a strategy to stabilize world population.* New York: Norton.

Brown, Lester; Patricia L. McGrath; and Bruce Stoker. 1976. *Twenty-two dimensions of the population problem.* Washington, D.C.: Worldwatch Inst.

Brubaker, Sterling. 1975. *In command of tomorrow: resource and environmental strategies for Americans.* Baltimore: Resources for the Future, and Johns Hopkins.

Buer, M. C. 1968. *Health, wealth, and population in the early days of the industrial revolution.* Repr. of 1926 ed. London: Routledge.

Calhoun, John B. 1962. Population density and social pathology. *Scientific American* 206: 32ff. In *Studies of crowding in rats, Scientific American* Offprint 506. San Francisco: W. H. Freeman.

Calvin, Melvin. 1974. Solar energy by photosynthesis. In Abelson, 1974.

Carey, James W., and Julian L. Simon. 1978. The church's responsibility to teach the value of life: a surprising dialogue between Catholic and Jew. Mimeo. Dept. of Economics. U. of Illinois, Urbana.

Carlson, A. J. 1955. Science versus life. *Journal of the American Medical Association* 147: 1440.

Carr-Saunders, A. M. 1922. *The population problem: a study in human evolution.* Oxford: Oxford U. Pr.

Chamberlain, Wilt, and David Shaw. 1970. *Wilt.* New York: Warner Paperback.

Chapelle, Anthony, and Georgette Dickey Chapelle. 1956. New life for India's villagers. *The National Geographic Magazine* 109: 572–95.

Chase, Allen. 1977. *The legacy of Malthus.* New York: Knopf.

Chayanov, A. V. 1966. *The theory of peasant economy.* D. Thorner et al., eds. Homewood, Ill.: Irwin.

Chenery, Hollis B. 1960. Patterns of industrial growth. *American Economic Review* 50: 624–54.

Chesnais, Jean-Claude, and Alfred Sauvy. 1973. Progrès économique et accroissement de la population; une expérience commentée. *Population* 28: 843–57.

Childe, V. Gordon. 1950. *What happened in history.* Harmondsworth, Eng.: Penguin.

Choldin, Harvey M. 1978. Urban density and pathology. *Annual Review of Sociology* 4: 91–113.

Clark, Colin. 1957. *Conditions of economic progress.* 3d ed. New York: Macmillan.

——. 1967. *Population growth and land use.* New York: St. Martin's.

——. 1978. Population growth and productivity. In Julian L. Simon, 1978c.

Clark, Colin, and Margaret Haswell. 1967. *The economics of subsistence agriculture.* New York: St. Martin's.

Claus, George, and Karen Bolander. 1977. *Ecological sanity.* New York: David McKay.

Cloud, Preston. 1969. Mineral resources from the sea. In National Academy of Sciences. *Resources and man: a study and recommendations.* San Francisco: W. H. Freeman.

——. 1971. Resources, population, and quality of life. In S. Fred Singer, ed., *Is there an optimum level of population?* New York: McGraw-Hill.

Coale, Ansley J., and Edgar M. Hoover. 1958. *Population growth and economic development in low-income countries.* Princeton: Princeton U. Pr.

Cohen, Bernard L. 1977. The disposal of radioactive wastes from fission reactors. *Scientific American*, June. Repr. in Raymond Silver, ed., 1980, *Energy and environment: readings from Scientific American.* San Francisco: W. H. Freeman.

Cohen, Mark Nathan. 1977. *The food crisis in prehistory.* New Haven: Yale U. Pr.

Commoner, Barry. 1972. *The closing circle: nature, man, and technology.* New York: Bantam.

Connell, K. H. 1965. Land and population in Ireland, 1750–1845. In D. V. Glass and D. E. C. Eversley, eds., *Population in history.* Chicago: Aldine.

Cook, Robert C. 1951. *Human fertility: the modern dilemma.* New York: Sloane.

Cook, Robert C., and Jane Lecht, eds. 1973. *People!* Rev. ed. Washington, D.C.: Columbia Bks.

Cook, Sherburne F., and Woodrow Borah. 1971. *Essays in population history: Mexico and the Caribbean,* 1: viii–82. Berkeley, U. of Cal. Pr.

Cornelius, Wayne A. 1977. Illegal migration to the United States: recent research findings, policy implications, and research priorities. Mimeo. Center for International Studies, MIT. May.

Daly, Herman, ed. 1973. *Toward a steady-state economy.* San Francisco: W. H. Freeman.

Darmstadter, Joel. 1972. *Energy.* In Ridker, 1972.

Darmstadter, Joel, et al. 1971. *Energy in the world economy.* Baltimore: Johns Hopkins.

Davis, Joseph S. 1953. The population upsurge and the American economy, 1945–80. *Journal of Political Economy* 61: 369–88.

Davis, Kingsley. 1970. The climax of population growth: past and future perspective. *California Medicine*, vol. 113, no. 5. pp. 33–39.

Day, Lincoln H., and Alice Day. 1964. *Too many Americans.* New York: Houghton Mifflin, p. 134.

Deevey, Edward S. 1960. The human population. *Scientific American* 203: 195–204. In Ehrlich, Holdren, and Holm, 1971

Denison, Edward F. 1962. *The sources of economic growth in the United States and the alternatives before us.* New York: Committee for Economic Development.

Dixon, Bernard. 1973. *What is science for?* New York: Harper.

Dorn, Harold F. 1963. World population growth. In Philip M. Hauser, ed., *The population dilemma.* Englewood Cliffs, N.J.: Prentice-Hall.

Dublin, Louis I.; Alfred J. Lotka; and Mortimer Spiegelman. 1949. *Length of life: a study of the life table.* Rev. ed. New York: Ronald Pr.

Easterlin, Richard A. 1967. Effects of population growth in the economic development of developing countries. *The Annals of the American Academy of Political and Social Science* 369: 98–108.

——— . 1972. Comment on Allen C. Kelley, Demographic changes and American economic development: past, present and future. In U.S. Commission on Population Growth and the American Future, *Economic Aspects of Population Change*, Elliot R. Morse and Ritchie H. Reeds, eds., 2:45. Washington, D.C.: GPO.

——— , ed. 1980. *Population and economic change in developing countries.* Chicago: U. of Chicago Pr.

Eckholm, Erik P. 1976. *Losing ground: environmental stress and world food prospects.* New York: Norton.

Ehrlich, Paul R. 1968. *The population bomb.* New York: Ballantine.

Ehrlich, Paul R., and Anne H. Ehrlich. 1970/1972. *Population, resources, environment: issues in human ecology.* 2nd ed. San Francisco: W. H. Freeman.

——— . 1974. *The end of affluence: a blueprint for your future.* New York: Ballantine.

Ehrlich, Paul R.; Anne H. Ehrlich; and John P. Holdren. 1977. *Ecoscience: population, resources, environment.* 2nd ed. San Francisco: W. H. Freeman.

Ehrlich, Paul R., and Richard L. Harriman. 1971. *How to be a survivor: a plan to save spaceship earth.* New York: Ballantine.

Ehrlich, Paul R.; John P. Holdren; and Richard W. Holm, eds. 1971. *Man and the ecosphere.* San Francisco: W. H. Freeman.

Eliot, Johan W. 1966. The development of family planning services by state and local health departments in the United States. In S. Polgar and W. Cowles, eds., *American Journal of Public Health*, Supplement (January) 56: 6–16.

Elliott, Robin; Lynn C. Landman; Richard Lincoln; and Theodore Tsuruoka. 1970. U.S. population growth and family planning: a review of the literature. In *Family Planning Perspectives*, vol. 2, repr. in Daniel Callahan, ed., *The American population debate* (New York: Anchor Bks., 1971), p. 206.

Epstein, Trude Scarlett. 1965. Economic change and differentiation in new Britain. *Economic Record* 41: 173–92.

Ericsson, Neil R., and Peter Morgan. 1978. The economic feasibility of shale oil: an activity analysis. *Bell Journal of Economics* 9: 457ff.

est. N.d. *The end of starvation.* Brochure of The Hunger Project.

Eversley, D. E. C. 1965. Population, economy and society. In D. Glass and D. E. C. Eversley, eds., *Population in history.* Chicago: Aldine.

Feiss, Julian W. 1963–65. Minerals. In *Scientific American* eds., *Technology and economic development.* Harmondsworth, Eng.: Penguin, in association with Chatto & Windus.

Fellner, William. 1970. Trends in the activities generating technological progress. *American Economic Review* 60: 1–29.

Fichter, George S. 1972. *The golden stamp book of earth and ecology.* Racine, Wis.: Western Pub.

Firth, Raymond W. 1936. *We, the Tikopia.* London: Allen & Unwin.

———. 1939/1965. *Primitive Polynesian economy.* London: Routledge.

Fischman, Leonard L., and Hans H. Landsberg. 1972. Adequacy of nonfuel minerals and forest resources. In Ridker, 1972.

Fisher, W. Holden. 1971. The anatomy of inflation: 1953–1975. *Scientific American* 225: 15–22.

Flesch, Rudolf. 1951. *The art of clear thinking.* New York: Harper.

Ford, Clellan S. 1952. Control of conception in cross-cultural perspective. *World population problems and birth control. Annals of the New York Academy of Sciences* 54: 763–68.

Frederiksen, Harald. 1968. Elimination of malaria and mortality decline. In Heer, 1968.

Freedman, Jonathan L. 1975. *Crowding and behavior.* New York: Viking Pr.

Freedman, Ronald, and Bernard Berelson. 1974. The human population. *Scientific American* 231: 30–39.

Frey, H. Thomas. 1973. *Major uses of land in the United States: summary for 1969.* Agricultural Economic Report No. 247. Economic Research Service. U.S. Department of Agriculture. Washington, D.C.: GPO.

———. 1975. *Cropland for today and tomorrow.* Agricultural Economic Report No. 291. Economic Research Service. U.S. Department of Agriculture. Washington, D.C.: GPO.

Friedman, David. 1972. Laissez-faire in population: the least bad solution. Population Council Occasional Paper.

Friendly, Alfred. 1970. British stand fast in battle against pollution of environment. *Washington Post,* February 5, p. A10.

Fuchs, Victor R. 1967. *Differentials in hourly earning by region and city size, 1959.* New York: Columbia U. Pr.

Fuller, Buckminster. 1969. *Utopia or oblivion: the prospect for humanity.* New York: Bantam.

Furnivall, J. S. 1957. *An introduction to the political economy of Burma.* 3d ed. Rangoon: Peoples Literature.

Glass, Donald V. 1964. Some indicators of differences between urban and rural mortality in England and Wales and Scotland. *Population Studies* 17: 263–67.

Glover, Donald, and Julian L. Simon. 1975. The effects of population density upon infra-structure: the case of road building. *Economic Development and Cultural Change* 23: 453–68.

Goeller, H. E., and A. M. Weinberg. 1978. The age of substitutability. *Science* 191: 683–89.

Goldman, Marshall I. 1970. The convergence of environmental disruption. *Science* 170: 37–42. Repr. in Robert Dorfman and Nancy S. Dorfman, 1972, *Economics of the environment: selected readings* (New York: Norton).

————. 1971. Ecological facelifting in the U.S.S.R. or improving on nature. In *Maison des Sciences de L'Homme Symposium*, 1971, *Political economy of environment: problems of method*, with an intro. by Ignacy Sach. Paris: Mouton.

Gourou, Pierre. 1966. *The tropical world, its social and economic conditions and its future status.* New York: Wiley.

Gregg, Alan. 1955a. Hidden hunger at the summit. *Population Bulletin*, vol. 11, no. 5, pp. 65-69.

————. 1955b. A medical aspect of the population problem. *Science* 121: 681–82.

Griliches, Zvi. 1958. Research costs and social returns: hybrid corn and related innovation. *Journal of Political Economy* 66: 419–31.

Habakkuk, John. 1963. Population problems and European economic development in the late eighteenth and nineteenth centuries. *American Economic Review* 53: 607–18.

Hagen, Everett E. 1975. *The economics of development.* Homewood, Ill.: Irwin.

Handler, Philip. 1970. Testimony before the Congressional Subcommittee on Science, Research and Development. July 21. Quoted by Wolman, 1971.

Hardin, Garrett. 1974. Living in a lifeboat. *Bioscience* 24: 561–67.

Hawkins, E. K. 1962. *Roads and road transport in an underdeveloped country.* London: Colonial Office.

Hawley, Amost H. 1972. Population density and the city. *Demography* 9: 521–30.

Haworth, C. T., and D. W. Rasmussen. 1973. Determinants of metropolitan cost of living variations. *Southern Economic Journal* 40: 183–92.

Hayami, Yujiro, and Vernon W. Ruttan. 1971. *Agricultural development: an international perspective.* Baltimore: Johns Hopkins.

Heer, David M. 1968. *Readings in Population.* Englewood Cliffs, N.J.: Prentice-Hall.

Heilbrun, Deborah. 1975. Calls lower birth rate key to world survival. *Jewish Notes* 23: 32.

Herfindahl, Orris C., and Allen V. Kneese. 1965. *Quality of the environment.* Baltimore: Johns Hopkins.

Hirsch, Werner Z. 1956. Firm progress ratios. *Econometrica* 24: 136–43.

Hirschi, Travis, and Hanan C. Selvin. 1973. *Principles of survey analysis.* New York: Free Pr.

Hirst, Eric, and John C. Moyers. 1974. Efficiency of energy use in the United States. In Abelson, 1974.

Hollingsworth, Thomas Henry. 1969. *Historical demography.* London: Hodder & Stoughton, p. 311.

Holton, Gerald. 1973. *Thematic origins of scientific thought.* Cambridge: Harvard U. Pr.

Houthakker, Hendrik S. 1976. The economics of nonrenewable resources. *Beihefte der Konjunkturpolitick* 23: 115–24.

Hoyle, Fred, and Geoffrey Hoyle. 1980. *Commonsense in nuclear energy.* San Francisco: W. H. Freeman.

Huxley, Julian. 1953. *Evolution in action.* Harmondsworth, Eng.: Penguin, in association with Chatto & Windus.

International Advisory Committee on Population and Law. 1977. *Annual review of population law 1976: constitutions, legislation, regulations, legal opinions and judicial decisions.* Law and population book series no. 20. Medford, Mass.: Tufts U.

International economic report of the president. 1974. Transmitted to Congress February 1974. Washington, D.C.: GPO.

Jablon, S., and Kato, H. 1970. Childhood cancer in relation to prenatal exposure to atomic bomb radiation. *The Lancet,* November 14.

Jacobs, Jane. 1961. *The death and life of great American cities.* New York: Random House.

Jaffe, Frederick S. 1969. Activities relevant to the study of population policy for the U.S. Memo to Bernard Berelson, March 11, 1969. In Elliott et al., 1970.

Jevons, W. Stanley. 1865. *The coal question.* London: Macmillan.

Johnson, D. Gale. 1970. Famine. *Encyclopaedia Britannica.*

——. 1973. World food problems and prospects. Mimeo. Washington, D.C.: Am. Enterprise.

——. 1974a. Population, food and economic development. *American Statistician* 28: 89–93.

——. 1974b. *World food problems and prospects.* Washington, D.C.: Am. Enterprise.

——. 1976. Food for the future: a perspective. *Population and Development Review* (March) 2:1-20.

——. 1980. The world food situation: developments during the 1970's and prospects for the 1980's. Mimeo. Office of Agricultural Economics Paper No. 80. U. of Chicago. March 5.

Jones, K., and A. D. Smith. 1970. *The economic impact of commonwealth immigration.* Cambridge: Cambridge U. Pr.

Jorgensen, Dale, and Zvi Griliches. 1967. The explanation of productivity change. *Review of Economic Studies* 34: 249-83.

Kahn, Herman; William Brown; and Leon Martel, with the assistance of the staff of the Hudson Institute. 1976. *The next 200 years: a scenario for America and the world.* New York: Morrow.

Kammeyer, Kenneth C. W.; Norma R. Yetman; and McKee J. McClendon. 1972. Family planning services and redistribution of black Americans. Repr. in Kenneth C. W. Kammeyer, ed., 1975, *Population studies: selected essays.* Chicago: Rand McNally.

Kanovsky, Eliyahu. 1966. *The economy of the Israeli kibbutz.* Cambridge: Harvard U. Pr.

Keyfitz, Nathan. 1966. Population density and the style of social life. *BioScience* 16: 868–73. Repr. in Reid and Lyon, 1972.

Kirk, Dudley. 1969. Natality in the developing countries: recent trends and prospects. In S. J. Behrman, Leslie Corsa, and Ronald Freedman, eds, *Fertility and family planning: a world view.* Ann Arbor: U. of Mich. Pr.

Kiser, Clyde V. 1970. Changing fertility patterns in the United States. *Social Biology* 17: 312–15.

Knodel, John, and Etienne Van De Walle. 1967. Breast feeding, fertility and infant mortality: an analysis of some early German data. *Population Studies* 21: 109–31.

Knodel, John and Etienne Van De Walle. 1967. Breast feeding, fertility and infant mortality: an analysis of some early German data. *Population Studies* 21: 109–31.

Korns, Alex. 1977. Coverage issues raised by comparisons between CPS and establishment employment. *American Stat. Assn. Proceedings,* Social Stat. section.

Krzywicki, Ludwik. 1934. *Primitive society and its vital statistics.* London: Macmillan, p. 216.

Kumar, Joginder. 1973. *Population and land in world agriculture.* Berkeley: U. of Cal. Pr.

Kunz, Philip R., and Evan T. Peterson, 1972. Family size and academic achievement. In Howard M. Bahr, Bruce A. Chadwick, and Darwin L. Thomas, eds., *Population, resources, and the future: non-Malthusian perspectives.* Provo: Brigham Young U. Pr.

Kuznets, Simon. 1960. Population change and aggregate output. In *Demographic and economic change in developed countries.* Princeton: Princeton U. Pr.

———. 1965. Demographic aspects of modern economic growth. Paper presented at World Population Conference, Belgrade. September.

———. 1967. Population and economic growth. *Proceedings of the American Philosophical Society* 11: 170–93.

———. 1971. *Economic growth of nations.* Cambridge: Harvard U. Pr.

Lader, Lawrence. 1971. *Breeding ourselves to death.* New York: Ballantine.

———. 1973. *The Margaret Sanger story, the fight for birth control.* Repr. of 1955 ed. Westport, Conn.: Greenwood.

Lancaster, Clarise, and Frederick J. Schewen. 1977. Counting the uncountable illegals: some initial statistical speculation employing capture-recapture technique." Paper given at Am. Stat. Assn.

Landsberg, Hans H. 1964. *Natural resources for U.S. growth: a look ahead to the year 2000.* Baltimore: Johns Hopkins. Published for Resources for the Future, Inc.

———. 1974. Low-cost, abundant energy: paradise lost? In Abelson, 1974.

Lapp, Ralph E. 1973. The logarithmic century: charting future shock. Englewood Cliffs, N.J.: Prentice-Hall.

Lebergott, Stanley. 1964. *Manpower in economic growth.* New York: McGraw-Hill.

Leibenstein, Harvey. 1972. The impact of population growth on the American economy. In *The report of the Commissions on Population Growth and and American Future,* vol 2: *Economic aspects of population change.* Washington, D.C.: GPO.

Lele, Uma J., and John W. Mellor. 1964. Estimates of change and causes of change in food grains production: India 1949–50 to 1960–61. *Cornell University Agricultural Development Bulletin* 2.

Leonard, Jonathon A. 1979. The "queen of diseases" strikes back. *Harvard Magazine* (July–August), pp. 20–24.

Leopold, Nathan F., Jr. 1958. *Life plus 99 years.* New York: Popular Lib.

Lesko Associates. 1975. Basic data and guidance required to implement a major illegal alien study during fiscal year 1976. Paper submitted to INS, October 15.

Lindert, Peter H. 1978. *Fertility and scarcity in America.* Princeton: Princeton U. Pr.

———. 1980. Child costs and economic development. In Easterlin, 1980.

Lipson, Gerald, and Dianne Wolman. 1972. Polling Americans on birth control and population. *Family Planning Perspectives* 4: 39–42.

Littlewood, Thomas. 1977. *The politics of population control.* South Bend: U. of Notre Dame Pr.

Love, Douglas. 1978. City sizes and prices. Ph.D. diss., U. of Illinois.

Love, Douglas, and Lincoln Pashute [Julian L. Simon]. 1978. The effect of population size and concentration upon scientific productivity. In Julian L. Simon, 1978c.

Maddox, John. 1972. *The doomsday syndrome.* London: Macmillan.

Malthus, Thomas R. 1803. Essay on population. *An essay on the principle of population, or a view of its past and present effects on human happiness.* London: J. Johnson. A new ed., very thick, enlarged.

———. 1817/1963. *Principles of population.* 5th ed. Homewood, Ill.: Irwin.

———. 1830/1960. *On population: three essays by Thomas Malthus, Julian Huxley, and Frederick Osborn.* New York: New American Lib., Mentor Bks.

Mamdani, Mahmood. 1973. *The myth of population control (family, caste, and class in an Indian village).* New York and London: Monthly Review Pr.

Manpower and Immigration. 1974. *Three years in Canada.* Ottawa: Information Canada.

Marshall, L. E. 1972. Sees hazards in overpopulation. Letter to the editor. *Des Moines Register,* July 12, p. 8.

Mather, Kirtley. 1940. The future of man as an inhabitant of the earth. *Sigma Xi Quarterly* (Spring), vol. 28.

––––. 1944. *Enough and to spare.* 2nd ed. New York: Harper.

McEvedy, Colin, and Richard Jones. 1978. *Atlas of world population history.* New York: Penguin.

McKelvey, Vincent E. 1973. Mineral resource estimates and public policy. *Summary of United States mineral resources.* U.S. Department of the Interior. Washington, D.C.: GPO.

McNamara, Robert S. 1973. *One hundred countries, two billion people: the dimensions of development.* New York: Praeger.

McNeill, William H. 1977. *Plagues and peoples.* Garden City, N.Y.: Anchor Bks.

Meadows, Dennis L.; William W. Behrens, III; Donella H. Meadows; Roger F. Naill; Jorgen Randers; and Erich K. O. Zahn. 1974. *Dynamics of growth in a finite world.* Cambridge, Mass.: Wright-Allen.

Meadows, Donella H.; Dennis L. Meadows; Jorgen Randers; and William W. Behrens III. 1972. *The limits to growth.* New York: Potomac Assoc.

Mera, K. 1970. Urban agglomeration and economic efficiency. *Economic Development and Cultural Change* 21: 309–21.

Merklein, Helmut A., and W. Carey Hardy. 1977. *Energy economics.* Houston: Gulf Pub.

Metz, William D. 1974. Oil shale: a huge resource of low-grade fuel. In Abelson, 1974.

Middle East Information Series. 1974. 26–27 (spring/summer).

Mitchell, Edward J. 1974. *U.S. energy policy: a primer.* Washington, D.C.: Am. Enterprise.

Mohr, L. B. 1969. Determinants of innovation in organizations. *American Political Science Review* 63: 111–26.

Morawetz, David. 1978. *Twenty-five years of economic development: 1950 to 1975.* Baltimore: Johns Hopkins.

Mowrer, O. Hobart. 1961. *The crisis in psychiatry and religion.* New York: D. Van Nostrand.

Mueller, Eva. 1976. The economic value of children in peasant agriculture. In Ridker, 1976.

Musson, Carole. 1974. Local attitudes to population control in South Buckinghamshire. In H. B. Parry, ed., 1974, *Population and its problems: a plain man's guide.* Oxford: Clarendon Pr.

Myers, Ramon H. 1970. *The Chinese peasant economy: agricultural development in Hopei and Shantung, 1890–1949.* Cambridge: Harvard U. Pr.

Myrdal, Alva. 1941/1968. *Nation and family.* Cambridge: MIT Pr. Repr. 1968.

Myrdal, Gunnar. 1940. *Population: a problem for democracy.* Cambridge: Harvard U. Pr.

––––. 1968. *Asian drama: an inquiry into the poverty of nations.* Vol. 1. New York: Pantheon.

Nag, Meni. 1962. *Factors affecting fertility in non-industrial societies: a cross-cultural study.* New Haven: Yale U. Publishers in Anthropology.

National Academy of Sciences. 1965. *The growth of U.S. population: analysis of the problems and recommendations for research, training, and service.* Report by the Committee on Population. Washington, D.C.: Nat. Acad. of Sciences — Nat. Research Council.

——. 1975. *Mineral resources and the environment.* Report by the Committee on Mineral Resources and the Environment (COMRATE). Commission on Natural Resources. Washington, D.C.: Nat. Acad. of Sciences — Nat. Research Council.

——. 1979. *Energy in transition: 1985-2010.* San Francisco: W. H. Freeman.

National Commission on Materials Policy. 1973. *Material needs and the environment today and tomorrow.* Washington, D.C.: GPO.

Nordhaus, William D. 1974. Resources as a constraint on growth. *American Economic Review* 64: 22-26.

North, David S., and Marian F. Houstoun. 1976. *The characteristics and role of illegal aliens in the U.S. labor market: an exploratory study.* Washington, D.C.: Linton and Co.

Novick, David; with Kurt Bleicken, W. E. Depay, Jr., Stanley A. Hutchins, J. W. Noah, and Mary B. Novick. 1976. *A world of scarcities: critical issues in public policy.* New York: Wiley.

Ohkawa, K. 1970. Phases of agricultural development and economic growth. In K. Ohkawa, B. Johnston, and H. Kaneda, eds., *Agricultural and economic growth, Japan's experience.* Princeton: Princeton U. Pr.

Oka, Takashi. 1976. Can the spread of deserts be halted? *Christian Science Monitor,* November 12, p. 16. Quoted in *The Other Side,* April 1977.

Olson, Mancur, Jr. 1965. *The logic of collective action.* Cambridge: Harvard U. Pr.

Olson, Mancur, Jr., and Hans H. Landsberg, eds. 1973. *The no-growth society.* Special issue of *Daedalus* (Fall) 102.

Olson, Sherry H. 1971. *The depletion myth: history of railroad use of timber.* Cambridge: Harvard U. Pr.

Opportunity Systems, Inc. 1975-77. *First, second, third, fourth wave reports: Vietnam resettlement operational feedback* (Washington, D.C.: Opportunity Systems).

Ortega y Gasset, José. 1961. *The revolt of the masses.* London: Unwin.

Osborn, Fairfield. 1953. *Limits of the earth.* Boston: Little, Brown.

Othmer, Donald F., and Oswald A. Roels. 1974. Power, fresh water, and food from cold, deep sea water. In Abelson, 1974.

Owen, Wilfred. 1964. *Strategy for mobility.* Washington: Brookings.

Paddock, William, and Paul Paddock. 1967. *Famine—1975! America's decision: who will survive?* Boston: Little, Brown.

Parsons, Jack. 1971. *Population versus liberty.* London: Pemberton.

Perkins, Dwight. 1969. *Agricultural development in China, 1368-1968.* Chicago: Aldine.

Petty, William. 1899. *The economic writings of Sir William Petty.* Ed. by Charles Henry Hull. 2 vols. Cambridge: Cambridge U. Pr.

Piotrow, Phylis Tilson. 1973. *World population crisis: the United States' response.* New York: Praeger.

Poleman, T. T. 1975. World food: a perspective. In Abelson, 1975.

Preston, Samuel H. 1980. Causes and consequences of mortality declines in less developed countries during the twentieth century. In Easterlin, 1980.

Price, Daniel O., ed. 1967. *The 99th hour.* Chapel Hill: U. of N. C. Pr.

Rainwater, Lee. 1965. *Family design: marital sexuality, family size, and contraception.* Chicago: Aldine.

Reed, T. B., and R. M. Lerner. 1974. *Methanol: a versatile fuel for immediate use.* In Abelson, 1974.

Reid, Sue Titus, and David L. Lyon, eds. 1972. *Population crisis: an interdisciplinary perspective.* Glenview, Ill.: Scott, Foresman.

Repetto, Robert G. 1976. Direct economic costs and value of children. In Ridker, 1976.

Report on the limits to growth. 1972. Washington, D.C.: International Bank for Reconstruction and Development.

Revelle, Roger. 1974. Food and population. *Scientific American* 231: 160–71.

Ridker, Ronald. 1972. Resource and environmental consequences of population growth and the American future. In Ronald Ridker, ed., 1972, *Population, resources, and the environment.* Vol. 3. The Commission on Population Growth and the American Future. Washington, D.C.: GPO.

——, ed. 1976. *Population and development: the search for selective interventions.* Baltimore: Resources for the Future and Johns Hopkins.

Robinson, J. Gregory. 1979. Estimating the approximate size of the illegal alien population in the United States by the comparative trend analysis of age-specific death rates. Paper given at PAA.

Robson, Geoffrey R. 1974. Geothermal electricity production. In Abelson, 1974.

Rose, David J. 1974. Nuclear electric power. In Abelson, 1974.

Rosenberg, Nathan. 1972. *Technology and American economic growth.* New York: Harper.

Ross, Edward A. 1927. *Standing room only.* New York: Century.

Salaff, Janet, and Aline K. Wong. 1978. Are disincentives coercive? The view from Singapore. *International Family Planning Perspectives and Digest* 4: 50–55.

Sanderson, F. H. 1975. The great food fumble. In Abelson, 1975.

Sauvy, Alfred. 1969. *General theory of population.* New York: Basic.

——. 1976. *Zero growth.* Trans. by A. Maguire. New York: Praeger.

Sax, Karl. 1960. *Standing room only: the world's exploding population.* 2nd ed. Boston: Beacon Pr.

Scherer, Frederic H. 1970. *Industrial market structures and economic performance.* Chicago: Rand McNally.

Schran, Peter. 1969. *The development of Chinese agriculture 1950–1959.* Urbana: U. of Ill. Pr.

Schultz, T. Paul. 1976. Interrelationships between mortality and fertility. In Ridker, 1976.

400

Segal, David. 1976. Are there returns to scale in city size? *Review of Economic Statistics* 58: 339–50.

Sheffer, Daniel, 1970. Comparable living costs and urban size: a statistical analysis. *American Institute of Planners Journal* 36: 417–21.

Shoji, Kobe. 1977. Drip irrigation. *Scientific American* 237: 15ff.

Silverman, Paul. 1970. Speech delivered at the U. of Ill. at Champaign-Urbana, Earthday.

Simon, Julian L. 1975a. *Applied managerial economics.* Englewood Cliffs, N.J.: Prentice-Hall.

———. 1975b. The positive effect of population on agricultural savings in irrigation systems. *Review of Economics and Statistics* 57: 71–79.

———. 1977. *The economics of population growth.* Princeton: Princeton U. Pr.

———. 1978a. *Basic research methods in social science.* 2nd ed. New York: Random House.

———. 1978b. An integration of the invention-pull and population-push theories of economic-demographic history. In Julian L. Simon, 1978c.

———. 1978c. *Research in population economics.* Vol. 1. Greenwich, Conn.: JAI Pr.

———. 1980. What immigrants take from, and give to, the public coffers. Report to the Select Commission on Immigration and Refugee Policy, August 15.

———. Forthcoming. The really important effects of immigrants upon natives' incomes. In Barry Chiswick, ed., *Conference on Immigration.* Washington, D.C.: AEI.

Simon, Julian L., and Roy Gobin. 1979. The relationship between population and economic growth in LDC's. In Julian L. Simon and Julie deVanzo, eds., 1979, *Research in population economics.* Vol. 2. Greenwich, Conn.: JAI Pr.

Simon, Julian L., and Adam M. Pilarski. 1979. The effect of population growth upon the quantity of education children receive. *Review of Economics and Statistics* 61: 572–84.

Simon, Rita James. 1971. Public attitudes toward population and pollution. *Public Opinion Quarterly* 35: 95–101.

Singer, Max. How the scarcity error hurts America. *Washington Quarterly,* Spring 1981.

Slicher van Bath, B. H. 1963. *The agrarian history of western Europe, A.D. 500–1850.* London: Arnold.

Smith, Adam. 1937. *An inquiry into the nature and causes of the wealth of nations.* Ed. by Edwin Cannan. New York: Modern Lib.

Smith, Barton, and Robert Newman. 1977. Depressed wages along the U.S.-Mexican border: an empirical analysis. *Economic Inquiry* 15: 56–66.

Smith, V. Kerry, ed. 1979. *Scarcity and growth revisited.* Baltimore: Resources for the Future and Johns Hopkins.

Smithsonian Institute Board of Regents. 1941. *Annual report showing the operations, expenditures, and conditions of the institution for the year ending June 30, 1940.* Washington, D.C.: GPO.

Solow, Robert. 1957. Technical change and the aggregate production function. *The Review of Economics and Statistics* 39: 312–20.

Sorokin, Pitinim. 1937. *Social and cultural dynamics.* 4 vols. Boston: Little, Brown.

Spengler, Joseph J. 1978. Population phenomena and population theory. In J. Simon, 1978c.

Steinmann, Gunter, and Julian L. Simon. Forthcoming. Phelps' technical progress model generalized. *Economic letters.*

Stevens, Jerry. 1978. Demographic market structure and bank performance. Mimeo. Dept. of Economics. U. of Ill.

Stryker, J. Dirck. 1977. Optimum population in rural areas: empirical evidence from the Franc zone. *The Quarterly Journal of Economics* 91: 177–93.

Stuart, Alexander. 1958. *Overpopulation: twentieth century nemesis.* New York: Exposition Pr.

Stys, W. 1957. The influence of economic conditions on the fertility of peasant women. *Population Studies* 11: 136–48.

Sveikauskas, Leo. 1975. The productivity of cities. *The Quarterly Journal of Economics* 89: 343–413.

Taylor, Carl E. 1965. Health and population. *Foreign Affairs* 43: 475–86.

Taylor, Gordon Rattray. 1970. *The doomsday book.* London: Thames & Hudson.

Terhune, Kenneth W. 1975. *A review of the actual and expected consequences of family size.* National Institutes of Health Publication No. 75-779. Public Health Service. HEW. Washington, D.C.: GPO.

Thomas, Dorothy S. 1941. *Social and economic aspects of Swedish population movements.* New York: Macmillan.

von Thunen, Johann H. 1966. *The isolated state.* New York: Pergamon.

UN. Dept. of Economic and Social Affairs. 1956. *The aging of populations and its economic and social implications.* Population Studies, no. 26. New York: UN.

UN. Food and Agriculture Organization. Various years. *Production Yearbook.* New York: UN.

UN. Fund for Population Activities. 1975. *Annual report.* New York: UN.

U.S. Congress. 1973. *Hearings on U.S. and world food situation.* 93rd Cong. 1st sess. October.

U.S. Council on Environmental Quality. 1975. *Sixth annual report.* Washington, D.C.: GPO.

———. 1976. *Seventh annual report.* Washington, D.C.: GPO.

U.S. Dept. of Agriculture. Economic Research Service. 1974. *Our land and water resources: current and prospective supplies and uses.* Miscellaneous Publication No. 1290. Washington, D.C.: GPO.

U.S. Dept. of Commerce. Bureau of the Census. Various years. *Population reports.* Washington, D.C.: GPO.

———. Various Years. *Statistical abstract of the United States.* Washington, D.C.: GPO.

U.S. Dept. of State. 1969. *Bulletin,* August 11. Washington, D.C.: GPO.

U.S. ERDA. 1976. *Energy and the environment.* Washington, D.C.: GPO.

U.S. General Accounting Office. 1978. *Reducing population growth through social and economic change in developing countries—a new direction for U.S. assistance.* Report to the Congress of the U.S. Washington, D.C.: GPO.

U.S. The White House. 1933. *Recent social trends in the United States.* Vol. 1: *The President's Research Committee on Social Trends.* Washington, D.C.: GPO.

——— . 1952. *Resources for freedom.* 4 vols. The President's Materials Policy Commission (The Paley Commission). Washington, D.C.: GPO. June.

——— . 1967. *The world food problem.* Vols. 1–2. Washington, D.C.: GPO.

——— . 1972. Population and the American future. *The report of the Commission on Population Growth and the American Future.* New York: Signet.

Van Vleck, David B. 1970. A biologist urges stabilizing U.S. population growth. *University: A Princeton Quarterly* (Spring): 16–18.

Villalpondo, M. Vic et al. 1977. *A study of the socio-economic impact of illegal aliens, County of San Diego.* San Diego: Human Resources Agency, County of San Diego. January.

Vogt, William. 1948. *Road to survival.* New York: Sloane.

——— . 1960. *People! challenge to survival.* New York: Sloane.

Wade, Nicholas. 1974. Windmills: the resurrection of an ancient energy technology. In Abelson, 1974.

Wagret, Paul. 1968. *Polderlands.* London: Methuen.

Ware, Helen. 1978. Personal correspondence, March 20.

Wattenberg, Ben J. 1974. *The real America.* Garden City, N.Y.: Doubleday.

Weber, James A. 1977. *Grow or die!* New Rochelle, N.Y.: Arlington Hse.

Wertham, Frederick. 1969. *A sign for Cain: an exploration of human violence.* New York: Warner Paperback Lib.

West, E. C. 1971. *Canada-United States price and productivity differences in manufacturing industries, 1963.* Ottawa: Economic Council of Canada.

Whelpton, P. K., A. Campbell Arthur, and J. E. Patterson. 1966. *Fertility and family planning in the United States.* Princeton: Princeton U. Pr.

Wildavsky, Aaron. 1980. Richer is safer. *The Public Interest* (Summer): 23–29.

Williamson, Francis S. L. 1969. Population pollution. *BioScience* 19: 979–83. Repr. in Reid and Lyon, 1972.

Willing, Martha Kent. 1971. *Beyond conception: our children's children.* Boston: Gambit.

Wilson, George W., Barbara R. Bergmann, Leon V. Hinser, and Martin S. Klein. 1966. *The impact of highway investment on development.* Washington: Brookings.

Winegarden, C. R. 1975. Educational expenditure and school enrollments in less-developed countries: a simultaneous-equation method. *The Eastern Economic Journal* 2: 77–87.

Winsche, W. E.; K. C. Hoffman; and F. J. Salzano. 1974. Hydrogen: its future role in the nation's energy economy. In Abelson, 1974.

Wolf, Martin. 1974. Solar energy utilization by physical methods. In Abelson, 1974.

Wolfers, David. 1971. The case against zero growth. *International Journal of Environmental Studies* 1: 227–32.

Wolman, Abel. 1971. Review of Paul R. Ehrlich and Anne H. Ehrlich, *Population, resources, environment.* In *Milbank Memorial Fund Quarterly,* vol. 49 (January), part I, pp. 93–97.

World food supply: PSAC panel warns of impending famine. 1967. *Science* 156: 1578.

Yaari, Shmuel. 1974. World over a barrel. *Jerusalem Post Magazine* 4: 4.

Yasuba, Yasukichi. 1962. *Birth rates of the white population in the United States, 1800–1860: an economic study.* Baltimore: John Hopkins.

Zajonc, R. B. 1976. Family configuration and intelligence. *Science* 192: 227–36.

Zimmerman, L. J. 1965. *Poor lands, rich lands.* New York: Random House.

Zimmerman, Erich W. 1951/1965. *World resources and industries.* 2nd ed. New York: Harper.

Zonis, Marvin. 1976. Petroleum and politics in the Persian Gulf. *University of Chicago Magazine,* March, pp. 14ff.

Index

Page Numbers in **boldface** refer to figures and tables.

Library of Congress Cataloging in Publication Data

Simon, Julian Lincoln, 1932–
    The ultimate resource.

    Includes bibliographical references and index.
    1. Population.   2. Natural resources.
3. Economic policy.   I. Title.
HB871.S573   333.7   80-8575
ISBN 0-691-09389-X

Julian L. Simon is Professor of Economics and
Business Administration at the University of
Illinois. He is the author of many books and
articles on the economics of population growth
and other subjects, and is a consultant to
various public and private organizations.